Happy
Birthday
Dad
with Love
Pam + Joe
1995

MAN ON EARTH

Number Ten

The Corrie Herring Hooks Series

JOHN READER

MAN ON EARTH

with photographs by the author

University of Texas Press

AUSTIN

Planned and produced by Robert MacDonald Publishing
Designed by Peter Campbell
Cartography by Chris Lovell

International Standard Book Number 0-292-75101-X

First University of Texas Press Edition, 1988
Requests for permission to reproduce material from this work
should be sent to Permissions, University of Texas Press,
Box 7819, Austin, Texas 78713-7819.

Typeset by Peter MacDonald, Twickenham
Origination by Adroit Photolitho Ltd, Birmingham
Printed and bound by William Collins Sons & Co Ltd, Glasgow

First published in Great Britain in 1988 by
William Collins Sons & Co Ltd

▪ CONTENTS ▪

▪ INTRODUCTION ▪

Man on Earth is an attempt to understand humanity and what is going on in the world. Why do people behave and organise their affairs as they do? Why do some cultures seem more bizarre than others? Why have some vanished while others continue to flourish? Do the problems that people perceive vary from place to place and age to age? Is mankind really likely to ruin the global environment?

Adaptation and regulation are the words that begin to answer these questions. The first refers to the talent that has enabled human beings to live permanently in a wider range of habitats than any other mammal, and the second refers to the systems of social and cultural practice by which people impose certain constraints upon the use and distribution of their habitat's resources.

In 1986 the scientific journal *Nature* published papers suggesting that everyone alive on Earth today is descended from a small number of men and women who emigrated from Africa – the acknowledged cradle of mankind – not later than 50,000 years ago. Biologists from the University of California at Berkeley have taken this proposition even further, presenting genetic evidence to suggest that the entire modern human population is descended from a single woman who lived in Africa about 200,000 years ago.

These hypotheses are as yet unproven, but they reflect a truth that is gradually beginning to dawn on mankind: despite all the apparent differences of race, colour, language and creed, the people of the world have much more in common than was formerly supposed. All mankind shares a unique ability to adapt to circumstances and resolve the problems of survival. It was this talent which carried successive generations of people into the many niches of environmental opportunity that the world has to offer – from forest, to grassland, desert, seashore and icecap. And in each case, people developed ways of life appropriate to the particular habitats and circumstances they encountered. A variety of distinctive physical, social and cultural characteristics evolved among groups isolated from one another, so that eventually the common inheritance of mankind was obscured by the bewildering diversity of looks, lifestyles, cultures and beliefs that divides and creates problems among people.

The talent for ingenious adaptation which initially enabled people to overcome the basic ecological problems of establishing themselves in a wide variety of habitats has always provoked a need of yet more ingenuity. In the first instance, the very success of an ecological adaptation inevitably

7

creates a need to develop some means of keeping population growth under control. It is a basic fact of human biology that people are capable of multiplying prodigiously under congenial circumstances. If modern humans were all derived from a single female as the Californian biologists suggest, and had produced offspring that bred at anything like the highest recorded rate for the species, their living progeny would have exceeded the present total of just over 4 billion in little more than 500 years.

Inadequate diet, disease and natural calamity are likely to have been the principle agents by which human population growth was restrained during most of the species' early history. And as human populations slowly expanded and dispersed around the globe, natural selection honed the adaptive talent of mankind, and people evolved strategies of control and regulation that were appropriate to their circumstances.

Farming, fishing, hunting, herding and technology are all expressions of the adaptive talent that has sustained mankind thusfar. Patterns of occupation and reward, birthright, marriage and inheritance, reinforced by systems of belief, education and government, are the strategies by which people have organised and regulated their affairs. Together, these aspects of adaptation and regulation constitute what is described as *culture*.

Man on Earth looks at culture from a functional point of view, examining the extent to which systems of adaptation and regulation have promoted the continuing existence of people in a wide variety of environments around the world. The islanders of the first chapter and the city-dwellers of the final pages actually have more in common than might at first be supposed, and though the chapters in between may at first seem to chart a progression from subsistence to cash surplus economies, they too stress the functional role of culture in human existence.

The book deals with cultures and habitats that vary considerably, but not every aspect of every culture is given equal attention. Common aspects – such as territory and population size, land ownership and food production, marriage and reproduction, inheritance, religion and government – are mentioned frequently, but covered in detail only where their functional relevence is most apparent. This does not deny their functional relevance in every other instance. In fact, the detailed coverage might inspire some thought about how they function in other cultures – particularly in our own.

Finally, it needs to be said that not every cultural strategy mentioned in these pages will find universal approval. Nor is every culture presently functioning in obvious accord with its circumstance: several are likely to change and some will disappear. But seeking the functional relevance of abhorrent strategies and negative developments should not be interpreted as an attempt to excuse them. They are presented in the context of culture as a dynamic phenomenon, rather than something on permanent display, always bearing in mind that the timescale of cultural change may be such that we cannot even distinguish its ebb from its flow in the short span of observation that is available to us.

John Reader, September 1987

CHAPTER ONE

ISLANDERS

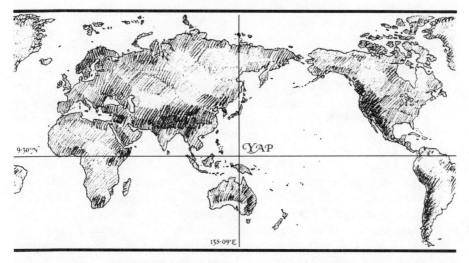

The island of Yap still retains many vestiges of the way people lived on remote Pacific islands before the advent of motorized transport, refrigerators and television. The road running down its length meanders through villages of wood and palm-thatch. Old tracks, paved with slabs of stone lead off to gardens in the shadowy forest. Wheels of stone money – for which Yap is renowned – stand at the roadside, blackened with age (some scratched with the names of today's youth), slowly sinking into the earth; timeless, like the air, the palms, the sea and the visions of south-sea paradise that Yap awakens.

The road ends at a small stream flowing to the beach, where a footpath leads across a bridge of two palm logs. Children swim in the lagoon. A breeze carries the scent of vanilla and coconut. Hibiscus, oleander and lemon grass line the path, and picking a sprig of hibiscus to carry through the village, as instructed, seemed a friendly enough gesture, though none of the villagers offered a greeting or even acknowledged our passing.

At Map, where the edge of the reef lies nearly a mile offshore, enclosing a large sheltered lagoon and a wide dazzling beach over which the palms sway in proper south-sea fashion, a group of men were building an ocean-going sailing canoe. The hull was high-prowed fore and aft, and carved with a twist along its length, like a propeller, so that each end leaned some degrees to opposite sides of the vertical and looked mistakenly constructed until one learned that either end would serve as the bow on a voyage, and the twist in the hull would always set the canoe accurately into the prevailing winds and currents whichever way it was sailing. Hibiscus cord laced the gunwales and leeboards to the hull. The outriggers were attached with lashings of coconut fibre string. The canoe was painted black, red and white and each prow was forked, like the upturned tail of the frigate bird.

The older men moved away from the canoe as we approached, and offered some refreshment. A number of coconuts were opened – the tops deftly sliced off to facilitate drinking – and handed round to all except John, our Yapese guide. For him, one of our hosts cut a small triangular section from the side of a coconut with three vicious slashes of the machete. The nut was passed around to John, but he left it untouched while we drank. Later, John explained that he was a stranger to the other men; and their treatment of his coconut was intended to indicate that his presence was tolerated only because he was accompanying visitors. John tried to laugh off the incident, but his attempts at levity were not helped by the casual remark that he would not have drunk from the coconut immediately anyway. No Yapese would eat or drink anything provided by strangers, he explained, unless able to establish that it was not poisoned.

In times past poisoning was a customary way of dealing with personal vendettas on Yap. Even during the 1980s there have been cases of sudden death which some feel can only be explained as poisonings, and further-more, crime statistics reveal an exceptionally high incidence of assault, homicide and suicide throughout the Micronesian islands.

There are, on Yap, none of the roadside food and drink stalls so common in tropical regions around the world – simply because no Yapese would ever patronise them. Visitors are advised not to stop, show a camera nor even acknowledge the presence of people in certain villages they pass through, and even that most comforting of human attributes – the welcoming smile – becomes suspect on learning that, in the Micronesian view, visitors should not smile so openly and so readily on a first meeting with strangers. Smiles give away too much, they say.

These attitudes do not simply indicate a dislike of foreigners, such as is found in places where tourists are unwelcome. They reflect a concern for territory that affects the islanders themselves much more deeply than it affects visitors. No islander would visit another village without an invitation from one of its residents, and even when passing through a village in the company of a visitor the islanders feel obliged to carry a sprig of hibiscus as a sign of benign intentions. And numerous accounts of violence among the islanders are likely to be heard. Recounted not apologetically, or with awe or surprise, but just cropping up in the course of conversation. On Ulithi atoll, boys learn to wrestle as though their lives may one day depend on it; and quite often they do. On Palau they learn to throw rocks with deadly aim – if a Palauan misses, it means he likes you, they say. And on Yap it was casually revealed that the host of a pleasant afternoon had recently served a six year gaol sentence for manslaughter.

Some 5,000 people live on Yap island, land area approximately 39 sq. mi. (100 sq. km.) A small place, little more than a village in demographic terms, where people are so tightly bound to their home ground that they cannot move freely about the island; where children grow up to accept violence as a means of resolving disputes, and where a large number of people can in all truthfulness say: 'yes, I know a murderer'.

Murder, manslaughter, suicide, rape, assault and theft all seem particularly reprehensible in the confines of a remote Pacific island, but violence occurs in all societies, and although its prevalence among the inhabitants of Micronesia may abuse some cherished dreams of paradise, it also presents some clear and unequivocal facts about human society. The realities of maintaining a reliable food supply and restraining population growth are stark and clear on a speck of land surrounded by a vast open expanse of ocean. The importance of developing appropriate techniques for securing food is inescapable. So is the need to develop appropriate social and cultural strategies by which the resources are apportioned among the island's inhabitants, and handed down from generation to generation. There is not much room for error on a small island, and the strategies by which generations of islanders have survived are therefore a good indication of the extent to which a particular kind of habitat can determine the behaviour of its inhabitants.

The Pacific Ocean is the greatest single feature on Earth. It covers fully one-third of the globe, an expanse of water so vast and voluminous that the entire land area of the Earth, along with all its most impressive features, could easily be accommodated within it. Mount Everest, for example, the highest mountain on Earth, would fit comfortably in the oceanic depths of the Marianas Trench (the deepest waters on Earth), with over two kilometres (a mile and a quarter) of water remaining clear between its peak and the surface.

Next to its sheer size, profound isolation is the most distinctive feature of the Pacific Ocean. Over 25,000 islands are scattered across its surface, more than in all the other oceans combined, but their land area adds up to little more than 125,000 sq. km. (48,000 sq. mi.), about the size of New York State, and their inhabitants total less than two million people, hardly an eighth of the number that live in the combined metropolitan area of New York City and northeast New Jersey alone. The oceanic islands of the Pacific are some of the most isolated places on Earth. Many are uninhabitable, by virtue of their small size and particular characteristics, but even the most favoured are very isolated fragments of land, strictly circumscribed by the ocean, strictly limited in terms of the numbers of people they can support. This basic fact of environmental circumstance has been the most pervasive influence in determining the social arrangements and cultural practices of the people that settled on the Pacific islands.

The peopling of the Pacific has been described as the greatest feat of maritime colonization in human history. Contrary to the conclusions of Thor Heyerdahl's *Kon-Tiki* expedition of 1946, the evidence of plant dispersal, archaeology, linguistics and genetics now shows quite conclusively that the Pacific was not populated from the east by South Americans who drifted in on balsa-wood rafts and the prevailing wind and current, but from the west, by groups from mainland Asia who gradually spread from island to island out into the Pacific. The process began over 40,000 years ago and reached Easter Island – the most isolated place on Earth – about

11

1,500 years ago. It ended about 1,000 years ago, when people first settled in Hawaii and New Zealand.

Simply surviving those ocean crossings of indeterminate length, in open canoes, to arrive on the shores of uninhabited and hitherto unknown islands, was a formidable achievement but, having found an oasis of land in the watery wilderness and floundered across the reef and up onto its shores, the survivors then faced a series of pressing problems for which solutions had to be found quickly if the small group of survivors was to become one of the vigorous self-sustaining island populations that greeted Magellan and the first Europeans that explored the Pacific extensively during the 17th and 18th centuries. The first settlers undoubtedly carried some equipment with them, tools perhaps, fishing lines and so forth; they also probably brought the roots of some basic food crops, but the most important attribute they carried was quite intangible, existing only in their minds – adaptability, the most important human characteristic of all: the ability to adapt a way of life to the prevailing circumstances; the ability to find a way of achieving desirable ends with whatever is available; the ability to perceive a problem and find its solution.

Though the inhabited Pacific islands may have been smothered in vegetation, they are not likely to have offered the voyagers cast up on their shores very much in the way of energy foods. Fish in the lagoon and offshore for protein, to be sure, but edible plants capable of providing the essential sugars and calories by way of their leaves, fruit or roots, were almost entirely absent. Purslane, seaweed and the *pandanus* nut were probably the only edible plants that reached the islands before the first human colonizers; a meagre larder. All of the islanders' staple food plants must have been introduced, for the simple reason that they could not have got there by any other means. The breadfruit, for example, is seedless and can only be propagated from shoots that grow from the spreading roots of the mature tree. Likewise, the banana can only be propagated from shoots, while taro, sweet potato and yams grow from tubers that could not have floated in and taken root on the distant islands – they must have been carried there. Even the coconut, possibly the most important item of all, may not have preceded man into the far Pacific. Although they may seem designed for dispersal by sea, some botanists have questioned whether or not drifting coconuts could retain their germinative powers long enough to establish spontaneous groves on island shores where they finally came to rest. Four months in the sea seems to be about the limit, which, however, may have been all that was needed, and a stand of mature coconut palms at the shore edge doubtless would have been a very welcome sight to prospective colonizers – promising something at least in the way of readily available food and drink.

Coconuts can supply a man's entire daily fluid requirement, and the nut itself can supply a good proportion of daily nutritive requirements as well, but to sustain even a small number of people calls for a luxuriant stand of mature nut-bearing palms. Of course, rainfall would provide an intermittent water supply, but without at least a moderate stand of coconuts palms to guarantee something of their daily liquid needs, the colonizers would not last long. Unless, that is, they had landed on a coral atoll and knew about the body of fresh water that floats above the saline water table on even the smallest, driest and most remote atolls.

Fresh water is just slightly lighter than sea water, by a ratio of 41:40, which means that 41 units of fresh water weigh the same as 40 units of sea water. In most circumstances adding fresh water to sea water simply dilutes the salt concentration of the latter, but in the case of an atoll, where the saline water table stands at the height of the surrounding sea level, rain falling on the island does not mix with the sea water as it percolates down to the water table but instead floats on top of it. Furthermore, because the specific gravities of fresh and sea water are in the ratio of 41:40, 40 parts of sea water are displaced for every part of fresh water collecting above the water table. So, if an island has a maximum elevation of say five metres (16 ft) at its centre, then a maximum 200 m. (650 ft) depth of fresh water may collect beneath it. This potential grades off towards the shore, reaching zero at the level of the water table itself, where the rain falls directly into the sea. Thus a lens-shaped body of fresh water collects beneath the atoll.

The principle by which fresh water displaces salt water on atolls and islands (coastal areas too) in this way is known as the Ghyben-Herzberg law, after the gentlemen who brought it to the attention of science, but it was discovered and exploited by the colonizers of the Pacific long before then.

In point of fact it is highly unlikely that any colonizers could have successfully established themselves on a Pacific atoll if they did not know about the supply of fresh water that lay hidden just a short distance beneath the surface sands. Whether they arrived already armed with the knowledge or discovered it shortly after their arrival, the hidden ground water was crucial to their survival – not only as a source of drinking water, but also for their food crops. Even coconut palms, whose huge wadded mat of fibrous roots is especially able to soak up and retain rainfall, benefits from the presence of additional fresh ground water; the breadfruit tree, with a spreading root system, is more dependent upon it while the banana can hardly be grown without it. The most crucial significance of the ground water, however, lies with the cultivation of taro, whose large starchy corm has long been a staple food of the Pacific islanders.

Taro, a swamp-dwelling member of the lily family that is believed to have originated in south-east Asia, will only flourish where its roots are completely flooded with fresh water a good deal of the time; even slightly brackish water will kill the plant. On the continental mainland and the high islands where its cultivation is presumed to have begun, maintaining a swampy root medium for taro was not difficult – indeed, it could hardly have been avoided. Growing taro on sandy atolls, however, was much more of a problem, and the solution was found in what is perhaps the most significant cultural adaptation of the Pacific islanders: sunken gardens.

At the centre of the island, where the ground water floats deepest and freshest above the saline, pits were dug down to the water table, and a muddy soil encouraged to develop. Leaves and humus from surrounding undergrowth were thrown in; algae proliferated at the surface, adding further nutrients to the sludge. Eventually, on islands far into the open Pacific, surrounded by an ocean of salt, the colonizers had perfected a method of recreating the freshwater swamps wherein taro had originated. The practice persists to this day. On small islands the pits may be only a metre or two across; on large islands like Nukuoro and Kapingamarangi they extend over hectares. Innovations that heighten production have evolved. In the Gilbert Islands (now called Kiribati), the taro corms are enclosed with a bundle of organic debris (leaves and humus collected from beneath specific trees) in a bottomless woven basket of pandanus fronds which is then staked to the muddy bottom of the pit, so that the taro effectively floats in its growing medium. A network of raised pathways traverses the sunken gardens, often planted with breadfruit and banana, which serve the important function of providing shade – for taro grows best when sheltered from direct sunlight. A mature plant stands up to two metres (six foot six inches) high.

Sunken gardens take time to establish. Taro takes time to grow and will not provide any substantial quantities of food for at least two years. Bananas take three years to fruit; a coconut palm may flower three years after germinating and taking root, but eight years is more usual – and even after the flower has been pollinated, the nut still needs a year to mature. Breadfruit – rich in carbohydrates and one of the highest yielding food plants – will not begin producing fruit for several years after planting.

So, even though fish were constantly available and wild-sown coconuts, pandanus and leaf plants may have provided an element of essential vegetative nutrition, establishing a good and sustainable food base on an uninhabited Pacific island was a problem of formidable proportions. As the colonizers sought and employed the solutions that they hoped might enhance their chances of survival, the limitations of the environment can never have been far from anyone's mind. There was little room for misjudgement or failure, and success was easily measured, consisting only of continued survival. It might be said that by hedging the colonizers round with the constant dire threats of starvation and death, the environment was selecting from available options those practices – solutions – that were capable of keeping people alive. By extension, then, the environment might be said to have selected for survival only those people who found appropriate solutions for their problems, and adapted their ways to the circumstances of the environment. Certainly, the environment would soon have inflicted severe penalties on those who did not adapt – and occasionally on even the best adapted. Typhoons, for instance, destroy indiscriminately.

Death – capricious or otherwise – was probably the fate of many who left their home populations with hopes of founding another, somewhere in the unknown. But clearly, some did succeed. Doubtless the practices that enhanced survival evolved progressively, as people extended the human domain further and further into the Pacific. Problems became opportunities, and the solutions to the problems became the customs – practices – which eventually became the sustaining culture of the group. More

14

individuals survived, nutrition improved and before long women began bearing children. The group of voyagers that had beached their canoe on the island was now on the way to becoming a viable population.

Considerable joy must have attended the birth of the first child on the island. In that single moment, all preceding effort and strife was justified. The birth simultaneously applauded past endeavour, present status and future hope. What more could the colonizers wish for? Here, surely, was the living expression, the only significant expression, of success and purpose in life? The group had found food and drink enough, shelter enough, care enough for its members to produce and raise children.

However, the first child born was also the first hint of a new problem for which a solution would have to be found. If a population is healthy enough to reproduce, its numbers will multiply. This is true of all forms of life, everywhere, but on an isolated island the effect is particularly problematic. Among a founding group of 20 men and women, for example, given adequate food and reasonable environmental conditions, births could exceed deaths to the extent that the population size would double with each twenty-five year generation span: 20 to begin with, 40 twenty-five years later, then 80, 160 and a living population of 320 individuals after only 100 years.

A doubling of numbers with every generation represents an annual increase of 2.8 percent, possibly higher than was likely, but even if the population grew at a more conservative overall estimate of only one percent per year, it would still number 100,000 living individuals after only 850 years.

Population growth is the most important single determinant of the way human societies are organised, and of the way people behave towards one another. It is equally fundamental to all societies, everywhere, but is most clearly demonstrated among an island community – on the island of Yap, for example.

Yap lies 1,000 km. (620 mi.) north of the equator and 13,500 km. (8,400 mi.) east of Greenwich. Politically, it is one of the four Federated States of Micronesia administered by the United States as a United Nations Trust Territory; geographically, it embraces over 1,000,000 sq. km. (386,000 sq. mi.) of the western Pacific – twice the size of France – though it offers only about 120 sq. km. (46 sq. mi.) of dry land, fully 100 of which are on Yap island itself, with the remainder distributed among 15 atolls and low islands, four of them uninhabited.

Yap is described as a high island, though in fact it is four close but separate islands of volcanic origin and unimpressive elevation, bound together by an encircling coral reef. Climate is distinctively tropical, with temperatures hovering around 27°C (81°F) all year and rainfall rarely falling below the 3000 mm. (118 in.) annual average. Winds are changeable, though predominantly from the northeast and rarely mounting to typhoon force. Being of volcanic rather than coral origin, warm and well-watered, Yap developed good stands of natural vegetation, and good soils. The reef, extending 1,000 m. (1,100 yards) or more from the shore all round the

15

island, supported sizeable populations of fish. In its pristine state of natural productivity, Yap offered its colonizers rare advantages of both space and opportunity.

The precise identity and origin of the first people to haul their canoes over the reef and settle on the shores of Yap is not known. The earliest firm evidence of human habitation on Yap consists of some pottery fragments found in deposits dated at 176 AD, though archaeologists suggest that people were established on the island for some time before then. The pottery fragments and artifacts that have been found, the stone paths that people long ago laid throughout the island, the house platforms they built, the fish traps, the taro pits – all indicate a long sustained human presence on the island.

Of their shadowy beginnings, Yap legend tells only of the ancestors having emerged and settled at a village called Ngolog, and later having re-emerged at another village called Tab after a flood had inundated the entire island. For the rest, the earliest history of Yap can only be deduced from an assessment of the island's environmental circumstances.

That the first colonizers arrived on Yap at all indicates that they were born and brought up among an established and successful group of people. The skills required to make, equip and sail an ocean-going canoe are not acquired overnight. Undoubtedly the colonizers brought along with their canoe other cultural artifacts and practices of the society they had left – not all of which need necessarily have been the most appropriate to the environmental circumstances they confronted on Yap. For instance, the abundance of shell implements that archaeologists have found in their digs on the island indicate that the colonizers had been accustomed to making and using shell tools in their home environment and continued to do so on Yap – even though Yap, a volcanic island, was littered with stone from which far superior and more durable tools could have been made. Having arrived with one skill the colonizers simply did not see the need or take the opportunity to develop another. Similarly, there may have been aspects of their social arrangements and culture that had evolved in the particular circumstances of their home environment, and functioned very well there, among an expanded and successful population, but which were of less value to a small group attempting to establish itself somewhere else. Thus it cannot be said that the pristine Yap environment was wholly responsible for the type of society and culture that developed among its inhabitants. Having been born and brought up elsewhere the colonizers brought a mixed bag of ready-made skills, ideas and beliefs to the island; and this cultural inheritance would have been the starting point for everything they attempted to do on Yap. Some skills might have been appropriate from the start; some might have been modified; others might have been abandoned. The result was a blend of cultural heritage and environmental influence such as is found among immigrants everywhere.

Good climate, fertile soils and a large expanse of coral reef – the colonizers thrived on Yap. It is impossible to say how rapidly their population grew, but it is certain that it eventually reached the carrying capacity of the island. From the evidence of house sites and other human

16

endeavour, archaeologists have calculated that, at its peak, Yap's population reached between about 28,000 and 34,000 people. By that time the island and the reef surrounding it had been transformed by the continuous labour of succeeding generations from a wholly pristine environment to a complex of food producing systems. Every available resource was utilized. Stone fish weirs had been built out towards the reef wherever they would be effective – walls of rough-hewn coral laid like arrows or zig-zags where the prevailing currents would head fish to traps set in the apex and corners of the weir. Taro pits had been excavated wherever feasible in the fertile alluvial soils of the coastal flats, carefully irrigated by freshwater channels to provide a year-round supply of the staple crop. Some 130 villages stood close by the shore, surrounded by luxuriant stands of palms, fruit trees and bamboo; row upon row of yam gardens had been laid out on every usable scrap of the high ground behind the villages; above and beyond the gardens rose intractable areas of steep forest and, surmounting all, a largely infertile plateau. In all, only about half of Yap's land area was suitable for cultivation, and of the cultivable land only about 20 percent was suitable for growing taro all year round, while the rest provided seasonal yam harvests.

But every cultivable scrap of land, every tree, every stretch of reef fishing was owned and used. A land survey of the Dalipebinaw district, for instance, shows that its land area of 5.5 sq. km. (2.1 sq. mi.) – 556 ha (1,375 acres) – contained 158 residential units with rights to 2,689 taro patches, 2,127 gardens and 177 stone fish trap sites. In many places around the coast people had dammed and filled in areas of the tidal flats to extend their arable land area.

From its fertile beginnings, Yap's expanding population probably inspired many ingenious and strenuous efforts to extend the island's cultivable land area and intensify food production, but once the limits of the resources had been reached the potential for innovation would soon have been exhausted. Thereafter, the people were concerned not with tackling new ground or unexploited resources, but with managing land and sea resources whose productivity was already extensively developed. Generation after generation of men, women and children were concerned principally with the production of food from the taro pits, gardens and fish weirs that had been built long before.

The environmental boundaries were well marked. Within them there was little opportunity to exercise explorative or exploitative talent, and possibly even less respect for it – so it is hardly surprising that the adaptations which served as solutions to the problem of containing a healthy expanding population within the rather narrow limits set by the island had more to do with social arrangements than with environmental matters. And Yap's high population growth rate potential on limited but fertile territory produced a social system of labyrinthine complexity, wherein every individual was from birth tied into a network of rights and obligations with 100 or more other individuals, and in which any piece of land might belong to one person, be subject to the consent of another, lived on by a third and cropped by a fourth.

Individual rights to occupy land and utilise resources were of course the crux of the matter, but, although it was the individual's urge to secure a position in the here-and-now that motivated the system, the Yapese made an important distinction between the permanent status of land and the transient nature of man. People come and go, they say, but the land remains forever, and the Yap system of allocating resources was more concerned with maintaining the productivity of the land than with fulfilling individual ambitions.

Broadly speaking, the Yap social system separated the responsiblity for land and people between the sexes: men were principal custodians of the land, women were custodians of the people. Everyone on Yap belonged to one or another of 30 or more clans, each tracing its descent through the female line, from mother to grandmother and so on back to one legendary ancestress. But, although mother and clan defined blood allegiances and historical status, individuals took their name and material status from the land their fathers occupied – not their father's name, but a name given to the land itself.

All the land on Yap is vested primarily in a series of named estates. The nucleus of the estate was the village land upon which the foundation of a house had been laid, but it also included taro patches, gardens, fish weirs, forest rights, sections of the lagoon and the mangrove swamps, which may not all be in the immediate vicinity of the village. In addition to the food and shelter it provided, the estate also conferred social status and authority on its occupants. The estates were ranked in an hierarchical order that matched their location and productivity, and their occupants were ranked accordingly – a chief was a man living on the estate of chiefs, and so on.

Estate rights and status passed from father to son. Daughters inherited nothing of the estate they were born on. Once past puberty women were obliged to seek a husband on another estate and take up residence there – a move marked by ceremonies and exchanges of rights and goods that established a complex series of claims and counterclaims between the two estates.

In essence, marriage was a trade-off between the value of a man's estate and the capacity of a woman to maintain or even enhance that value with her labour and the production of children. But since all the occupants of both the groom's and the bride's estates were obliged to contribute towards the cost of guaranteeing that the marriage was a good deal, and since every individual was likely to become involved with the obligations (both shared and reciprocal) for several marriages over the years, a great deal of mutual interest and obligation developed among the estates and their occupants. The productivity of the land and the health of its occupants were always central to these concerns, for neglect of either would leave an individual severely disadvantaged in the exchange of guarantees.

Yap's social system may have acknowledged the paramount importance of productive land and water, but it also made some people more important than others. Where and how an individual lived, the quality of life, and – to a certain extent – whether or not a person lived at all, was defined by social status. The hierarchical ranking of estates and their occupants fell into a

descending order of seven social castes, that were qualitatively described
as *tabugul* – pure – at the top end of the scale, and *taay* – impure – at the
lower end, and this distinction eventually pervaded all aspects of life on
Yap. There were differences of degree, but in the end all things were either
pure or impure. Land, resources, produce and people – everything. Certain
lands produced crops that only the pure could eat. Certain seafoods, such
as turtles, were available only to the most pure, while eel, sharks and squid
were eaten only by the impure. A man was considered pure, and his wife
impure. Their house was divided down the middle into its pure and impure
halves. The wife's kitchen was outside, her husband's inside. His food
came from his pure gardens and sea portions, hers from the impure; it was
cooked and eaten from separate pots – pure and impure. At the same time,
however, man and wife were themselves pure and impure with respect to
others of their clan and estate. There were people the husband could not
eat with, and others that could not eat with the wife.

Similarly, there were areas where the impure may not venture, paths
along which they may not walk, and places where if they encountered
someone of higher caste they must bow low and look away.

Taboos such as these are a common feature of island societies throughout the Pacific, indeed the word derives from the Polynesian term *tabu*. On
Yap in particular the combined effect of taboos, caste, land and clan
distinctions left little opportunity for people to venture beyond the clearly
defined limits of their social and territorial status. With every person and
every piece of land hedged round with restriction and taboo, trespass was a
very serious offence. Simply to enter another estate without good reason
could mean death. Thus it was quite possible that an individual from one
end of the small island might never visit the other end. Though Yap's
environmental boundaries enclosed such a limited land area, social
boundaries made the island a larger world than one person could
encompass.

For the most part, enforcement of the taboos was rarely necessary, for
everyone believed that infringement would cause actual harm – impure
food was actually tainted and would poison; trespass would affect
productivity of the gardens; fishing would fail; typhoons would destroy
plantations; disease and disability would afflict the guilty. Society could
and did punish misdemeanour with fines, banishment and even death if
the offence was serious enough, but the fear of some natural punishment
usually sufficed – especially since there was no time limit on the
punishment: an unexpected death could be due to an offence committed
years before, it was believed, and could affect not only the guilty party but
also any other member of the family.

Though Yap's social system was structured to the requirements of high
population density it would be wrong to suppose that the population was
always very large and always nicely contained within the carrying capacity
of the island, providing its inhabitants with a Utopian existence wherein
all were happy, well-fed and cared for. No, the population size appears to
have fluctuated widely, and life at times was very hard for some, and very

19

easy for others. There are tales told on the island of when Yap was so crowded that men and families were disinherited, destitute, and forced to live off rafts in the mangrove swamps. There are other tales told of the good times, when young men had little to do, young women wanted only to play and neither saw any need to take on the responsibility of marriage and raising children. These tales are a measure of the parameters within which the norms of Yap's social system are set. The parameters were wide enough to include both a disinherited, lower caste of people that served, it has been said, as a sump which absorbed and disposed of excess population in times of hardship, and sexual and abortion practices that restrained population growth when times were good.

The Yap social order of rank, estate and clan acknowledged the boundaries of environmental circumstance and maintained the high productivity of land and lagoon. But there was a price, though only one section of the population was expected to pay it.

It might be imagined that Yap's stratified caste system would have been designed to allow a degree of social mobility, rewarding the commendable with a move up a rung or two on the social ladder, and punishing the less diligent with a move downward. But in fact, upward movement occurred only when a woman married a man of a higher caste (and was never available to men because for a woman to marry a man of lower caste was a social offence punishable by death). Downward movement was a constant threat to everyone, a fate to be avoided, but for some the unavoidable consequence of pressure on land and resources at times when Yap's population density was critically high.

When population growth strained the boundaries of environmental capacity, social constraints ensured that some people were squeezed out of the system before the environment's productivity was harmed. If a man's landholding was too small to divide among his sons, for instance, the younger of them were expected to leave and support themselves – making coconut fibre rope, perhaps, or undertaking tasks for families better endowed. Similarly, women were required to marry off the household estate and into another once they became eligible; and until she left, a marriageable young woman was considered the most impure of the estate's occupants – confined to certain areas, allocated specific resources and cooking area, no longer allowed to eat of even her mother's food, required to crawl on hands and knees past any men she was incautious enough to encounter. Thus the estate's fertile young women, the individuals most likely to add more numbers to a growing population, were rated the least wanted members of the household. Marriage onto another estate was of course the customary way out of the fertile young woman's despised status, but marriage was not always possible.

Ultimately, however, unmarried women had to leave their natal estate. Outcast and landless, they joined the disinherited sons of the smaller estates and together these individuals developed into a shifting population of landless people that survived in servitude.

Thus, in all important respects there are just two classes of people on Yap: the high-caste landowners, who are called the *pilung*, which means

essentially *the voice of the people*, and the low-caste *milingai*, said to
mean *to run a place*.

In return for work and service the milingai were allowed to establish villages of their own on pilung estates. They exchanged servitude for security, but in a society that regarded land as the measure of all prestige, their status was little more than that of slaves. The milingai were summoned for all kinds of menial work; they were expected to keep their masters supplied with turmeric, pottery, woven mats and baskets; they were required to carry away and bury the corpses of the high-caste dead. In times of dispute between high-caste villages, the milingai were obliged to form the front line of both warring parties and to open hostilities by flinging stones at one another. The low-caste cut their hair short to ensure they could not wear the comb that was the privilege of the high-caste, and were forbidden to wear any other ornaments, or to tattoo themselves with certain high-caste designs. Milingai women were obliged to squat at the roadside when high-caste people were about; a low-caste man had to walk behind a high-caste woman. The food the milingai were given in return for work had to be taken from the daughters' plot (the most impure on the estate); their coconuts had to be collected from the women's side of the garden. The land they were allocated was often inland and poor, any fishing rights they were granted were restricted to certain places, to certain net sizes and to certain kinds of fish. Flying fish, and most reef fish were absolutely taboo for the milingai. From the sea, those that were permitted to fish at all subsisted mainly on shark, stingray, squid and eel, all impure food that the high-caste would not touch. The residents of some inland villages trapped and ate rats as a protein substitute for the fish they were denied.

During the periods when Yap's population was relatively low, when rainfall was high, when fishing and harvests were consistently good, some benefit inevitably found its way down to the milingai. Then they were allowed to move onto better land; some acquired coastal sites and access to fishing. Life improved, marginally, for a time, but their inferior social status did not change. The milingai remained the outcasts of Yap society; an example of what might happen to those who pressed too hard against its boundaries. They were a useful source of labour, and always the people who suffered most when circumstances took a turn for the worse.

When conditions deteriorated, the landless low-caste became a buffer between the privileged high-caste and the boundaries that the environment was tightening around them: a buffer that absorbed most of the pressure and for which the high-caste need feel no great sympathy. After all, the landless outcasts had been snared beyond the boundaries long ago, and trapped there by taboo and social convention for so long that now they seemed like different people. A distinct race of people perhaps, impure and manifestly destined to bear the brunt of the violence that the environment occasionally inflicted on its inhabitants. What more should the privileged high-caste feel for them? There were no reciprocal land ties that could provoke concern, and few blood links strong enough to evoke any sense of mutual responsibility.

21

In the early days of settlement on the island the birth of child signified the success of the lifestyle that the settlers had established. It was a magical event, full of promise and hope. As the population approached the maximum density that Yap could support, however, births became rather less desirable. Each birth represented not only another mouth to feed, but also another obligation, another threat to individual status, another person with whom resources would have to be shared. From the individual's point of view, so long as there were enough hands around to perform essential tasks, it was best to control the number of additional individuals joining the group. Thus the individual's wish to retain an allotted share of the available resources accorded precisely with the group's need to restrain its population growth.

But the means that evolved to achieve and maintain this essential balance between individual wish and group need was not instruction, order, taboo or edict directed specifically towards the problem, telling people that they must not have children. No, it was much more subtle than that. Entirely indirect, even unconscious, the necessary practices developed from the selfish pursuits of individuals, and they persisted because in this case individual selfishness served an altruistic end — enabling the group to remain secure and healthy within the boundaries of its environmental circumstances, reproducing enough to guarantee the existence of future generations, but never so much as to overstrain the capacity of the system.

Essentially, the means that served this end were social devices ensuring that the most fertile members of the group looked upon raising children as the least desirable of the activities open to them. This was not difficult to achieve, (though it needs to be stressed again that it was not a conscious decision directed towards a particular end so much as a series of preferences that persisted because they served that end).

With the resources of land and sea brought to maximum productivity, marked out, allocated and managed, prestige eventually became the dominant feature of Yap's culture. And prestige was measured and ranked along every conceivable axis of the island's highly structured, stratified, formal and conservative system of landholding and social organization. Within the family and the clan, the estate and the village, the district and the island, every individual and every plot of land held an assigned rank and status of prestige. Older people, both men and women, held more prestige than younger, simply by virtue of their years, and the old men held most prestige of all. Old men and the elder heads of family achieved the ultimate prestige of chieftainship and high office. It was they who sat around in lengthy council of family and village heads, debating rights and obligations, assigning privilege, planning exchanges and occasionally plotting wars. None was likely to be less than 50 years old, and since the various positions passed from a man to his brothers in order of descending age, as they died, then to the oldest among the sons of all the brothers, and so on — prestige could be a very long time coming to even the most deserving and ambitious individuals.

Prestige was closely related to responsibility. Technically, a young man

22

was considered to be a man only when he became the head of a family or village group, and was responsible for its prestige and status. Until then he was still a young man, even though he might be over 50 years old.

While the population of Yap remained within the island's carrying capacity, everyone had enough to live on, whatever their rank and prestige – or lack of it. Prestige was linked to the management of group resources, not to the individual possession of produce; it bestowed no direct advantage upon the prestigious, so prestige was sought for political, rather than for material ends. Conversely, within the security of productive estate and well-managed clan, a lack of prestige brought no material problems, no want that could translate into a driving ambition to acquire prestige status. The positions of prestige were well known, their incumbents visible for all to see. The succession was clearly defined; a young man might see a long line of uncles and male cousins standing between himself and manhood but there was little he could do to hasten the process. He might plot and scheme, he might resort to magic, sorcery, chicanery or even poison, but his accession was answerable to more than just his position on the line – there were other measures of suitability to be taken into account and in a closed society where not much could be hidden, he had better wait his turn, passing his fertile years as a young man with no responsibilities.

Childhood on Yap was a protracted affair, for both sexes and in more than one sense of the term. For a boy it extended well into the late teens. His food was prepared by his mother, he had few duties and no responsibilities. Between the age of fifteen and twenty he would build a house for himself on his father's estate as far as possible from his parents' dwelling. Taro pits, yam plots and coconuts would be set aside for his use. He would fish, and might be called upon to fight in village disputes, but for the most part there was little call on his time and an elaborate round of love affairs became a major preoccupation. As a youth he would already have had one lover, and would certainly seek others. He would have learned that girls are demanding and inconstant – hard to attract and harder to hold. Even if he could persuade a girl to live with him, her affections were still likely to wander.

Young women were similarly free of duty and responsibility while they lived as children with their mother. At the onset of her first period, however, a young women moved out of the village to a specially designated menstrual area, where she remained for an entire year. Here she was visited by friends, and love affairs became a consuming interest. No man could claim her exclusive affection during this year (even though she might be married), and she was likely to spread her favours widely, seeking broad experience in love and sociability.

At the end of the year the young woman returned to her father's estate, if resources were adequate, where a house would have been built specially for her. Or else she might have chosen to live with a lover, in which case she was considered as married to him, although her way of life was not radically altered until the couple solemnly undertook the ceremonial exchanges of rights and obligations between the families. Until then the young woman need not tend or prepare her husband's food – his mother would happily do so. She was expected to be faithful, but either party could end the marriage at will.

The Yap system acknowledged that most young people start marriage more to facilitate their love affairs than to undertake the serious responsibilities of home and family. No criticism attached to couples that terminated their marriage after a week, a month, or a year. Even if the ceremonial exchanges had taken place, the couple were still free to part – provided no children had been born. More than any other factor, children brought responsibility to marriage, confirming a man's obligation to provide food for his wife; binding a woman to her husband, effectively tying her down to one man. Children also made divorce a much more serious matter. A child stayed with its father when a couple separated – except if it was still suckling, when the mother was allowed to take the child with her but was obliged to return it when weaned.

Thus, the social constraints that evolved to contain Yap's population growth included a good deal of sexual freedom and lack of serious responsibility during an individual's most fertile years, along with considerable social pressure to assume responsibility if a child should be born. Faced with a choice between responsibility and freedom, most couples chose the latter and took care not to produce children. Their affairs followed a pattern of social scheming, conversation and the exchange of gifts. Couples met in secluded parts of the estate, where they avoided the reproductive consequences of their coming together by concentrating their attention on the pleasurable external aspects of sex. The Yapese speak shyly of a traditional sexual practice that gives heightened pleasure to both partners and avoids conception. Though never perfectly described, a prolonged embrace and slow friction of penis against clitoris seems the essence of the procedure. Ejaculation need be internal only when intended. With a skilful partner the female's pleasure is said to be particularly intense, but, since young men acquire the necessary skill only with much practice, youthful love affairs tend to become impassioned pursuits of an exquisite pleasure that is often talked about but rarely experienced – especially from the females' point of view.

Traditionally, young female entertainers were installed in exclusive club houses, with whom the young men of the village could satisfy their sexual desires and learn about the most satisfying practices without having to worry about the demands of an aroused and impassioned woman. It was all considered quite proper and above board. The young ladies were accorded the respect due to any who fulfil important roles in society.

The practice of installing young ladies in club houses specifically to aid and tutor young men in sexual matters was deplored by European missionaries when they arrived on Yap and was eventually abandoned. But the stories of traditional sexual practices persist, and women can still become very demanding, it is said, in their pursuit of the complete sexual satisfaction that tradition promises. For their part, men on Yap have always believed that after the first flush of youth and early adulthood, sex is debilitating and can be harmful. Once a man has married or assumed a

24

degree of social responsibility, many taboos affect his sexual activity. He is expected to refrain from coitus while constructing a canoe, building a house, laying a road, or gathering certain shellfish, for example, and must stay away from women completely while preparing for a fishing expedition. Thus there are occasions when a man must refrain from sex, and a married man may often refuse to satisfy his wife in the prolonged traditional manner, for fear that she will insist upon it too often, with detrimental effect on his work and well-being.

In effect, sex was both carrot and stick in a complex of social ethics that served to control Yap's population size. While the unmarried and those without social responsibility could satisfy their sexual desires as they pleased so long as they did not produce any children, married partners were free to produce children but could not copulate as much as they might have wished. Individuals undoubtedly believed that the concessions granted, prestige bestowed and restraints imposed all served principally to further individual interest. The unmarried would hardly need to be told that babies would hinder their freedom and pleasure, while a married man truly believed that too much sex would harm his health and threaten the success of his endeavours.

Yap's population growth was further restricted by the fact that birth was not the inevitable consequence of conception. Many unmarried women chose to terminate the pregnancy instead, and even a married woman might want to restrict the size of her family. Children increased the burdens of gardening and cooking considerably, not so much because there were more mouths to feed, as because Yap's emphasis on the separation of rank and sex within the clan and estate meant that the mouths of each sex and age-grade had to be fed with the produce of separate gardens, cooked over separate fires, served from separate pots. Complying with these social strictures involved a great deal of work that most women preferred to avoid; many openly expressed the hope of having only a few children, significant numbers of them resorted to abortion as a means of ensuring the hope was fulfilled.

Though publicly deplored, deliberate abortion fits very neatly into the Yap social scheme. Married men wanted children. A husband would expect his wife to be fertile, and probably would hope that she was fecund too, able to produce children as often as their limited copulation allowed. He might beat or divorce a wife that attempted abortion, and such a woman severely jeopardised her chances of ever making a stable marriage. Nonetheless, any woman who wished to abort a pregnancy could easily do so without much risk of discovery. It was the Yap attitude to menstruation that made this possible.

Menstruating women were regarded as impure, and were obliged to seclude themselves in a specially designated menstrual compound at the onset of their period each month, and to remain there until it was over. Nothing, it was believed, could affect a man and his endeavours more adversely than the proximity of a menstruating woman. At the same time, if a woman did become pregnant it was customary for her to conceal the fact for at least the first three months, during which it was believed that

25

both she and her child were most susceptible to sorcery. So a pregnant woman would still retire to the menstrual compound each month when her period was normally due. So far as her husband was concerned she was menstruating normally, and while in seclusion could terminate the pregnancy with little risk of discovery.

Induced abortion was a relatively common practice among the densely populated islands of the Pacific. Drinking concentrated sea water and vigorous massage were two methods frequently employed, but on Yap another technique was devised. A thin roll of hibiscus leaves was inserted into the mouth of the cervix. The leaves expanded as they absorbed moisture, stretching the cervix which was then scratched with a sharp stick, stone, fingernail or other object until blood flowed. The local infection resulting from this self-inflicted injury was usually enough to induce abortion.

Amid the plethora of obligations and rights in which everyone on Yap partook there was a need for some sort of token that could be seen, handled and even exchanged as evidence that the obligations between people and groups indeed had been fulfilled. The token should be rare and durable, but of no practical purpose, so that it was valued only for the obligations it represented – rather than for any intrinsic attribute. Such tokens are a feature of most human societies, they take many forms and collectively are known as money. On Yap, shells were the first items to be used as money – a practice the first settlers probably brought from their original home. They used the rare flat mother-of-pearl shells, and naturally, the size and condition of the shells varied – making some more valued than others. The value of one shell and another was comparable, so therefore were the obligations – or payments – that they represented.

Shell money is common throughout the Pacific, but at some stage in their history the Yapese introduced to their dealings a form of currency that is found nowhere else – stone money. Discs of stone the size of millstones, though sometimes much larger, with a hole through the middle. Called *rai*, the stone money of Yap has all the virtues of a sound and dependable currency: hard to make, difficult to counterfeit, and not easily lost, stolen or destroyed. Nor, however, are rai easily transported. With a pole through the central hole they can be carried between the shoulders of two men, but it is simpler to leave them in one known place – in the bank, as it were – while their ownership changes hands. Thus rai are found all over the island, ranged along pathways, leaning decoratively against houses, vanishing beneath enveloping vegetation.

Precisely when stone money was first used on Yap is not known, nor is there any idea of where the practice originated. Because their form resembles that of the pierced jade discs from ancient China, called *pi* (the origin of which is in turn traced back to the early stone age mace), some see in Yap's stone money an indication that the first settlers may have had links with continental Asia. Yap myth ascribes the invention to a wise old man called Anagumang who, guided by the Pleiades, long ago found caves of beautiful shining rock on a distant island. He set seven men to quarry

26

and fashion the rock with shell-axes. First they made fish, then crescent
moons, and finally a disc, round as the full moon, that Anagumang found
most to his satisfaction. With a hole cut through the middle to facilitate
transportation, the disc was ferried back to Yap – and people have been
fighting for them ever since, some narrators will add.

The intrinsic value of the stone money lay principally in its manufacture. Hard to credit, but the rai were quarried not on Yap, but from
limestone caves on Palau, an island that lies 400 km. (250 mi.) across open
ocean to the south west of Yap – at least five-day's sailing under the most
favourable conditions. The stone itself is aragonite, a dripstone hard as
marble that creates the spectacular stalagmites and stalactites that are
found in limestone caves. The first rai may have been simple slices of
stalagmite or stalactite, but cutting them with shell tools can never have
been easy – in one legend those condemned to the Yap version of hell must
eternally break stone on Palau. Permission of the Palauan chiefs had to be
traded for with dyes, betel nut and labour. Fires were set to split the rock,
the discs were laboriously shaped with shell tools, polished with pumice
stone and the hole drilled through with pieces of reefstone. The canoes
that carried the rai were sunk in tidal channels to facilitate loading, then
baled out for the voyage back to Yap.

The problems of manufacture and transportation severely limited both
size and number of rai in the early days. Discs of about 120 cm. (48 in.)
were the largest the canoes could carry, most were considerably smaller
and all were extremely rare – owned only by chiefs whose estates produced
enough to send men on such distant and extravagant voyages. Andrew
Cheyne, a British sea captain visiting Yap in 1843 reported that the stones
were very rare and highly prized, their possession the cause of much
jealousy between the chiefs. In the 1860s, Alfred Tetens, a German trader
remarked that the limited amount of available stone money assured 'a
controlled financial system', though Tetens himself assured the beginning
of its rapid devaluation.

In 1865, Tetens carried a group of ten men and their rai back from Palau
to Yap. By then European traders had brought iron tools into the Pacific.
On Palau, iron of course hastened the production of rai, while the advent of
trading ships allowed the carriage of much larger coinage. The culmination
of this trend came in the 1870s, when an enterprising Irish-American
trader by the name of David Sean O'Keefe struck bargains with the chiefs
on Yap whereby he would underwrite the production and transportation of
stone money from Palau, in return for all the copra (the dried oil-bearing
core of the coconut) and dried *beche de mer* (the sea cucumber, a delicacy
in China) they could provide. Thus O'Keefe cornered the market for
himself, and sealed the fate of Yap's unique monetary system.

A craze for the stones broke out. Between 1872 and 1901, when he
disappeared and is presumed to have died, O'Keefe ferried literally
thousands of rai into Yap, most larger than previously known. At one time
there were over 400 men working in the quarries on Palau, it is reported.
After O'Keefe's disappearance, a larger German vessel took over the trade,
bringing in rai up to four metres (13 ft) in diameter. Devaluation eventually

ended the trade with foreigners. From an item of rarity in the 1840s to a common feature when quarrying stopped in the early 1900s, numbers soared from perhaps hundreds to a total of 13,281 when officials counted them in 1929.

Despite the effects of foreign trade, however, stone money has persisted as a token of traditional exchange among the Yapese. Aged and pitted like old marble, draped with creeping vegetation, they seem more the relics of a past era than the tokens of current transactions. But in fact, their ownership is still transferred against the obligations of clan and estate. The stones identifiably made before O'Keefe's time are valued most highly, but every piece has its price.

The first explorers of the Pacific may have evoked images of paradise when they described the islands they discovered – but the traders, whalers and adventurers who followed in their wake found a different reality. An early visitor likened the Gilbert Islands to a 'madhouse, with the different wards each at war with one another'. D. Parker Wilson, doctor on an American whaling voyage to the Pacific during the years 1839 to 1843, writes of islands where people were 'sorely straitened for food'. He tells of his vessel finding a canoe with five living and 13 dead that had been set adrift from an island nearly 3,000 km. (1,860 mi.) away, with just coconuts and some bamboo containers of water to sustain them. Wilson found forced emigration, abortion and even infanticide to be common practice among the Pacific islanders, and he had very little doubt as to their motive: '... I believe nearly all the South Sea islanders destroy their female children immediately they are born.... Did these people not destroy their offspring, they would become vastly too numerous... as it is, however, they often times become over-populous, and hard necessity requires the sacrifice of some, and the lot falls upon families to abandon their place of birth... in fragile canoes... in search of more bountiful lands.'

Yap was one of the most bountiful islands that drifting emigrants could have hoped to encounter – extensive and productive enough to support a large population. Many generations passed between the arrival of the first settlers and the refinement of the strategies that served to maintain a stable population, and when European visitors first attempted to settle on the island late in the 19th century they encountered a highly ordered, self-regulating community – though they certainly did not understand Yap's social system as anything other than a contrast to their own, and tended to view it as an example of exotic barbarism.

By then the island had probably sustained its maximum carrying capacity of between 28,000 and 34,000 people for a very long time. The limitations of the island environment, and the constraints of its social system, were recognized and accepted by everyone. Yap was an enclosed and introverted community. Strange foreign visitors who arrived in fantastic sailing ships, and left again soon after, were tolerated, but the first strangers who attempted to settle on the island were treated no differently from islanders who attempted to trespass from one part to another.

Islanders killed a number of the Spanish soldiers and missionaries who

28

attempted to establish stations on Yap in the late 1800s. The Spanish responded with larger, fiercer forces, however, and fear of retaliation soon tempered Yapese violence to pragmatic acceptance of the Spanish presence. Foreign rule has been continuous ever since. As Spain's colonial decline coincided with the rise of Germany's colonial ambition under Bismarck, the administration of Yap and all the Caroline Islands, passed to Germany in 1899. At the onset of the World War I, the islands were taken over by Japan; at the end of World War II they became a trust territory of the United Nations, administered by the United States. And at present, though aspiring to independence within the Federated States of Micronesia, the islands remain economically dependent on the United States.

The predominant effect of foreign influence in the Pacific has been a calamitous drop in the number of people living on the islands. Wherever Europeans landed the effect of their arrival was deathly. On Yap, the number of people declined from an estimated minimum of 28,000 before 1850 to a total of just 7,808 when Spanish missionaries conducted a census in 1899. Twelve years later the German adminstration counted 6,157 people on the island. Under the Japanese the population fell to 4,401 in 1925, and to 3,556 in 1935. By 1946, when the Americans made a census, the total number of people living on Yap had fallen to 2,582 – for every thousand people the island supported before 1850, 92 descendants were alive in 1946.

The diseases that Europeans carried to the islands were the initial cause of population decline. Lacking any inherited resistance, the islanders succumbed in their thousands to measles, smallpox and tuberculosis. But more pernicious than the deaths, however, was the lack of births. During the years from 1917 to 1930, for example, when the crude death rate stood at 40 per thousand the birth rate was only 15 per thousand. A study conducted by researchers from Harvard University in 1948 found that among women of child-bearing age and above on Yap, 34.4 percent had never given birth, compared with an average of about 15 percent among women of other population groups around the world.

Disease was partly responsible for the declining birth-rate, just as it had been largely responsible for the rising death-rate, for the Europeans had also introduced syphilis and gonorrhea, and these often cause sterility. But in the final analysis it was social practice rather than disease that held Yap's population in steady decline. As numbers dwindled, life became easier for those who survived, high- and low-caste alike. Prestige accrued more speedily, but responsibility was less pressing and even less desirable than before. Young people enjoyed their freedom more than ever, and no woman needed to assume the burden of a large family.

With improved health care, the American administration succeeded in reversing Yap's population decline. From the low of 2,582 in 1946 the number of people on Yap rose to 5,142 by 1973, and on to 7,298 by 1986. A number of immigrants from other Micronesian islands contributed to this increase, but a continuing decrease in the death rate, coupled with an increase in the birth rate, accounted for the major part of it. But although more individual women have children, families remain small – and seem

29

to be getting smaller: the 1973 census recorded an average of five persons per household, in 1980 the figure stood at 4.8 per household.

Yap is considered to be one of the most conservative of the Pacific islands. But to describe Yapese society as conservative is really just another way of saying that it is rigidly adapted to a set of environmental circumstances that no longer pertain. Adaptations evolve slowly, over generations. Present-day Yap society, with just a few thousand members, essentially is still adapted to the problem of sustaining many times that number, and the lessening of environmental problems, combined with the advent of a new economic circumstance has, if anything, reinforced the conservative nature of that society. The free-for-all of the modern cash economy favours the high caste; prestige these days is measured more by tangible material possessions than by the assumption of intangible responsibility. Mutual obligations that the traditional subsistence economy once imposed have lapsed, broadening the gulf between high and low caste. Education is available to all, but an egalitarian society is still some way off. Though introduced to an ethic of individual advancement, young people remain constrained by the traditional system their parents still adhere to; the conflict strains some to the point of suicide. Though subject to the officers of a democratically elected administration, much of the island's real authority is still vested in the traditional system. It is very difficult for outsiders or low-caste individuals to uncover the evidence that would enable them to solve crimes and enforce the law, and while Yap society unites in this way against what it sees as external authority, the divisions within it harden and are expressed with impunity in the social violence that Yap traditionally condoned: a distrust of strangers, social segregation, physical violence, murder.

Yapese society is presently in a state of flux; making the transition from one environmental circumstance to another. The process is inexorable but ponderous; the evolving pattern of adaptations may eventually exclude every vestige of the caste system that still stipulates precisely how a man should live, and with whom he may sit and eat, but they may be slow to arrive. In the meantime, John's coconut should have come from a woman's palm tree. He belongs to the low-caste, and therefore should not drink with the high caste men even though he had joined them in the company of a visitor.

CHAPTER TWO

SWIDDENERS

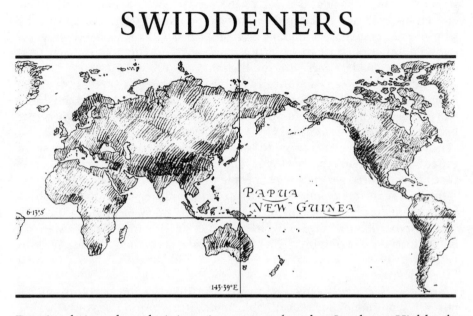

Despite being the administrative centre for the Southern Highlands Province of Papua New Guinea, Mendi has an aura of impermanence – as though it would disappear very quickly if the administrators were to vacate it for a while. The clouds rolling about the top of the valley walls seem more firmly attached to the landscape than does the town sited beneath them. The houses are prefabricated and most of them are elevated above the rough ground on stilts, often with an accumulation of odds and ends below that appear to have been put ready for a not-too-distant day when the owners will move on to another posting in the post- colonial network of itinerant administrators, teachers, medics, missionaries and international development aid experts.

Possibly the most permanent feature of post-colonial endeavour in Mendi is the corps of 23 Australian army engineers, men who have volunteered for a spell of road-building and vehicle maintenance in the highlands as part of the Australian government's aid programme. The military men have their families with them (single men are discouraged) and live in a discreet section of town where the roads are noticeably well maintained, the gardens are neat, and small notices announce precisely who lives where.

The presence of the Australian army in Mendi, along with the few shops, the post office, the police station, the smart new provincial government buildings, (and even the sprinkling of white expatriate faces) all contribute to an impression that Mendi is situated where people have always gathered, and grew from the needs of the people living around and about. A visitor might suppose that Mendi, like most towns, is an expression of its surroundings, dynamically integrated with the broader context and with

31

the economy upon which it depends. But in the case of Mendi such impressions are a delusion. The town in the valley did not rise of its own impetus from the social context of the people living there: the site was chosen because it was flat and extensive enough for use as an airstrip by administrators given the task of civilising the highlands. Mendi serves a national function, bringing the national government and the national economy to this last corner of the highlands.

Mendi is of course economically active, but not as an expression of the economy prevailing among the local people; it has brought God, business and politics to the region, but only a limited number of people derive direct benefit from these activities. The rest may welcome the health care and education that have also come to Mendi, but for the most part they serve the town more than it serves them. They are still dependent upon the land that has supported generations of people in the highland forest. For several thousand years they practised shifting horticulture, clearing a patch of forest to make a garden, cultivating a wide diversity of food plants for a year or two, then moving on to clear another patch while the first was left fallow for a decade or more. The practice is also known as slash- and-burn agriculture or, less pejoratively, *swidden* – an old Northumbrian word for a forest clearing.

Swidden is a highly effective means of utilising a forest environment, but it is a viable and sustainable agricultural economy only where population densities are low, and where the gardens are not expected to fuel a cash economy or satisfy any other excessive demands on their productivity. In the Mendi region, however, the people are now some distance from the perfection of the classic swidden economy. During the past 300 years, a sequence of economic, social and cultural developments has left the people increasingly dependent on canned and processed foods that have to be bought, while – paradoxically – large amounts of land and energy are devoted to the production of food for cultural exchanges which have outlived their usefulness and do little to nourish the people.

The modern prefabrications of Mendi have been set down on an environment of profound antiquity. The clouds rolling about the tops of the valley wall, 700 m. (2,300 ft) above the town, are the most important feature of that environment. The clouds bring rain most afternoons; they billow up the valley from the south, sweeping away the bright sunshine with which most days begin. People have cleared large gardens high up on the steep slopes of the valley, near white cliffs where the limestone structure of the mountains breaks through the thick natural vegetation. Trees line the ridge; beyond lies the forest. The nights are cool, but the days are always warm and moist. There is a sense of great natural fecundity in the highland valleys – even where a town has been built.

A market has been established beside the road that leads north from Mendi. Fenced and orderly, it levies a small fee from each vendor, most of whom are women sitting patiently among their cabbages, tomatoes and onions – the produce they value more as cash than as food. Traditional clothes predominate; the *bilum* (a large string bag) hanging from the head, shell necklaces. One woman, sitting against the trunk of a large eucalyptus

32

at the centre of the market ground, is in mourning for the death of her husband; she wears a grass skirt, her face and body are smeared with grey mud, and from around her neck hang innumerable strings of the polished grey seeds that are called the tears of Job. She will remove one string as each day passes, and when the last one has gone her mourning will be complete.

Some of the men at the market are in western clothes, others are dressed just as they would have been before development brought markets to Mendi. The cloth they wear around the hips is called *laplap* in the pidgin English that serves as *lingua franca* throughout Papua New Guinea; a bunch of large leaves tucked through the belt at the rear is called arse-grass, while their thick beards and moustaches are known as face-grass. Some men have large crescents of pearlshell hanging at their throats, its yellowish iridescence rubbed over with red ochre. As one man turns his head a spot of light shines through the neat round hole in his nasal septum; on another occasion he might adorn himself with a cassowary quill – or a ballpoint pen – passed through that hole.

The United Church, established in 1966 when the Methodist and Congregational missions pooled their resources, occupies a stretch of rising ground beside the road a short distance out of Mendi. The senior missionaries are expatriates from Australia, Canada and Europe; they provide medical and educational services for the local people, as well as running a large proportion of Mendi's commercial activity – including its service station, supermarket, hardware store, and guest house – to the tune of two million US dollars a year. On Sundays the missionaries conduct rousing church services which residents of the guesthouse cannot avoid. The services are enlivened with a good deal of singing, clapping, hallelujahs, handwaving and smiling. The blood of Christ runs freely through the imagery of sermon and service, and the congregation is encouraged to believe that this will wash them clean of sin. By way of confirmation, a man who had recently completed a two year sentence for robbery and rape told how, yes indeed, hallelujah, the blood of Christ had saved him.

The tarmac ends a few hundred metres beyond the mission, and thereafter the road bears less and less witness to the town it left behind; the people walking along it are country dwellers, some have returned from Mendi or the market perhaps, but they all belong to the houses and gardens that are set back among the undulations of the valley floor.

Down a footpath near the group of houses called Tente – more a hamlet than a village – a huge fire of split logs is burning over a pit in the corner of a garden that seems hedged with salvia, the blossoms bright red and shoulder high; there is a cane fence, with banana trees, hibiscus and ginger growing alongside it. A man and two women arrive, each leading a pig tethered by its foreleg. Some boys set rocks to heat on the burning logs. When the fire burns through, the rocks and coals at the bottom of the pit will be thickly covered with banana leaves enclosing quantities of pork and sweet potato. Sealed over with earth, in a few hours the oven will provide a feast for the wedding of Popi Diso and her groom, Moni Dima.

While the wind stirs the casuarina trees and threatens to blow in a

33

shower or two, the representatives of the clans to which Popi and Moni belong set out a long table on which the relatives participating in the customary exchanges may lay out their contributions to the brideprice. In the highlands a wedding is an exchange of family wealth as well as the conjugation of two individuals. Earlier negotiations between the various parties have already assessed the values of bride and groom; all relatives will both give and receive, and everyone involved will have a good idea of the minimum that must change hands. While bride and groom stand quietly alone and to one side, Moni dressed in dark trousers and open-necked shirt, Popi wearing a pale yellow frock, their relatives proceed with the negotiations. The tone of the discussions is intense, but the volume surprisingly muted. Moni's family contributed 12 pigs, 30 pearl shells and 2,000 Kina (£2,857 sterling) to the exchange, 'that is what she cost me' he says. Popi is Moni's second wife; she previously worked at the guesthouse, and now becomes a measure of Moni's standing in the community. She will have to go and work his land, she says, growing sweet potatoes and raising pigs (as well as children) to increase his wealth and prestige, but still cherishes a hope that she might also be able to continue working at the guesthouse. Moni is a clerk in the offices of the Provincial Government.

That there were more than one million people occupying 850,000 sq. km. (328,000 sq. mi.) of Papua New Guinea's mountainous interior was not known to the outside world until the 1930s, though the island had long been the subject of colonial attention. Following the surveys and forays of explorers around the coasts of New Guinea in the 18th century, the Netherlands claimed colonial rights over the western portion of the island in 1828 (now called Irian Jaya and a part of Indonesia). When Germany claimed the northeastern portion of the island in 1884, together with the adjacent island archipelagoes, naming the territory German New Guinea, Britain hastily conferred the status of protectorate on its holding of the southern and eastern sections of the island, and formally annexed the country in 1886, calling it British New Guinea.

In 1906, British New Guinea became the Territory of Papua, under Australian administration, and following the defeat of Germany in the First World War, Australia took over the former German New Guinea as well. At independence, in 1975, the country was united in name as well as in territory and became Papua New Guinea.

The line separating British from German New Guinea was drawn through the high interior of the country, but no one had ever been there. On the maps of early colonial times the boundary traverses a blank space with an assurance that belies the reality. Mountains rise steeply to 3,000 m. (10,000 ft) and above from the coastal plains, mountains so rugged and densely covered with vegetation that no one imagined the interior to be inhabitated. Explorers had attempted to travel up the major rivers flowing from the interior – the Sepik and Ramu in the north, the Fly and Purari in the south – but were thwarted by impassable waterfalls and rapids, and discouraged by the hostile behaviour of some New Guinea inhabitants.

Even the people of some accessible coastal regions had an unsavoury reputation for collecting heads and eating people, (a fate suffered by the reverend James Chalmers, a pioneer representative of the London Missionary Society who was killed and consumed by the inhabitants of an island in the Gulf of Papua in 1901), and the fear of what might lie beyond the known fringes of habitation was a considerable deterrence to exploring the unknown interior – especially among the porters who would be needed to carry an expedition's wherewithal.

Gold prospectors have taken most of the credit for opening up the interior, though they were often aided and preceded by missionaries and government officers. From the turn of the century, a series of small gold strikes led, in 1926, to the discovery of a major alluvial deposit at Edie Creek in the mountainous region of the former German territory. A goldrush ensued. The deposits lay at an altitude of well over 1,000 m. (3,300 ft) in the valleys above the Bulolo river, more than 75 km. (47 mi.) from the coast; all equipment and supplies had to be carried in on the backs of porters, and when the diggings were taken over by large companies with international finance in the early 1930s, the vast complex of essential machinery was actually flown in – the world's first airlift.

The Edie Creek experience created a few millionaires, killed some men and left a select few with a taste for the pursuit of gold in the most inhospitable mountains. Among them was Michael Leahy, whose story is told in *The Land That Time Forgot* (London 1937). In a series of expeditions from 1930 to 1934 Leahy, together with his brothers and associates, travelled thousands of kilometres through the mountains; panning for gold along every river, traversing the high ridges to check the headwaters of each tributary. They found several workable pockets of alluvial gold, and some hopeful veins of gold-bearing quartz in the mountains, but never enough to halt their search for more.

The early expeditions encountered several groups of hitherto unknown people, and more than once their supposition that any unknown group

35

could be aggressive was proved correct. Their camps were attacked; porters were killed, Michael Leahy himself suffered a blow from a stone club that left him alive, but with a dented skull and a dull roaring in the left ear that never disappeared. They killed people too, but more often endeavoured to dispel any ideas of attack with a demonstration of rifle power on non-human targets.

In 1932 the Leahys found promising gold deposits at a place called Bena Bena on the high reaches of the Tua river. But they still looked westward, towards the region in which there were mountains now known to be over 4,000 m. (13,000 ft) high – truly the heartland of the country.

A preliminary expedition over the western divide revealed a succession of steep timbered ranges and finally a precipitous corridor, heading westward between steep limestone escarpments to a broad valley whose limits were obscured in a distant haze. The people across the divide were unlike any the prospectors had previously encountered. The men were particularly well-built and much less fearful of the visitors; their heads were decorated with birds' wings, feathers and beaks; short strings of shell hung from pegs stuck in holes that pierced their noses. Many were tattooed with a pattern of curves radiating from the corners of the mouth. The men carried bows and arrows, and stone axes with long blades fashioned from hard black basalt and a green stone, narrow and blunt at one end and finely tapered to a broad cutting edge at the other, 10 cm. (4 in.) broad and ground sharp as a knife. The villages were strategically placed on the brows of ridges, and the surrounding lands were impressively cultivated; groves of casuarina trees grew among the houses, and ornamental shrubs had been planted along the paths.

Leahy was convinced that the valley he had seen from the divide must be the route to the still unexplored interior. With the backing of a gold mining company he planned a major expedition into the area, but first he flew over the area with his brothers and the company's general manager.

'We saw a great, flat valley, possibly twenty miles wide and no telling how many miles long, between two high mountain ranges, with a very winding river meandering through it', he later wrote in his book. 'Below us were evidences of a fertile soil and a teeming population – a continuous patchwork of gardens, laid off in neat squares like chess-boards, with oblong grass houses, in groups of four or five, dotted thickly over the landscape. Except for the grass houses, the view below us resembled the patchwork fields of Belgium.' A second flight spanned the length of the valley. 'The flat and thickly populated area appeared to be roughly sixty miles long by twenty miles broad', reported Leahy, 'an island of population so effectively hemmed in by mountains that the rest of the world had not even suspected its existence'.

In early 1933, an expedition arranged jointly by mining and government authorities, led by Leahy and Assistant District Officer Jim Taylor, became the first party to explore the great valleys of the Western Highlands. On a subsequent expedition the Leahys found rewarding quantities of gold at Ewunga Creek, near Mount Hagen at the heart of the New Guinea highlands, and settled there to make their fortunes.

During the next year or so, two missionaries, three prospectors and one government official were killed in the highland regions that the Leahy brothers had opened up. The government responded by declaring the highlands a closed region – although the Leahys were allowed to continue working their claim at Ewunga Creek, since access was by air and they maintained good relations with the local people; even so, they were restricted to the vicinity of the airstrip. The highlands remained closed for some years; parts of the Mendi region were the last to be opened – non-government personnel were not allowed on the Nembi Plateau, which lies a short distance to the south of the town, for instance, until 1965.

The exclusion of outsiders from the New Guinea highlands was inspired as much by the difficulties of administration as by any concern for the well-being of either highlanders or outsiders, but among other effects it did leave some large samples of human society all but untouched by modern civilisation until after the Second World War and well into the 1960s and '70s. These societies subsequently became the subject of extensive research in the fields of human geography, biology, sociology, anthropology and ecology and have provided some unique insights into the relationships between social systems, cultural behaviour and the environments that sustain them.

Some of the most remarkable facts to have emerged from the many studies of Papua New Guinea are concerned with its linguistics. More than 1,000 languages have been recorded in Papua New Guinea and Irian Jaya – a quarter of the world's total shared among four million people, a tiny fraction of the world's population – making it the most complex and varied linguistic region of its size in the world. The languages divide into two broad groups: 250 or so belong to the Austronesian Group, whose realm extends from Madagascar, through southeast Asia and across the Pacific to Hawaii and Easter Island; and 750 belong to the Papuan Group, which is restricted to Papua New Guinea. The Austronesian languages are comparatively closely related, though spoken by only about 15 percent of the population. Among the Papuan languages, on the other hand, most are mutually unintelligible and more than half of them are classified in nine groups which are not related to each other in any way. Thirteen are what linguists call phylum-level isolates, single languages with very few words in common (between seven and 12 percent), and almost no grammatical agreement with any other language. Within the context of New Guinea, these isolates are as distinct as, say, Finnish and Hungarian in Europe.

Apart from sheer number, the languages are also unevenly distributed throughout New Guinea. Three of the Papuan languages are spoken by more than 100,000 people each; about 50 are spoken by more than 10,000 people; but the remaining 700 or so are spoken only by small communities, ranging in size from a few dozen to a few thousand people, who live in relatively isolated and restricted regions – though often in quite close proximity to each other. Many of these are found in the highlands, where the inhabitants of one valley may speak a language that is unintelligible to the people who live in the next valley.

37

The number and diversity of languages in Papua New Guinea confirms the potential for rapid change that is basic to the human capacity for speech. Given enough separation in either time or space, similar languages will soon begin to sound very different. The Atlantic keeps British and North American English apart. Geoffrey Chaucer and Ernest Hemingway both spoke English but could not have understood one another had they ever met. In less than 600 years the language changed a great deal (even though the advent of the printed word must have slowed the process considerably).

Language diversity in Papua New Guinea serves to separate people who are otherwise very similar, apparently confirming a separation that geography alone might have imposed. This is especially true of the highlands.

The central highlands are the most densely populated non-urban area of Papua New Guinea, holding a full 39 percent of the country's population. People were attracted to the highlands at a fairly early stage of man's migration through the island, probably to escape the effects of malaria, which is endemic in the hot wet climate of the lowlands, and is thought to have been the most important determinant of population distribution in the country. The people of Papua New Guinea lack the sickle-cell gene which protects some African populations against malaria; babies and young children are particularly susceptible and in one lowland region an infant mortality rate of 571 per 1,000 births has been attributed to the effects of malaria. Immunity develops in individuals who survive past the age of five, so lowland populations persisted, but significant numbers of early immigrants must have moved on into the highlands, where the effects of malaria decrease with altitude, becoming insignificant above 2,000 m. (6,500 ft).

The first inhabitants of the New Guinea Highlands were nomadic hunters and gatherers. Archaeologists have found stone tools, rock shelters and evidence of forest burning, indicating occupation of the highlands going back to 15,000, 20,000, and possibly even 30,000 years ago. There is some tenuous evidence suggesting that the domestic pig was introduced to the highlands about 10,000 years ago, and firm evidence that it was widespread from around 5-6,000 years ago. But the most remarkable conclusion to be drawn from archaeological investigations in the highlands concerns the origins of agriculture in the region. At Kuk, a swampland in the upper Wahgi valley near Mount Hagen, there is evidence of bush clearance and drainage systems dating back to between 9,000 and 10,000 years ago. This suggests that while the inhabitants of northern Europe were still foraging and hunting mammoths across landscapes from which the glaciers of the last Ice Age had only recently retreated, the highlanders of New Guinea were already growing crops – probably taro. This agricultural activity predates even the cultivation of grain in the 'fertile crescent' of the Middle East which is generally assumed to have marked the beginnings of agriculture.

The incentive for growing crops lay in the particular circumstances of

38

the New Guinea environment: there are no large animals such as have
been an important source of protein for human populations in other parts
of the world. In fact, the vertebrate fauna of New Guinea is described as
one of the poorest in the world. None of the large Asian mammals, such as
elephant, rhinoceros, tiger, apes and monkeys are found on the island,
there are no deer of any form, and no fossil evidence to suggest that any of
these creatures ever lived there (the pig is an introduced species). The
native fauna of the island consists only of spiny anteaters, some species of
kangaroo, rats, mice, and bats – and not all of these were present in the
highlands. There were some reptiles and frogs, but no fish of any size in the
rivers. Bird life was extremely rich, with over 2,000 species and sub-species
including the cassowary, many beautiful birds of paradise and numerous
pigeons and parrots, but these alone could not have provided a sufficient
source of food. In the final analysis there was very little animal fare to
sustain a band of hunters in the New Guinea highlands.

But there was plenty of vegetable food to be gathered. The New Guinea
flora is as rich as the fauna is poor, especially in the highlands. With the
benefits of an equatorial climate, including year round high temperatures
and high levels of almost continuous rainfall (never more than nine days
without rain in five years at one highland meteorological station), an
extremely productive tropical rainforest has evolved to clothe the mountains of Papua New Guinea. A survey of its vegetation lists 650 species of
plants (representing 378 genera and 134 families) that are used as food,
medicine and raw materials in the highlands. These include nuts, seeds,
leaf and root plants, all of which can still be gathered from the wild forest
although, as the archaeological evidence from Kuk reveals, for the last
5,000 years or more human subsistence in the highlands has been
dominated by agriculture.

The predominant form of agriculture in the New Guinea highlands –
which, on the evidence, also seems likely to have been mankind's earliest
form of agriculture – was swidden. The old Northumbrian term was
resurrected in 1951 as a substitute for the more common 'slash-and-burn',
which by then had acquired a decidedly prejorative connotation. To
colonial administrators stationed among people dwelling in tropical
forests, the widespread practice of clearing a patch of forest with axe and
fire, planting crops for a year or two then moving on to another patch
seemed wasteful and destructive. Slash-and-burn destroyed forest, ruined
soils, and supported only a fraction of the numbers of people that could live
from the produce of a well-run farm, they said.

But slash-and-burn was only half the story; the other half, largely
ignored by the critics, consisted of the peoples' very deep knowledge of the
land and its potential. Postwar researchers have found that slash-and-burn
– or swidden – is by far the most effective and efficient way of using the
natural habitat, especially in the tropical rainforest environment.

At its best, swidden agriculture is a functional imitation of the natural
environment; transforming the natural forest into a harvestable one by
substituting a diversity of edible plants for the diversity of forest plants
that had previously grown there. In an extensive study of swidden

practices among the Hanunóo of the Philippines, Harold Conklin recorded more than 1600 plants that were used at one time or another, including 430 cultivars of which up to 150 may be planted during the first year of cultivation in a new clearing. In one three-acre (1.2 ha) swidden plot monitored by Conklin, the careful intercropping of 40 crop plants ensured a continuous, year-round supply of food. Fruit trees, bananas, vines, beans, grains, root crops, spices, sugar cane, tobacco and other non-edible items grew simultaneously, their distribution through the garden replicating not only the diversity, but also the canopy architecture of the natural forest they had temporarily replaced. The apparently random pattern of differing plant heights in the garden served to moderate the rain wash-off and weed growth that would defeat single-crop production in an open clearing.

Most of the nutrients in a tropical rainforest are locked up in the trees. The soils are relatively poor – good for making bricks but not much good for growing food crops. Thus burning the trees not only clears the land, it also releases nutrients to the soil, and the productivity of a swidden garden is demonstrably related to the completeness of the burning. But the nutrients released are sufficient only to grow crops for a short period. In an early 1960s study of swidden agriculture as practised among the Maring people of the central New Guinea highlands, anthropologist Roy Rappaport and geographer William Clarke found that 85-90 percent of a garden's total yield is produced in the year following the fifth month after planting. After two years the garden is abandoned to lie fallow; secondary forest quickly reclaims the clearing, which is not cultivated again for many years. Clarke found that the gardens then in use had lain fallow for at least 15 years, while some had not been used for 40 years or more.

The long fallow period required in swidden agriculture imposes an obvious constraint upon the number of people it can support. Around 50 per sq. km. (130 per sq. mi.) is reckoned the maximum sustainable density, though it is often less. Among the Maring, Rappaport and Clarke reported population densities of about 30 to each square kilometre of land in use (80 per sq. mi.) with a good deal more land available – even allowing for extended fallow periods.

Life is not especially arduous for swiddeners. The Maring gardens, for instance, produced about 17 times more energy than was spent on clearing and tending them. Feeding the entire population called for an average of only about 9.5 hours of food-producing work each week from every able-bodied man and woman, with perhaps another six hours to be expended weekly on cooking and household chores.

In general, more food was grown than was needed for immediate human consumption. The surplus of course served as a buffer against unantici-pated need or disaster, but since it consisted of perishable vegetables and root crops that would not keep long in the hot damp equatorial climate, storage might have been the problem. The solution, however, was simple: the surplus production was fed to the pigs which every household kept. And as a means of storing perishable food crops and feeding people there is little to beat the pig.

Pigs are the most useful source of animal protein ever domesticated: 35

percent of the food that a pig consumes as it grows to maturity is converted to meat, compared with 13 percent for sheep and 6.5 percent for cattle. Furthermore, it breeds prodigiously; from a pregnancy of four months each sow produces an average of eight piglets which can each be fattened up to a weight of 400 pounds (180 kg.) in a further six months. Thus a pair of pigs can produce up to 3,200 pounds (1,450 kg.) of meat in ten months. A cow, by comparison, is pregnant for nine months, and usually produces a single calf that takes a further four months to attain a weight of 400 pounds – which makes the pig over ten times more useful as a meat producer.

The pig's only drawback as a domestic animal is that it is not much use for anything but producing meat and hunting truffles – it gives no milk and cannot be ridden or used to haul a cart – and in the absence of natural forest fare must be given the kind of cultivated foods that people eat. In a series of celebrated publications, anthropologist Marvin Harris has suggested that the pig's general uselessness for anything but meat production, and its competition for human food resources were the inspiration for the ritual taboos that were imposed on its consumption in the Middle East, where it was indigenous and had flourished until the vast forests of the region shrank drastically as a result of climatic change and human activity. In Papua New Guinea, where swidden agriculture had left the productivity of the forest environment essentially unaffected, the demands of the pig inspired a quite different cultural response. When the number of pigs around the homestead began to impinge upon the food requirement of the people themselves, all but the breeding stock were slaughtered and eaten in a grand feast that in turn provided ample opportunity to invite the neighbours in, and thus establish, reinforce or repair social bonds between individuals and groups.

Furthermore, because the pigs were a means of storing surplus garden production, they were also items of value that could be exchanged – a form of wealth. And being wealth, they were also a measure of status. The more pigs a man owned, the more respect and authority he gained. The man with the most pigs was effectively the leader of his community. Reasonable enough: pigs are a store of surplus food, which in turn must represent productive and well-managed gardens; a man capable of managing his gardens better than any other should be best able to run the wider affairs of the community as well.

Such men became known as big-men. Every group in the fertile highland valleys had one or several big-men. They controlled affairs within their group and, on a broader scale, managed the relationships between groups. The establishment of big-men was the culmination of the process by which swidden agriculture has determined the social organisation and culture of the Papua New Guinea highlanders.

Swidden calls for a relatively small number of people to be concentrated around patches of active cultivation in a relatively large area of land that is currently out of use. Since people first began cultivating the highlands of Papua New Guinea, this inherent isolation has been intensified by the mountainous nature of the terrain. Numbers grew slowly, so isolation was

41

long term as well as intense – factors which no doubt contributed to the development of so many different languages, but which also produced a social system based on the blood relationships and affiliations of the clan. Clans consisted of a number of related sub-clans, each of which was, in effect, an extended family. Common descent from a founding ancestor, told in the stories that trace individual descent five or six generations back down the male line, bound the members together, but sub-clans tended to split when their numbers increased beyond a critical point. This was almost certainly a response to population density, and thus an acknowledgement of limited carrying capacity in the swidden system. Among the Mendi it has been found that the territorial resources and social harmony of a sub-clan were strained when its numbers exceeded 100 members.

And so the highlands supported numerous sub-clans, each holding an acknowledged tract of land, but all linked by a history of blood relationships, and politically united as the segments of a clan. Beyond the clan – both in terms of territory and genealogy – were other clans. Again, the fact that many of them relate the same mythical stories of their origin, and tell of their descent from the same ancestral founders, suggests that the clans share blood links too, but the links are too distant to have much effect on clan relationships (except on the broadest scale – when clans sharing these features will unite to deal with another discrete groups of clans on what might be called the tribal level).

Basically, the members of one clan regarded neighbouring clans as a source of brides, warfare, and wealth; three interrelated factors which lay at the root of the system and were themselves dependent upon the productivity of the swidden gardens.

First the brides. Marriage in highland society is exogamous, outward, meaning that no man may marry a woman from his own clan, and women must join their husbands' households and bear children for his clan. The acquisition of women called for some payment, however, and this could only be the surplus produce of their gardens – food, and especially pigs. Thus a cycle was established: the gardens required more hands, the hands must be purchased with garden surplus which in turn required more hands to produce...

The second factor determining the relationships between clans of highlanders – warfare – initially arose from territorial dispute, and thus was directly related to population densities and the productivity of the gardens. War ended many lives. The anthropologist M.J. Meggitt analysed the genealogies of the Enga highlanders and has concluded that prior to 1947 as many as 20 percent of the adult male population died in battle with neighbouring clans; a large number of the victims were young bachelors, or married men without children – the least experienced and most dispensible members of the clan. The Enga occupy one of the most intensively exploited and densely populated regions of the highlands, with densities of up to 115 people per sq. km. (300 per sq. mi), and Meggitt found that in pre-contact times clan territories had altered continually in response to the shifting economic, political and demographic fortunes of individual clans.

Warfare was an important mechanism in the redistribution of people, possibly the prime mechanism. When there was no vacant land for it to occupy, a growing clan could expand only at the expense of a weaker clan; and a declining clan could not long survive the pressures exerted by stronger neighbours.

But warfare was also commonplace between clans under no territorial pressure. Seeking the ecological perspective of warfare among the Maring clans studied by Rappaport and Clarke, Andrew Vayda found that of the 39 wars to which causes could be attributed, 22 had been provoked by murder or attempted murder, and the remainder by a variety of offences, including the abduction of women, rape, crop theft, sorcery and insult. Only two wars had been provoked by territorial encroachment.

There is more than a suspicion that, by the time the white men first reached the highlands, warfare had become an end in itself among the people living there. Certainly, warfare appears to have been a commonplace activity. References to it appear in virtually every academic study and popular book on the highlands. Some give detailed accounts, but none give a more dramatic and sobering sense of its ever-present shadow in pre-contact times than the recollections of one of its exponents, Ongka, as transcribed by Andrew Strathern from tape recordings.

'We burnt houses, slashed banana trees, tore the aprons off women and raped them, axed big pigs, broke down fences, we did everything', says Ongka. The enemies retaliated. 'When we left our women and went out to fight, they were in danger. Men came to find them, chasing them down to the edges of streams till they seized hold of them... Twenty men might lay hold of the same woman, pulling her around for a day and a night, and then letting her go, saying "We've had intercourse with you, but you're not dead, so it doesn't matter, you can go home now"'. One war lasted five months. 'There was no sweet potato; all the gardens were burned off... hunger tore at our insides... Older men pushed leaves into their bark belts to fill out the space between their stomachs and their belts. They declared they were pleased to be hungry, and went out to fight again.... All this time we had to keep fighting, the enemy came with drawn bow, we faced him and drove him back, then he drew his bow and came forward again. Eyes were put out and legs were lamed; we had to cut out arrows stuck fast in flesh... in the fifth month both sides were tired of it, and began to slacken'. Later, Ongka's clan made a surprise attack on their enemy. 'We charged over to their settlements', he recalls, 'We swept over them, raped their women standing up, chopped bananas, axed pigs, fired houses. They fled like wild pigs from all their settlements'.

And so it went on throughout the highlands. A sickening history of killing, rape and pillage to which survivors were proud to add tales of their exploits, and to which boys were keen to add their contribution. Why was it so?

Organised warfare is one of the most extreme aberrations of human cultural behaviour, but anthropologists, social scientists and ecologists have found it difficult to provide more than a simplistic explanation of the phenomenon as a means of population control – and even then science is

43

accused of seeming to condone the practice. No one would want to provide the intellectual base from which warfare might be instigated as a rational or desirable course of action, scientifically approved, and attempts to explain warfare dispassionately, as a functional element of human ecology, are a revealing instance of science rasping against the tender sensibilities of mankind.

The instances of warfare that Rappaport studied among the Maring people, however, show signs of human aspiration ultimately directed towards peace. A negotiated truce brought most wars to an end, and even those which ended with the outright victory of one side were followed by extended periods of peace during which warfare was ritually proscribed. These periods lasted ten years or more; the rituals included the sacrifice of pigs to the spirits of ancestors believed to have assisted the war effort, pig feasts to reward allies, and the payment of negotiated compensation to victims of the war. There was, however, an element of functional practicality about these periods of ritual peace: it took time to accumulate the frequently very considerable amount of wealth that had to change hands. The wealth had to be grown, quite literally, in gardens that may well have been neglected or even destroyed during the war, by a clan whose workforce may have been seriously reduced by death and injury.

The Maring evidence even suggests that peace lasted only as long as it took to pay off the debts incurred in the previous bout of warfare. Informants told of wars that began within two or three months of the pig feasts that marked full and final settlement of war debts and dues.

Whatever the true functional or ethical explanations of warfare may turn out to be, there is no doubt that it could not be waged in the New Guinea highlands (or anywhere else for that matter) without a sound agricultural base on which to raise and feed warriors, buy weapons, recruit allies and compensate victims. Which brings us to the third factor of society and culture that is closely related to the demands of agriculture in the highlands – wealth.

Wealth among highland swiddeners was originally an expression of surplus production, stored principally in the form of pigs, but also in pearlshell traded up from the coast, and in the bird of paradise plumes and other items of extravagant decoration with which the highlanders adorn themselves from time to time. Every man needed to accumulate some wealth – to buy a wife, to contribute to clan obligations, to repay a debt – but it accrued principally to the big-men; and indeed it has become a measure of big-man status.

Everything has its price in highland society – brides, murder, rape, insult – and while individuals handled their affairs within the clan, the emergence of wealthy, authoritative and shrewd big-men was an impor-tant factor in the managing of relations between clans. With a prodigious memory for bloodlines and past events, subtle exploitation of conflicting pressures, appeals for clan solidarity, coercion, persuasion, threat and promise – the big-men effectively controlled social relations throughout the highlands. They sanctioned the extension of land holdings, arranged marriages, settled disputes, declared war against other clans, made peace

44

and assessed compensation. Prior to the arrival of the Australian administration, the big-men recognised no other authority but their own, and they competed to become the biggest of the big-men. From the basis of his home settlement, each endeavoured to build up wealth and prestige by extending his landholdings and by buying wives to grow food and raise more pigs. They manipulated allegiances, schemed and wrangled to accumulate wealth. And, once having accumulated enough, they gave it away in a complicated series of exchanges that repaid debts and established credit.

The exchange practices in the highlands are known by the general title of *moka*. Their most important rule is that a man must be exceedingly generous. To make moka he must give away a great deal of wealth – much more than he received in the previous round. The network is vast, operating among blood and social relations at all levels. Each gift is, of course, also an investment, for the recipient will be obliged to pay it back eventually, with interest. Organising the moka requires an enormous amount of time and effort, leaving the principal participants little time for anything else. Moka culminates in a grand festival, when literally thousands of pigs are slaughtered, some to be eaten by those present, others to be sent to the most distant parts of the moka network. But despite all the effort that the moka exchanges demand, and the virtually continuous flow of meat and goods that they instigate throughout the highlands, the benefits that moka exchange bestows upon the people at large seem decidedly limited.

The largest pig feasts are infrequent, occurring perhaps two or three times in the course of a man's life; many people have died after eating great amounts of meat at a feast from the effects of *pigbel*, a form of enteritis to which children between the ages of three and 14 are particularly susceptible. The meat often travels so far that much of it goes rotten before it can be consumed. 'Such pork stinks so horribly that we have to carve it under water lest we vomit on it', Enga clan members told M.J. Meggitt. The meat gets eaten nonetheless since, to the highlanders, all pork is by definition 'a good thing'.

It is not difficult to see that the social and cultural practices of the New Guinea highlanders probably began in the swidden gardens, as a 'good thing'. But when it comes to the accumulation of wealth, the highlanders seem to have taken the fundamental good sense of the system well beyond its initial justifications. In effect, they have turned the system on its head. Whereas pigs and wealth were once simply the surplus of good productive management, in the modern era they have become the primary requirement, serving not as food reserves but as the principal element in extravagant exchanges of wealth that serve only to bolster the prestige of the big-men. It is estimated that between 40 and 60 percent of highland agricultural production is now used to rear pigs for moka, while many of the people who produce the food are under-nourished. What went wrong?

The explanation almost certainly lies with the introduction of the sweet potato into the highlands some 300 years ago. The sweet potato is more productive than the traditional swidden crops, and it will grow at higher altitudes, under a wider range of environmental conditions, but the initial appeal of the new crop was probably as a means of feeding pigs and thereby increasing scant supplies of essential fats and proteins, rather than for the direct sustenance of people. In a number of highland languages the word for sweet potato also means pig fodder, and it is certainly true that pigs thrive on the entire plant of the sweet potato – leaf, vine and tuber – and, furthermore, will eat it raw, unlike the traditional staple, taro, which pigs find unpalatable in its raw state.

The new crop enabled highlanders to produce more food with less labour from the same area of land, and these advantages encouraged the decline of the intercropping and diversity essential to the swidden system in favour of intensified sweet potato production. New methods of cultivation evolved. In one area, a grid-iron system of tillage was developed; in another, planting sweet potatoes in mounds composted with old vines and other vegetation became customary practice. Fields were fenced, and cultivated almost continuously, with only short intervals of fallow. The sweet potato rapidly became a predominent crop in many areas, while the pig ceased to be merely the repository of surplus produce and became the key element in a new social order. Pigs featured ever more prominently in marriage, child and mortuary payments, they were used as compensation payments for death and injury in war, and as items of competitive exchange among the big-men – a role which has become crucial since warfare was outlawed and the big-men have tended to fight with pigs rather than with axes, as one anthropologist has put it.

Eventually, the social demands of pig production began to match the human demand for sustenance, creating the extraordinary circumstances which prevail today. But there is no reason to suppose that the process of social and cultural evolution that produced the present state of affairs has now come to a stop. The existing highland society and culture is the product of the human and ecological factors that prevailed in the past; similarly, the present state of affairs must contain the discernible seeds of future development. And indeed it does. On the Nembi plateau to the south of Mendi, for instance, the demand for sweet potatoes to fatten pigs for the moka exchange system has impoverished the soil, made slaves of the women, depressed the birthrate and increased infant mortality. This is the mechanism by which human biology will rein back the excesses of human culture in the highlands of Papua New Guinea.

The Nembi region bears little resemblance to the flat tableland that the term 'plateau' usually brings to mind. The Nembi plateau is a land of high limestone hills, cliffs and steep valleys, but at a general altitude of between 1,600 and 1,800 m. (5,200 to 5,850 ft) it does stand 2-300 m. (650-1,000 ft) above the adjacent landscape and is thus isolated by its terrain to the extent that even vehicles gain access only with strain and difficulty, while most people must walk in and out.

The king parrot, a beautiful bird distinguished by its dark red chest, dark green upperside and long tail is occasionally seen gliding at the forest edge above the sweet potato fields; there are sulphur-crested cockatoos on the plateau as well, though they are rare now that their plumage has become such a desirable feature of decoration. The people live in small hamlets scattered across the plateau, linked by a network of footpaths, each occupied by a man, his wives and extended family. Pe's houses stand on a bluff at a place called Uba. Down the path from Uba is Kongip; here the houses are built in the old style, much lower than Pe's, and with thatch rather than tin roofs. They are long and very low; split timber posts form the framework, and the walls are mats of woven cane. Women, children and pigs live at one end of the house, men at the other. Bananas grow in the small garden adjoining the houses and next to them there is a small stand of coffee, which does well at this altitude where there is little disease and few pests – apart from a feral guinea pig population which is descended from the two pets that escaped from the mission some years ago and which now regularly strips the flowering branches of the coffee.

In the high cliffs across the valley there is a cave where the remains of a Nembi big-man were deposited, with considerable effort and ceremony, when he died in 1980. Below the cliffs, women are busy in their sweet potato fields, ridging the soil over piles of compost in preparation for planting. The blades of their spades are worn short and shine like stainless steel from so much heavy, daily use.

'The human ecology of the Nembi plateau is very simple', a long term observer remarked, 'the men buy wives who work the land to produce the crops that feed the pigs which make the men wealthy in the eyes of other men'. A man's gardening obligations are limited to the initial heavy work of felling trees and grubbing out roots to clear land for planting. He will do this when he gets married, but will expect to repeat the exercise only under exceptional circumstances. This cultural pattern is found throughout the highlands and it places increasing pressure and strain upon the women.

Pe has bought eight wives in the course of his adult life; one died and one has left him, but the remaining six reside with him still at Uba. His wives have borne 33 children; six died during infancy or childhood, five are grown up and have left home. Twenty-two are still dependent upon him – 15 boys and seven girls. He is the big-man of the Palam clan, with power enough to authorise a pig kill, or instigate a fresh round of fighting in the warfare that remains unsettled on the plateau. He was born and raised before the region was pacified by the Australian administration, when warfare was commonplace. Show the slightest interest and he will proudly display his arrow wounds and launch into a story of past exploits.

In a grand ceremony that took place during March 1984, Pe killed 20 pigs that his wives had raised from the sweet potato gardens at Uba. Asked to give them a cash value, he said the pigs had been good animals, worth 5,270 kina in all – £UK7,528. The highlanders put a very high value on their pigs. Pe valued his at around £UK7.50 per kg. (£3.40 per pound) live weight, more than double the cost of a prime joint of pork at Harrods in 1986. And Pe's valuation is not simply a figure that has no real foundation – pigs actually are sold at those prices, for cash; but not to feed people, only to meet traditional exchange obligations.

A survey conducted by geographer Michael Bourke, from the Australian

National University, reveals that, in addition to their ceremonial contributions, the ten heads of household at Uba handed over another 29 pigs in brideprice and moka transactions during the first ten months of 1984. During the same period they also paid out 2,060 Kina in cash (£2,942) and 353 pearlshells. They received some payments through the moka network, but not as much as they paid out; over the ten months the ten houholds were, in fact, 600 Kina, 96 pearlshells and one pig out of pocket on their transactions. The men earned several hundred Kina from their coffee and sundry work, but this money was spent on promoting their own affairs and contributed very little to the household economy. Thus the responsibility for feeding the families and raising the pigs for the men to exchange and kill at some extravagant feast for the benefit of other men, fell upon the women and the gardens – both of which were being worked to the point of exhaustion.

Geographer and economist Robert Crittenden has documented the changing status of the Nembi in a number of publications. Before the white man's world began to influence affairs on the Nembi Plateau some 30 years ago, the Nembi held a strong position on the traditional north-south trade routes along which prized pearlshell and an especially valued tree oil were brought up from the lowland to be traded for the highlanders' stone axes, salt and pigs. Proximity to these routes enabled the Nembi to achieve virtual control of the trade, taking a slice of profit from its movement in both directions. While still subsisting on their agricultural base, they became wealthy in terms that measured not their own surplus, but that of the traders they exploited. This rewarding state of affairs changed dramatically when the Australians came to the highlands.

First the traditional currencies were devalued to the point of ridicule; pearlshell arrived by the planeload; likewise, vast numbers of steel axes rapidly knocked the bottom out of the stone axe market. Second, the power of the whites and their weapons was allied from the beginning with the producers and traders that the Nembi had previously exploited, thus effectively undermining Nembi authority. And third, such trade as did continue in the highland moved principally on an east-west axis, leaving the Nembi high and dry on the old north-south routes.

The decline in Nembi status culminated with the establishment of Mendi as administrative centre of the region, and the general acceptance of money as the medium of exchange. Money replaced pearlshell and steel axes in official payments for land, produce and labour in 1962, and by the late 1960s had also begun to feature in bridewealth and other traditional exchanges.

Thereafter money became increasingly important to the Nembi, but they found themselves with very limited access to it. Some men were attracted by the inducements offered by labour contractors, and went away to work on mines and construction projects; others planted coffee, seeking the sustained cashflow offered by agricultural economists, but neither strategy lived up to expectations. Money simply did not accumulate fast enough, while the importance of wealth and status became, if anything, more firmly entrenched than ever before. In a pattern familiar throughout the highlands (and indeed elsewhere in the world), disillusionment with the new system produced a vigorous return to the old, traditional, system.

'The economy turned in on itself', Crittenden reports. As the traditional trade that supported the Nembi was replaced by a dependence on money, the pursuit of prestige and power intensified. But since trade and exchange could no longer support those pursuits, the demands placed increasing pressure on the sole remaining economic base, the gardens, and soon began to affect the long term prospects of the system at its most vulnerable point – the nutritional status of its children. And it is from here that the balance ultimately will be redressed. While pigs are fattened for moka, pregnant women, babies and young children on the Nembi plateau are inadequately fed and therefore prone to illness and premature death.

On the Nembi plateau in particular, the strain on the women is heightened by a combination of planting and cropping cycles which calls for the greatest labour input between August and early December, when there is a substantial gap in the food supply and women have least food available for their families. Furthermore, since this combination of food shortage and excessive workload always comes about six months after a time when women were relatively well fed and therefore most likely to conceive, it also strikes a cruel coincidence with the overall pattern of pregnancy on the plateau, leaving pregnant women starved and over-worked during the critical final months of their babies' development.

The Nembi call this gap in food supply the *taim hangri* in pidgin English; they insist it never occurred before the arrival of the white man, which may or may not be true, but it is also undeniably associated with their increasing insistence on the cultivation of sweet potato at the expense of the broad variety of crops that characterises the well-managed swidden garden.

This has meant that, during the months when women might have been harvesting other crops, the gardens are filled with sweet potato. Taro, the traditional staple food of the highlanders, could supplement the food supply during the taim hangri, but that too has been ousted by the demand for more sweet potato to feed more pigs.

A study published in 1980 found that sweet potato occupied 75 percent of the cultivated land on the Nembi plateau. The large open gardens had been producing sweet potato continuously for between 15 and 20 years – and even longer in some cases. The traditional swidden mixed crops occupied only about 20 percent of cultivated land, and were fallowed for only between two and five years after just one year of cultivation. Not surprisingly, production is low. In 1982 the sweet potato yield was found to be 7.1 tonnes per hectare (2.8 tons per acre) – one of the lowest ever recorded in Papua New Guinea, where 15 to 20 tonnes per hectare is considered a reasonable yield. The tubers themselves are small, most weighing less than 100 gm. (3.5 oz) each, tubers that elsewhere in the highlands would be fed only to pigs but on the plateau must feed people too. 'Our ground is sick', the Nembi complain, again attributing the cause

49

to the changes that followed the arrival of the Europeans. Yet the men raise more pigs, and tend to keep them longer as the difficulties of accumulating the desirable amounts of wealth during times of shortage lengthens the period between transactions.

Meanwhile, the people are becoming sick too. It has been estimated that in the highlands generally, pigs consume 64 percent of all sweet potato and absorb 40 percent of agricultural labour; and although Crittenden has found that pigs consume only 38 percent of the average family's sweet potato crop on the Nembi plateau, the fact that so much ground and labour are devoted to producing such a meagre crop exacerbates the extent to which raising pigs affects people on the plateau.

Sweet potato comprises between 40 and 60 percent of the Nembi's year round diet, and the proportion may rise to 80 percent during the taim hangri season, when the variety of other foods available is low. Such quantities of sweet potato may satisfy the needs of the average person, but it is significantly inadequate for some members of the community, particularly during the most critical time of the year.

Nutritionist Janis Baines has found that, in the course of a year, pregnant women on the Nembi plateau received on average 41 percent of the recommended energy requirement, 74 percent of the recommended protein, and 62 percent of the iron they required. During the last months of the taim hangri the deficiency increased, and the women were found to be receiving just 31 percent of the energy, 49 percent of the protein, and 41 percent of the iron requirements recommended for pregnant women.

This alarming deficiency occurs, of course, at the time of year when the women are obliged to work hardest in the gardens. They work to the point of exhaustion: 95 percent of all women lost significant amounts of weight during this period, and the effect is severe – on the women themselves, on their expected babies, on the infants they may be breast-feeding, and on children recently weaned.

In a survey conducted from 1979 to 1981, Crittenden and Baines found that birth weights on the Nembi plateau averaged 2.8 kg. (6 lb 4 oz), while 27 percent of all babies weighed 2.5 kg (5 lb 8 oz) or less, an exceptionally high proportion indicating considerable nutritional stress in the system. Crittenden estimates that one in five babies die before the age of five. Among those who survive, nutritional status declined rapidly for the first 18 months after birth, then slowly levelled out to leave between 33 percent and 43 percent of all children significantly stunted by the age of five. The loss is never recovered, and there is growing evidence to suggest that such nutritional deprivation during the first years of life also affects the individual's ability to attain full mental potential. And quite apart from the dietary inadequacies of the sweet potato, some workers have suggested that small children are simply incapable of eating a volume large enough to satisfy their needs.

Many children of all ages on the Nembi plateau are close to the deprived nutritional status at which the risk of death from disease is substantially increased, as has been shown in another highland group, where Peter Heywood found that as the weight-for-height assessment of children falls from 90 percent to 80 percent of the desirable norm, the death rate among them rises from 60 to 230 per thousand.

Of the survivors on the Nembi plateau, the girls will grow to help their mothers and perhaps dream of escaping, like Popi, in a modern marriage. The boys will grow up to the resounding tales of their fathers' exploits. Some of them might escape too, and find a job, as Moni did. The remainder are trapped in an anachronistic system that no longer makes sense, and which their reduced numbers, reduced state of health and reduced enthusiasm for the old ways must surely bring to an end.

The dynamics of human ecology insist that culture cannot stand still, locked in some timewarp that preserves forever both its ancient justification and its most flamboyant expression. The social arrangements and cultural practices of the Papua New Guinea highlanders were founded in the swidden cycle of root crops feeding pigs which in turn forged social links and helped to ensure the continuing viability of the highland swidden gardens. But these arrangements and practices have ceased to be viable now that pig production has overwhelmed the system, and the highlanders' fantastic adornments and extravagant rituals are, in fact, prime examples of the extent to which selfish interests can encourage people to pursue the cultural artifices of tradition beyond their functional justification.

51

CHAPTER THREE

THE RICE GROWERS

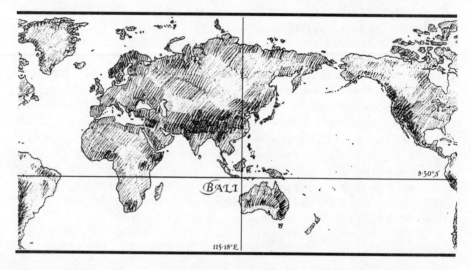

The time zone seven hours ahead of Greenwich makes a large deviation eastward between eight and ten degrees south of the equator. The bulge is designed to keep the islands of Bali and Lombok on the same time as the portion of the Indonesian archipelago which extends 3,200 km. (2,000 mi.) westward, but it also ensures that the sun rises on the islands very early each morning. In villages throughout Bali, where cockfighting remains an officially sanctioned part of the social order, the cocks usually begin crowing to one another before four o'clock, silencing the frogs and rousing the dogs. People begin to stir; muted voices are heard through open windows and, indeed, through the walls, which often consist of woven palm mats. Dawn advances with surprising speed as the sounds of human activity gain volume and conviction.

The air is exquisitely cool in the dawn hour, while the sun is still hidden and the humidity that characterises the daily, year-round climate of the island is still held in the mist over the rice terraces. On a slight rising breeze, the mists drift gently through the valleys, creating a shifting pattern of grey, soft-green shapes that condense here and there to the form of houses and trees, and then dissolve again into the mist. In the village, smoke begins to mingle with the mist, hanging among the branches of the huge banyan tree that stands close by the temple.

As the sun dries the mist from the terraces, a line of noisy white ducks waddles from the village, followed by a boy carrying a tall bamboo pole with a white flag tied at the top. They head for a field from which the rice has been recently harvested, where the boy plants the pole firmly in the ground, and the ducks will forage among the stubble all day, unattended, returning to gather around the pole for the walk home as dusk approaches.

At the edge of the village a man opens the sluice on the south side of a rice field and the water begins to flow away from the tall green stems and into the next field in the progression of terraces. There are burbling streams and irrigation canals at every turn; the landscape runs with water. Lower down, a canal crosses the valley by means of a bamboo aqueduct and carries water to irrigate yet more fields. A farmer is driving his bullock through a flooded field, levelling the knee-deep mud with a large board float. On another field, a group of five men have tucked their sarongs up to the waist, in the fashion of the Indian dhoti, and are planting out rice seedlings, rich green slender plants thrust down into the mud.

With the sun now risen well above the shoulder, a family has appeared on a field high on the opposite valley slope and begins to harvest the ripe grain. With a slight jolt of surprise, the visitor might now realise that all stages of rice cultivation are occurring simultaneously in just this one small area. The harvesters cut the head of grain and a few centimetres of stalk with a deft flick of a blade held in the palm of the hand. They thresh the grain by slapping it over boards propped up at 45 degrees on a spread of cloth. The old Balinese rice was cut and carried home in bundles, but the new strains drop the grain too readily, and must be threshed in the field.

Rice cultivation is a labour intensive activity. Small fields, lots of people working together cooperatively, a few animals for the heavy work, but very little opportunity for mechanisation. The Japanese have invented a diesel-powered rotovator, but it is expensive and not entirely effective. For the most part, hands still do the work in the rice fields, and just as the landscape is carefully moulded to carry water to the fields, so the paths winding through it are constructed to accommodate human feet striding one before the other, with very little room wasted on either side. The modern tarmac road is a fairly recent innovation in Bali, still barely extending the realm of the tracks along which carts always travelled from village to town, and for the most part leaving the rice terraces accessible only by foot. In the more distant fields you can hear only faint voices and laughter; birds, and the intermittent clatter of the miniature windmills that farmers erect to scare birds from the ripening grain. At the corner of one field, a single red hibiscus grows beneath a simple bamboo construction that serves as a shrine to the rice goddess.

Every morning, in each compound along the earthen track that runs through the village, women prepare offerings for the gods whose influence pervades every aspect of Balinese life; and the same scene occurs in virtually every compound throughout the island. A few grains of cooked rice laid on small squares of banana leaf are placed at significant points in and around the compound. These are the offerings that must be made each day to the ancestors, to the guardians of the compound, and to the spiritual brothers and sisters of the family. An offering to Brahma, the god of the hearth, is laid at the fireplace; an offering to Wisnu, god of water, is laid beside the cistern; an offering to Dewi Sri, the rice goddess, is placed in the granary. These offerings acknowledge the gifts of food and well-being that sustain people. To accept such gifts without offering thanks would be as bad as stealing, the Balinese believe.

The women perform their daily ritual duties with the speed and efficiency that long practice brings, but also with the grace that devotion bestows on any task. They move swiftly about the compound, confined to brisk movement by the sarong that wraps them tightly from waist to ankle, laying out the offerings with a bow, a curtsey, and a silent prayer over hands held palm to palm in the penitent's clasp. Sometimes a woman may add a flower to the offering, a purple bougainvillea, perhaps, or a richly scented frangipani blossom. On days of especial significance, she will fashion a number of small delicate baskets from strips of freshly cut palm leaf to hold the offering, which will include flowers, fragant oils and sandalwood water, as well as cooked rice. And when there is a festival at a temple to which the family is attached, she will make elaborate confections of flowers, fruit, palm-leaf and rice, which will be taken to the temple and offered there.

Every day the women make the customary offerings; every day is especially important for some households, and every day there is a temple festival somewhere not too far away, so that the ritual of the offering, at all levels, is always evident in Bali – along every path, beside every house, in every field. The combination of skill, devotion and long practice that women apply to the daily ritual offerings is echoed in all aspects of Balinese life. In dance, painting and sculpture it attains all the grandeur of art, but very often its connotation is purely functional. The woman preparing a pineapple on the verandah of her house in the village, for instance, cuts a sequence of deft spiralling grooves down and around the fruit which not only creates a most decorative effect, but also removes the skin and fibrous indentations in a most swift and efficient manner.

Most people have returned to the village by 11 o'clock, leaving the fields empty but for the man working the bullock and the family busy gathering its harvest. The day is hot and extremely humid, but its activities are far from over. A period of celebration approaches. A huge tower, bedecked with a profusion of floral tributes sways into view, followed by an excited crowd and a larger-than-life effigy of a bull, covered in bright yellow cloth and sporting a prodigious red-tipped penis. The bull stands on a framework of bamboo poles which rest on the shoulders of numerous young men – singing, shouting and laughing. Riding astride the bull are two more young men, both cheering and singing, while within it, one learns, lies the body of their friend who was drowned in the treacherous surf at Sanur beach some days before. As the procession advances up the track, the bull charges from side to side, twists and turns to the exhortations of bystanders and followers. On the open space above the village, between two grand banyan trees, tower and bull are connected to a pressurised supply of paraffin and set alight. There are one or two pockets of sadness among the crowd of onlookers as the flames roar skyward, but plenty of customers for the food and soft drink stands and an abiding sense that, for the Balinese, a cremation marks a moment of joyous transformation.

Later, as the day cools towards evening, family groups gather at the confluence of two irrigation canals and bathe, with plenty of soap and jolly playful behaviour among children and parents, and quite without any embarrassment at their nakedness. Indeed, it is clear that they feel as private and contained in the fresh open air as they would in an enclosed bathroom – embarrassment can only accrue to the onlooker whose glance lingers a second longer than politeness permits.

By seven o'clock it is dark and blessedly cool; the humidity has dropped and a light breeze wafts scents of perfume and food through the village. A woman hurries past with a suckling pig, roasted golden brown and running with fat. People strolling by, conversing, stop to buy banana pancakes from one of the stalls at the side of the road. At Peliatan a crowd is gathering for a performance of traditional Balinese music and dance, once a relatively infrequent event, but weekly now that the tourists have shown such enthusiasm for it; audiences always include a sizeable proportion of appreciative Balinese, however.

As the warrior performs the intricate and abrupt movements of the *baris*, flamboyantly dressed, immobile between movements, staring un-blinking into a prospect only he can see over the heads of the audience, he awakens a most unusual sense of rapport – as though the message of this strange dance were perfectly understood while its language remained totally incomprehensible. Similarly with the *Barong* and *Rangda*, wild and exotic representations of good and evil respectively, which engage in battles that neither ever wins. The Barong is a glorious creation of cloth and carved wooden mask, garishly decorated, and operated – like a pantomime animal – by one man at the head and another at the rear. The precise derivation of the Barong is obscure. It is most commonly said to represent a lion or a tiger, but has been most evocatively described as a cross between a puppy dog and a dragon. The Barong is large and powerful, but its demeanour is very sympathetic, even playful. It shakes its head a lot, snaps its teeth and stumbles about. The front and hind legs are never quite in step, as though, like humanity perhaps, it is full of good intentions but never well enough coordinated to apply them. Rangda, on the other hand, is fully applied to the purpose of evil. She has a thick mass of stiff white hair, bulging eyes, wide nostrils and fanged teeth. Rangda feeds, it is said, on corpses and the entrails of young children. Her movements are determined and abrupt, sharpened by flicks of her long cruel fingernails, and she has an eerie laugh. Rangda terrifies young children, but she never quite manages to defeat the Barong; nor, on the other hand, does the Barong ever do more than hold Rangda at bay.

The dance, with its fantastic extravagances of music, costume and performance, gives a strong impression that the machinations of violence and evil would soon take over the world were they not repeatedly confounded by the baffling power of innocence and goodwill.

Like all good theatre, Balinese drama and dance at its best leaves its audience with a sense of having been seduced by an excellent performance into the contemplation of truths that are not often thought about. Much of Bali is like that. The thousands of temples and the extravagant cultural activity that pervade Balinese life do not set Bali apart from the rest of world, as one might at first suppose, like some sort of exotic museum. No, they are the touchstones of a cultural system that seeks to confine the diversity of human behaviour within the same limits of human existence that prevail everywhere. Theatre, dance, music, paintings, gods and devils carved in stone, the daily round of ritual offerings – even the work on the rice terraces – all have their place in a strictly ordered system of ties and obligations that everyone acknowledges.

The American anthropologist Clifford Geertz, who began studying social and cultural aspects of life in Bali and Java in the late 1950s, has described the cultures of the islands as examples of cultural involution; an instance in which cultural patterns, having reached a definitive form, continue to develop by becoming internally more complicated, turning inward upon themselves like the twists and twirls of Arab architecture and Maori carving, weaving an incredibly complex web of ritual and social demands around the participants. The reasons for this process, first expounded by Geertz in his book *Agricultural Involution* in 1963 and much developed since then, are complex too, founded in the religious and social history of the islands, and powerfully accelerated from about 1830 by the policies of the Dutch colonial government. But they stemmed initially from the fact that the cultivation of rice as practised by the Javanese, and especially by the Balinese, can sustain very large populations on a relatively limited land area.

While the swidden gardens of a tropical rainforest can sustain no more than about 50 people per sq. km. (130 per sq. mi.), rice grown where tropical rainforest once stood in Bali can support well over 1,000, year after year with almost total dependability. But rice cultivation demands a much larger labour force, and people must work together in a very well organised and coordinated manner, building and maintaining terraces, ensuring adequate water flow, synchronising the planting and tending of the crops to ensure maximum production all year round. Once these essentials have been established, the process is virtually self-perpetuating. A surplus accumulates, the population grows, spreading labour demands, leaving more and more individuals free to pursue other activities. Confined to a limited patch of land, the culture turns in on itself. Practices that once persisted primarily because they met the demands of a society subsisting on rice cultivation now became an end in themselves; ritualised in religious and social behaviour, given form in sculpture and painting, acted out in dance and drama.

Like the beautiful tail feathers that the peacock and the birds of paradise display, the complexities of the involuted culture do seem to exceed the need by some distance. But at the same time, the complexity also seems to add resilience. The threads run so tightly through all aspects of the society and culture that it is difficult to imagine their ever falling apart. Certainly they have proved remarkably resistant to external attempts to pull them apart – even in the modern age of global economics and tourism.

Bali is not a large island. Roughly diamond-shaped, it measures about 140 km. (87 mi.) from east to west, and about 80 km. (50 mi.) from north to south. No part of the island is more than about 30 km. (19 mi.) from the

sea, which on clear days is always visible from the chain of high mountains
which runs along the east-west divide of the island. The total land area is
5,632 sq. km. (2,174 sq. mi.) and the present population is estimated to be
2.3 million, an overall density of just over 400 per sq. km. (1,000 per sq.
mi.). A full 80 percent of Bali's population, however, lives in the south of
the island, hemmed in by a ring of mountains rising 2,000 m. (6,500 ft) and
more in the north, which help to ensure an annual rainfall of about 2,500
mm. (98 in.) spread fairly evenly throughout the year. Within this compact
area of about 1,200 sq. km. (460 sq. mi.) are the island's capital, Denpasar;
the beach resorts of Sanur and Kuta to which the government has decreed
that tourist development should be largely confined; several other large
towns, and the major rice-producing lands of the island.

The landscape rises sharply from the coastal plain, and is divided into a
series of steep ridges and deep ravines by the fast-flowing rivers that splay
outward from the mountains. There are cascades of rice terraces below the
villages that line every ridge. Coconut palms and bananas edge the
terraces; stands of bamboo and other natural vegetation cluster at
uncultivable corners and along the steepest ravines. There is little seasonal
change this close to the equator; year round temperature averages 26°C
(79°F); rain falls on an average of 200 days each year, and the humidity is
always correspondingly high – between 70 and 80 percent. It is a beautiful
and very fertile corner of the world. Clifford Geertz sums up very aptly:

'If ever there was a forcing house for the growth of a singular civilisation,
this snug little amphitheatre was it; and if what was produced turned out
to be a rather special orchid, perhaps we should not be altogether
surprised'.

The overall form of Balinese culture and social order lies rooted in the
Hindu religion which invaders from India brought to Bali sometime
around the 9th century AD, when terraced rice cultivation was already
well developed. But the Hindu religion did not swamp the pre-existing
social order so much as it was absorbed into it. Since then Hinduism in
Bali has become quite unlike Hinduism anywhere else, and Bali remains
the only one of the many regions in southeast Asia where Hinduism has
persisted beyond the influence of the conquerors who brought it, and the
only major island of the 10,000 in Indonesia that remains actively Hindu.
As the Dutch progressively displaced the Indic kings during the 19th
century, the Balinese continued with the elaborate worship of their deities,
even though the self-proclaimed earthly representatives had long been
dispossessed.

Perhaps the most obvious aspect of religion in Bali is the extent to which
it pervades all aspects of life. While the Christian world, for example, has
very largely succeeded in separating the realms of secular and spiritual
activity, Bali has integrated the two. For the Balinese there is no difference
between a person's spiritual and secular life. In fact, there is no such thing
as a secular life. From the Balinese point of view, the entire universe is an
expression of enormous spiritual capability. Everything owes its existence
to the power of overriding spiritual forces; everyone must at all times
remain aware of their debt to those forces. This integration of the spiritual

and the secular tends to make the world a very complicated place, imbuing everyday life with the kind of moral and ethical rectitude that modern Christian societies by and large prefer to restrict to expressions of determination in church on Sunday mornings, but in Bali its demands have produced a society in which everyone knows their place – in all senses of the term.

Jane Belo, an anthropologist who studied Balinese culture during the 1930s noted that 'the most striking characteristic in the ordinary behaviour of the Balinese is the absolute poise and balance of his bearing, noticeable in his posture, his walk, his slightest gesture. All mature men and women have this [and] small children develop it with remarkable rapidity. [There is] poise, but a *carefulness* too, as if each foot were placed in its appropriate place, each turn of the head or flick of the wrist calculated not to disturb an equilibrium delicately set up, and hanging somewhere unseen within the individual'.

The sense of orientation that Jane Belo had discerned is crucial to the maintenance of the Balinese social order – and not just geographical orientation, but social and temporal orientation as well. In terms of geography, the Balinese align their lives and behaviour to the slopes that fall from the mountains to the sea. The mountain peaks are the abode of the gods, they believe, the highest and most holy places. The sea and the shore, on the other hand, are unholy; the places where rivers deposit their filth, and where monsters and demons dwell. Between these two extremes, the gradient of the slope defines a gradient of holiness. The higher things are, the more holy they are; the lower, the more profane.

The mountains are quite literally the central feature of Balinese life. The direction in which they lie, along with the orientation of east and west are the basis of even the simplest household instruction. A visitor might be asked to move a little to the south-west as he takes a seat, or a child instructed to pick up the spoon to the east of its plate. Houses are orientated towards the mountains; the beds within them are placed so that people sleep with their heads towards the mountains. It has been said that a dancer cannot perform in a strange place if he is unable to determine in which direction the mountains lie.

Although reverence for the mountains and maintenance of a good sense of orientation are undoubtedly motivated from day to day by purely spiritual or ritual considerations, they do have a secular relevance too. The mountains are volcanic in origin, (and therefore the source of Bali's exceptionally fertile soils); some are still active and several fierce eruptions have occurred in historical times. Therefore it might be as well to develop the habit of keeping them in mind. The most recent eruption occurred in 1963, when Gunung Agung erupted with a force exceeded only by that of Krakatoa in 1883. An enormous black cloud soared into the atmosphere, blotting out the sun up to 300 km. (nearly 200 mi.) away, and subsequently affecting solar radiation readings from the South Pole to Hawaii. Lava and sulphurous ash devastated the north east of the island; killing 1,100 people, while 67,000 were evacuated from the area and 400,000 left destitute. Amazingly, the most holy place in all Bali, the temple complex at Besakih, high on the slopes of Gunung Agung itself, escaped destruction. The temples were covered in ash; thatch roofs and some wooden structures were set alight, but the holiest sanctuaries were spared. An ornamental gateway built near the temple to honour the then president Sukarno was totally destroyed, however, an event which, along with the eruption itself, was broadly interpreted as a divine judgement on the corrupt Sukarno regime, which was overturned soon thereafter.

The Balinese have a word, *kaiket*, which the anthropologist J. Stephen Lansing suggests is one of the most important words in the Balinese vocabulary. Kaiket means, literally, 'to be tied' and refers to the position and status of the individual. It applies to the geographical orientation mentioned above, insofar as that is an indication of status at any given time, but it refers most especially to social position. From the moment of birth the Balinese are tied, as Lansing puts it, 'to a bewildering variety of obligations, duties, organisations, temples, places, people and things'. From the Balinese point of view, kaiket is not a restriction, however, for it is precisely the fact of being tied into these clearly defined networks of behaviour that frees the spirit and enables people to function properly as human beings. Everyone knows where they stand. And the very complexity of the system, baffling though it may seem to the outsider, in itself serves to provide a multitude of reference points by which the insiders orientate themselves confidently and with precision.

The ultimate purpose of Bali's complex system of behaviour and beliefs is spiritual, they say, but the function is undeniably social. In a densely populated community requiring a good deal of cooperative effort among individuals to maintain food supply and services, such common obligations create a desirable degree of social cohesion. Being kaiket, tied, quite literally holds the system together. Paradoxically however, the system is most simply explained with descriptions of the factors that set people apart.

Of primary significance perhaps is the caste system that operates in Balinese society. It is derived from the Hindu system which prevails in India, but has been modified to Balinese conditions. There are four castes, hierarchically established and each traditionally assigned to a specific role. In descending order these are the *Brahmins* (priests), *Ksatriyas* (rulers or warriors), *Wesya* (traders), and the *Sudra* (farmers). There is no *Harrijan* (untouchable) caste in Bali. Their names make the functional significance of the caste groupings immediately obvious, but caste distinctions are blurred in modern Bali; they do not appear to mean much in terms of education and the distribution of wealth and power. The first three groups constitute about ten percent of the population, and are known collectively as the *triwangsa*. All the rest belong to the sudra caste. Each of the four castes is divided into sub-castes, and among the sudra these are very numerous indeed, each with a specific name, specific duties and a specific position in the caste hierarchy. The names may vary from place to place even though duties and hierarchical status remain the same, and such is the complexity of these variables that the religious knowledge of the priests consists very largely of information concerning the location (in

59

terms of geography, duty and status) of the multitude of sudra caste groupings. In other words, the priests provide a reference for the kaiket of the various groups. Only Brahmins may become priests (though many do not), and they are tied to high standards of behaviour which balance the inherent authority of their position.

The high and low connotations of caste have an obvious correlation with the concerns for geographic elevation that run through the Balinese social order, and they translate directly into modes of social behaviour. 'Where do you sit?', the Balinese will ask on first meeting a stranger, meaning not simply the immediate location, but location in three senses of the term – geographical, social and temporal. Each person politely places the other at mutually understood reference points in the social order. Conversation proceeds once the reference points have been established, but until then the conversants are more-or-less tongue-tied, for 'where they sit' may also oblige them to use a different form of the Balinese language. There is high Balinese, low Balinese, and even middle Balinese and a number of regional variation of all three. When a person of low caste is conversing with someone of high caste he should use high Balinese, while the high caste person he has addressed will reply in low Balinese. If however both parties wish to be especially polite and avoid reference to caste, they will both employ middle Balinese. Further, if either party should need to talk about themselves, they will use low Balinese, regardless of their own caste or that of the person they are addressing. The complexities of Balinese languages are particularly evident in the theatre, where the three grades of Balinese are supplemented by old and middle Javanese, Sanskrit and modern Indonesian to add layer upon layer of meaning to the text.

Quite apart from the complexities of caste, there are several other orders of function and obligation by which the Balinese orientate themselves in the social system. In the village there is the *banjar*, a social organisation composed of anything from a few dozen to several hundred families – usually the same family lines for generation after generation. The banjar is the basic unit of administration at the village level, and its function has been integrated into the system of national government. The banjar has the authority to make and enforce laws, impose taxes and penalties, and to call upon its members to assist in communal work projects. But all banjar decisions require full agreement of all married men belonging to it, which slows down the introduction of new ideas, the Balinese admit, but does ensure that change is well-considered.

Most banjars have a gamalan orchestra and a dance group; some, like the group at Peliatan, achieve wide renown, but all are established primarily for the benefit of the immediate community. Dancers and musicians are recruited at an early age from the two youth organisations that exist within every banjar, and of which membership is compulsory for every boy and girl until they marry. There are other organisations within the banjar that accommodate all members of society. It is an extremely cohesive unit; a point of reference, and a refuge in the event of misfortune.

Running parallel with their obligations to the banjar, every villager also belongs to a number of temple congregations and is obliged to contribute

60

towards their maintenance and perform ceremonies there at specified intervals. Most Balinese belong to at least six congregations. Three of these will be the founding temples of their own village, but the others may be widely scattered, according to the affinities of the individual – farming temples, water temples, state temples, caste temples and so on. There are over 20,000 temples in Bali, several dozen in every typical village. Individuals must know precisely at which temples they are entitled to perform their rites, for it is customary to advise people of their errors only after the mistake has been made. No one wants to blunder into the wrong temple, so all are particularly concerned to remain aware of where they may and should worship.

Beyond the banjar and the temple organisations there are also voluntary organisations which are formed, as Lansing notes, 'by anybody and for any purpose, from the earth-shaking to the utterly trivial'. By way of example, Lansing mentions a bicycle-buying organisation he encountered, wherein complicated arrangements for regular payments into a common treasury and a schedule for buying bicycles spared individual members the bother of saving up and buying a bicycle independently. But with restrictions: the rules of the organisation apparently obliged one betrothed couple to postpone marriage until both partners had qualified for their bicycles.

Caste, banjar, temple – even bicycle-buying organisations – all tend to diminish the status of individuals, leaving them with a set of responsibilities and obligations, together with all that is required to fulfil them, while not encouraging any kind of self-aggrandisement. The Balinese tend to dislike and distrust people who project themselves above the group as a whole, and where power has to be exercised they tend to disperse it very thinly.

Temporal location in Bali is hardly less complicated than the social kind, and the implications are equally demanding. The year is a round of rite and anniversary. Every one of the 20,000 temples has a day of celebration each year, lasting three days or more at the most important temples, and for every activity an offering must be made at the appropriate time of year. The arts must be honoured, for instance, and offerings must be made to the musical instruments, the dance costumes and the masks that have been the source of enjoyment during the year. There are days on which divine implements must be reconsecrated, others when appeals are made for successful cattle breeding, and when offerings are made to fruit trees, palms and gardens. On *Saraswati*, a holy day commemorating the goddess of learning, no reading or writing is allowed, and all books must be offered for blessing. On *Pagerwesi*, prayers and offerings are made for the protection of the family, the village and the world at large. On *Soma Rimek* the goddess of rice and fertility is honoured and the milling or selling of rice is forbidden. There is even a day when cars are blessed (an occasion when visitors may find their hired car mysteriously unavailable one day, and bedecked with flowers the next).

The list of obligatory offerings and celebrations is very long, and many of the events require elaborate preparations, and possibly some travelling too,

61

so that due notice of their advent is important. Notice is provided by one or other of the two traditional calendars that the Balinese employ, neither of which is the western calendar which regulates the official life of the island. In effect, there are three measures of temporal location in Bali.

The traditional calendars are the *saka*, which is of Hindu origin, and the *uku* calendar, which is an ancient Javano-Balinese construction. Saka is a solar/lunar calendar of 12 months with 29-30 days each, which is brought into line with the solar calendar every 30 months by adding an extra lunar month. The saka calendar determines the scheduling of harvest festivals, some temple festivals, and the advent of the Balinese New Year, *nyepi*. Nyepi falls on the first day of the tenth month, immediately following the new moon closest to the spring equinox, and therefore marks a degree of seasonal variation. Old Year's night is noisy, but throughout the island nyepi is a day of fasting and silence, when it is hoped that devils and demons, which the clamorous celebrations of the previous night were intended to arouse, will now quietly disappear.

The uku calendar is rather more complex, with 30 individually named weeks of seven days each; 210 days in all. There are no months as such, but the uku year is divided into six cycles of five seven-day weeks, along with which special note is also taken of other units of time, especially the three-, five- and six-day cycles. The coincidence of certain days within these cycles is deemed auspicious for the performance of certain rites – when, for instance, the fifth day of a five-day week coincides with the seventh day of a seven-day week. Other coincidences are deemed inauspicious. When the third day of the three-day week falls on the fifth day of the five-day week, for example, people must take care. The effect of this particular coincidence on the Balinese has been likened to the uneasiness that some westerners still feel about Friday the 13th (the combination of seven- and 28/31-day cycles); an important difference, however, is that the Balinese example occurs every 15 days.

Every household is expected to be aware of all the simpler and most important combinations of days and weeks, and the women will prepare and make the appropriate offerings accordingly. There are some events however, for which favourable days are not fixed by the calendar – social events such as weddings and cremations, for instance, and these must be scheduled by consultation with the priest, who will refer to the *tika*, a wooden counting panel on which the days and weeks of the saka year, together with all the significant coincidences are shown in detail.

A particularly revealing expression of the Balinese tendency to suppress individual interests beneath the greater significance of the group is to be found in their system of naming people. Individuals are known not so much by a personal name distinct to themselves as by a name denoting their birth order. There are four of these: Wayan, for the first born; Njoman is the second-born; Made the third and Ketut the fourth. These are the boys' names, for girls the prefix ni- is added: Niwayan, Ninjoman, Nimade and Niketut. If a couple have more than four children the cycle is repeated, so that the fifth and ninth children would be called Wayan (or Niwayan, as the case may be), along with the first; similarly, the sixth and tenth would be Njoman, or Ninjoman, and so on.

People are given personal names at a ceremony that takes place 105 days after their birth (105 is a particularly auspicious coincidence of three-, five- and seven-day cycles), but the personal names are very rarely used, and then only to distinguish between individuals with the same birth-order name: 'I mean Njoman Warse', someone addressing a group of children might say, 'not Njoman Umi'. And while people grow up with names that principally denote their location in the birth-order, once they have children of their own they lose even that identity and are known instead by names denoting their positions in the generation-order: a man becomes 'father-of-Wayan', his wife becomes 'mother-of-Wayan', and so on. When the children themselves marry and have children the identity of their parents changes again, and they are called 'Grandfather- and Grandmother-of-Wayan'. Adults who have no children retain their birth-order name, and with it the sense that they are, in some way, still children, subtly accorded less respect or authority in village affairs.

Of course the names by which people are known in Bali are not properly names at all – they are titles indicating the individual's position in the family line. They denote status and position in the social network more than they mark individual identity, providing yet another dependable reference point in the maze of interaction and obligation that cultural involution has produced in Bali. The system effectively affirms the greater significance of the whole over its parts.

To western eyes, wherein the distinctive potential of each separate human being is seen almost to be a sacred thing, the individual in Bali may seem diminished to the status of a mere cog in the wheel. But to the Balinese, whose traditional need of extensive cooperative effort in food production has always been high, the muted nature of personal identity in Bali acknowledges that fact that individual human existence is a very transient affair, while the system that sustains individuals is much more enduring. People come and go, but the system persists.

The functional advantages of an outlook that puts the significance of the system above that of the individual in this way are obvious (and have appealed to political theorists throughout history), but in Bali the starkly functional aspect of the strategy is wrapped around with yet another layer of cultural invention that protects everyone from the dangers of seeing themselves as mere transient functionaries – religion, offering the individual an afterlife in paradise as recompense for all the cooperative effort that is expended on earth during a brief lifetime. The promise is eternally unverifiable, but it stretches human imagination to soaring heights of expectation. For the gifts that dreams of heaven offer, a few years of drudgery on earth are a small price.

The religious world of the Balinese is at least as complex as their social world – and no less real to them, for the simple reason, as mentioned earlier, that the Balinese make no distinction between their spiritual and their secular lives. Over the last thousand years, while western societies

63

have been struggling to disentagle the secular from the religious, the Balinese have been assiduously integrating them.

Despite the popular misconception of Hinduism as a faith with innumerable quite distinct gods and goddesses, it actually has just one absolute divinity, which in Bali is called *Sangyang Tunggul*. The deities that people worship and make offerings to are simply manifestations of the one god; the radiating divinity of Sangyang Tunggul, as perceived from a specific location in the planes of geographical, social and temporal dimension in which the Balinese must constantly orientate themselves. The Balinese word for god – *dewa* – comes from the sanskrit *dev*, meaning ray. *Bhatara*, goddess, comes from *bhatr*, meaning protector. Extensive though the Balinese panoply of gods may be, it is not its numbers but its diversity that is most important. There are very few (if any) aspects of the natural and supernatural worlds that the Balinese are willing to take for granted. Gods tie people to the realities of human behaviour, to the world they occupy – and, not least, to the volcanoes that created Bali.

The home of the gods is Gunung Anung, the most holy mountain, the volcano which is, the Balinese believe, the mother of the entire world. But Gunung Anung is only the home of the gods in the sense that it is the highest place on Bali and therefore their most appropriate resting place. The manifestations of Sangyang Tunggul do not reside only on Gunung Agung; they are ever-present, everywhere. As Lansing puts it, 'they blow like the wind over Bali, without personality until they alight at some particular spot.... The location defines the personality: a god may come to a certain temple for a brief "visit" and acquire thereby a definite name and personality, but when he visits a different temple a few miles away he will have a different name and a different, utterly distinct personality'.

These ethereal gods, blowing like the wind, shining like the sun, blessing the earth with rain, represent the ideal and eternal good of the world that the Balinese occupy. They are the pinnacle of the hierarchy of power and being that comprises existence. The Balinese believe that people are ranked some distance below the gods in this hierarchy, and just below people are the evil spirits, which are held to be the intangible but powerful enactors of bad human feelings and thoughts. Below the evil spirits are the witches, physical manifestations of bad feelings and thoughts, and right at the bottom are the animals, which are believed to be the physical form that witches often assume while pursuing their malevolent intentions.

So the Balinese view grants humanity only a very tenuous position in the world. There is a good deal of malevolence below, sublime perfection above, and maintaining a position in between requires constant attention to matters of kaiket. But the system acknowledges the realities of human existence to a greater extent than might be supposed. It places the darker aspects of human nature firmly in a context where their unyielding persistence is explained, but never excused. The selfish and instinctive appetites of animals are extreme metaphors for the lowest kinds of human behaviour. But animals are an integral part of the system. And the selfish instincts of mankind are as much a part of the living world as are the animals upon which people feed. Every farmer is well aware that the filth of rotting decay fosters new growth. But while the base instincts cannot be expunged from mankind, they cannot be allowed to rampage unhindered either. So, they are given a physical existence in drama, painting and sculpture, where ugly hairy bodies, protruding eyes, fanged teeth, lolling tongue and ridiculous gait embody every trait the Balinese deplore. These devils and demons are the epitome of brute instinctive behaviour and its consequences and, as such, provide forceful reminders of the human obligation to restrain selfish instincts for the benefit of social harmony. People, unlike animals, must live by the rules, not their instincts: kaiket – tied, secure in a system that regulates realities as well as urging the pursuit of ideals.

The ultimate link between the secular and spiritual worlds of the Balinese lies in their belief that the traditional gods are actually deified human beings. Ancestors, in fact, who are present in both worlds at all times; though no one can be certain precisely which ancestors are the gods at any specific moment. The gods actually represent the distant founders of family lines, and this accounts for both the plethora of gods and temples in Bali, and for the variety of titles they hold for similar roles: as families multiplied, diverged and spread across the island, each lineage created its own panoply of gods. The Balinese believe that people are ordinarily reborn into their own families every five generations; a gap small enough to permit grandparents to compare grandchildren with memories of their own great-grandparents, but too distant – after a few generations – for anyone to be sure precisely which generation represents the reincarnation of the ancestral god. All that anyone can know is that everyone must have children – to provide a vessel for the reincarnated spirits of the ancestors – and that every individual is closest to the gods at birth, and at death.

Life, then, is a cycle not a progression. There is no accumulation of worth with age, just a gradual move away from pure holiness during the years to middle age, and a gradual return to holiness as death approaches. In this scheme of things, it is no accident that people are believed to be furthest removed from the divine state in their middle years, when they are likely to be at the height of their earthly powers; it is just then that they are likely to need most restraint, and must be treated most cautiously. The sequence of individual life is utterly predictable, amounting to a series of set positions in the social and temporal order, with the transitions from one to another marked with appropriate ceremony – the rites of passage.

A baby is the most holy object in the living world of Bali; an object of sublime innocence, blemished only by the means of its passage into the world. It must be cleansed and blessed. The afterbirth is buried under a stone in the compound, (to the right of the entrance if the infant is a boy, to the left if it is a girl), where it becomes a physical symbol of the four ethereal brothers or sisters, one guarding each cardinal direction, who will accompany the child through all the days of its life. Seven days after birth the infant is given bracelets and anklets of black string, symbolically tying it to the world of human obligation. At 42 days, these are replaced with

65

items of brass and silver. The ears are pierced and a thread passed through, so that the child may later wear tiny gold earrings, shaped like flowers. A necklace of amulets, including a silver tube containing a piece of the infant's umbilical cord, glass beads, an ancient coin perhaps, and a tiger's tooth or a piece of tiger's bone, is hung about the infant's neck – all intended to diminish the effect of the child's inevitable decline from the state of perfect innocence.

At 105 days, the child is literally planted on the earth for the first time, and *Ibu Pertiwi* – the Earth Mother – is asked to accept and take care of this most precious offering. Throughout the first months of its life, the infant is believed to be closer to the divine than to humanity, and nothing must mar that all-too-fleeting state of near perfection. It is deeply loved; distress and tears are held to be the fault of the parent, not the child, and western parents visiting Bali are frequently chided for their readiness to chastise and actually provoke their childrens' unhappiness. The Balinese child is never allowed to crawl, for crawling resembles the behaviour of animals, but is carried everywhere until able to stand and walk.

The first haircut, the emergence of the first deciduous tooth, and later the first permanent tooth, are all moments that are deemed to require special rites to ensure the safe passage of the developing child from one state to another. Puberty is especially important, and a most significant ceremony occurs sometime later, when the canine teeth are filed level with the tooth row, thus removing the animalistic fangs and symbolically levelling the last extremes of personality in preparation for adulthood. Later comes marriage and parenthood; then death and finally cremation, when the spirit is liberated for a sojourn with the gods, looking after and over things, before returning to enact them once again.

Of all the features that attract the visitors' attention in Bali, the love and care that parents bestow on their children strikes the deepest chord. Not every child behaves like a little god all the time, nor are they always treated like one – predictably, there are exceptions – but parents do seem deferentially concerned for the wellbeing of the child. And any parent who feels ritually obliged to carry an infant until it can walk, lest it should behave like an animal on the ground, must surely become more firmly tied to the child than would otherwise be the case. It is tempting to believe that the Balinese are nicer people, and care more for each other, because of the way they treat their children and once were treated themselves; but quite apart from the sentiment, caring for other people actually plays an important functional role in Balinese society: it encourages the co-operation which is essential to maintaining production of the island's staple food crop – rice.

Rice is the world's major food crop. It provides nearly one third of all the calories that mankind consumes – 656 calories for every man, woman and child on earth, every day. Rice is the only crop grown almost exclusively as human food, and for three out of every five of the world's inhabitants, it is the indispensible staple food. One in ten of the earth's arable hectares is devoted to the cultivation of rice. A string of impressive statistics can testify to the importance of rice in human affairs. More unexpected perhaps, is the fact that over 97 percent of the world's rice is eaten within the borders of the country where it was grown; most of it within five kilometres (three miles) of the very field. It has been calculated that under the methods of cultivation still prevailing where over 90 percent of the world's rice is grown, every hectare requires anything from just under 1,000 to over 2,000 man- or woman-hours of labour to produce one harvest. One hectare (2.47 acres) of the traditional rice varieties produced between one and two tonnes of rice per harvest – which is a relatively small return for so much labour. But if labour and production were meticulously organised, that same hectare would produce three harvests each year, and would do so year after year – for centuries.

The extraordinary productivity of rice has been recognised for a long time, and one has only to look at a population density map of the world to see the extent to which the potential of rice has been exploited in the regions where it grows best. But just *why* rice should be so productive remained a mystery until the 1970s. How was it that rice could produce the same dependable harvest, year after year from the same field? Researchers at the International Rice Research Institute in the Philippines have supplied some of the answers. In the first place, rice has evolved special adaptations enabling it to grow in flooded and waterlogged conditions that would drown most other plants (taro, the root crop that sustained dense populations on the Pacific islands, is the only other food plant adapted to such conditions). Rice has a system of air passages from leaf to root ten times more efficient than is found in barley, for instance. This means that even when the roots are in waterlogged, oxygen-deficient (anaerobic) soils some distance under water, the plant still receives sufficient oxygen from the leaves above water to respire aerobically (with oxygen), to utilize carbohydrates efficiently, and to grow. Some varieties of rice are able to flourish where the water floods up to five metres (16 ft) deep, and can grow at rates of up to 25 cm. (10 in.) per day in order to keep some leaves above the rising waters.

There are varieties of rice that thrive under dryland cultivation, but it is in artificially flooded terraces that the natural adaptations of rice are most greatly enhanced. Controlled flooding produces a sequence of cumulative effects on the nature of the field, some decidedly beneficial. In the first instance, the action of the farmer and his animals working back and forth through the flooded field eventually turns the land into a pond of knee-deep sludge, the consistency of a malted-milkshake, with a densely compacted layer of subsoil underneath. Few nutrients are leached away through the subsoil, as happens in dryland farming, while the sludge minimises the exchange of air between the atmosphere and the soil in which the plant is growing, so that the loss of nutrients in a gaseous form is also inhibited. And from these physical advantages of flooded culti-vation stem benefits of a chemical nature, for while flooding prevents nutrients escaping from the system into either the subsoil or the atmosphere, it also renders them more readily available within the system. For instance, in a flooded field, soluble iron, aluminium, manganese and

67

calcium freely release the phosphorus that in dryland conditions remains chemically bound up with them. Phosphorus is the second-most important plant nutrient. Far and away the most important is nitrogen and, fortunately, it is in the supply of nitrogen that the strategy of controlled flooding has its most beneficial effect in wet-rice cultivation.

The atmosphere is 80 percent nitrogen, but very few plants are able to absorb atmospheric nitrogen directly. For most plants it has to be 'fixed' first. Lightning does a certain amount of fixing, but the principal agent is the host of specialised microorganisms that live in the soil and produce ammonium compounds as they decompose dead organic matter. The ammonium produced by the microorganisms is unstable, and quite rapidly oxidises into nitrates, from which plants are then able to assimilate nitrogen. However, the soil itself cannot hold the nitrate, so if it is not soon absorbed by plants the nitrogen is quickly leached away, or reverts to a gaseous form. Under dryland conditions this process rapidly produces an impoverished soil, (forcing swidden farmers to shift to new land), but at the bottom of a flooded rice field the process is slowed down considerably. The stubble and other organic matter that the farmer ploughs into the mud decomposes very slowly, and with minimal amounts of oxygen available, the ammonium oxidises to nitrates at just about the rate at which the plants can assimilate them. Very little is lost, and the rice flourishes.

And while a depth of water slows down the nitrogen cycle at the bottom of the flooded field, it also supports some very useful forms of life at the surface. Foremost among these are a tiny water fern called azolla, and a microscopic blue-green alga which lives in a symbiotic partnership with the water fern. Azolla and the blue-green alga possess the rare ability to fix nitrogen direct from the atmosphere. It has been estimated that under good conditions they can fix up to three kilograms of nitrogen each day in every hectare of flooded rice terrace (2.7 pounds per acre); nitrogen which becomes available to the rice as the azolla and algae die and decompose.

So all in all, the flooded rice terrace enjoys a remarkably continuous supply of nitrogen. The supply can amount to as much as 100 kg. per ha (89 pounds per acre) which greatly exceeds the quantity of artificial fertiliser that subsistence farmers would expect to scatter on their fields (and in fact scientists at the International Rice Research Institute have found that the addition of artificial fertiliser actually inhibits the natural production of nitrogen in wet-rice fields), but under average conditions the supply is between 20 and 40 kg. per ha (18-35 pounds per acre). As it happens, rice needs about 20 kg. of nitrogen per hectare to produce one tonne of grain. And so the various processes of natural nitrogen fixation and retention that rice farmers have engendered in their flooded fields have been enough to produce one or two tonnes of grain per hectare per harvest, two or three harvests a year, every year, from the same piece of land for centuries.

The farmers who founded and refined the wet-rice system and maintained its high levels of production for centuries knew nothing of nitrogen cycles and oxygen transportation in plants. They worked purely by trial and error. In the process, however, they acquired a sound appreciation of just what made the system work, and of how to keep it working. In

68

Vietnam, for instance, farmers founded a temple in which the virtues of
the little water fern, azolla, are extolled and honoured. In Bali, where
maintaining high levels of wet-rice production in a relatively small area is
made more complex by the rugged nature of the terrain, farmers have made
a religion of their activities. Rice in Bali is not grown according to any
production timetable that the modern agronomist might work out, but
according to the stipulations of the temples and the rice goddess – and with
very good effect. No Balinese rice farmer ever needs to consider the
technical details of how rice should be grown to produce maximum crops
from his land – precisely when to plough, when to flood, when to plant,
when to drain and so forth. All he has to do is follow the calendar of *Dewi
Sri*, the goddess of rice and fertility, and the crops are virtually guaranteed.
Rice cultivation is the ultimate expression of the Balinese readiness to
follow the edicts of some greater authority: the cult of the rice goddess not
only demonstrates the integration of the secular and the spiritual worlds of
Bali at the most fundamental level, it also provides an eloquent example of
the functional significance of religion in human ecology.

The cult of the rice goddess ensures that every farmer proceeds in a
manner that will ensure one or two tonnes per hectare wherever the land is
capable of growing wet rice, and the key to its success lies in the way it
promotes optimum use of fertile mountain slopes and copious rainfall.

Bali enjoys a remarkably consistent climate. The temperature rarely
rises much above or falls much below 26°C (79°F). Over a ten-year period,
Geertz found that the annual rainfall was never less than about 2,200 mm.
(87 in.), never more than about 2,500 mm. (98 in.). Monthly rainfall was
also extremely consistent, almost unvarying, with almost precisely the
same amounts falling each January, each February, and so on, year after
year. Over millenia the inherently fertile volcanic soils have been enriched
by the accumulating humus of natural vegetation. Under these conditions,
plants can grow all year round. Farmers do not need to consider seasonal
factors – they can plant and harvest continuously.

Rice, indigenous to the region, is the obvious choice for a staple crop
under such conditions. There is water enough, and warmth enough, for it
to flourish productively. There are two problems, however. Firstly, the
nature of the landscape, with a narrow coastal plain backed by steep,
deeply fissured mountain slopes, makes cultivation difficult. Secondly,
although rice grows in a depth of water, the field must be dry when the
grain is harvested, and must remain dry for a brief period before the next
crop is planted. So, although the water is available all year round, it is
needed in each field only part of the time. The solution to these problems
was, of course, the construction of terraces on the mountain slopes, and an
irrigation system that controlled the flow of water down the slope,
flooding and draining fields as required.

Ideally, the irrigation system should be arranged so that maximum
production is sustained on every terrace down the slope. When the high
terraces are flooded and prepared for planting, the crop should be
well-advanced on lower terraces, and ready for harvesting on the lowest. In
this respect, the timing of cultivation throughout the system is as

69

important as the water supply. Growing cycles should be staggered from terrace to terrace so that some are flooded while others are dry, aiming to ensure that the system as a whole uses a relatively constant amount of water at all times, year after year. If water-flow and cultivation cycles are not coordinated in this way, but left subject only to the decisions of individual farmers, there would be a danger of the water resources being seriously overtaxed should a majority decide to plant simultaneously, for instance, and woefully underused when the same majority harvested their crop. The ideal arrangement, however, would sustain a continuous cycle of maximum production on each terrace, to the benefit of individual and group alike. The Balinese have achieved this ideal with a secular organisation called the *subak*, which functions in accordance with the spiritual edicts of Dewi Sri.

Subak means 'irrigation society', it is a completely independent social organisation devoted exclusively to irrigated farming, imposing its own obligations and demands upon the individual – another point of reference in the social grid. A subak comprises all the terraces that are irrigated from a single water source, usually a dam constructed high on one of the many gorges which cascading rivers have cut deep into the mountain flanks. The dam may be 15 km. (10 mi.) or more above the fields, and the canals carrying water from it may have required the construction of tunnels and aqueducts, as well as the precise levelling needed to keep the water flowing at optimum speed throughout. Just above the fields the water flow is divided among two or three smaller canals, and each of these may be divided again and again, depending on the size of the subak, creating a number of separate flows into the terraces. Each inlet is called a *tempek*, and its flow is divided and sub-divided, as size demands, into smaller units called *ketjoran*, 'water neighbourhoods' as Geertz describes them, within which the water is yet again divided to supply the gentle flow that each terrace requires. This final unit of the subak is called a *tenah*, a word which also serves as the measure of several other things. A tenah of land is the area that a tenah of water will irrigate; a tenah of seed is needed to plant that much land, and a tenah of rice is the yield it will produce.

A typical subak illustrated by Geertz, shows its water supply divided through five stages to produce 240 tenah, each of which should receive precisely the same amount of water from the subak dam (and in general they do, Geertz reports). The technical difficulties of dividing a flow of water accurately, combined with the need to regulate the timing of the supply – so that different terraces are flooded at different times, call for complex arrangements within the subak. And since there are thousands of subaks in Bali (the average measures just 80 ha; 200 acres), many with dams on the same watercourse, and all ultimately deriving the bulk of their water from one or other of two crater lakes in the mountains there must be a good deal of cooperation between subaks as well, if maximum production is to be maintained on every terrace.

Each subak has a council controlling the technical aspects of its irrigation system, collecting taxes to finance upkeep and improvement, and empowered to call for maintenance and construction work from its

members as required, according to a rota of individual and group obligations. There is a written constitution (an agrarian bill of rights, written
on a palm-leaf, is how Geertz describes it); each member casts a single vote
on matters of policy and in the election of officials, regardless of the size of
his holding. Fines are imposed for infraction of subak rules.

As Geertz stresses, the subak is not a collective farm, however: it
regulates the water supply to ensure that every field gets its fair share, and
that is all it does. Subak land is freehold, and ownership is unaffected by
social status or place of residence. A farmer may be of any caste; he may
own land in several subaks, and every subak has members from several
different villages. Members are free to sell land, farm it themselves,
employ others to farm it, or rent it out, as they please. They may consume
the rice it produces, sell it, or give it away – the subak is not concerned.
The subak sets the context within which maximum production is
maintained – nothing more.

But the Balinese have set the context of the subak itself in the realm of a
transcendent authority – Dewi Sri, the goddess of rice and fertility. Every
stage of water division, from dam to canal, from canal to tempek, from
tempek to ketjoran, from ketjoran to tenah is marked by ritual ceremony;
so too is every stage in the development of the growing rice. Farmers erect
shrines in their fields, some permanent, some temporary. The subak builds
temples at appropriate points on the subak lands (there were 13 in the
subak that Geertz describes), where priests officiate in the major ceremonies, and members are obliged to participate.

The water temple ceremonies are scheduled according to the Balinese
calendar, with its year of 210 days, and it is surely no coincidence that the
growing cycle of Balinese rice spans precisely half a year – 105 days.

On the appointed day each Balinese year, the heads of all participating
subaks make the arduous journey up the steep forested sides of the
mountains to join the priests at the lake temple in ceremonies that will
invite down the gods designated to reside there, and ask them to arrange an
adequate and effective water supply during the forthcoming growing
seasons. At the same time, while the mountain-top rituals 'open' the
waters of the lake to feed the dams on the water-courses down below, the
subak chiefs use the gathering as an occasion on which to confirm the
sequence by which individual subaks will open their canals from the dams.
This in turn determines precisely when the canals should be opened to the
tempeks and so on, right down to the tenah, where the individual farmer
must arrange his labours to coordinate with the water supply.

The schedules of the various stages and water-openings are all set by the
cycle of religious occasions that farmers are obliged to acknowledge with
prayers and offerings. Included among these occasions are the days on
which the ground should be broken (and not before), when the field should
be flooded, when seed should be planted, and when the young seedlings
should be transplanted. A large ceremony is held in the main subak temple
when the rice is about to flower, and a full scale three-day festival takes
place when the seed is set. There are lesser ceremonies, (pleading for good
growth and for protection from pests, for instance), made at shrines in

every field, and other large ceremonies are held as the crop ripens, when it is harvested, and when it is placed in the granary. Geertz lists nine, and another authority 16, specific religious occasions on which every subak member must make obeisance to the appropriate gods.

All these religious occasions are scheduled in the Balinese calendar according to the cycle of the rice goddess, and it will be no surprise to learn that this religious cycle closely matches the growing cycle of rice. The 'Opening of Openings' at the high mountain lake temple locks every subak and terrace into a single coordinated rhythm of cultivation. Once the waters of the lake have been ceremonially opened, this rhythm predetermines exactly when each subak should open the waters into its canal, and thereafter proceed with the cultivation cycle according to the events specified in the Balinese calendar for its particular temples. Once the ritual cycle has been initiated at the lake temple, nothing can interrupt its progress down the mountain to the sea, as it initiates cascading cycles of ceremony and cultivation in every subak it touches.

Furthermore, the cycle initiated at the 'Opening of Openings' serves to stagger the subak cycles so that, at any given moment, the sequence of cultivation throughout the drainage area falls into a stage-by-stage progression down the slope. When the high subaks are flooding their terraces ready for ploughing, for example, those lower down are still clearing the land; when the lower terraces are planting, those higher up are already preparing for the harvest. And since there are just two lake temples at which the 'Opening of Openings' is celebrated; Batu Kau serving western Bali, and Ulun Danau serving the rest of the island, the rituals lock rice cultivation throughout Bali into one grand, coordinated and extremely productive system.

So, behind all its ceremony and complex ritual, the cult of the rice goddess is basically a functional device that maintains rice production at the highest possible level, principally by keeping water use consistent with water supply throughout the year; never over-taxed, never under-utilised. The functional link between spiritual conformity and the fulfilment of secular demands is undeniable; they must have developed together, and now the ritual of one and the technology of the other are so entwined that neither could exist alone.

In the 1970s, foreign advisors persuaded some farmers to stop growing rice according to the ritual schedules of the Balinese calendar and plant as frequently as they could, using fertilisers and pesticides to produce more rice. The farmers did so for a time, and prospered. But then continuous cultivation began to encourage the build-up of pests and predators (especially mice), which had regularly starved and died out during the fallow periods that the ritual calendar ordained. Frogs disappeared, mosquitoes multiplied and malaria became prevalent. Soil conditions changed, making fields harder to plough. Before long the costs of cash input, manual effort and environmental effect began to work against increased output. Productivity dropped. By 1979, all those involved had reverted to the temple calendars.

CHAPTER FOUR

ALPINE PASTORALISTS

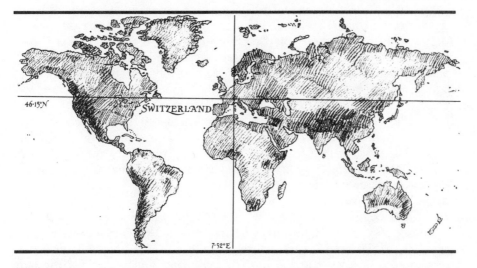

The larch is an oddity among conifers for, unlike the pines, it drops its needles in late autumn and acquires a new set each spring. The new growth is still soft and bright green in early summer, sprouting thickly around the branches, and cheeringly prominent among the sombre shades of the forest above Törbel, a Swiss alpine village in the valley of the Mattervispa, which flows from the glaciers of the Matterhorn. During winter and early spring, snow and then melt water heap the fallen larch needles against the upper sides of the tree trunks – convenient for collection by villagers farming the land below who still use larch needles as stall-bedding for their cows. Most have abandoned the practice, but in former times the forest floor was raked clear of needles to its least accessible corners. A family might collect ten cubic metres (13 cubic yards) or more, transporting it down the mountainside in large baskets, and once the needles had served their purpose in the stable, soaking up the manure, the material was composted and spread on the vegetable plots, the vineyards, the grain fields and the hay meadows. Thus, by providing bedding and helping to maintain the fertility of the land, the oddity of the larch has a useful application among alpine communities.

The trees are useful in other ways too. Simply by standing firm on the steep slopes, they lessen the chances of an avalanche engulfing the village; they also provide fuel, and timber that splits straight and easily along the grain, hardly needing the saw or the adze to square the logs of which the village houses are built. The resin of the larch is a fine natural preservative which, with time, colours the houses a deep rich brown.

The multiple application of the larch is just one example of the extent to which the natural environment is integrated with the lives of the people

73

who inhabit the high alpine villages of Switzerland. Not just the larch, every part of the alpine environment – land, water, vegetation, animals, people – are integrated in a pattern of strictly regulated self-sufficiency so effective and durable that its influence has reached beyond the alps, becoming a fundamental part of Switzerland's political system.

People have been living at Törbel for over a thousand years and although the pattern of their lives has changed significantly during the past 50 years, the continuing existence of the community is in itself a token of the success with which earlier generations used the limited resources available to them. The land area of Törbel is limited to about 800 hectares (2,000 acres); its population is limited to about 500 men, women and children. The land owned by the community abuts the holdings of adjacent communities – boundaries that were marked out centuries ago, since when there has been no room for expansion. The amount of food the land produced was also brought to its maximum limit many years ago, by a process of intensification, as the villagers exploited the full potential of every square metre and intensified production by judicious land-use, irrigation, and manuring.

Acknowledging the limits of its land and defining a set of regulations according to which the resources of that land could best be exploited, has enabled the Törbel community to sustain a healthy population on the same 800 ha for a thousand years. The same land, and essentially the same people, too. The present population of 530 men, women and children are spread among 160 households, among which are found just 12 family names. Every one of those names is to be found among the signatories to a document dated 1483 that laid down some important land-use regulations. The document is preserved in Törbel's village archives, along with many others relating to village affairs, the earliest of which dates from 1224. Doubtless each document was drawn up as events called attention to some aspect of Törbel life that needed to be defined and regulated for the wellbeing of the community. Individual land ownership, for example, would not have required precise definition until the growing population encountered increasing pressure for land, and disputes within the community had begun to herald the limits of expansion. Likewise, the rights to use common resources such as water and forage need not have been allocated until the benefits of intensified production became obvious to the community. The documents must have been based on the accumulated knowledge and experience of the community, and, as such, they may have simply formalised arrangements that had already been in existence for some time. But more than that, those ancient scraps of parchment, neatly written in Latin, bear witness to the fact that when people have reached the limits of their territorial expansion, and have increased their food supply to the limits of intensification, then only one option remains to ensure continued well-being: regulation of access to the resources.

Centuries before the word ecology was coined and achieved common usage (and frequent mis-usage) among the fashionable environmentalist movement of the 1960s and '70s, the residents of Törbel understood the laws of ecology that govern relationships between organisms and their

74

environment very well indeed. They knew that their existence and the prospects of future generations depended upon keeping their population size and the exploitation of resources balanced within the limited carrying capacity of their environment. Fundamentally, they had to define and enforce regulations that would establish a lasting balance between what individuals put into the community and what they took from it, between individual benefit and communal responsibility.

The problem of individual versus communal interest afflicts every social group, no matter how large or small, but its significance is most potently revealed in circumstances where its effects are ecological and have a direct bearing on the size and durability of the community, such as is the case at Törbel. And successful resolution of the problem is also well demonstrated at Törbel, where reasoned regulation has produced remarkable continuity – the same 12 family lines sustaining themselves generation after generation, through the centuries, from the produce of the same piece of land.

Robert Netting, whose studies of ecological change and continuity at Törbel contribute significantly to this chapter, writes of the individual family interests running parallel to and supporting community interests 'in an ecosystem as finely calibrated ᵍand dependable as an old Swiss watch'.

By late June the green of the new needles on the larches is darker, less luminous, in the forest under the alp. Kingcups gleam amid reeds and cotton grass; there are violet gentians blooming on the open ground. Pockets of snow persist in north-facing corners of the forest, but the vines at the valley floor are already advanced enough for Roman Wyss to spend his mornings tying in the new growth. The school is closed for the summer, and three generations of the Seematter family head for their meadows on the low valley slopes, where the hay is already cut and dry enough to carry into the barn. A tree laden with ripe cherries stands in the wall bordering the small meadow, frequently distracting the children from the main purpose of the afternoon's endeavours.

Young potato plants are prominent in the gardens that occupy the limited expanse of relatively level ground below the village. Beans are breaking through the soil, Klara Kalbermatten is planting out lettuces and the apple tree adjoining her plot has set a noticeably good crop of fruit. Ignaz Lorenz is driving his two cows from the barn near Feld, where they have been feeding on the last of the previous year's hay, to his meadow some distance below, cut last week and already grown well enough to provide grass for two cows while he mows yet another meadow. Above the village the hay stands uncut, rich with the colour and variety of plants that characterise old meadows – clover, buttercups, camomile, harebells amid verdant grass.

Throughout the summer, each weekday from eight in the morning until four in the afternoon, the peaceful village activities are overhung by the explosive rattle of pneumatic drills and the rumble of heavy lorries leaving the excavation site beside the school and community offices, where contractors are mining deep into the granite to make a nuclear shelter large enough to accomodate the entire village population for at least 14 days after a nuclear attack. The communal shelter is in addition to the one that anyone building a new house is obliged, by law, to construct.

On Saturday morning, while wraiths of a cool mist still hang over the uncut meadows above the village, Oswald Seematter, who works at the La Roche chemical factory in Visp, 20 km. (12 mi.) away, where the Mattervispa flows into the Rhone, is milking the cow he has named Paris. He leans his head against her rump, talks to her while she munches at the fresh hay he has put in her bier. Daniel, his six year old son stands alongside, silently watching the milk foam in the bucket. Oswald's brother, Philemon, clears out the stall – not needles but straw these days, when jobs outside the village provide the cash to ease tasks within it. Across the cwm, where the sun is just striking the larches and houses that stand below the fall of the Törbelbach at Alpji, groups of people and cows begin to converge on the track that leads to the alp. Within 30 minutes, cows and people are appearing from all directions. From tracts of land distinguished to outsiders only by the fences between them, or by one or two larch-log cabins, but known by name to Törbel residents – from Alpji, Blattegga, and Wängerle they cross the Törbelbach and follow the track across the voralp to Hannig; from Furren, Bina, Burge, Brunnen Ze Springu, and Törbel itself they move up along the switchback road. The cows are a mixture of alpine breeds, stocky, short-legged animals with heavy shoulders and rumps – built more like beef than milch cattle.

Oswald has finished milking; several litres of Paris's milk is given to her calf, the remainder is for the house. He grooms her, smoothing away the patches where a night in the stall has roughened her immaculate coat, scratching in the curls that rise between her horns, talking to her, coaxing, as he straps a cowbell round her neck and a bridle over her head. Oswald hands the bridle to his son who, with no hesitation, tugs the enormous cow from her barn.

By now the groups of cattle approaching from all corners of the Törbel territory have converged on the road above Oswald's barn, mingling with an equally large number of people and vehicles. Progress is slow, with the cowbells offering more appropriate accompaniment to the procession than the snorting exhausts of the cars on the steep incline. At the corner where the road takes a hairpin bend up from the steep sloping land they call Schatze, larch pole fencing and a length of dry stone wall enclose a section of meadow; 105 cows are led into the enclosure and left standing free – looking rather forlorn in this bare, slightly abandoned place where the only company is a water trough hewn from a whole log in the manner of a dugout canoe, while around the enclosure are clustered large numbers of noisy spectators. There are hotdogs, coffee and beer for sale, and a carnival air prevails. The cows meanwhile are beginning to assess one another, and their relative positions, in the enclosed meadow. Soon, fights break out between individuals, each accompanied by a round of cheers from the crowd as the cows charge at each other, heads down, horns rampant, more in the manner of Spanish fighting bulls than Swiss cows. The cows are establishing their order of dominance (their 'pecking order', though the established ethological term hardly seems applicable to the massive cows of Törbel) for the 12 weeks of communal life that they will spend together on the alp, after nearly 40 weeks of solitary confinement in barn and meadow as the private responsibility of their individual owners. The owners, meanwhile, are assessing the condition of the animals, gauging how well their cows measure against the others, and against the standards of previous years, comparing notes with other owners, eating, drinking, laughing. The event is something of a carnival.

This Saturday at the end of June marks the first day that the herd of privately owned animals will begin to crop the resources of the communally owned alpine pastures. From that day until the herd is brought down again in the autumn, the cows will be in the care of one herdsman and any young helpers he may recruit (there is usually no shortage of volunteers). The herdsman is paid a negotiated wage from the funds of the alp association; he must ensure that the alpine pastures are grazed judiciously, that the cows get the best of the new grass as it grows, but without over-tiring them on long treks to and from pasture. In the evening the herd retires to the recently built and fully mechanised milking stable at Chalte Brunne, where the herdsman is assisted with the milking by a group of adult volunteers from the village. The milk is pumped through a stainless steel pipeline down to the dairy and cheese-making facility in the village. The stable is hosed down, and the resultant manure sludge is pumped out onto a grazed portion of meadow through a mobile pipeline that will be moved and extended across the accessible pasture as the season and grazing advance. After milking, the cows are put out to graze again in the vicinity of the barn, and gradually the adjoining road fills with a line of parked cars.

Throughout the alpine season individuals, couples, and whole families regularly make an evening excursion to watch the cows on the alp. They wander across the meadow, seeking out their animals, patting them, talking, checking their condition.

The evening excursion to the alp has an air of ritual about it. The people stand, infants in their arms, young children playing, amid bells gently ringing and an aroma of cows and sweet manure. They talk and point, but essentially, for perhaps an hour or so, they seem to commune with the cows; the contemporary representatives of 12 family lines that have lived with their cows on this piece of land for a thousand years. Carlen, Hosenen, Juon, Lorenz, Kalbermatten, Petrig, Schaller, Zuber, Seematter, Wyss, Ruff, and Summermatter. No other families are entitled to use the alp. The herd is smaller now that the modern Swiss economy provides cash incomes to replace the hard round of self-sufficiency, but such a long history of mutual dependence, man and cow, has left its mark on the people living there today. They stand about the meadow, wrapped up in factory made goods against the evening chill, and gaze at the cows now grazing the land — demonstrating an affinity that there is limited opportunity to exploit in the modern age. As dusk advances they return to their cars and drive home to the village.

Oswald is making raclette, facing the open side of half a round of Törbel cheese to the coals of the barbecue he has built outside his new house, which stands just above his parents home at Furren, on the northern edge of Törbel. As the cheese melts and toasts a little, Oswald scraps it onto plates, together with boiled potatoes and rye bread, and serves his guests. The cheese is made in the village throughout the summer months when milk is plentiful, and distributed to each household in direct proportion to the amount of milk that the household has contributed to the communal effort. In 1986 Oswald contributed nearly 3,000 litres (5,280 pints) of milk and received 350 kg. (770 pounds) of cheese; 60 heavy wheels that he stores and ripens down in the cellar. The cellar is actually a nuclear shelter, with walls of reinforced concrete nearly one metre (three feet) thick, but Oswald has disguised its function with rough wood panelling, from which hang cow bells and certificates of merit won by his cows at country fairs. He stores his potatoes there too, and has built shelves like ladders which hold his cheeses upright on their edge – the way they mature best. There is a bar in one corner, with small casks of his father's wine standing in line behind it. The nuclear food store and water supply is unobtrusively situated along the rear wall of the shelter-cum-cellar, with the air conditioner outlet nearby.

There are no facilities for nuclear protection in Roman Wyss's cellar. He is a tall, vigorous man with hard-worked hands, living with his wife in an old double storey log-built house at the heart of the village. The house is reached via several tortuous flights of steps, past small garden patches of cabbage and lupins. A plum tree grows beside his front door, the highest fruit tree in Törbel, marking the limit at which fruit will grow on the ascending altitude and descending climatic gradients of the village environment.

Access to Roman Wyss's cellar is via the living room, preceded by an hour or so of conversation across a table covered with a heavy wool cloth. A television set stands on the sideboard. Mrs Wyss remains in the kitchen; greeted, but unseen. Mr Wyss converses slowly, in a regional Swiss-German dialect of open vowels that is hard to follow at first, even though he moderates it for the ears of his German-speaking guests. He brings out photographs of the village taken in the early 1920s by Gottlieb Fritz Stebler, who wrote a book on the region entitled *Die Vispertaler Sonnenberge* – the sunny mountains of the Vispa Valley. An old man, but endearingly reluctant to reveal his age, Roman Wyss speaks of the early decades of the century, when self-sufficiency was still the absolute requirement of existence – in Törbel and virtually every other alpine community.

Salt was the only item from the wider world that Törbel could not do without, he said. Cheese will not cure without salt, and cheese was the best way of storing the milk that cows produced during the short summer. Along with potatoes and rye bread baked from homegrown grain, cheese was an essential part of the diet that sustained Törbel through the long winter months – probably *the* essential part. Each household might have a pig or two, which was turned into bacon and hams, and each would sell calves and make sausage from cows that had passed their most productive years, but a good stock of cheese in the cellar was the best insurance against the vagaries of the future. Well-made cheese would keep for a decade or more, growing more flavourful and more treasured – like vintage wine – as the years passed and the stock diminished. Down in his cellar Roman Wyss cut slivers from a variety of aging cheeses, and poured glasses of wine from a range of casks. In a house built long before the days of electricity, the ceiling of the cellar is so low that the light bulb swings at his shoulder; the floor is earthern, a covered pit in the corner holds a store of potatoes. He laughs about the old days when there would have been a store of rye bread here too, growing tougher as it dried and ultimately requiring a woodsaw to slice it and jaws strong as a vice to chew it. Customarily, each household baked its bread in the communal oven just four times a year, in batches of 50 loaves or so, and the bread from the preceding batch had to be finished before the next was begun. Sometimes the bread would be half a year old before it was eaten. Frugality and thriftiness were the village virtues, he said; everyone deplored waste and extravagance.

In the final analysis, the amount of cheese a family had in the cellar represented the number of cows they owned and, most important of all, the amount of grass they were able to provide for the cows to eat. In an environment where neither root crops nor grain grows well enough to produce large quantities of food, grass is the ultimate resource, and the domestic cow its processing plant. Thus Törbel has always depended upon its cows and the management of its meadows. The growing season is short, just four or five months a year when the cows may actually graze fresh grass. For the remaining seven or eight months of the year they must be provided with hay.

The amount of work involved in watering, mowing, raking and storing hay is such that individual households could never make enough hay in the four or five months of summer to feed their cows through the rest of the year if they also had to tend the cows and make the cheese that they themselves needed for the winter. At the same time, individual households could not afford the time to graze their cows individually on the very useful high alpine pastures. The solution to these problems has been to establish the alp as communal property and responsibility, where all the cows are left in the care of one or two herdsmen while the villagers mow their hay meadows, which are privately owned.

Viewed today from the vantage point of its success, the regulated balance of communal and private landholding and resource utilisation at Törbel seems obvious and highly desirable, but of course it is simply the product of human interaction with the environment. The system evolved as the environmental limits were perceived; it was not imposed, fully fledged, upon the land and its inhabitants.

Looking down on Törbel from the high track through the larch forest, people appear to be disproportionately small parts of the ecosystem – mere bundles of energy scurrying about between the meadows and the cluster of houses. From that distant perspective, the principally regulatory significance of human beings on this Earth is quite clear: they keep small parts of it ticking over in a fashion they find beneficial. Seeking a more substantial token of human existence, a visitor might retire to the village graveyard, expecting to find a mass of weathered stones recalling the existence of venerated ancestors from the early years of the Wyss, Seematter, Karlen and other founding families of the community. But the graveyard is surprisingly small – and extremely neat. There are no gravestones, just a series of identical metal crosses, and closer inspection reveals that none records an internment of more than 25 years ago. Törbel has no land to spare for its ancestors – the ancient scraps of parchment that regulate the community's existence are the ancestors' best memorial. Taking a pragmatic view, the village long ago adopted the practice of using the same piece of burial ground over and over again. The members of each passing generation occupy the small plots just long enough to be venerated by those who remember them most dearly – their children.

Switzerland is an exceptionally well regulated country. The towns are clean; the roads are excellent; trains and buses run on time; a letter posted anywhere in the country will be delivered to any other part of it next morning; people tend to keep the appointments they make, the coffee is always hot, the cakes never stale, and the Banks have lots of money. Switzerland undeniably holds unique and enviable status in the world. Its citizens enjoy a higher standard of living than any in Europe, and earn a larger per capita income than any but the citizens of the oil states and the phosphate-laden island of Nauru in the Pacific. Why? Switzerland has no natural resources that could have produced its wealth. No oil, no minerals; no vast cereal-producing plains, no ranching land, no fisheries, no forests of valuable timber. Where did Switzerland's wealth come from? The answer is that in the almost total absence of any material resources that it could sell, Switzerland was obliged to earn its money in the service of other economies. To give just one set of examples from the modern era, one might say that Switzerland supplies the world with watches to regulate its activities, Nescafé to drink when it needs a break, and tranquillizers – Valium and Librium – to calm its nerves when the pace gets too hectic.

But Switzerland is full of paradox and contradiction: though neutral in two world wars, for instance, Switzerland was the nation most prepared to deal with German ambitions in 1939, with ten percent of its population armed, and its entire army in operational position when Britain declared war. As Machiavelli wrote: 'the Swiss are the most armed and the most free'. Every male citizen is obliged to do regular military service throughout his adult life, and keeps his equipment at the ready, at home. Every supermarket is obliged to maintain strategic stocks of food, at all times. Switzerland is the only country in the world committed to providing every citizen with the means of surviving nuclear war. Then again, Switzerland does not belong to the United Nations, yet it is an important venue for international deliberations – neutrality is marketable too, it seems.

And the country itself, though only 41,285 sq. km. (15,936 sq. mi.) in extent, is inherently fragmented. It consists largely of high mountains split

by deep valleys. Two major religions and four national languages –
German, French, Italian and Romansch – cut deep divisions through the
population. Dialects compound the distinctions, and a profusion of local
newspapers promote regional interests. Noting the existence of so much
human diversity within the boundaries of a single nation, an observer
might reasonably wonder what holds it together.

Switzerland, like most countries in Europe, is a political, rather than a
geographical entity – but one in which geography and environment have
been more than usually important in the creation of its political system. It
is more a matter of deficiencies than of assets. The Alps, being high and
remote, with scanty patches of relatively poor soils, offered few attractions
for the feudal system that dominated Europe during the Middle Ages.
These mountain fastnesses remained the property of self-sufficient peasant
communities who owed allegiance to none but their own interests. They
did, however, occupy a strategic position. The Alps form a crescent of
obstruction between Italy and the rest of Europe. As wealth and power
became increasingly concentrated in the cities of medieval Europe, a good
deal of it needed to cross the Alps from time to time in pursuit of personal,
national or religious interests. By the middle of the 13th century, a
network of routes had been established across the Alps. Traffic was well
regulated, and the levying of tolls was a very rewarding activity, principally controlled by bishops based in the trading towns that had grown up
in valleys leading to the passes. Waves of urban foundation followed the
development of Switzerland's present total of over 50 major and minor
alpine passes. In some instances, subsequent urban growth was spectacular. In less than 100 years following the opening of the St Gotthard Pass in
the early 13th century, for example, the city of Luzerne grew to almost its
19th-century size.

The commercial exploitation of the passes depended upon a good deal of
cooperation between the rural mountaineers who maintained the passes
and escorted travellers across, and the urban managers who regulated trade
and collected tolls. The relationship was not always an easy one, and in
1291 three valley communities for whom alpine trade was especially
important determined to strengthen their position by setting out on a piece
of parchment the terms under which they would henceforward regulate
their affairs:

In view of the evil times the men of the valley of Uri, the Landsgemeinde *of
Schwyz and the community of the lower valley of Unterwalden... in common
council have with one voice sworn, agreed and determined that in the above
named valleys we shall accept no judge nor recognise him in any way if he
exercise his office for any reward or for money or if he is not one of our own and an
inhabitant of the valleys.*

This document, subsequently became the foundation of Switzerland's
political system. In 1393 the Swiss Confederation was created – a unique
independent republic that grew increasingly wealthy in the service of
Europe's trade, and increasingly powerful in the exercise of its military
might. Occupying the strategic heart of Europe, capable of raising an army
of 80,000 men, surrounded by countries that war had impoverished, the

81

Swiss Confederation became the richest and most formidable power in Europe. The essence of its military successes lay in the strength and stamina of its soldiers, most of whom were recruited from among the alpine peasant community under terms whereby political freedom involved a degree of military obligation to the common cause. The Swiss alpine peasant soldiers were the top military force of the late medieval period.

The Swiss Confederation maintained its dominant position in European affairs throughout the 15th century, but eventually the diversity of independent interests that had been purposefully submerged when the cantons united to repulse foreigners, re-surfaced among individual ambitions to invade foreign lands. The expansionist ambitions were not universally shared; some cantons declined to supply soldiers for adventures in France and Italy and, thus weakened, the hitherto invincible Swiss armies suffered defeat. Though never conquered, by the mid-16th century the Confederation was once again a small neutral state dependent on trade. But with a difference. While 17th-century wars of political ambition and religious reformation laid waste to much of Europe, the Swiss Confederation, though not untouched, found itself a political entity, isolated within well-marked boundaries. The agreements that had been made within and between communities and cantons during the Confederation's years of ascendancy in Europe, now proved to be an excellent basis of stability and profit during the years of Europe's decline. The key point was that they regulated power by putting final authority in the hands of the people. Neither the community, nor the canton, nor any larger entity could commit the national interest to any course of action without the agreement of all its independent parts. This did not eliminate internal dissension – some of which was very fierce indeed – but it did prevent the emergence of any one absolute authority. The Confederation survived the vicissitudes of religious, social and economic development, and went on to construct an imaginative and energetic service economy on the foundations of a sound, self-sufficient agricultural tradition.

People of frugal and thrifty background are among the first to appreciate the value of luxuries – especially when it comes to selling them. When they turned to trade, the Swiss specialised in luxury goods. They had little choice, as the Cambridge historian Jonathan Steinberg has pointed out, because their natural environment was poor, their markets far away and transport costs correspondingly high. The linen industry of St Gallen, for instance, could not have supported the cost of transporting the material to the distant markets if it had produced anything less than prime quality (the identifying stamp on St Gallen cloth in the 15th century was Europe's first seal of quality). Subsequently the value of linen was raised to luxury levels with the embellishment of fine embroidery. The same is true of virtually all Swiss endeavour – textiles, printing, engineering, chemicals and – of course – watchmaking. Since all the raw materials had to be imported, none of these industries could have survived competition from manufacturers based nearer the market without some extra feature that would cover transportation costs. Excellence was about all that the Swiss could add to their products.

In the early days much of Switzerland's industrial effort was as firmly based in the rural community as its political system. Some 4,000 bar looms were at work in peasant cottages around St Gallen in the mid-19th century, for example, and it has been estimated that even at the turn of the century more than 50 percent of all people engaged in the Swiss watch industry worked from home – specialist craftsmen making mainsprings, escapements, hands, cases and so on, assemblers, finishers, polishers, all working independently to a required standard of excellence.

More than most nations, the character and status of modern Switzerland is quite obviously the product of geographical location and human astuteness fortuitously combined. By acknowledging the human tendency to differ, by treating diversity as a positive factor to be accommodated rather than a negative aberration to be eliminated, the Swiss have created a system of remarkable resilience and durability. The system is not perfect, by any means, but its strength surely lies in its communal structure. Growing from free peasant or urban associations has made the system bottom-heavy, as Jonathan Steinberg remarks. 'Rather like those dolls which spring up no matter how often the child pushes them over. The weight is at the base. The communities have a deep equilibrium to which, as the point of rest, the social and political order tends to return'. Fundamental to this stability, then, is the kind of ecological equilibrium that persists in places like Törbel.

The land that has been supporting the Törbel community for so long is nicely placed; a triangle of alpine slope facing due south across the Mattervispa valley. The triangle inclines steeply upward from the Mattervispa river, at about 900 m. (3,000 ft) above sea level, to the irregular edge of the larch forest at 1,900 m. (6,250 ft). The village stands at 1,500 m. (5,000 ft) and even in mid-winter enjoys seven hours of sunshine while Stalden, in the valley below, shivers with just 30 minutes. The sunny south-facing position also enhances the productivity of Törbel's 800 hectares, matching the gradient from river to alp with a temperature gradient that brings almost mediterranean conditions to the lower fields, where vines are well advanced before even the snow has melted from the alpine meadows 1,000 m. (3,300 ft) above.

The village itself is a tight cluster of multistorey log houses and barns, deep brown and blackened with age, many perched on small columns and slabs of the local tabular stone – assembled like mushrooms – to keep out mice and rats. The buildings are stone-roofed too; irregular diamond-shaped slabs mostly covered with lichen but glinting where the sun catches flecks of quartz in the stone. A patchwork of vegetable gardens and hay meadows, dotted with barns and fruit trees, surrounds the village. At a slightly greater distance are small satellite villages – Feld, Bad, Brunnen, Bine, themselves surrounded by gardens, meadows and barns, in which the villagers would spend some weeks each summer as they followed their cows and the demands of haymaking around their segments of property in the village lands. Above the village the triangle opens into an amphitheatre of gentle gradients ringed by forest, with a scattering of barns and chalets. These high meadows lie just below the summer grazing grounds and are called the *voralpen*. The alp itself runs along a line of glades, patches of forest, small hills and lakes, sweeping around and above the culivated land to the top of the Mossalp headland, which on a fine day affords a distant view of the Matterhorn.

The annual cycle of the village turns around the needs of the cows. Of Törbel's 160 households only 75 owned cows in 1984, when the village herd totalled just 105 animals, compared with 263 owned by 105 households in 1844, and 205 owned by 103 households in 1946. But although total numbers have declined over the years, the patterns of ownership remain remarkably consistent. From his analysis of stock records, Robert Netting found that the cows averaged 2.50 per owner in 1844-5, and 2.43 per owner in 1970-1. Thirty-eight percent of the owners had just two cows each in both 1844-5 and 1970-1; only eight percent owned more than four cows in 1844-5, only two percent in 1970-1.

The cows spend the winter months in shelter, moving from barn to barn on the fields around the village where their owners have cut and stored hay. In the spring, as soon as the grass begins to grow on the lower meadows, the cows are put out to graze. As spring turns to summer they are moved to higher meadows while the lower hayfields are mown and the hay stacked in the barns that the cows have vacated. By midsummer, the lower meadows are being irrigated for a second crop of hay, the mid-level fields are ready for mowing, the cows are on the voralpen and the vegetable gardens are well advanced. This is the busiest time of year. Every family has every available member at work – milking, mowing, watering and hoeing. By late June, however, there comes relief. Though snow still lies on the peaks and in shaded crevices down to 2000 m. (6,500 ft), the grass has begun to grow on the alp. The length of the day and the intensity of the light at that altitude more than counter the effect of still relatively low temperatures. Growth is prodigious. The glades are quickly covered with lush grass, smothered with a flush of wild flowers. As soon as the cows have been moved up to graze the communally owned alp, to be tended and milked by one or two herdsmen, the rest of the village is freed to attend to the pressing demands of their private lands below.

The alpine season is brief, however, ten or 12 weeks at the most, and by late September when the grass has ceased growing on the alp the cows are brought down again, following the retreat of growth down the slope just as they had followed its advance upward in the spring. First they graze the voralpen for a week or so, then the middle meadows, and finally the lower meadows before retreating to the barns for the winter. In this way a meadow can provide four crops (two major and two minor) in a season – an early minor crop grazed by the cows in the spring, two major crops of hay reaped in the summer, and a final minor crop grazed in the autumn.

Törbel is a classic example of the 'storage culture' that Ellen Weigandt defines in a study of the alpine subsistence economy she published in 1977. The community must store sufficient produce from a very short

84

growing season for consumption during the non-productive months. The
slope and the sun extend both the season and the range of crops that Törbel
can produce, but, nonetheless, its staple crops have to grow fast and store
well. Grass is the most productive crop in the alpine environment, the first
to start growing in the spring and the last to stop in the autumn.
Unsuitable for direct human consumption, of course, but conveniently
converted to milk by the cow, and thence to butter and cheese by the
farmers, grass sustains the community. Rye, potatoes, wine, sausage, ham,
all provide valuable supplements, but it is grass that fuels the system, cows
that keep it going. And of course grass for the cows must be produced and
stored in sufficient quantities too.

In addition to the grass that it consumes during the summer grazing,
each Törbel cow requires, on average, nearly three tonnes of hay for the
seven or eight months when it will be largely confined to the barns.
Multiplied by the number of cows owned by the community, and then
divided among the relatively small total area of land available for hay
meadows, the winter hay requirement thus places a heavy demand on both
farmer and field. The average figures of holding and productivity recorded
by Robert Netting indicate that every farmer must make and store about
7.5 tonnes of hay for his cows' consumption during the winter, and,
relating that figure to average land ownership, every hectare of meadow
must therefore produce about eight tonnes of hay (about 3.25 tons per acre)
on average – year after year. Mechanisation has eased the farmer's load, but
demands on the field have remained unchanged for centuries.

Documents preserved in the Törbel archives show that by the 12th
century the community was already feeling this pinch of environmental
constraint. It is impossible to know whether the problem was one of too
many mouths to feed, not enough land, or not enough hands to work it. To
what extent the land was communally or privately owned is not known
either. One might suppose that by then the community had already
expanded its landholdings as much as was feasible, and irrigation from the
Törbelbach was probably increasing the yields of the village fields, but all
that is known for certain is that, in 1270, the community took a bold step
to intensify the productivity of its resources with the purchase of water
rights in the Embdbach, a stream rising in the Augsttal, six kilometres
(3.75 mi.) down the valley. The purchase required the construction of ten
kilometres (six miles) of major canals to bring the water to the village lands
and a complex network of channels and sluices to distribute it among the
fields. The main canal was named the *Augstbordwasserleitung*, after its
source, but it is still referred to as *die Niwa*, the new one, which rather
implies that it replaced or augmented an older system. In 1948 an
underground pipeline was installed, and die Niwa ceased to be used,
though its course across the upper alp can still be followed.

Drought is not a factor that springs to mind when considering the alpine
environment, but lack of rain severely restricts productivity in the
southern Swiss Alps. The mountains deflect rain-bearing clouds from the
Mediterranean and the Atlantic so that the Vispertal, for instance, has the
lowest rainfall in Switzerland. It is estimated that Törbel receives an

average of only about 50 cm. (20 in.) a year. And of course not all the rain falls during the growing season. Furthermore, the region sees far more cloudless days that the rest of Switzerland and without additional water, crops growing on Törbel's sunny south-facing slopes would soon wither in the heat. With intensive irrigation, however, their yield is increased four- to five-fold. Grass will then grow where previously only vegetation adapted to near drought conditions could survive; meadows will produce grazing and two lush harvests of hay.

The purchase of water rights in Augsttal over 700 years ago probably brought Törbel to the limit of the potential for intensified production on its lands. It was an astute investment, doubtless expensive in cash and the commitment of labour at the time, but permitting to this day the intensive exploitation of land that otherwise could have been of only marginal use. (In the 1950s the investment even produced a cash return, when Törbel contracted to supply water from die Niwa to industrial sites in the valley below).

In 1514 another bold purchase brought an element of expansion to the strategies employed by the Törbel community – they bought 350 ha (865 acres) of land on the Grimsel Pass, three days march away, for 850 Bernese pounds (equivalent to 19,000 modern Swiss francs). The document recording the purchase notes that Törbel expected to graze one-third of its stock on the land for 65 days each summer, as well as gaining some hunting and fuel collecting rights. The purchase of summer grazing, at such a distance and at such a price, was almost certainly undertaken to relieve pressure on Törbel's home resources. Netting reports that the document recording the purchase lists the names of 74 community members (presumed to be heads of household) who did not have enough pasturage for their needs on the Törbel lands. By modern reckoning, 74 households would account for nearly half the community; in 1514 the proportion is likely to have been even higher – certainly high enough to encourage the maximum expansion, intensification and – most important of all – regulation of the exploitation of the community resources.

Community affairs in Törbel were (and are still) regulated by written statute. The documents are an eloquent testimony to the power of the written word, and also demonstrate that it is not ancestral blood, so much as good common sense that merits long-term respect. The earliest document, from 1224, records an agreement with the church in Visp to provide fighting men and grain in exchange for a share of the tithe. A string of documents from the 1300s record land transfers wherein individual landowners effectively mortaged their land to the Törbel community. By 1483 Törbel was referring to itself as a *Bauernzunft*, a self-governing peasant corporation, with eligibility and conditions of membership precisely defined. A regulated balance between the ownership of private land and the use of communal resources was a crucially important element of the terms laid down by the Bauernzunft, perhaps more responsible than any other for the durability and resilience of the system. Community landowners had the right to graze cattle on the alp, but anyone who sold their land thereby relinquished that right.

The precise extent of Törbel's forest and alpine pastures was written down in 1519, 'on the sworn testimony of eight honest men', as Netting records, and probably in response to an unacceptable degree of individual encroachment. The terms under which community members could use the alp were established two years before, in a document that ties the number of animals allowed to graze the communal alp directly to the amount of land that is privately owned. 'No one is permitted to send more cows to the alps than he can winter', the regulation of 1517 declares.

By this simple regulation the number of animals owned by community members was strictly tied to private, not common, landholding, and most directly tied to private meadows and the amount of hay they could produce to feed the animals through the winter. Community members could enlarge their herds and thus their share of the communal grazing only by acquiring the land to produce sufficient winter fodder. There was no incentive to keep more calves than there would be hay for; no one could fatten an animal on the alp during the summer for sale and personal profit in the autumn. Acquisitive individual ambitions were thus neatly confined to the private sector, while the common land remained a summer retreat, carefully exploited to the benefit of the entire community.

The documentary evidence shows that from early in the 16th century, and probably for some time before then, Törbel was a closed community. The regulations carefully spelled out on so many pieces of parchment in effect erected a barrier around the community. While land-use regulations controlled the exploitation of resources within the community, regulations controlling membership and inheritance kept the size of the community within the limits of available resources. In theory, a man from another community could buy land in Törbel, or marry into the village, for example, but the practice was not encouraged. Outsiders were granted rights to the alp only if all community members agreed, and then only in exceptional circumstances and on payment of substantial fees in addition to the initial land purchase. A man could marry a woman from another community and bring her to live in Törbel, but she gained no rights thereby, though her children would be community members by birth.

The effect of Törbel's membership and landholding regulations has been to produce and sustain a community of remarkable stability. Examining parish records for the past 300 years, Robert Netting found that 86 percent of all marriages have been between members of the community. Only three men from outside have married into the community and produced children since 1700; one subsequently left with his family, another had children but no grandchildren, and the third established Törbel's Weisshorn hotel in 1963.

Törbel families have tended to be large, which ensured that each household had all the labour it required, but people started their families relatively late, for couples did not marry until they had a house to live in and land enough to support a family. Thus human birthrate and population growth was also directly related to the amount of available resources. Only people with land could have children, while those without the prospect of inheriting enough land could not even marry. In times past excess women

87

remained unmarried and largely childless, while excess men joined Switzerland's renowned fighting forces. In modern times both sexes are likely to emigrate or find work in cash economies beyond the community boundaries.

Parents generally divided their property equally among all their children, male and female alike, when they made their wills. With a relatively small total land area to divide among relatively large families, this practice of partible inheritance through the centuries has fragmented land-holding every bit as much as might be expected.

The Törbel lands are presently divided into over 5,000 separate parcels, all individually owned, all documented, some no more than 20 m. (65 ft) square. And as with the land, so too with the barns. Only rarely is a barn owned outright by one family; usually it is divided up into quarter, eighth, even 16th parts – the shares exploited in terms of days and weeks, in most cases, rather than spatially. It seems clear that this fragmentation of land – so demanding of transport and labour – must have arisen from each household's need of not only an absolute totality of land but also of holdings in each of Törbel's quite distinct growing regimes on the alpine slope: every family needed pasture and meadow, garden, grainfield and vineyard. Fragmentation inevitably increased demands on labour and productivity, but in the long term it has proved surprisingly beneficial. With so many marriages contracted within the community, both partners have generally brought several parcels of land to the union; through the centuries these have tended to give each household a good mix of landholdings and barn space throughout the climatic spread of the slope. A few families have more than 100 separate parcels; most have considerably fewer. Oswald Seematter makes use of 19 holdings immediately around the village and further afield.

Oswald's grandfathers were the last full-time farmers in his family line; they both died in 1974 at the ages of 94 and 76. Oswald remembers them fondly and would prefer to be a full-time farmer himself, as they had been, rather than spend so much of his life in the chemical factory. 'I don't make full use of our land', he says, 'I'm just a hobby bauer'. Even so, in the dead of winter he still puts in three hours a day, tending the cows, and in summer the family has no spare time for anything but farming. He and all the other part-time farmers of Törbel feed into the system funds that they earn outside. They are no longer self-sufficient, but their farm produce is an indispensible element of their household economies, further aided by federal social schemes designed to benefit communities like Törbel. Oswald and Törbel are part of a larger community now, but as long as the system continues to make sense, they will work their part of it.

■ CHAPTER FIVE ■

NOMADS

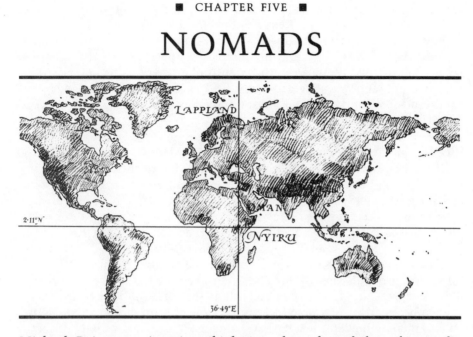

Michael Rainy, an American biologist whose knowledge of nomadic pastoralism gathered during 20 years of living and working among the Samburu people of northern Kenya forms a large part of this chapter, tells of an occasion when he took a visitor to meet a group of elders on the Lerogi Plateau. After a polite exchange of greetings, the visitor contributed little to the gathering – except as a figure of curiosity to the children – until he drew a handkerchief from his pocket and proceeded to blow his nose. Eyes turned in his direction, conversation ceased and, aware of the attention he had attracted to himself, the visitor refolded his handkerchief with particular care before returning it to his pocket. Then an elder leaned across to Michael – 'Tell me', he asked, 'why does this man wish to keep the substance that comes from his nose?'

Nomadic pastoralists like the Samburu are as human as the rest of us, but they have a very distinctive view of human affairs and priorities. They survive at the margins, utilising land which otherwise supports only scrub bush and wild animals adapted to thrive in conditions of heat and aridity. Rainfall is erratic, ranging between 150 and 800 mm. a year, and often brought by storms which produce brief torrential floods between periods of extended drought.

In such regions, cultivated crops would fail in four out of every five years, and in dry years and seasons even the natural vegetation barely provides enough grazing for the small docile cattle, sheep and goats upon which the Samburu depend. Wet years generally refund the losses which droughts incur, but there is little surplus in the system. Fat rarely accumulates on their animals, and almost never on the people. In common with nomads everywhere, the environment has obliged the Samburu to

89

adopt a severely functional view of the world and its possibilities. There is little in their lives that does not serve some definable purpose.

The climate of northern Kenya is hot and dry, the grazing is sparse, widely dispersed and not at all well watered. And yet the Samburu manage to keep dairy herds alive and productive on these extremely marginal lands. Dairy herds! While western agriculture reserves its lushest pastures for milk production and grazes only beef cattle on its rangelands, the Samburu consistently produce substantial quantities of milk from what is essentially semi-desert.

The Samburu eat meat (particularly as a protein tonic after childbirth or illness), and in times of hardship will drink blood taken from living animals. In modern times, their diet has been significantly supplemented by maizemeal, but milk remains their staple food. Maintaining a constant and adequate supply of milk means that the Samburu herds must always contain a critical number of cows that have recently calved, along with others that are pregnant and will take over the milk supply in due course. But cows will conceive and produce calves successfully only while they are reasonably well nourished, which in turn means that Samburu survival ultimately depends upon their ability to keep enough cows in a reproductive state – no mean feat in conditions that often kill beef cattle.

Even beef cattle are a practical proposition in semi-desert regions only on commercial ranches, where they can range widely at a density of about one animal to every 20 hectares (50 acres) – and then only provided there is supplementary drinking water available. Maintaining the nomadic pastoralist's dairy herd at productive levels under such conditions is quite another matter. The grazing is scanty, but security in a region still populated by lions, hyenas and stock raiders demands that nomadic cattle must graze close together nonetheless. The nomad's herd also must be driven to and from water (often many hours away) every second or third day, and each night they must be confined within the high thorn fence of the settlement for milking and protection.

The advantages of a nomadic pastoralist strategy based on milk, rather than on meat, in arid regions are considerable: milk protein is produced five times more efficiently than meat protein; milk can be harvested daily, whereas a cow supplies meat only once in its lifetime, and milk production resumes within days of a drought breaking, while muscle tissue takes months to regenerate. But the difficulties of keeping cows well nourished impose heavy demands upon every group of nomadic pastoralists, and particularly upon the men who lead them. The pastoral leaders must have profound knowledge of their land, its climatic cycles, of their herds and of the people who will tend them. It is not enough to know where there is grass available today. They must know where it will be available in the months ahead, how long it will sustain how many cows, where there will be sufficient water, when the herd must be taken to the sparsely distributed salt pans. The leaders must calculate with some precision when the herd should leave for the new pasture, always bearing in the mind the quality of grazing *en route* and the dangers of hurrying the herd. They must know when calves are due and which cows will soon come into

90

heat. They must plan herd movements in good time so that they are unhurried, imposing no undue stress on the animals or their herders.

Each group is generally an extended family unit – so the wishes of brothers and married sons must be accommodated too, and a family must coordinate its movements with other families of the same clan; the clan must take into account the likely movements of other clans, and the clans as a tribe must be prepared for the encroachment of rival pastoralists into their territory.

The anthropologist Paul Spencer, who studied the Samburu in the early 1960s, described Samburu society as a gerontocracy: one that reveres its elders. And no wonder. The elders are an invaluable source of essential knowledge, and in an environment that by its very nature allows only a narrow margin for error, the oldest survivors must possess the most valuable knowledge of all. The elders know their environment intimately – every lie and twist of it. The land, the water, the vegetation; trees, shrubs, herbs – nutritious, medicinal, poisonous. They know each cow, and have a host of specific names for the distinctive shape and skin patterns of each animal in just the same way that Europeans distinguish individual plants within the general term flower, or tree.

Samburu elders note the phases of the moon and the movements of the stars and planets, using them as a calendar of the seven seasons they recognise as when rain might fall each year, and the periods in between which they call long and short hungers, according to the severity of the drought they must suffer.

There is nearly always a period of drought and hunger between one rainy season and the next, but when the rains fail to replenish the grass for more than nine months (the gestation period of people and cows) – as they often do – then the elders begin to talk of the killing cycles that the climate inflicts upon the region. At the level of highest frequency and least intensity there is the calf killing cycle, which may come round twice in every seven years, when fetuses are aborted, udders dry and calves die. Then, three times in the lifetime of a man (74 years), annual rainfall can be expected to decline and remain below normal for seven successive years. Each year, less grass and milk are available. Many cattle die in these cycles and the Samburu become increasingly dependent on sheep and goats.

Finally, there is the bull killing. When bulls have died, people have died too, in large numbers, and although it is considered a bad omen even to speak of the bull killing, it persists in the memories of the elders, and in the warnings given to sons by their dying fathers, as a cycle that brings tragedy every 100 years. The last was in the 1880s, when epidemics of smallpox and rinderpest almost eliminated the Samburu and their cattle, and the 1980s are not finished yet.

The cycles of climatic influence and effect turn concurrently, but at varying speeds. They may afflict all or part of the region at any one time, and their advent can sometimes be foreseen in the juxtaposition of certain stars, the elders say, but beyond that the Samburu believe their fate lies in the hands of their deity, Nkai, whose name also happens to be the Samburu word for rain.

91

A visitor might find a degree of contradiction in the restrained but obviously deep sense of religious devotion that the Samburu manifest. They live in a marginal environment, often at the very edge of starvation; a hard existence in which there is no room for anything not functionally appropriate. And yet, where one might expect a hard intolerant manner, with little evidence of sympathy or smiles, an air of grace prevails. Grace – there is no better word for it. When elders meet, their greetings take the form of responses – asking after the settlement, the family, the livestock, the land. The replies are positive (any matters to the contrary that need to be discussed will be broached later), accompanied by a slight bow of the head and the word Nkai, Nkai, repeated in supplicatory tones. On parting, senior individuals will offer blessings, and again the response is Nkai, Nkai. A young man will ask for a blessing when he feels the need. Children will walk up to newly arrived elders and stand silently awaiting the blessing of some quietly spoken words and the right hand placed lightly on the head, to which, once again, the response is Nkai, Nkai. So the name of god and the word for rain are constantly repeated in the Samburu community; it is impossible for them to speak of rain without there being some reverential connotation. Similarly, whenever they call for god's blessing they bow to the overriding authority of rain in their lives.

Nkai is believed to reside in a cave high on Mount Nyiru, the holy mountain of the Samburu which rises to nearly 3,000 m. (10,000 ft) above the arid semi-desert at the southern end of Lake Turkana. And indeed, Nyiru *is* a paradise. The slopes are cloaked with forests of cedar and podocarpus; burbling brooks lace the glades and meadows of the summit plateau. There is honey and wild fruit, and the Samburu cattle give rich milk when drought drives them up from the plains to graze the Nyiru meadows. Nyiru is the final dry season retreat of the Samburu. When grazing for cattle is finished everywhere else, there is always some on Nyiru. The Samburu have ritualized the significance of Mount Nyiru in their lives. A man returning from the mountain will take a sprig of cedar to wear in his hair; and in distant parts a sprig from any cedar tree will be worn as a sign of reverence for Nyiru. The direction in which the mountain lies is always known; the entrances of all initiation houses face Nyiru, after a meat feast, *moran* – the warriors of the tribe – will place the skull of the animal they have consumed in a tree, again facing Nyiru. God and rain have blessed Nyiru, the Samburu believe, however much they may have wrought devastation on the land around.

The rangelands of northern Kenya have experienced several periods of drought during the last 20 years, and famines have struck the human population (which has grown continuously during that time). Season after season the rains failed to materialise, or else brought only a few showers that caused the grass to sprout then left it to wither. 1976-83 were wetter years, enabling many people to hold their own, and some definite recovery was under way when, in 1984-85, there came the 24 months of continuous hard drought that moved people around the world to contribute to relief aid programmes in Africa. During this drought, pastoralists in northern Kenya lost over 80 percent of their cattle, 40 percent of their sheep and goats, and five percent of their camels. Many people died too; but deaths would have been much more numerous without famine relief.

Although the droughts of 1984-85 seemed a new phenomenon when they reached the television screens of the world, extreme drought was nothing new to the nomads; each generation hears from its elders the sombre stories of similar disasters that afflicted previous generations. There is no doubt that the influences of modern medicine, veterinary care and supplementary foods enlarged the dimensions of the 1984-85 disaster by encouraging larger populations of stock and people than the land could support, but, while not wishing to diminish the human tragedy of the drought, it should be noted that suffering was greatest where people had lost the means and freedom of pastoral movement, and least where they followed traditional strategies.

Paul Robinson, whose research for a PhD thesis on the survival strategies of the Gabbra people in territory to the north of the Samburu coincided with the worst years of the drought, documents a complex pattern of 14, 35, 42, 63 and 80 to 100 year cycles which the Gabbra have perceived in the erratic and seemingly random sequence of rain and drought that their region experiences. Knowledge of these cycles is the basis of Gabbra survival strategies, and enabled their most knowledgeable elders to foresee and survive the drought of 1984-85.

During 1983, Yatani Sorale and other revered Gabbra elders saw an ominous conjunction of cycles ahead and predicted that the region was entering a prolonged drought which would be relieved by only intermittent and insufficient rain. In November, Yatani and the groups associated with him, moved from the Hurri Hills to areas near Lake Turkana which are traditionally reserved for periods of severe drought. Others, who did not hear or heed the warnings of the elders, made only the shorter journey to the Chalbi lowlands, planning to return to the Hurri Hills with the seasonal rains which could be expected to fall there towards the end of most years.

The rains failed over most of the region. By early 1984 even the Lake Turkana rangelands were seriously depleted, and some of the groups who had accompanied Yatani decided to return to the Chalbi region in anticipation of the rains they felt certain must fall by April. Yatani and several other elders, however, chose to make a far longer and more arduous trek over parched and insecure terrain towards the Ethiopian border near Sabarai, then beyond to Gorai and Tertalle. They were following the strategy of those who had survived similar droughts in the 1890s and 1920s.

Light rains fell north of the border in April and May 1984, but none at all fell in the Chalbi lowlands or on the Hurri Hills. By May, people there had lost 95 percent of their cattle, 60 percent of the goats, 40 percent of their sheep and five percent of their camels. Their plight was desperate: only relief aid averted widespread starvation and, by August, 7,000 people were receiving famine relief from one distribution point alone.

Seasonal rains fell on the Hurri Hills and the Chalbi lowlands in late 1984, as expected, but not enough to alleviate the crisis, and, significantly,

93

those following the traditional regime did not turn back in anticipation of them. In September 1984, Yatani Sorale and the groups with him headed north and east again, towards the Borana highlands, though fully aware that the region was still in the grip of protracted drought and that the Borana – their traditional allies – had already lost most of their stock.

But the move was well-judged. Good rains fell on the Borana highlands in late 1984; the Gabbra found ample browse for their stock and were even able to fulfil their traditional obligations to give the Borana animals with which to re-build their herds.

No group survived the drought unscathed, but Yatani Sorale and the elders who accurately assessed the probable scale of the disaster, and followed the difficult and dangerous strategies that their knowledge of the region's climatic cycles called for, suffered only a fraction of the losses that afflicted those who elected to remain in the Chalbi lowlands. No Gabbra had ever accepted famine relief before but, by August 1985, over 50 percent were dependent upon it, their chances of rebuilding their herds entirely in the hands of the other 50 percent who had followed traditional strategies, and whose livestock was poised to benefit from the good rains which eventually must replenish the land.

The Gabbra elders correctly predicted that the drought would continue through 1985, finally breaking with the rains of April 1986. Furthermore, 1987 marked the peak of a 35 year cycle which would bring very good rains, they predicted. And indeed, as a dry March and April encouraged meteorologists to speak of the rains failing yet again, widespread rain fell in May and Kenya experienced the wettest June for many years.

The settlement was situated on the southern edge of the El Barta plains and a good 1,200 m. (4,000 ft) above sea level. There was a body of warmth among the cows crowded into the thorn enclosure, and the low windowless huts maintained a comfortable temperature day and night, but the air was cold in the early morning. Before she began milking, Nankarusi warmed her hands in a stream of urine flowing conveniently from one of the cows. She massaged the teats, then directed the milk into the long polished gourd; just a few cupfuls – the small Samburu cows seldom give large quantities of milk. The skin of a young calf killed by cheetahs the previous day had been sewn up and stuffed with grass overnight; now the surrogate form was laid before its mother, who nuzzled it and obligingly let down her milk. When the milking was finished and the herd left the settlement, the women gathered up the wet dung from the enclosure and plastered it over the walls of the huts, filling cracks, patching holes.

At the brink of an eroded gulley a short distance from the settlement, the leading animals of the herd suddenly shied back, all together in one movement – like dead leaves caught in a gust of wind – and soon afterwards their sense of danger was confirmed by the appearance of two moran bearing a fresh lion skin wrapped around the pole they carried between them. The previous day three lions, two female and one male, had killed and eaten a cow some distance down the gulley, it transpired, while the young herdboy had looked on helplessly. When a group of moran had

94

tracked down and confronted the culprits later that evening, the females had run away, but the male had stopped to fight and died with seven spears in him.

Out across the plain, some groups of zebra were grazing; they lifted their heads as the herd approached and strolled peaceably out of its path, not greatly disturbed. As the day advanced, a line of quivering white heat rose from the ground, slicing the distant Ndoto Hills from the landscape. There was no sign of rain. Red sand, humps of grey scrub bush, acacia trees with thorns standing out like bleached fishbones... amidst all the aridity the cattle somehow found something to eat.

Lesipin, a man whose ability to interpret the juxtapositions of the stars is highly respected, had said that it must rain before the horn of the Pleiades fell below the horizon or it would not rain at all that season. For the past week the clouds had seemed to be gathering and growing thicker over the Ndotos and Nyiru each day, but now they had thinned out again and the horn of the Pleiades had fallen the night before. There was still heavy cloud piled over the highland to the south and tumbling back from the west escarpment of the Rift Valley, but the prospect of rain on the El Barta plain seemed slim now, and the next chance of rain was four or five months hence.

Several herds were already drinking at the dam below Koitokol when Linolosi arrived, and not all of them were Samburu. Koitokol marks the point at which the Samburu territory merges with that of the Rendille and the Turkana. From the retaining wall of the dam, other herds could be seen approaching across the plains, raising great clouds of swirling dust, Turkana from the west, Rendille from the north and east, Samburu from the south and east.

When the rains are adequate, the three tribes are ecologically separated by the characteristics of the different rangelands they occupy, and by the different mix of livestock they keep. The Samburu are able to keep cattle as well as sheep and goats (and a few camels) in the relatively high rainfall regime of the high lands they occupy, but only camels can sustain the Rendille in the drier lowland Koroli and Kaisut deserts to the north of the Samburu territory, while the Turkana, who range about the southern end of Lake Turkana and down the Suguta valley, lead a rather more opportunistic life, subsisting largely on sheep and goats, but keeping cattle and camels where and when they can – often acquiring them in raids on neighbouring communities. The division between the three tribes is essentially ecological – each subsists on the most productive stock that the environment can sustain – but for the people themselves the division is primarily cultural. The Rendille, or 'people of the camels', share many tribal affinities with the Samburu, or 'people of the cattle'. They are traditional allies against the Turkana, who have proved capable of sustaining life in an extremely harsh environment, and are noted primarily for their lack of cultural cohesion – they do not circumcise, have few food taboos, and will even eat fish! Samburu elders point out with disgust.

Now, at the height of the drought, the Turkana and the Rendille were invading Samburu territory. Their own pastures were close to devoid of

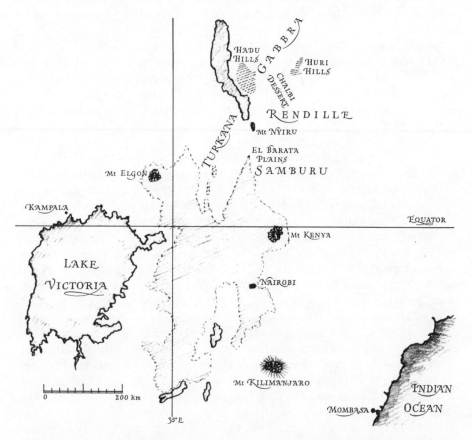

nourishment for their stock, but while grazing in the highland was running
short for the Samburu cattle, there was still enough for camels and goats,
which browse on bushes more than they graze. From the Rendille and
Turkana point of view there was no choice – they had to move on to
Samburu territory, but their intrusion was not welcomed. At the dam,
stories were told of bloody skirmishes between Turkana and Samburu
warriors; spears had been thrown and men wounded near Isiolo; Turkana
encampments had been established in several parts of Samburu territory.
Feelings ran particularly high around the last remaining sources of water,
where the herds and herdsmen mingled. The diplomatic skills of the elders
were called into play time and again as Samburu moran became increasingly excited, and called for the order to take their spears and attack the
invaders.

There were outbreaks of fighting in which some warriors were killed,
and some cattle raids, but then the peaceful wishes of the elders prevailed.
Samburu cattle moved up onto Mount Nyiru, and flourished there for a
time, while Turkana goats and Rendille camels browsed on the scrubby
bushes of the Samburu plains below. Why did not cattle stay on Nyiru all
year round? Linolosi was asked. Because they sicken and scour if kept too
long on a rich diet, he explained, because ticks and disease build up rapidly

96

in the damp pasture, and because a dry season reserve that is used all year round would be less able to serve its need in a really severe drought.

Nomadic pastoralism is a way of life in which the interaction between man and environment is very direct. Until relatively recent times there was only a very narrow margin separating success from failure; nowadays the margin is broadened by the availability of supplementary foods and the blandishments of the cash economy. The nomads are no longer so absolutely dependent upon their livestock; health care – from childbirth to old age, from the treatment of illness and snake bite to the removal of arrows inopportunely encountered in cattle raids – keeps more people alive. But they remain a very small fraction of the national populations of East Africa, occupying a disproportionately large fraction of the land.

Among a total of about 200 distinct tribal groups in East Africa, only 15 are pastoralists, and 12 of those range across the semi-desert regions of northern Kenya. Their numbers are relatively small, totalling about 1.2 million people, six percent of Kenya's total population, but the land they occupy is vast – about 421,000 sq. km. (162,500 sq. mi.) – which amounts to 85 percent of the national land area. The pastoralists' population density is thus about three people to every square kilometre (just under eight per sq. mi.). Meanwhile, the rest of Kenya's population, numbering some 20 million, is crammed onto the other 15 percent of the land area at a density of about 120 people per sq. km. (310 per sq. mi.). The differences in population density between the two areas are directly related to rainfall and productivity. The most densely populated regions comprise the most productive arable and agricultural land of Kenya, and the people occupying it constitute about 30 tribal groups which, when compared with the 12 groups occupying the far larger pastoral regions, is an interesting note on the way people will split into distinct groups under circumstances of high population density. The agriculturalists are not only more numerous in Kenya, however, they also took over all major positions of political, administrative and economic power in the transition from British colony to independent nation. (The balance has been redressed slightly in recent years by the appointment of several ministers of pastoralist stock).

The agriculturalists were always inclined to look upon the pastoralists as little more than dangerous and wasteful vagrants; a point of view that was initially derived from a long and painful history of enmity between the two groups, and was subsequently compounded by the views of the western experts who came with international development aid packages. With shamefully little respect for the very special characteristics of semi-desert regions in equatorial Africa, indigenous politicians of an agriculturalist background, and western experts with limited experience of Africa, set about imposing the strategies of temperate agriculture and husbandry upon the pastoralists. As they saw it, the problem was quite straightforward: the herds were too large and the cattle therefore of inferior quality. Fewer cattle of better quality was the answer and the marketing of such animals would provide cash to replace the traditional milk supply. The nomads should settle down on demarcated land and concentrate on the production of high quality beef cattle; they should send their children to school, grow a few crops and join the tourist industry. They might even considering harvesting and marketing the meat of the wildebeeste, eland, impala and gazelle that were so plentiful, and consumed so much grass.

The integration of the nomads into the cash economy was the declared aim. A livestock marketing board was established to buy and market beef from the more remote regions. All over Kenya, land previously held in common by tribal groups was demarcated and allocated to group ranching endeavours (and many of the wettest portions subsequently sold or rented to agriculturalists). In the early 1970s, the Food and Agricultural Organis-ation of the United Nations funded an extravagant attempt to devise procedures for harvesting game meat. It was estimated that between ten and 30 percent of the standing population of antelope and gazelle could be cropped each year; but the project ended in farce, with the cost of the manpower, vehicles, helicopters, fuel and water required to catch and prepare the meat for sale far exceeding its value in the marketplace – where not many wanted to buy it anyway, even when it was pointed out that the tapeworm larvae with which it was infested were specific to lions and hyenas and would not infect humans.

Kenya's development programme for its marginal rangelands has not been conspicuously successful. Insofar as the pastoralists have been integrated into the cash economy of the country at all, most money has been flowing the wrong way – from the national coffers into the pastoralist regions – which is ironic when one considers that, of all the groups that lived in Kenya prior to its colonisation and independence, the pastoral nomads were the most self-sufficient – fiercely so – and might therefore have been expected to impose the least drain on the national economy. But, though well intended, the development philosophy that independent Kenya inherited from its colonial overlords never stood very much chance of success – simply because it failed to accommodate the ecological circumstances of the system it was attempting to change. The develop-ment proposals were based upon the agricultural strategies of temperate regions, where the growing season might be short but always produces enough each year. In temperate regions, the seasons vary relatively little from year to year; one spring is always much the same as the next, people are able to assess the production capability of their land with a fair degree of accuracy, and can regulate their strategies accordingly, with a fair prospect of achieving and maintaining maximum possible production.

In a word, *maximisation* is the basic strategy of the temperate agricul-ture that the development planners brought to Africa. In arid tropical rangelands, however, *survival* is the basic strategy that the nomadic pastoralists must respect. Their system is regulated not by human plans and rules designed to maintain maximum production, but by the vagaries of climate and the environment, which can be assessed only in terms of evidence from the past, and must be accommodated in terms of the worst that they might inflict in the future. Every aspect of the nomadic pastoralist lifestyle is a measure of human ingenuity endeavouring to assess and accommodate environmental constraints.

98

The most fundamental strategy employed by the nomads is in the variety of stock they herd – camels in the driest regions, cows where there is more rain and therefore more grass, sheep and goats throughout. Then there is the important question of numbers. In regions where rainfall may vary from none to average, to above average and back to none again in the course of a few years, with no reliable forecasts available, the size of a man's herd is, in effect, a measure of the breeding capacity that the rainfall of past seasons endowed. The pastoralists' aim must always be to raise as many animals as possible, for next year it might not rain at all, nor the year after. The pastoralists' urge to keep large herds is often criticised, on the assumption that nomads regard livestock as a form of wealth and that large herds are therefore a sign of avarice. This is wrong. Such wealth as livestock represents to the nomadic pastoralist is as paid-up insurance, redeemable only in the event of disaster. One typical Samburu elder had 200 cattle when the 1984-85 drought set in, for example; he lost 80 percent of them, and so still had 40 animals – the best of his stock – to keep his family alive when the drought ended. Had he started out with only 40 (a number that western agro-economists might recommend as being most likely to maximise cash returns from the land), and lost only 50 percent, he and his family would have found it hard to survive and re-build the herd from the remaining 20 animals.

Small stock – goats and sheep – are another important aspect of the nomads' survival strategy. Goats in particular are often criticised by development aid personnel because, it is said, they breed too fast and degrade the environment. But goats are the vital safety net of nomad strategy; they are extremely hardy, and able to survive where other animals quickly expire. Most important of all, they continue breeding when worsening conditions have long since rendered the larger stock barren. Goats are the last to cease giving milk as drought advances, and the first to commence again when conditions improve. Their gestation period is short, and pregnant goats can produce milk within days of the first good rains. The Samburu built up large flocks of sheep and goats during the dry years of the 1970s. These animals survived the 1984-85 drought which killed their cattle, and large numbers of them were subsequently traded for the Somali and Ethiopian cattle with which the Samburu replenished their herds.

The nomadic pastoralists have developed the only feasible strategies by which people can sustain themselves exclusively from the resources of arid regions. Their population density is low, but that is a measure of the environment, not a defect in the strategy of nomadic pastoralism. But what of the future? It is unlikely that any other means of exploiting the food potential of the land could actually support more people. Enterprises such as large-scale ranching or irrigated farming might produce more cash from the land for a few individuals, but neither activity would employ as many people per square kilometre as nomadic pastoralism supports. Meanwhile, although the resources of the land remain finite, the population is growing. There are more people and more cattle than ever before living in the semi-deserts of northern Kenya, despite a cycle of devastating drought, and clearly they cannot all be accommodated within the narrow margins of survival that traditional nomadic pastoralism has developed. The system has expanded and intensified to its limits – now further regulation seems desirable. Marketing enterprises (with increasing pastoralist participation) have already begun to take surplus male livestock from the system. More schools and more economic growth might provide skills and jobs which take more surplus people from the system too – but, however it is achieved, a large degree of regulation must be forthcoming, though it probably will be called development.

Development is an unfortunate word, for it suggests that the existing state of affairs is undeveloped, possibly even primitive. But there is hardly a system of human existence more highly developed than nomadic pastoralism, so it is encouraging to find that, whereas Kenya's 1978-83 Development Plan unequivocally stated that development for the nomads meant abandoning their traditional strategies, the Five-Year Plan published in 1984, (at the height of the drought), acknowledges that nomadic pastoralism is the best possible method of using semi-desert environment and therefore must be incorporated in development plans for the region.

Nomadic pastoralism was once common in the Middle East, where its terms – lamb, flock, shepherd – and sensible ecological strategies subsequently became a fundamental part of the ethics and morality that the christian world has espoused. Islam similarly sprang from the strictures of nomadic life. With the advent of farming and the inevitable competition for land as settled agriculture inhibited nomadic movements, the nomads' tendency to take arms, attack and fight for the land they once freely ranged no doubt encouraged the farmers to live together in groups, with a wall round them that could be defended. Thus nomads quickened the pace of organised warfare, and hastened the establishment of towns and city states. Furthermore, their cattle provided the basic terminology of urban capitalism. Pecuniary, meaning to do with finance, is derived from the Sanskrit *pacu*, meaning cattle, via the old Latin *pecu* meaning cattle as moveable wealth and property. The word money is derived from *moneta*, the name of the Roman goddess in whose temple *pecunia* was minted.

But of course it is not only cows and camels, sheep and goats that the nomads have herded; they have also exploited the potential of yaks, horses and reindeer; and it is not only into the deserts that they have followed their livestock – the Bakrwal of northern India, for instance, shepherd flocks of sheep in long nomadic migrations between high and low mountain pastures in Kashmir; and the seasonal movement of cows in the Alps is a form of nomadism that anthropologists have dubbed transhumance (-*humance* here is derived from *humus*, the Latin for ground). And all around the landmasses of the north nomads have followed the reindeer far into the high Arctic.

The reindeer provides a compelling example of an animal that sustains and buffers mankind against the most extreme rigours of the environment. The average year-round air temperature of the Arctic tundra regions that the reindeer (called the caribou in North America) inhabit is -5°C (23°F), and the annual range far exceeds anything encountered in the equatorial deserts. The temperature can exceed 30°C (86°F) in sheltered corners that catch the full mid-summer sun, and it can drop to below -60°C (-76°F) in mid-winter. Rainfall varies according to topography – averaging 1,500 mm. (59 in.) each year on Norwegian mountain plateaux, but less than 300 mm. (12 in.) on some parts of the open tundra – barely matching the rainfall that keeps the Samburu alive. But of course there is little or no evaporation in the tundra. On susceptible soils, such precipitation as does occur maintains the body of frozen earth that lies a few centimetres beneath the surface – the permafrost – and thus leaves the soil always moist enough for the plants that are adapted to grow under Arctic conditions – sedges, grasses, scrub willow and birch, juniper, cloudberry, blueberry, cranberry, fungi and lichens. Surprising though it may seem, the productivity of tundra environments is prodigious. Though the growing season is very short, its days are very long, and tundra vegetation grows for 24 hours a day at mid-summer.

The tundra environment provides bountiful food for the huge flocks of migratory geese and waterfowl that each year nest and rear their young in the high arctic latitudes; it supports hordes of insects and vast numbers of hares, squirrels, voles and lemmings. But the reindeer is the only large mammal that the tundra sustains in comparable numbers.

Though at first glance a clumsy and unattractive beast, the reindeer is supremely well adapted to its environment. The bedraggled look of summer, when the coat is moulting, quite belies its splendid adaptation to winter, when a fur coat four to five centimetres (1.5 to 2 in.) thick, with wool packed to the skin at a density of over 2,000 hairs to the square centimetre (13,000 to the sq. in.), enables reindeer to thrive in temperatures down to below -60°C (-76°F). The reindeer can run at 80 kph (50 mph) if it needs to, and large splayed hoofs enable it to travel long distances at a steady speed of around 40 kph (25 mph) over deep snow fields and ground that humans find virtually impassable (in anything but an aircraft). The hoofs also enable the reindeer to swim very well, and most important of all – large splayed hoofs enable reindeer to dig through deep snow to the lichen that sustains them through the winter.

Lichen is not a year-round food for the reindeer, but primarily a winter food, and even then constitutes only about 60 percent of the diet, the balance consisting of buds, woody plants, herbs, and such grass and leaf litter as might be found along with lichen beneath the snow.

Ideally, reindeer should be in peak condition by the end of autumn, with a good reserve of fat, for their winter diet is not well balanced. Lichen is virtually all carbohydrate (over 90 percent) – an energy food – and very low in the protein (about two percent) needed for the growth and replacement of body tissue. Reindeer are endowed with the ability to digest up to 90 percent of the carbohydrates in the astringent and bitter-tasting lichens they consume (by comparison, sheep and cattle can utilise only 50 percent at best), but even so, lichen only keeps them going – nothing more. A controlled experiment showed that even 8 kg. (18 pounds) of lichen a day is not enough to maintain the weight of mature reindeer, and it is estimated that under natural conditions a reindeer weighing 100 kg. (220 pounds) in the autumn loses at least 10 kg. during the course of the winter.

Observations have shown that reindeer spend on average about ten hours a day digging for lichen during the winter months. While digging they trample and destroy as much lichen as they consume, and since lichen regenerates slowly – in some instances requiring 30 years of undisturbed growth to regain moderate grazing volume – it follows that a herd of reindeer requires a very large expanse of lichen pasture to sustain it through winter after winter – at least ten hectares (25 acres) per reindeer, according to one estimate.

Lichen sees the reindeer through the arctic winter and thus enables them to live year-round where they otherwise could not. But its limited availability, nutritional deficiencies and slow regeneration strictly control the size of the reindeer population.

Reindeer calves are born between May and mid-June, and although they are usually weaned by the late autumn, they remain with their mother until the following spring – dependent upon her for access to lichen. The reindeer's gestation period is about seven and a half months, and in a normal year between 50 and 80 percent of mature females will be pregnant. So each winter, the most important members of the reindeer population – pregnant females – confront a season of inadequate diet in a condition of high nutritional demand, with a calf in the womb and possibly the added burden of another to find food for. They are well prepared for it, however: female reindeer are the only females of the deer family that grow antlers each year, like the males. Furthermore, they retain their antlers longer than the males, so that by the end of a hard winter season, when competition for diminishing supplies of lichen becomes intense, the females are equipped to defend the holes they have dug for themselves and their calves in the snow, and may even evict males from the lichen patches they have uncovered.

Individual males might thus find themselves doubly disadvantaged as winter approaches. First, the competition of the autumn rutting season, when males regularly fight to exhaustion for access to females, will probably have left them less than adequately nourished for survival through the winter. And second, if the winter is hard and long, with deep snow making lichen difficult to reach, the females are likely to deprive the males of the food they need. In the natural order of things, therefore, many males are likely to die during a hard winter. The extent of this male redundancy in reindeer populations was dramatically demonstrated by the herd of 29 reindeer that was put ashore on St Matthew Island, in the Bering Sea in 1944 by United States coast guards.

The uninhabited island was 331.52 sq. km. (127.97 sq. mi.) in area, all virgin tundra. By 1957 the original 29 reindeer had multiplied to 1,350; by 1963 there were 6,000 on the island and the lichen pastures were seriously depleted. Only 42 reindeer survived to be counted in 1966 – all but one of them female.

Reindeer usually give birth to equal numbers of male and female calves, but it is estimated that for every 100 females only four or six males manage to breed. All the males of course have a role to play during the rutting season, when competition selects the males that will breed, but once the females have been covered the surplus males can as well be removed, for the system is resilient enough to absorb the loss of substantial numbers in a hard year.

Wolves have been the principal removal agent during most of the reindeer's evolutionary history – though not only of males, of course. By weeding out the easily caught weak and sick animals, catching females and calves as well as surplus males, the wolves have served a selective function too, their predation contributing to the maintenance of a viable age and sex structure within the population, and generally helping to keep population in balance with the carrying capacity of the environment.

During the past few thousand years, however, people have taken over from the wolves as the principal agent of control in reindeer populations. The Lapps are the best known and best documented example, but throughout the circumpolar regions – Scandinavia, northern Russia, Siberia, Alaska, Canada, Greenland – numerous groups of people have devised the means of subsisting on reindeer in the tundra environment – Eskimo, Athapaskan, Chuckchi, Tungus and Yakut, as well as Lapp, to name just a few of them.

The subsistence strategy that the Lapps traditionally employed was nomadic pastoralism, like the Samburu, but with some crucial differences. The Lapps did not drive their stock from pasture to pasture, so much as they tracked the animals' seasonal migrations. They did not depend upon milk so much as upon meat. The Samburu and other similar groups are milch pastoralists. Lapps, like wolves, are carnivorous pastoralists.

The Lapps' style of pastoralism is essentially an extension of the hunting and gathering strategies that first took people into the circumpolar regions. It began a long time ago. Man and wolf are believed to have stalked reindeer for at least 270,000 years, moving south and north with the advance and retreat of the Ice Ages, developing different styles of exploitation, according to the nature of the terrain that the reindeer themselves exploited. In the forests and mountains the Lapps pursued an essentially sedentary form of pastoralism, for example, establishing settlements and trapping the reindeer as they passed on their relatively short seasonal migrations. Out on the tundra they were obliged to adopt a more nomadic form of pastoralism.

The reindeer which exploit the resources of the open tundra are said to be the world's most gregarious and most constant migrants. In eastern Siberia, herds of up to 12,000 animals have been recorded moving over 30 km. (19 mi.) a day. In northern Scandinavia, distances are less vast, but the movement is as persistent and the motive the same. In winter the reindeer are kept on a constant move by the search for lichen; in spring they move to the fawning grounds and the tundra where the new vegetation first appears; by summer they are forced to retreat daily before the hordes of black fly and mosquitoes that plague them. High ground and woodland provide respite and grazing until the insect numbers fall to less pestilential proportions in the cooler air of early autumn. Then there are berries to be gorged upon, before the rigours of winter come round again.

Within the broad pattern of reindeer migrations, the Lapps occupying the coastal rim of northern Scandinavia enjoyed a particularly advantageous set of circumstances. The coastal tundra plain is relatively narrow, affording the reindeer easy passage between high and low ground, and the people ready access to the produce of both land and sea. There were fish – especially Atlantic salmon – to be harvested during summer, even a limited amount of agriculture was possible where the Gulf Stream warmed the land sufficiently. In autumn there were cloudberries, blueberries and cranberries to be gathered. The reindeer provided meat, some males were castrated to be used as draught animals, some females were kept to provide milk – exceptionally rich in its protein and fat content (10.3 percent and 22.5 percent respectively, compared with 3.5 percent and 3.7 percent for the cow).

The coastal Lapps were but semi-nomadic, however, following the herds only to round up and mark the new calves in the summer, or to take out animals for slaughter in the winter. And although the reindeer remained essentially wild, each animal was individually owned. The herds ranged over land to which individual families and communities held the rights in common. Each round-up was a communal effort, because it required a large number of people, but once it was complete and the animals marked, each individual was free to do as he pleased with his own animals – they were his own private property.

Within the boundaries of the ecosystem it exploited, with an essential mix of landforms, climate, vegetation and animal life, the Lapps' strategy of nomadic pastoralism regulated human activity to the level at which it was self-sustaining. But the system could remain in balance only so long as it remained closed to outside influence. Outside influence eventually proved unavoidable, however, and by the beginning of the 19th century the Lapps' nomadic pastoralism had begun to break down. With the approval of national governments, settlers moved into the Lapp regions, taking over land and steadily eroding the common access principles of Lapp social order. The boundary between Finland and Norway was closed to reindeer herders in 1852, denying the Lapps access to land they had previously held in common amongst themselves, and the closure of the Finland/Sweden border in 1889 brought further division of Lapp interests and appropriation of their common land.

By the end of the 19th century, many Lapps were living in permanent settlements, with little or no access to the reindeer migrations upon which previous generations had depended. The reindeer still roamed, however, and during the 20th century, as more and more Lapps were obliged to join the cash economy, it has been cleverly transformed into a luxury item – its meat more expensive than beef; its fur more valuable than mink, and its antlers the basis of a valuable souvenir market. Consequently, the profit motive tends to dominate reindeer-herding these days.

Some degree of traditional herding is still practised in Norway and Sweden, where government-controlled migration routes are maintained, and vestiges remain of the cultural system that once regulated exploitation of the reindeer throughout Scandinavia, but in Finland all has long since been handed over to the profit motive. The traditional Lapp rights to reindeer and pasture were abolished in 1898, when a system of herding districts was introduced. Since then, Finnish Lapps have been denied even the option of their semi-nomadic lifestyle, and are obliged to take up permanent residence in the vicinity of their designated herding district.

The boundaries of Finland's herding districts were established primarily along geographical features – roads and rivers, for example, – with little or no reference to the migratory needs of the reindeer. The reindeer are still individually owned, and are still managed by the collective effort of all owners under the direction of the herding district council, but the motive is now exclusively profit and, inevitably, some members are more powerfully motivated than others. Reindeer tend to concentrate in the hands of large owners, not all of them Lapps. Though there are only about about 3,000 Lapps in Finland, there were 7,066 registered reindeer-owners in 1982.

Young Lapps, married with families they would like to support on the resource they see as rightfully theirs, complain bitterly of how impossible it is for them even to consider the prospect. A family would need at least 400 animals, they say, and none has much chance of raising the capital required to purchase a herd and sustain themselves while it builds up to economically viable numbers.

Meanwhile, reindeer have become big business in Finland. The national affiliation of herding districts meticulously records and publishes the vital statistics of reindeer numbers, offtake and productivity. A member can see at a glance that 0.07 man/days per animal were expended on a herd of 8,798 reindeer in the Paistunturi herding district of Utsjoki, in the far north of Finland, during 1982, for instance. Paistunturi slaughtered 1,355 calves and 1,844 animals one year old and over that year. Details of marketing and of incomes accruing to the district's 123 members are all carefully noted. The statistics even record that 25 of the Paistunturi reindeer were killed by cars during the year; while in Kallio, further south, 57 were killed by trains.

At Karagasiemi Ailigas, near the Norwegian border, when the members of the Paistunturi herding district round up their reindeer for marking in early July, the scene has more the aspect of a rich man's pastime than of the rural subsistence from which it is so recently derived. While the reindeer run nervously around the pen, pursued by clouds of mosquitoes, the owners arrive in their Volvos and Mercedes and wait in their caravans for the time when the herd is deemed calm enough for the calves to be separated from their mothers and marked. Hans Vuopio and his sons drink tea and eat salted trout; from time to time the radio-telephone in the Mercedes jangles with some message from the tourist lodge that Hans owns nearby. The herd has been brought in from the tundra by young men on motor cycles over a period of days, and the separation takes place at night, when heat is least likely to cause the animals any distress. The animals are completely wild, so that identifying and marking the calves is

105

a long and tedious procedure. First, small groups of animals must be herded into separate pens, where a large numbered card is hung about the neck of each calf; then calves and adults are kept apart until they are calm enough for the next stage, which consists of releasing the calves to join their mothers and noting by number which calf is associated with the notched ear marking of which mother. Later, the calves will be separated again and their ears notched with the individual owners' marks of the females to which their number has been allocated.

As calves and mothers try to locate each other the herd circles the pens continuously for several hours, while the sun begins to rise again from the northern horizon and the owners stand about the high ground, wrapped up warmly against the bitter cold night air of midsummer. They scan the herd through binoculars, making notes from time to time like punters at a race meeting – though there is not much of a gamble involved in modern reindeer herding these days; profit is an odds-on certainty. Or at least it was until 1986, when fallout from the Chernobyl disaster irradiated the lichen pastures of northern Scandinavia and rendered reindeer products unsuitable for human use.

The Lapps, largely dispersed and almost wholly dispossessed of their tradition and rights have re-grouped as an essentially tribal entity called the Sami, a name by which they prefer to be known and which in their language means, simply, 'we people'. Like the Samburu, they have found a measure of support for their struggle with the economic forces that threaten their existence. And at a further extreme, in the Arabian deserts, the Bedu also have to contend with the effects of an economic system that has rendered their traditional lifestyle largely redundant.

The wealth of oil has removed the survival incentive of the nomadic pastoralism that the Bedu refined to such a high art. But the practice has not disappeared. The Harasiis Bedu of Oman, for example, still herd their camels and goats across the Jiddat-il-Harasiis. The practice began some generations ago, initially as a consequence of growing pressure for land and grazing in the mountains to the south, or on the coastal plain in the east, it is believed. Subsequently the Harasiis reversed their strategy, adopting the Jiddat as their proper home, and using the coastal plain as a summer retreat from conditions which even they found hard to tolerate.

The Jiddat-il-Harasiis is the flat barren fringe of the Empty Quarter, a vast arid gravel plain of nearly 40,000 sq. km. (15,440 sq. mi.) in area, and certainly among the most demanding of environments for human habitation. Temperatures regularly exceed 30°C (86°F), even in winter, and the average June shade temperature reaches 45°C (113°F). Rainfall is extremely intermittent – none at all at the Al Yalooni research station in 1984, 165 mm. (6.5 in.) on a single April day in 1983, 38 mm. (1.5 in.) in 1982 – and grazing is correspondingly sparse. There was no surface water available in the desert, and the Harasiis developed the ingenious practice of squeezing their water supply from blankets carefully laid over bushes to collect the copious early morning dew. The heavy dew which regularly condenses over the desert in winter is a unique feature of the Jiddat-il-Harasiis –

106

without it, people could not have survived there. Dew provided the stock with enough water wherever they were in the desert, allowing them to graze more widely, free of the limitations that fixed water supplies impose. The Harasiis never drank water in the desert, not even dew, they boast, but derived their liquid needs entirely from goat and camel milk.

In the 1950s and '60s wells were sunk at a number of sites throughout the Jiddat as part of the oil exploration programme. The wells are sparsely distributed; few supply sweet water, while most provide but limited access to brackish water for the stock – and even these wells had to be shared, on not altogether friendly terms, with neighbouring tribes. Nonetheless, the wells enabled the Harasiis to stay in the desert longer each year, while the people of the coastal region became increasingly reluctant to allow the Harasiis access to grazing in their retreat from the desert. Finally they were denied all access and obliged to remain in the desert all year round – 2,000 people, 40,000 sq. km., sparse grazing and only two wells to which they had uncontested access – one sweet and one brackish.

Their confinement to the desert was closely followed, however, by the influx of wealth that events of the early 1970s brought to the oil-producing countries. By the end of that decade, the Harasiis found themselves sharing the desert with not only several oil wells and a newly-built adminstrative centre complete with school and medical facilities, but also with a research station at Al Yalooni, established to fulfil the Sultan's wish that the arabian oryx should once again roam the wastes of the Jiddat-il-Harasiis, from which hunters had eliminated it.

These developments have brought the Harasiis a source of cash income, either by way of employment or in the form of government aid. The Harasiis have shown little inclination for the settled life, however. They have not moved into the air-conditioned cement-block houses that are available at population centres. Families still live out in the desert, in their open encampments, following their goats and camels on the search for grazing that has become seriously depleted from overuse and is given little chance of regeneration. But the nomadic existence is considerably less arduous than before, the Harasiis having applied the facilities of the new order to their old lifestyle with remarkable alacrity. Children learn to drive at an early age, families generally own several vehicles and think nothing of travelling in a few hours the distances that previously took weeks. Men transport truckloads of water across the desert for their stock and family every few days. Camels are valued for their perfection of form rather than simply for their capacity to provide milk, and one of racing potential may be worth several thousand dollars. The meagre grazing that the desert provides for the stock is supplemented by a regular supply of commercial feed. The camels are given enriched bran pellets, while each goat might receive a handful or two of dried sardines in the evening. The sardines are brought up from the coast over 100 km. (60 mi.) away, where they cost about one dollar a kilo.

Samburu, Sami, Harasiis – each group of people developed the means of surviving, generation after generation, in environments that otherwise would have been uninhabitable. Their ways of life were adaptations to the limitations of the environment. Individual lives were regulated by the clear understanding that the future existence of the group, and of the individuals therein, was determined by its ability to subsist on the very minimum that the environment might provide, not by its ability to take all it could get from the land. Any fool could turn the resources of a marginal environment to profit when times were good, but only the truly wise could survive when times were hardest – and then only by regulating their affairs to conform with the limitations of the environment.

The same is true of minority groups around the world, virtually all of whom have seen their traditional patterns of subsistence and self-sufficiency disrupted by the acquisitive ambitions of the global cash economy in the space of a few decades. All together, they constitute a tiny proportion of the world population, but their fate strikes a sympathetic chord of concern wherever long term views are not swamped by short term demands for cost-effectiveness. It might seem odd that the remnants of such hard and unforgiving cultural adaptations can arouse any concern at all in a world of essentially comfort- seeking disposition. But it should not. Minority groups in general, and nomadic pastoralists in particular, are shining examples of mankind's capacity to discover, acknowledge and make appropriate adaptation to the constraints of the environment. Their sturdy survival strategies demonstrate that mankind is capable of devising ingenious cultural solutions to the most intractable of problems. They might even represent a kind of cultural 'dry-season retreat' in the sub-conscious of sedentary man – providing the evidence of proven adaptations in which the species could find the means of surviving disaster, just as Nyiru enables the Samburu to survive the hardest drought.

CHAPTER SIX

FISHERMEN

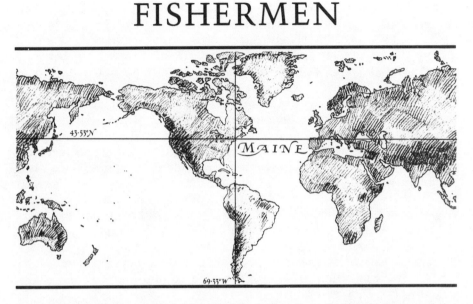

Leaning against the rail of the wooden dock, about half way between the shed where the fishermen unload their lobsters and the rough and ready establishment in which the tourists sit down to eat them, the dealer suddenly became suspicious. 'Are you one of those environment and ecology people?' he asked. 'Because if you are, I tell you we don't need any more environment and ecology round here, thank you. We've got enough of it. Just mind your own business and leave us to get on with ours.'

The dealer's business was lobsters, and he controlled a substantial part of the lobster trade in that part of Maine. He supplied fuel and bait (and on credit too, he would add) for the professional fishermen using that harbour, paid a fair price per pound for every lobster they brought in, sold a large number in the establishment he had built on the dock, but most through wholesalers in Portland and Boston. His family had lived in the small harbour town for generations, always actively involved with the fishing and lobster business, and, as the present custodian of family fortune, the dealer was also very actively involved with local affairs. He was a prominent member of the local town Board of Selectmen – where the combination of his family and business status lent more weight to his opinions than might otherwise have been the case.

Right now, he was incensed by Federal and State regulations that inhibited building and development along the coast of Maine. The business community wanted to develop the region, he said. This meant clearing land and putting up buildings. He gestured expansively to the bluffs and inlets of the enclosed natural harbour in which dock and town were situated – a beautiful place of rock and wooden houses delicately poised between the water and a rising backdrop of spruce, maple and oak.

'Look at it', he said, 'we could get twice as much building along that waterfront. We would have to cut down a few trees – but what's so special about a tree?' he demanded, 'and who are the environment people to tell us what we can and can't do? Our people have been living here longer than any goddamn tree. We own this place'.

The extent to which civic law regulates the exploitation of private land in modern society brings an ironic twist to the relationship between common and private holdings that underpins western capitalism. Where once private ownership was seen as the most satisfactory means of regulating the exploitation of resources, and thereby averting the more tragic consequences of common use, subsequent events have often shown that private interest is not always the best custodian of common good. Private owners have often needed to be restrained from exploiting their property in a manner that is commonly held to be undesirable. Laws enacted in the British House of Commons make it illegal for farmers to clear listed woodland, or to plough up sites of special interest, for instance. Property owners throughout Europe may not make unauthorized alterations to listed buildings; environmental concern increasingly restricts the activities of industry in Europe and America, and small communities along the coast of Maine may not pursue private development at the expense of the common environment – no matter how old and effectively self-governing they may be.

The story is the same everywhere – in the modern world more and more private action is subject to common approval – but it is especially revealing in the communities that have grown and flourished about the lobster fisheries of Maine, for the private wealth the fishermen and dealers have accumulated, and wish to exploit on land, is actually the product of a common wealth they exploit at sea and – furthermore – one which they actively regulate to serve their own private interests. By law, the coastal waters of the United States are the common property of every citizen. Anyone who takes out the appropriate state licence is entitled to catch a share of the resources those waters provide, but the innocent citizen who attempts to exercise this common right by trapping lobsters along the coast of Maine will soon find that his activities are less than welcome. Discouraging remarks at the public dock will be the first impediment, one that even vacationers wanting to catch their own lobster for supper will encounter; a mounting sequence of threats, cut lines, damaged property and even physical violence will confront citizens who attempt to take anything approaching what they might consider their fair share of the common resource.

The fact is that the dealer and the fishermen regard the lobsters as their private property, and the waters in which the lobsters are found as their private territory.

From each of the limited number of sheltered harbours along the storm-prone rocky coast, dealers and fishermen operate in what the anthropologist James Acheson has termed harbour gangs, restricting access to the common resource at sea no less vigorously than the environmentalists restrict the dealer's development of his private interests on land.

110

The sea: 'a vast and terrible water that sustains fishes and destroys men', as Heraclitus put it, is popularly believed to be a wonderfully fertile resource that mankind has scarcely begun to tap. The received wisdom of old (and some not-so-old) textbooks says that the oceans are responsible for 70 percent of the earth's primary production, thereby sustaining stupendously rich food chains which adequate technology would readily link to the secure future of mankind. But modern research has shown that the received wisdom is misplaced – derived from the combination of imprecise measurement and enthusiastic over-estimation that distinguished subsequent calculations. It is now known that the oceans are responsible for just 25 percent of the earth's production, in spite of the fact that they cover just over 70 percent of its surface.

The deep blue open waters which comprise over 90 percent of the world's oceans are virtual deserts, so deficient in nutrients that their primary production barely exceeds that of the earth's terrestrial deserts. Furthermore, the primary production of the open oceans consists of microscopic plankton, which must pass through several links of the food chain before its energy is available in a package large enough to be convenient for human capture and consumption. One authoritative study suggests that five or more such links are required, each of which serves to reduce the efficiency of the system to the extent that the fish population of the deep blue open oceans is estimated to be no more than 0.6 percent of the world total.

The most productive parts of the oceans are found where upwelling currents of cold water continuously bring nutrients from the ocean floor to the surface – along the Pacific coast of South America, for example. In the rich waters of such upwellings primary production may match that of the tropical rainforest; and since it consists of relatively large plankton, which can sustain relatively large fish, fishermen take their catch from the end of a relatively short food chain. Upwelling areas comprise only 0.1 percent of the world's oceans, but they produce fully 50 percent of the world's renewable fish supply.

The continental shelves, estuaries and reefs that surround the landmasses of the earth constitute a third class of oceanic environment. These coastal zones add up to about 9.9 percent of the world's ocean area, and are reckoned to produce about as much fish as the upwellings (though, of course, they occupy 99 times more space). Their productivity has to do with their location. In the coastal zone the inherent sterility of the sea is tempered by a flow of nutrients from the land and by the greater complexity of the food chains that can be sustained in shallower waters.

The coastal zone is a classic example of an *ecotone*, the name ecologists have given to the transition zone between one kind of environment and another. An ecotone can derive benefits from both the systems that it joins, and is characterised by a large diversity of species – both floral and faunal – and a correspondingly high energy turnover. There are ecotones at the boundary of the plain and the forest, and where a field of potatoes touches the meadow, but the ecotone that marks the transition from land to sea is the most dramatic and richest of all.

The coastal zones are arguably the most dependable sources of human sustenance that the earth has to offer, but strangely they seem to have been the least subject to human regulation. Perhaps this is because they have constituted only a basic subsistence resource for most of humanity's evolution, and became susceptible to exploitation for profit rather than for individual consumption only with the development of modern technologies and marketing techniques. And yet, of all the environments that mankind exploits, fisheries are especially susceptible to over-use.

Throughout the world there has been over-exploitation of fisheries, often with disastrous results, and the common ownership aspect of the marine environment is generally held to be the cause. Where fisheries are open to anyone, a fisherman has no incentive to restrict his activities when catches decline, for there is no guarantee that his restraint will bring more profitable catches in the future. The fish he leaves in the water today most likely will be taken by someone else tomorrow.

National disputes, such as Britain's 'Cod War' with Iceland which saw the deployment of gunboats in defence and pursuit of fishing rights, have demonstrated the value attached to the resource; and continuing efforts to establish a 'Law of the Sea' have demonstrated international determination to place the resource firmly in some kind of regulatory context. Within each national community, however, where the law pays such concern to the ownership and control of terrestrial resources, the aquatic resources lying below the high tide mark of the coastal zones remain common property, their exploitation unregulated by law and effected principally by private interests. The Maine lobster fishery is a case in point, but here the value of the fishery and the nature of the environment have combined to produce regulations that go a long way towards conserving the resource, even though they are, strictly speaking, against the law. The studies of James Acheson have shown that the extra-legal arrangements concerning territory and fishing rights which have developed among the harbour communities have a significant impact on the fishery. Biologists have focused on the effects of environmental factors such as water temperature, food supply and natural predation on lobster stocks and landings, but Acheson's work suggests that fishing rights are a critical factor.

Dan keeps his boat at Poverty Knob, around the head from Pemaquid Harbour. At six on a September morning, the sky is just gaining a lighter tinge of magenta above the trees to the east, the air is still, with a chilly touch of moisture in it, and the water dead calm. A light shines through the window of the tackle shed, where Seth is preparing extra pots to be set out on the haul that morning. The tackle shed is a neat and strictly functional square wooden structure, roofed and walled with shingles, no guttering, no downpipes, leaning slightly backwards from the edge of the wharf on which it is perched – a displacement from the perpendicular that is emphasized by the angle the lines of the shed make with its perfect reflection on the surface of the pond below. Not a ripple; hardly a sound until Dan arrives to help Seth heave crates of bait down to the boat.

Dan is something of a sophisticate among lobstermen. With the aim of achieving a degree of independence from dealers and market fluctuations alike he has dammed the small cove that breaks into the stretch of coastline he owns to make a tidal pond (a 'lobster pound'), wherein he holds his catch, and can select from them for sale by size and to order at a negotiated price – rather than handing over every day's catch to the dealers at prices they impose. Dan tries to hold his catch while the price is low in the late summer and fall and aims to sell only when prices inevitably rise. He smiles non-committally at questions concerning the success of the strategy, and talks instead of its problems. The tide doesn't always freshen the pond as much as would be desirable, he says; lobsters die when it gets crowded and the weather is warm, and he doesn't particularly enjoy having to don wetsuit and aqualung when it becomes necessary to take out the corpses. Still, we manage, he says, and turns to the 'phone that is ringing at the door of the tackle shed.

Time was – and not so long ago, either – when all lobsters were caught in wooden traps a little under a metre long, made of spruce slats over a half-circle frame of oak. The traps were made in the region, often by the lobstermen themselves, to a pattern that had remained unchanged for a hundred years or more. The slats were spaced about four centimetres (1.6 in.) apart, so that undersized lobsters could escape. A funnel-shaped net fixed at one end of the trap allowed the lobsters easy access to the bait, but prevented them getting out again. Such traps are still in use, but not so many are made any more; as they wear out they are dumped (or cleaned up for the souvenir stores) and often replaced with traps made of plastic-covered wire mesh. Less attractive, agrees Dan, but much easier to handle.

Across the Johns River channel from Poverty Knob, and into the surprising expanse of the enclosed bay between the Johns and the Damariscotta rivers, the waters are littered with buoys marking the traps set out by hopeful lobstermen. There hardly seems to be a ten metre square that does not hold at least one trap. About 35 men fish the Pemaquid territory, Dan explains, and between them they set at least 10,000 traps. The Johns river estuary is maybe five miles (8 km.) long, and much less than one mile wide on average. From the mouth of the estuary the territory extends about eight miles (13 km.) out to sea and is perhaps a little over three miles (5 km.) wide. All in all, the Pemaquid men fish about 29 sq. mi. (75 sq. km.) of coastal waters – but they cannot use all of it all the time. The lobsters move in- and off-shore with the seasons. In summer and autumn they can be taken in relatively shallow inshore waters; as winter approaches they retreat to the deeper waters, several miles offshore, which remain relatively warm while the inshore bays are often close to freezing. The lobstermen follow their prey. Fishing is hard in the winter, with prices – though high – scarcely rewarding enough to merit the work involved, so most concentrate their effort on the summer season; packing their traps in among the other 10,000.

Each buoy is marked with its owner's registered colours, and every man knows every other man's markers; there can be no mistaking them – the

113

fluorescent colours stand out vividly, especially in the grey early morning light – and intruding boats or foreign buoys would be recognized instantly. Dan's buoys are orange and white. His son Mark fishes luminous yellow buoys with a green band.

At the head of the bay Dan begins to haul. He catches the buoy with a boathook, loops the line over the snatch block, gives it two turns round the power winch and quickly lifts the trap onto the gunwale as it breaks the surface. Two lobsters of legal size go into the barrel, their pincers deftly secured with elastic bands. One obviously under-sized, is thrown back; another is checked with the gauge – found to be under-sized and thrown back. Seth strings in a fistful of bait, closes the trap, and lets it drop into the water at Dan's instruction. Next one. One lobster and three crabs. Next, empty. Next, three lobsters. Next two; then three, three, four and two. 'I always get a good haul just here', Dan explains.

Some traps are dropped back in the waters from which they were hauled; others are moved to different places. Dan scans the seascape, handles the boat, hauls the traps; Seth fixes the bait and drops the traps back into the water. A rhythm is soon established and they will probably haul 200 traps on a good morning with barely a word between them. The lobstermen prefer to work the morning hours, before conditions roughen up.

In the shadow of the extraordinary towerhouse which stands on an island opposite Pemaquid harbour, a young lad was hauling traps into a skiff, struggling a little to manage the boat, keep the outboard engine running and handle the traps on his own, all at the same time. He had traps piled in the bows and, having hauled the last of a string, puttered off to set them out further offshore. 'Thats how we all learn about lobsters,' said Dan. 'You give a lad a few traps and the use of a skiff when he's 12 or so, and if he takes to it, he'll be earning a good few dollars before long. Then he'll buy more traps and take over a bigger boat when he's ready. Like an apprenticeship – he's worked his way into the business. Its the best way to learn, and no one can argue about his right to set traps around here. They usually begin by setting them right next to their Dad's. I always know when Mark's not doing so well: he puts his traps on top of mine.'

Out in the open water of Johns Bay, between Thrumcap Island and Pemaquid Point, where you get a view of Monhegan Island on the southeast horizon, Dan begins to pay more attention to his depth-sounder as he set the traps. There is a point around the submerged Pemaquid Ledge, about a mile offshore, where the sea bottom rises sharply from 120 to 60 feet (36.6 to 18.3 m.), and Dan likes to set some traps along the steepest edge of the transition. He weaves the boat back and forth across the line – 60, 120, 60 120, 60 – as Seth tips the traps over the side. Another boat is in the area, but there are few traps so far out yet; most of the Pemaquid men are still content to reap the smaller pickings inshore, but with the cold season approaching Dan is hoping to get the first of the larger lobsters that are moving offshore.

The Pemaquid territory that Dan fishes is penned between the New Harbour territory to the east, and the Little River territory to the west. Inshore, and up into Johns Bay it is undisputed Pemaquid territory, defined

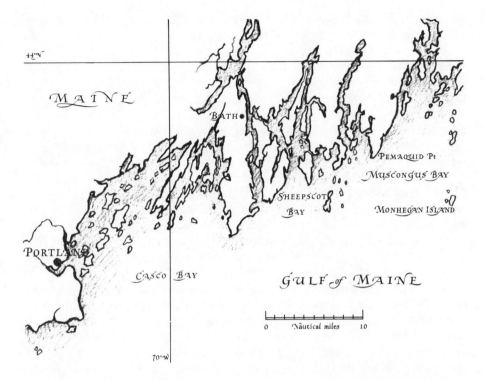

to the metre by reference to distinctive features of the shoreline. Boundaries are known intimately and no outsider would dare invade the inshore territory. But offshore, the boundaries are less clearly defined and often overlap. 'That's where you get the trouble,' Dan remarks. 'You know exactly where you are inshore, and if you go out far enough the whole ocean is yours, but in between it gets difficult. There's always someone trying to set his traps a little further over than before. And when it goes too far, there'll be trouble.'

Dan's brother was embroiled with a spot of trouble at that time, as a result of having persistently set traps closer to Damariscove Island than the Boothbay boys were prepared to accept. He was warned off at the beginning, with a couple of half hitches tied around the spindle of the offending buoys. Then there was a shouting match over the radio, and after that the aggrieved parties initiated the retaliatory escalation of first cutting trap nets, so that they caught nothing, and then cutting each other's traps loose so that the gear was lost altogether. But a man has to be very careful, Dan explained, he can never be certain exactly who cut his traps loose, so he might choose the wrong traps when he retaliates. And if he cuts two, the other fellow might cut ten. There's a lot at risk for the sake of a little extra sea bottom. His brother was looking for support from other members of the Pemaquid gang, with little success, it transpired. Dan, though family, felt not the least desire or obligation to join the campaign.

Dan and Seth hauled and re-set about 200 traps that morning, and were out from Poverty Knob for just over seven hours. Dan would speak only

115

vaguely of the morning's catch: average, he said, seeming uncertain as to whether he should exaggerate or understate the case. At a guess, there were 200 lobsters in the barrel, which at the average for the fishery would have weighed into a dealer's scales at 240 pounds (110 kg.), worth $2.50 a pound ($5.50 per kg.) – though of course Dan might expect his marketing arrangements to produce a better than average price.

Eating lobster is something of a rite for Americans, especially for those with New England connections. 'Perhaps we take a certain atavistic satisfaction in eating lobster', a writer reports. 'There's never any need to wonder or ask, "Is it fresh?". When we buy it, it's alive. We no longer buy beef on the hoof or kill a chicken for dinner, but it is possible to select our lobster live from a tank.... This is a noble animal, a feisty creature in keeping with the rocky shore, the recalcitrant, changeable mood of the New England Atlantic, the stubbornly independent way of life New Englanders take such pride in. This is a creature that is part of the regions's heritage, a delicacy since the days of the Pilgrim'.

Gratifying this lingering atavism of America's huge and hungry consumer society has become very big business indeed. Jimmy's Harborside place in Boston reckons to serve an average of 10,000 lobster meals every month of the year – and Jimmy's is only one of many thousand speciality restaurants in New England and across the United States to which modern transportation methods have made live New England lobster available.

The United States lobster industry landed 42 million pounds (19 million kg.) of lobster in 1986 – around 34 million individual lobsters. Not surprisingly, there is growing concern about the ability of the lobster to sustain this seemingly insatiable demand. At present, the only regulation directly affecting the number of lobsters taken from the water is one concerning their size. The carapace is the measure; from eye socket to the end of the carapace, where the body joins the tail, a lobster must be more than 81 mm. (just over 3 in.) but less than 127 mm. (5 in.) long. The idea is that any lobster over 127 mm. is definitely breeding stock and therefore should be preserved (though they are also very large and correspondingly difficult to sell), while any under 81 mm. have yet to reproduce at all.

These regulations were laid down at a time when very little was known about lobsters beyond what could be learned from them as they made their journey from trap to dinner plate at the age of about seven years. By the early 1970s, however, there were clear signs that the regulations were inadequate. Between 1969 and 1973 the New England catch declined from 19.8 to 16 million pounds (10 to 7.3 million kg.), even though the number of traps in operation during the same period leapt from 819,000 to 1,747,000. Research into the life and times of the American lobster, *Homarus americanus*, has intensified considerably since then, generating ever more strident calls for greater State and Federal control of the nation's common lobster resource.

Marine biologists have found good reason to suppose that the extraordinary productivity of the inshore lobster fishery is based not so much on the resources of the inshore waters *per se*, as upon the fact that the inshore population is regularly replenished by deep water breeding stocks that lie offshore. If this is indeed so, then it is a wonderfully productive system. Each year the fishermen effectively clear out the inshore waters, and each year brings a new stock in from offshore. The lobstermen in effect harvest a surplus, and even if their catch included large numbers of immature lobsters they could not harm the long-term stability of the system so long as they confined their activities to inshore waters. But there's the rub. Although lobstering traditionally has been an inshore business, with prevailing conditions and available equipment offering little incentive to venture into offshore waters, by the late 1960s bigger and more powerful boats, along with radar and depth-sounders, made offshore lobstering perfectly feasible. At the same time, rising prices and soaring demand made it an extremely attractive proposition. Biologists from the Northeast Fisheries Center laboratories at Woods Hole estimate that, by the mid-1970s, 30 percent of the lobster catch came from offshore waters; by the mid-1980s the proportion was reckoned to be approaching 50 percent, and alarming consequences threatened. If the offshore population does indeed replenish the inshore stock and equal numbers of sexually immature lobsters are being taken from both populations, then the American appetite threatens to reduce the reproduction pool of the New England lobster below the point at which it can sustain itself. Then, after centuries of stability and a few years of phenomenal growth, the fishery will collapse.

Biologists are convinced that collapse can be averted by increasing the 81 mm. size limit. Their findings show that at least 90 percent of all lobsters are caught in the first year after they have moulted into the legal size bracket. But only six percent of females are sexually mature at that size, whereas virtually all are mature by the time their carapace measures 98 mm.(3.86 in.), about two years later. This means that only around ten percent of female lobsters stay in the water long enough to reproduce. If the carapace limit was raised to 88.9 mm. (3.5 in.), suggest the biologists, then at least 60 percent of female lobsters would have an opportunity to bear eggs at least once.

Since lobsters with carapaces larger than 88.9 mm. currently constitute less than 30 percent of the catch, lobstermen are understandably appalled by the biologists' proposal, seeing little future for themselves in a 70 percent catch reduction, whatever it might mean for the future of the lobster. The biologists counter with the suggestion that the limit need not be raised in one step, the increase could be spread over several years, they say, with minimal effect on annual incomes. No matter, reply the lobstermen, 88.9 mm. makes a big lobster, an expensive luxury item that people simply will not buy. Yes they will, say the economists, there is no limit to what people will pay for their luxuries – look at the price of vacation homes on Nantucket, look at what people will pay for exclusive Swiss watches, for reindeer meat from Lapland and lobsters in Sweden, where fishermen get $20 a pound ($44 per kg.) at the dock.

There is general agreement among biologists, legislators and fishermen that the New England lobster fishery needs some form of regulation, but just what it should be, when it should be introduced and how it should be enforced remains undecided. Meanwhile, James Acheson has been looking for clues in the regulations that the lobstermen have developed among themselves.

Maine is far and away the leading producer of lobsters in the United States, supplying 47 percent of the annual harvest in 1986. The state issues and renews over 10,000 licences each year, of which about 2,500 go to full-time fishermen; the rest are held by schoolboys and other part-timers. Every licence holder is subject to the few conservation laws that the state of Maine has passed: boats, buoys and traps must be marked with licence number and assigned colours; a lobster's carapace must fall within the set size limits if it is to be taken; regardless of size, egg-bearing females must be returned to the water, with two notches cut in the flipper; notched-tail lobsters may never be taken. These laws are obeyed by everyone – full- and part-timers alike, though the state employs only 37 Sea and Fisheries wardens to enforce them along its entire 2,500 mi. (4,000 km.) of coastline. Much more meaningful, however, is an additional set of laws controlling the Maine lobster fishery which have never been formally promulgated, are never publicised, but which are actively and continuously unheld by every member of the 2,500-strong full-time fishing force.

If the general public is aware of these laws at all, the awareness is usually derived from an outraged account of some unhappy vacation experience. Every summer, a significant number of visitors buy a lobster licence and set a few traps for the sport, and every summer police and wardens along the coast dutifully record complaints of traps damaged, cut loose, or even removed entirely. The visitors always have the law on their side, but never have the evidence that would enable the police to confront the law-breakers, and when they complain to the local people they are doubly outraged to find *themselves* labelled outlaws – *not* the men who cut their lines or stole their traps. Thereafter they soon learn that it is simpler to buy lobsters from the dealer on the dock, because Maine lobster fishermen regard extensive tracts of the ocean as their own private property.

But the informal laws excluding part-timers from the lobster fishery also impose very formal restrictions on those within it: to belong they must conform. Despite the widespread and persistent image of the New England lobsterman as a rugged and taciturn individualist with little time or respect for the ideas and expectations of others, he is in fact hemmed round with obligations to conform with accepted modes of behaviour. In the broad sense, these modes of behaviour are the same as those of all middle-America – namely, the pursuit of success and affluence. But while middle-class America is largely free to migrate to and fro across the country in pursuit of its chosen goals, the lobsterman is confined to a very much smaller pond. He spends his working life chugging just a few miles to and fro across a strictly demarcated stretch of coastal water, conforming to social rules that are no less strictly defined. He probably began as a schoolboy part-timer, following the trade of his father, his grandfather and possibly even more distant antecedents. Very few lobstermen find any

118

other way into the business. 'Out-of-towners', 'summer people', and worst of all, 'people from New York' stand little chance, and even the son of the local and long-term resident doctor might find entry impossible – unless he happened to spend his summers fishing with local boys and thereby grew up into the business with them.

The harbour gang to which a man must belong if he is to catch lobsters at all typically comprises about 30 full-time fishermen, and the group keeps the individual under great pressure to conform with the accepted norms of behaviour. The operational part of the business is lonely, secretive and highly competitive. The successful fisherman is the man who sets his traps where there are most lobsters, and in the confined waters of the harbour territory he is always competing directly with the other 29 members of the gang. Every man will have a very good idea of exactly where every other man is setting his traps, and the material affluence that middle-America's cultural ambition demands will always give an indication of success. Within the gang, success is admired – but only so long as it denotes skill tempered by respect for the group. Every man is entitled to earn a 'fair living' from the fishery, they say, but no one should take more than his 'share of lobsters'. A man who has many more traps than anyone else, or who goes out in bad weather that keeps the rest of the gang at home, soon becomes the subject of intense bad feeling. 'A bristleman [pig]', they call him, 'a man who wants to take something that belongs to everyone to live better than the rest of us.'

Exactly what constitutes a 'fair living' or an appropriate 'share of lobsters' is never precisely defined, though the notions clearly occupy prominent positions in the concensus opinion of the group. But, of course, by remaining undefined the notion remains open to interpretation according to circumstances, and there is little doubt as to what circumstances are undesirable. The men know that someone with a lot of traps eventually may invade the territories of adjacent harbour gangs. Trap cutting, and even a 'cut war' involving dozens of men could result, and the gang will apply pressure on the culprit before circumstances become dangerous. 'A couple of our men are fishing upriver', an informant told James Acheson, 'and it is just a matter of time before those river rats come down here. When they do we'll have to push them out. I wish they'd stay to home', he concluded, referring to his gangmates.

Related to the fear of invasion and retaliation is a sound appreciation of the fact that having a lot of traps makes no sense at all in terms of cost and productivity. The lobstermen are fully aware that there is only a finite number of legal-size lobsters to be caught in a given area and they can see that individuals will catch about the same number of lobsters when each has 300 traps as when each has 2,000. The only difference would be the increased cost and effort involved. The trouble is, however, that once the process of trap escalation has begun it is difficult to stop. One man with more traps will obviously catch more lobsters, and others will feel compelled to follow suit.

Some degree of trap escalation has occurred all along the Maine coast. In some parts, men feel obliged to set over 2,000 traps to catch their share of the lobsters, with vastly increased costs producing virtually the same income as before, but escalation is least evident among relatively small harbour gangs with clearly defined and vigorously defended territories.

James Acheson began his research into lobster fishing practice and productivity along the Maine coast in the early 1970s, and encountered a good deal of initial reluctance and negative comment – 'You professors have a long way to go to understand this business', commented one interviewee. No one readily reveals details of personal income and expenditure, least of all the taciturn, self-employed New England lobsterman, and the enquiries were not helped by the fact that, in 1973, they coincided with United States Inland Revenue Service decisions to investigate the Maine lobster industry. In the course of these investigations a very large number of Maine lobstermen were "overhauled", as they put it, by the IRS. Many were obliged to pay additional taxes and several were charged with criminal fraud.

Despite the setbacks, however, Acheson has over the years brought together a substantial body of evidence showing that the regulations harbour gangs impose upon their members are good for the lobsters and good for the lobstermen. The best fisheries are those whose boundaries are most clearly delineated and the most vigorously protected. The territories around the islands of Penobscot Bay, for instance – Monhegan, Matincus, Metinic, Green Island and Little Green Island – are known to the metre, and the harbour gangs exploiting them have a notorious reputation for violence. To all intents and purposes this jointly-held resource is 'owned' by the families that own land on the islands – even to the extent of their renting such fishing as they cannot exploit themselves to other fishermen. Many of the lobstermen who fish the Metinic waters in fact rent the fishing from the two families that own the island. In some cases, the families have supplied capital equipment and take 50 percent of the gross income; furthermore, the rights to rent are traditionally held, and although formally untestified, they pass from father to son with as much certainty as United States law affords the inheritance of land property rights.

The assumption of private ownership in the ostensibly public waters of the Maine lobster fishery has been taken to its farthest extreme by the 12 fishermen on Monhegan Island, who successfully petitioned the state legislature to declare a closed season on lobster fishing from June to January for the waters up to two miles off the island. At a stroke they not only achieved what surely amounts to legal recognition of their fishing rights, but also arranged the fishing to their utmost benefit. They now fish in the winter only, when prices are highest and territorial invasion is least likely and most easily repelled. In summer they service the lucrative tourist industry that Monhegan Island attracts, while state wardens must take over the responsibility of keeping fishermen out of the islanders' lobster territory.

Acheson's findings show that fewer boats per square mile operate in the most strictly regulated territories than in territories that are loosely defined or overlapping. The men catch about 25 percent more lobsters per trap hauled, the average lobster is significantly heavier and the men earn around 30 percent more. It is clear that regulation is good for the resource and good for the men exploiting it. Acheson believes that regulation was always an important aspect of the lobster fishery.

Fifty years ago lobster fishing was a summer only activity, undertaken by small groups of men who were confined to very small territories and defended them vigorously. The early lobstermen worked from sloops or dorys; winter fishing was all but impossible and even in summer the lobstermen could never venture far. They mapped the sea bottom and located the lobster holes with a lead line. Since a family's income was dependent upon a very small stretch of inshore water and a good measure of experience, territorial boundaries were vigorously defended; fishing rights were held by small bands of kinsmen and passed directly from father to son. This strictly regulated system began to change as technology broadened its options.

By the 1950s, motorboats, depth finders and improved navigation aids had made territorial expansion perfectly feasible, and by the 1960s increasing demand had made intensification of the fishery highly desirable. The result has been predictable. By the mid-1980s the Maine lobster fishery was showing signs of extreme over-exploitation. Regulation was urgently needed. But what sort of regulation? The only proposal that found general approval is one limiting the numbers of traps a lobsterman may set, but since it had been shown that trap limits have no effect on the size or composition of the total catch, serving principally to reduce the lobsterman's costs (and thereby increase his profits), clearly other measures were needed as well. The biologists said an increase in the legal size limit was essential; anthropologists such as Acheson recommended that the lobstermens' own territorial arrangements should be formalized in some way; administrators suggested limiting entry to the industry, such as had been done in the state of Massachusetts, where existing commercial licences are renewed while those not renewed are cancelled and new licences issued at a rate of 80 per year from a waiting list that currently had nearly 3,000 names on it – so that anyone wanting to join the Massachusetts lobster fishery will have to wait well into the next century. Some sort of tax was proposed, with universal condemnation from the lobstermen on the grounds that they, not the government owned the fishery. 'No man can collect rent on a house he doesn't own', said one man, 'and the government can't collect a tax on the ocean'.

Ownership is the crux of the matter. If the lobster fishery is truly a common resource, owned by the nation, then the government has a perfect right to legislate for its control. But patently it never has been a common resource since the New Englanders started exploiting it, though the rights to its use have never been formalised to the same extent as land rights. In the confusion between common and private ownership, the lobstermen have seen their resource over-exploited and their rights eroded. They have complained, and occasionally have taken the law into their own hands. Now they are caught in an uncomfortable bind – for accepting the protection of the law means tacitly handing the resource over to the control of the government and abandoning their claim to private rights.

CHAPTER SEVEN

THE SEASHORE

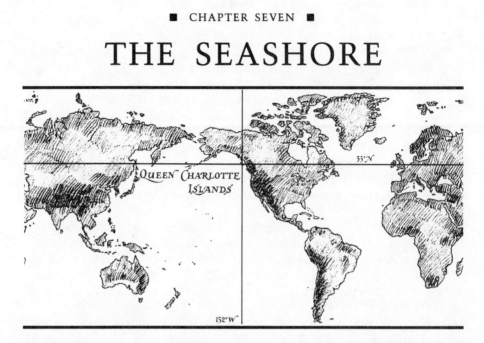

In 1776 Captain James Cook made his third voyage to the Pacific, at the command of the Crown and with instructions to head for the northern limits of the Pacific, where he was to search out the northwest passage which, it was believed, must link the Pacific Ocean to Hudson's Bay and the Atlantic. Immense strategic, political and economic advantage would accrue to the nation that discovered and controlled a short-cut between the Pacific and the Atlantic. Cook did not find a way through the ice beyond the Bering Straits, and was murdered on the shores of the Sandwich Islands (now Hawaii) on the return journey, but he did discover an exceptionally valuable resource on that fatal voyage – the thick lustrous fur of the sea otter which inhabits the waters of the northwest Pacific coast.

When Cook's ships had anchored off the southwest coast of what is now called Vancouver Island in February 1778, his crews had been at sea for the best part of two years, their clothing was badly worn and quite inadequate for a voyage in the arctic regions they were scheduled to explore. For the exchange of a few trinkets, the ships' companies acquired a quantity of furs from the Indians, which served well as clothing and bedding during the voyage to the north. While calling at Macao on the China coast to re-provision for the voyage home, Cook and his crews found that the best of these furs – the prized sea otters – were each worth several years of a seaman's wage. In all, £2,000 was paid 'for what was in the ships', Cook reports in his journal, 'and that after at least two-thirds of the quantity we had originally got from the Americas were spoiled and worn out, or had been given away and otherwise disposed of'.

'The rage with which our seamen were possessed to return... and, by another cargo of skins, to make their fortunes, at one time was not far short of mutiny', Cook reported, going on to propose that a good return could be made on the £6,000 that he estimated would be needed to purchase and equip two ships suitable for trading between China and northwest America. The cost of the necessary barter goods was 'scarcely worth mentioning', he wrote, pointing out that 'six of the finest skins purchased by us were got for a dozen large green glass beads, yet... the fancy of these people for articles of ornament is exceedingly capricious', he went on, suggesting that since iron goods are the only sure commodity it would be a good idea to take along 'five tons of unwrought iron, a forge and an expert smith, with a journeyman and an apprentice to forge such tools as the Indians were most desirous of.... To this might be added a few gross large-pointed case knives, some bales of coarse woollen cloth... and a barrel or two of copper and glass trinkets'

The sea otter is the delightful, playful creature that is often seen on film performing its trick of cracking open sea urchins with a stone on its belly while floating on its back. Its fur is smooth and short-haired, glossy jet-black flashing with silver when blown open; the pelt of a full grown animal is about 150 cm. (5 ft) long and between 60 and 80 cm. (2 ft and 2 ft 6 in.) wide.

It is difficult to give a measure of the trade in sea otter furs from the northwest coast of America to China following Cook's discovery of the potential market, but the following instances taken from voyage reports and from Paul Phillips' review of the subject in his two volume work on the fur trade do provide an indication of the terrible depredations that the animal suffered. The first ship expressly intended to exploit the trade, a British owned vessel of 60 tons named the *Sea Otter*, sailed from the China coast in April 1785 and was back by December of the same year with 560 skins which sold in Canton for 20,600 US dollars. In 1785 two vessels also set sail from France, ostensibly on a voyage of exploration but ultimately collecting 600 sea otter skins 'of very inferior quality' it is reported, which sold in Canton for a mere $10,000. Meanwhile, in 1786, eight British vessels sailed from China, and during the succeeding years disputes arose among the competing parties involved as to which had the greater 'right' to collect skins along the northwest coast. Those with trading licences issued by the East India Company or the South Sea Company claimed exclusive rights; others avoided the issue by flying the Portuguese flag and selling their skins at Macao instead of Canton. A trading station was established at Nootka Sound, on the west coast of Vancouver Island in 1787, from which thousands of skins were shipped out. Prime pelts cost a few cents – paid for in trinkets and ironware, especially chisels – and fetched more than $100 each. The trade was generally peaceful, though the Indians soon acquired a reputation for wily theft, and as competition for skins increased among traders the Indians became more demanding, haggling from ship to ship for the best terms. There were clashes, and several bloody incidents mark the history of the maritime fur trade.

In 1787 the New Englanders joined the trade, sailing round Cape Horn to collect skins on the northwest coast, then setting course for Canton, where they sold the skins and purchased tea, porcelain and silks for an even more profitable voyage home to New York or Boston. In 1790, Captain Robert Gray acquired 200 prime skins for 200 chisels, and subsequently sold them in Canton for $100 each. In 1791 Captain Joseph Ingraham obtained 1400 sea otter skins, many of them at a rate of three for each of the polished wrought iron collars that the ship's blacksmith made by twisting together three lengths of half-inch diameter iron rod. Between 1793 and 1818, over 100 American vessels were engaged in the northwest coast trade. Huge profits were made. One voyage returned $120,000 profit on an investment of $40,000; another made $156,743; another $206,650.

From about 1800, the sea otter trade was conducted almost entirely by American ships, and one of very few available estimates suggest that they bought and sold at least 100,000 skins in the eight years between 1804 and 1813 alone. 'Vast herds of sea otters' were located along the shores of Alaska, and so long as the Russian authorities claiming control of the territory allowed, Aleutian Indians trapped them for the Americans by the thousand – virtually to the point of extinction. Widespread and indiscriminate slaughter made a collapse of the sea otter trade inevitable. Shipments fell to 6,200 skins in 1814, to 2,488 in 1820, and down to just 300 in 1832.

Meanwhile, as sea otters became more difficult to find, the Indians satisfied their needs from less demanding sources of trade. Salmon and beaver were much more readily available, and found a steady market with the traders who by then had reached the Pacific coast by the overland route. The Hudson's Bay Company established its first trading post on the coast in 1827, and thereafter became an increasingly important conduit of the northwest fur trade. The Americans continued to compete, sea otter skins were still highly valued, but the period of fantastic maritime trade was finished, having lasted little more than 25 years.

The fur traders took a luxury item from the northwest coast, but they hardly touched the resource base that had enabled the region to support a high population density. While settlers in New England had declared themselves owners of land, and had assumed the right to impose and administer laws that ultimately drove the Indians close to extinction, no settlers were attracted to the northwest coast. Europeans hardly knew of the region's existence until the late 1700s, when sea otter furs became fashionable, and even the fur traders were mostly seasonal visitors, many of whom did not so much as set foot ashore. Some trading posts were established, it is true, but in these the whites were principally concerned with their trade and their safety; they did little or nothing to influence the Indians. Even missionary activity was slight. In terms of their lifestyle, the northwest coast Indians were left almost entirely to their own devices, and thus were uniquely able to incorporate the economic benefits of foreign trade in their cultural systems without suffering the disruptive effect of foreign influence that usually ensues.

There is no doubt that the fur trade affected the northwest coast Indians profoundly, but while some early authorities were inclined to believe that much of their culture – the clan system, and totem poles, for instance – did not exist before the time of contact and was, therefore, a product of the fur trade, the concensus today takes the view that the fur trade caused no fundamental change in the existing culture of the Indians, but simply produced 'an expansion and an intensification of prevailing cultural emphases and directions'. In other words, whereas the influence of settlers and trade in northeast America virtually swamped the Indians and their culture, on the northwest coast, the fur trade stimulated indigenous cultures to grow along existing and very distinctive lines.

From the Indians' point of view, the northwest fur trade simply brought added wealth to a society already organised around wealth. The new tools and the guns increased their capacity to harvest a resource – sea-otter fur – not crucially important to their welfare, and increased productivity brought increased returns. The extra wealth strengthened existing social and economic systems, since the chiefs, who controlled sea otter hunting and trade relations, became richer and more secure. More wealth meant a more active social, commercial and ceremonial life, with more demand for craft skills and artistic talent. 'Northwest Coast society rushed out to meet the sea otter trade, to use it, and to shape it to the society's own ends', writes anthropologist Joyce Wike.

This is not to diminish or gloss over the less favourable effects of the fur trade on the Indians of the northwest coast. The traders brought smallpox, venereal diseases and alcohol, along with the trinkets and iron tools; the guns they provided killed people as well as sea otters. Combined, the long-term detrimental effects of the fur trade served to reduce the Indian population of British Columbia, for example, from an estimated minimum of 80,000 (and probably substantially more) prior to contact, to 28,000 when the first accurate censuses were taken in 1885, and on down to 22,605 in 1929, since when numbers have steadily increased, to 40,800 in 1963 and 59,543 in 1982.

There was a time during that first hundred years, however, when despite the detrimental effects of the fur trade, the northwest coast Indian culture burgeoned. Like a river swelling on an incoming tide it embraced the extra flow and, still nourished by its own resources, achieved a brief moment of splendour. And then the tide swept it away.

The northwest Indian culture was most highly developed along the northern coast from Vancouver Island, and the mouth of the Fraser River, to southeast Alaska. Along this coast, rising sea levels in prehistoric times flooded the lower parts of deeply glaciated valleys, creating fiord-like inlets that penetrate 150 km. (90 mi.) or more into the coastal mountain range. Former high ground was cut off from the present mainland by the rising waters to form intricate chains of small inshore islands, and the large outlying masses of Vancouver Island, 482.7 km. (299.8 mi.) long, in the south and the Queen Charlotte Islands, 289.62 km. (179.85 mi) overall, to the north. The mountains rise sharply from the coast to a range of peaks reaching 3,000 m. (10,000 ft) and more, with long steep ridges cutting off the deep inlet of one drowned valley from the next. Innumerable mountain streams drain into the inlets, but very few large rivers provide valley

125

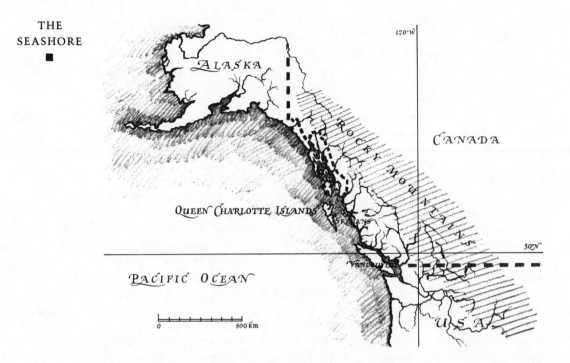

routes through to the interior. Between the Fraser river, at whose estuary the modern city of Vancouver is situated, in the south, and the Skeena river 800 km. (500 mi.) farther north, not a single river breaks through the coastal mountains to reach the sea. The inhabitants of these coastal regions were always, therefore, isolated from the interior. Furthermore, even short journeys from one part of the coast to another were more easily made by water than by crossing the steep ridges that cut off one valley from the next.

But land and climate combined to provide the means by which such journeys, and indeed much else of life along the northwest coast, could be effected: timber – for canoes, housing, clothing and equipment. Timber was the mainstay of northwest Indian life.

The predominantly cold conditions usually encountered 60 degrees north of the equator are modified along the British Columbia coast by a branch of the warm Japanese current, and by westerly airstreams which bring wet but mild weather in from the Pacific. Winter frosts are usually brief and snow does not lie long at low altitudes. Fog and mists are common, however, and the high mountains induce very heavy rainfall on their seaward slopes, especially during the winter months, when the westerly winds are strongest. Annual rainfall on the seaward slopes of Vancouver and Queen Charlotte Islands and on parts of the mainland reaches 2,500 mm. (100 in.).

This damp and relatively mild climate produces the most luxuriant forest growth in north America. Forests of spruce and cedar clothe the landscape from the shoreline to the mountain heights. Individual trees

126

grow to over 80 m. (260 ft) tall. Straight-grained, with trunks often two metres in diameter, the cedars and spruces provided good, easily worked timber. Trees of appropriate size were transformed into canoes, the sides smoothed in pre-contact times with shell, stone and elk-horn adzes, the interiors alternately charred with fire and dug out with hand tools. When the sides were sufficiently thin the canoe was filled with water which was then heated with quantities of hot stones; as the hull softened, cross pieces were forced in to give the canoe a greater beam than the diameter of the trunk from which it had been fashioned. Prow and stern pieces were hewn separately, and sewn to the hull with cord made of spruce root, through holes and grooves bored so deep with bird-bone gimlets that the stitching would be unnoticed unless deliberately looked for. The Haida Indians of the Queen Charlotte Islands were the most accomplished canoe builders, constructing some craft over 20 m. (65 ft) long, and capable of carrying 100 men, in which they frequently voyaged to the mainland and along the length of the coast.

Timber of course provided housing too, set along the shore, in villages of perhaps 30 or more buildings that might house a population of several hundred people. The longhouses – as they were known – were up to 20 m. (65 ft) wide and some were 100 m. (325 ft) long; the framework consisted of massive cedar tree trunks, up to eight metres (25 ft) high; lighter poles supported the roof, which was made of planks perhaps one metre broad and several centimetres thick – as were the walls. The planks were split from felled tree trunks with wedges.

Outside the houses stood massive totem poles, each carved with complex designs of heraldic significance which, in their stylized renditions of animals, birds and fish, represented the status and ancestry of the family living within. Inside the houses, furniture, plates and bowls were also made of wood. Cedar boards were adzed to minimal thickness, cut to a pattern, steamed and then ingeniously folded and stitched with spruce-root cord to form storage boxes. Watertight buckets were made in similar fashion and, in the absence of metal, wooden potboxes served as cooking utensils too, water in them boiled and food cooked as stones hot from the fire were dropped in. Baskets and cloth were woven from beaten cedar bark; fish hooks, fashioned from bent wood and bone, were ingeniously contrived to catch the different kinds of fish. Wood played such an important role in the everyday life of the northwest coast Indians that their enthusiasm for the iron tools – especially axes and chisels – offered by the fur traders is easily understood. At first contact the exchange of a few skins for items of such utility must have seemed an extraordinarily good bargain; after all, skins were an element of the natural resource – there for the taking.

Women gathered a rich harvest of vegetables and berries during the summer, a good proportion of which was preserved to provide a much-needed element of vegetable food in the winter diet. Nettle leaves, bracken roots and edible seaweed were gathered freely, but tracts of land especially rich in valued wild produce were claimed as private property, and payment was demanded of outsiders wishing to exploit them. Patches of wild clover root, for instance, were fenced and weeded to encourage good growth, while wild hyacinth bulbs, which grew prodigiously in the south, were a medium of barter with northern groups.

Elk, deer, mountain sheep, goats, bears and other animals were hunted to varying degrees, but nowhere in the coastal regions did hunting provide a major part of the diet. Fur, horn, bone and sinew were the principal objectives of the hunt and, indeed, some of the tribal groups are believed to have had a definite aversion to meat and to have held those who ate it in low regard.

Throughout the region, fish was the most important source of sustenance, making the northwest coast a classic example of the ecotone and its benefits: the resources of the land – principally timber – providing the means of living; and the resources of the sea – fish – sustaining life itself.

There was a seasonal round to the fishing. From March to June halibut were caught in large numbers with set lines attached to floats, or with weighted hooks trolled behind slow-moving canoes. Cod were speared after being lured to the surface with a bait of live herring. Sometime between March and May, shoals of herring swam into the bays and inlets to spawn, where they were caught in nets, or, if the shoals were especially dense, 'raked' from the water with long flat-sided poles to which rows of sharp bone spikes had been fitted. A single sweep of the fish-rake could transfix several herring. When the herring were about to spawn, leafy hemlock branches were sunk in the shallow waters they habitually used, and the spawn subsequently collected from the branches to be dried and stored.

In spring the candlefish, or olachen, just 20 cm. (8 in.) or so long but rich in edible oil, came from the sea into the rivers to spawn. When the fish were running, great numbers were caught each day in bag nets extended across the rivers. The candlefish were left to decay for a week before they were boiled in wooden troughs or canoes with heated stones, the oil was then skimmed from the surface, squeezed from the boiled fish, and stored. Candlefish oil keeps well, and was an important supplement to winter diets otherwise very low in fats, but large candlefish runs occurred only on relatively few rivers, and then not every year, so that the large quantities of oil produced in favourable years would become items of an important and far-flung trade in subsequent poor years.

Mammals were taken from the sea too. Seals and sea-lions were usually harpooned or clubbed when they came ashore early in the year. Porpoises and seals were also harpooned from canoes and the sea otter – very wary – was sometimes found sleeping on the surface and harpooned immediately, but more often had to be pursued for hours before it could be shot with an arrow as it surfaced to breathe. Some Indians, notably the Nootka, hunted whales – an extremely risky undertaking to which much prestige and ritual was attached.

The several species of salmon that ascend the rivers to spawn were the most important resource that the sea provided. And the fishery is still a resource of prodigous proportions; in 1985 British Columbia's commercial

fishery, for instance, landed 104,013 tonnes of salmon – a good indication
of the fish stock that was available each year to the 80,000 Indians
estimated to have inhabited the northwest coast prior to contact (by
comparison, Government statistics reveal that the fishery 'directly supported' about 22,000 people in 1986, and another 25,000 'indirectly').

The Pacific salmon, unlike their Atlantic cousins, return to the river of
their birth to spawn only once, and invariably die shortly thereafter. Since
the spawn of only a very small percentage of the run would suffice to
replace the entire stock (each female produces about 1500 eggs per kg. –
700 per pound – of bodyweight), all but a very small percentage of the fish
entering the rivers are available to feed whoever can catch them. Such is
the bountiful surplus that the ocean brings to the coast of northwest
America.

Chinook, sockeye, coho, pink and chum – the different species of
salmon arrive in their thousands at the estuaries of tidal rivers at different
times of year, providing an almost continuous run of some fish from March
to December, but most intensively during the spring and autumn. At the
height of the runs, narrow stretches of river are literally packed with
salmon, fat and in finest condition, fighting their way towards the
spawning beds upstream. At such places, at such times, they could be
speared, netted, gaffed and otherwise lifted from the water, but dams and
traps were always more effective. The catch that particular sites should
provide, the time of year and day on which they could be exploited most
profitably, and the habits of the various salmon species, were all known in
thorough detail. Husbandry was practised too. The Nootka, for instance,
would re-stock streams on which the run seemed to be failing with spawn
from other beds, which they carried to the depleted stream in moss-lined
boxes.

The salmon resource, though huge, was not universally available,
however; nor was it the common property of all who lived along the coast.
River dam sites, estuaries, and even open water were held and recognised
to be the private property of individual groups. Those who held very
productive sites had in them the wherewithal to barter for goods they did
not possess in such quantity; conversely, groups that had limited or no
access to salmon trapping were thereby motivated to produce something
they could barter for a share of the resource. Salmon, dried, smoked or
otherwise preserved, was the one essential item that a group had to have in
store, in sufficient quantity, by the late autumn if it was to survive the
winter, when fresh food of any kind – terrestrial or marine – was distinctly
hard to come by. Thus, like villagers in the Swiss Alps, the northwest coast
Indians depended upon a storage strategy. Salmon was their mainstay, and
probably the main component in a network of trade linking numerous
groups along the coast long before the fur traders arrived on the scene.

Survival on the northwest coast depended very heavily upon cooperative
effort. From felling a tree to catching and preparing enough salmon while
they were available and in best condition, there was little that one
individual – or indeed one family – could handle alone. Accordingly, social
groups tended to be large enough to ensure an adequate level of available

labour at all times. Village and settlement groups remained relatively small, nevertheless, (perhaps as a result of splits that arose from internal feuding as numbers increased), with no overall political organisation uniting them. Each village group was effectively a law unto itself. And, it has to be said, conflict and warfare and the taking of captives to provide slave labour at home seem to have been as characteristic of interactions between groups as was the mutually beneficial barter and exchange of goods.

The resources of each village – its fishing, hunting and collecting grounds – ostensibly belonged to a few families, whose leaders were accorded the status of chiefs, along with a good deal of prestige and privilege. The chiefs regulated the affairs of the village community, controlled its productive activities and determined its relationships with neighbouring groups. They could initiate ceremonies, and were entitled to assume traditional crests and insignia as their family devices to be carved on canoes, housefronts and totem poles. Status and privilege were highly respected. Within and between communities there was a distinct under-standing of chiefly ranking, and a chief's position in the hierarchy directly affected the standing of all his family members in their communities. But rank was not a family arrangement that passed to an individual at birth. It could pass from generation to generation within a family line, but the assumption of rank placed considerable obligations upon the individuals involved, and since there was always rivalry and competition for and between the various ranks in the hierarchy, even maintaining a particular status inevitably involved still more obligations. If one individual felt more entitled than a relative to hold the rank of family chief, for instance, then he would strive to take over the position. If one chief felt more powerful than a neighbour, he would endeavour to demonstrate the fact.

The means by which rank was achieved and maintained was the *potlatch*, a Chinook Indian word meaning 'gift' which has become the accepted term to describe this aspect of northwest Indian culture, although, according to one author, the true Indian word is not potlatch but *passapa*, which also means gift, but more precisely 'a gift with an elastic string attached to it, so that it will come back with interest'.

Within every family aspiring to chiefly status, every important social event demanded a distribution of gifts to other members of the clan and community – the birth of a child, the naming of a young person, the assumption of a predecessor's rank, the completion of a new house, the raising of a totem pole – and the more a man gave away, the greater right to hold rank he demonstrated. Occasionally property was destroyed as well as given away; in especially profligate displays of generosity, a chief might deliberately hack a canoe to pieces, break his most precious possessions and pour quantities of olachen oil onto to the fire so that flames leapt to the rafters and no witness could deny that here was a man who, in effect, had money to burn.

There was, however, a catch to all this generosity – not so much for the donor, whose status was assured by his extravagant gestures, as for the recipient, to whom custom denied any right of refusal while at the same time imposing an obligation to return the gift or gesture at some future date – with interest. 'Gifts make slaves', the French anthropologist Claude Levi-Strauss once remarked, and in the case of the northwest coast Indians this was especially true. The gifts people received at the potlatch were not really gifts at all, but might more accurately be described as enforced loans at a very high rate of interest. Whatever gifts a man had received, or gestures he had witnessed, he would be expected to return with greater generosity or profligacy – to do otherwise would be to admit the greater glory of the initial donor. Thus at any one time the communities might be both riven and linked by an intricate network of status rivalry and obligation: a dynamic situation in which those aspiring to assume a rank to which they might be entitled must accumulate a good deal of material wealth before they could do so, while those already holding high rank must always be ready to counter a challenge. And the giving itself was tempered by the awareness that, while a gift might be returned twofold, this in its turn would have to be returned at some future date – fourfold. The restraint that the potlatch imposed upon the ambitions of chiefs among the Indians of the northwest coast echoes, conversely, the restraint to which the lobstermen of the east coast are subject as they contemplate invading a neighbouring territory or cutting loose a trespasser's traps – if the gesture is overdone it is very likely to rebound upon its progenitor.

During the pre-contact days from which the potlatch originated, the gifts were, of course, derived from the natural resource – food, oil, skins, canoes and carvings, for example, along with slaves taken in raids on hostile groups and, most precious of all, flat, shield-like ceremonial objects beaten from the nuggets of natural pure copper that were found in certain parts of the region. Under these circumstances, the capacity to host a potlatch was directly related to a family's ability to accumulate a conspicuous surplus of natural produce over and above its subsistence needs. In these terms one might say that the potlatch provided an incentive to exploit natural resources to the full, while the environment itself served to regulate the social ambitions of the people involved. A chief's generosity was always limited by the productivity of the territory he controlled, by the extent to which he could barter for produce not immediately available to him, and by his capacity to commission the construction of material goods such as canoes and ceremonial items. Therefore, along with its obvious social function of defining resource ownership, establishing rank hierarchies and maintaining bonds between individuals and groups, the potlatch of pre-contact times also served the very important function of encouraging production and distributing surplus produce more broadly through the barter system than would otherwise have been the case. Not all surplus produce stored well anyway, and much might otherwise have gone bad. Furthermore, the potlatch would have served to even out annual variations in the availability of resources throughout the region. This was particularly significant in the case of the salmon.

Overall, the annual salmon migrations are always substantial – but they vary considerably from river to river and from year to year. Canadian Department of Fisheries statistics for the rivers exploited by 16 distinct

131

groups of Southern Kwakiutl Indians, for instance, have shown that, over a period of 17 years, the median number of salmon returning to spawn in the various rivers ranged from 5,400 up to 241,000, while the actual number of fish arriving in any one year varied from less than half to more than double the median number. Setting these assessments of salmon resource size and variability against what is known of early population size and relative cultural ranking of the 16 groups, anthropologists Leland Donald and Donald Mitchell found a 90 percent correlation, suggesting that control of a large and/or less variable salmon resource enabled a group to sustain a larger population, accumulate more goods and thus hold the potlatches that granted them high status and prestige. Correlation does not necessarily prove causation, as Donald and Mitchell are careful to point out, but their findings do support the idea of the potlatch as a cultural device serving to distribute produce and stabilise social relationships in an environment that was always subject to wide and unpredictable fluctuations in the availability and amount of the resources it provided.

So long as they subsisted on their own renewable resources – the fish, the trees, berries, roots and furs – the northwest Indians were part of a closed system. Their social relationships were determined by the potlatch, their numbers and ambitions were tempered by the constraints of the environment. But the fur trade changed all that. Within decades, the iron chisels and other foreign elements that the traders bartered for skins had ruptured the system. Goods that had previously circulated within the system and maintained a balance between the demands of the people and the supply capacity of the environment, poured out to satisfy the demands of a quite foreign system. As the resource was depleted, demands upon it were distorted, and cultural aspirations were exaggerated. The introduction of foreign goods effectively transformed the potlatch from a social strategy operating to the benefit of the system, into a cultural artifice that could be exploited by ambitious men.

By the time the first serious anthropological studies of the northwest Indians were undertaken in the 1880s, potlatch exchanges were no longer measured in the produce of the system itself but in the cheap white woollen blankets that the agents of the Hudson Bay Company supplied. A boy was obliged to distribute several hundred blankets among his clan on assuming the name to which he became entitled at the age of 12. One copper shield alone was valued at 7,500 blankets in 1893; another was said to be worth 6,000, another 5,000.

There is nothing inherently wrong with blankets; they keep a person warm, are easily stored and will not go bad. But, of course, along with everything else that the traders offered to the northwest Indians, they were an import that could only be acquired by the export of some natural product from the system. First it was furs, then it was food, labour and souvenirs. Social aspiration, however, remained largely unchanged. The acquisition of privilege and prestige was still the motivating force of northwest Indian society, and the potlatch was still the medium by which privilege and prestige were acquired.

Subsequently, as the population fell drastically from the effects of

132

disease, the potlatch became a grotesque exaggeration of its former self. No longer tied to the resource base by the need to sustain large numbers of people on a fluctuating resource, no longer entirely dependent on the closed system for the goods that were to be given away or destroyed, ambitious individuals among the survivors used the potlatch to vie for the prestigious positions that the ecological balance of the system had previously defined. It is from this period that the accounts of potlatch excesses are derived. Thousands of blankets, bags of flour, sides of salmon, gallons of oil, given away, thrown away, and destroyed. 'Fighting with property', one anthropologist has called it; a 'will to superiority' and 'unabashed megalomania', wrote another.

A shortcoming of the early interpretations and eye-witness accounts of the potlatch is that the observers were principally concerned with the social context of the phenomenon, attempting to understand its effects on social relationships while overlooking the significance of its original, environmental context. The post-contact potlatch was, no doubt, a bizarre and fascinating affair, but it was an aberration: more an example of what can happen to cultural strategies when their context is distorted by foreign influence, than a record of pristine cultural practice.

By the time academics began to consider the complexity and social significance of the potlatch it was already far removed from its environmental context, and, like a fish out of water it floundered extravagantly, stranded on the shores of a foreign cultural system for which it was not at all well adapted. To the white colonial administrators of British Columbia the potlatch was little more than an extraordinarily profligate waste of resources that should be stopped, and it was eventually outlawed under the Indian Act of 1874. A revision of the Indian Act passed in 1951 omitted the sections banning the potlatch, but by then the ceremony – like so much else of the northwest coast Indian culture – was little more than a folk memory.

There lay the town of Skedans....
And he told his son-in-law to bring him a box which was near the wall. And, when he brought it over to him, he took four [more boxes] out of it in succession, and began pulling from the innermost the feather clothing of an eagle. Then he gave him one among them in which fine black feathers were mixed with white.

Then he went outside, put it on, and flew up to a high frame in front of the house. He flew easily. Then he flew down.... then he sat at Skedans point....

By and by some children came to him. And the children shot up at him with blunt arrows. But every time they shot at him he sat lower down.

Presently the boys were forbidden to shoot, and the grown people began shooting at him. Every time they shot at him he came lower. When a big crowd was about him, he seized one person by the top of his head. And, when he flew up with him, some one seized his feet. In the same way they all seized one another's feet until he flew up with the whole town. Then he flew seaward with them and let them fall there. They became islands. The town of Skedans became empty.

This is part of a Haida story recorded by John Swanton of the Smithsonian Institution during the winter of 1900-01, in the Queen Charlotte Islands.

133

It was related by the chief of a clan known as Those-born-at-Skedans, and is but one of close on a hundred Haida texts and myths that Swanton recorded.

It is estimated that more than 8,000 Haida Indians were living on the Queen Charlottes when they were visited by Captain George Dixon in August 1787. Dixon was the first fur trader to explore the region and he named the islands after his ship and his Queen. Less than a hundred years later, the official census of 1885 put the total population at 800 men, women and children living in a scattering of small settlements around the island shores. In the following decades, numbers dwindled still further and shortly before 1900 the survivors of the dying Haida villages were persuaded to abandon their ancestral homes and join the remnants of the Haida Indian population in two main centres – Skidegate and Old Masset. The 1915 census counted just 588 individuals; by 1982 numbers had increased to 1,634 – though only 838 were actually living on the islands at the time of the census and most of those were concentrated around the main population centres.

In recent years, the increase in Haida numbers has been accompanied by strident calls for increased recognition of Haida identity and rights. Like a number of Indian tribes in Canada, the Haida never signed a treaty formally ceding their rights to the government and still see themselves as the beneficiaries of a Proclamation issued by King George III in 1763 which reserved 'such parts of our Dominion and Territories... not having been ceded to or purchased by Us' for the Indians' exclusive use. Though subsequent legislation was supposed to nullify the terms of the 1763 Proclamation it left loopholes large enough for some tribes to win multi-million dollars awards from the government. The 327 Fort Nelson Indians, for instance, have concluded a long-term $100 million royalty deal on the natural gas that will be extracted from beneath their ancestral lands in the foothills of the northeastern Rockies. In the early 1980s the Haida Indians began campaigning for a deal of similar proportions on the oil and gas that lies beneath the offshore waters of the Queen Charlottes, and the Canadian government responded by putting a moratorium on all oil exploration and development in the region. The Haida are also calling for a greater interest in the fish and timber resources of the islands.

Success in these claims would re-establish Haida identity, they say. It would also make some individuals very rich. Meanwhile, the ancestral village sites remain deserted, and rarely visited – mere patches of shoreline that seemed to have shrugged off virtually all sign of human habitation.

In late November, when a rare day of clear sunshine and a calm breeze permits a landing at Skedans, deer tracks across the sandy north beach are the most immediate sign of occupation, and where old photographs show dugout canoes hauled up before a line of totem poles and houses on the south shore, a mass of logs now rolls ponderously against boulders in the high-tide swell. The village site was very well chosen. A narrow neck of land extends seaward from high wooded cliffs which provide shelter from northwest gales, while the crescent-shaped beaches on the north and south shores would permit the landing and launching of canoes in virtually any weather. Halibut, herring, cod and salmon are plentiful in season and the rocky shores are rich with abalone, scallops and mussels. Sizeable trees have grown up where the longhouses once stood. Moss covers the lengths of rotting timber that lie about the grassy depressions where families spent their time together. There are no voices, beyond what is heard in the slap of the sea and rolling logs, but a sense of the stories they told is very strong: 'There lay the town of Skedans...'.

Young trees have grown up around the totem and mortuary poles that are still standing – the rough bark of living trees enwraps smooth weathered carving. Where a pole has fallen, a tree actually stands growing from the base; one long thick root stretches along the upper surface of the pole and lateral roots drop down each side like cords lashing it to the ground, as though fearing it might disappear, as has so much else of the Haida world.

To a European eye, accustomed to seeing art and artifacts preserved in museums, where they will be venerated for generations to come, it is profoundly unsettling to see such rare items decaying back into the environment that bore them. Unsettling, not because they will be lost forever, but because the sight provokes the thought that decay is the more natural, least disruptive and possibly most appropriate fate.

In the hollowed end of one fallen mortuary pole there is a human skull, completely covered with a skin of soft green moss. The skull lies on its right side, blind eyes turned away from the sea and the offshore islands that the chief of Those-born-at-Skedans had spoken of – and an eagle circles the bay until a thermal lifts it westward and out of sight.

CHAPTER EIGHT

HUNTER GATHERERS

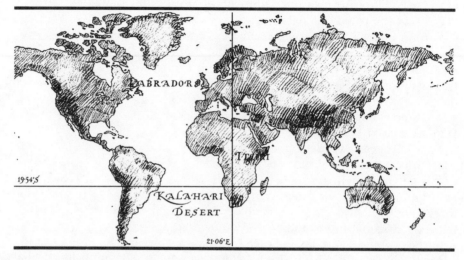

The day-to-day life of individuals depends as much upon what they *believe* to be right, proper and consequent as it does upon what they *know* about their physical requirements and the world they inhabit. Religion, prophecy, divination and magic are powerful forces in the ordering of every human society. Among many groups of people, special powers of counsel and prophecy are vested in particular individuals. And the shaman, medicine man, witch doctor and priest inspire faith in their pronouncements with the aid of ritual, ceremony, oaths, a scattering of bones or the bloody slaughter of an animal.

Divination and magic are forms of belief that seem to call upon powers beyond the capacity of human reason, and which arouse a shiver of apprehension. No one who has had a divining stick placed in their hands, and felt it pulling down over a bowl of water, can deny the power of the occasion. Perhaps it was just a trick, perhaps it really happened – whatever the case, it demonstrated a powerful capacity for belief. And some people who were children in London during the post-war years still have vivid memories of Sunday afternoons, when, after a tea of mustard-and-cress sandwiches with a plate of cockles and winkles from the cart in the street, an aunt would swirl the dregs in the bottom of the teacup, tip off the excess liquid, and then proceed to read future events from the pattern that the tea leaves had formed around the inside of the cup. Perhaps it was just an entertainment for when conversation flagged in the days before television, but it made a strong impression on young minds.

No one reads the tea leaves any more – it's not only flavour that teabags have banished from the English ritual of afternoon tea.

The beliefs that pervade human society have been extensively recorded,

136

beginning most impressively perhaps with the twelve volumes of James
Frazer's *The Golden Bough* published between 1890 and 1915, which
presented comparative accounts of ritual and belief from around the world,
and continuing in anthropological studies to the present day.

The function of these beliefs is less well studied, however, though the
cult of the Rice Goddess in Bali (see Chapter 3) is a good example of how
religion can have a very practical role. A convincing explanation of how
magic may also have a practical application has been drawn from Frank
Speck's classic study of the Naskapi Indians, published in 1935.

The Naskapi Indians occupied the inland regions of the Labrador Peninsula, a glaciated plateau of tundra, lake and forest bounded by Hudson Bay
to the west, the Atlantic Ocean to the east and the Gulf of St Lawrence to
the south. Eskimoes lived along the shorelines, while the Naskapi ranged
in small bands across the hinterland: semi-nomadic, following the seasonal round of hunting and gathering that the environment dictated. Speck
described the Naskapi as 'savages... to be ranked among the earth's
lowliest, even crudest peoples'. 'Sheltered only in draughty caribou-skin or
bark tents, clad in caribou-skin raiment, using mostly bone and wooden
implements, and professing neither political institutions nor government,
they follow no occupation or industry other than hunting wild animals and
fishing amid the most physically exacting and rigorous climatic environments of the globe,' he wrote. Speck judged the 'one yearning of the
Naskapi mind [to be] subsistence while living and postponement of death.'
Unlike the better- known Indian tribes of north America they had no
resonant history of warfare, nor the pursuit of property, territory or
retribution to give death a gloss of honour or glory, Speck remarks. The
Naskapi expected to die as a result of some accident or mishap from which
freezing, starvation or disease ensued. Child mortality was very high and
life expectancy very low. So, reconciled to the severity of life, with an open
eye too realistic to foster fear of death, the Naskapi attached their esteem
to the continuity of human existence: 'from great-grandparents to great-
grandchildren we are only knots in a string', they believed.

Among their neighbours 'Naskapi' was a term of disdain, denoting an
afflicted and impoverished state of life totally lacking the fundamental
assets of possession, invention, or even opportunity. Numerous visits to
the Naskapi between 1908 and 1932 convinced Frank Speck, however, that
the disdain was entirely misplaced. He concluded that the severity of their
environment had inspired in the Naskapi a greater resourcefulness than
was to be found among their detractors 'who boast the protection of more
numerous acquired inventions'. Furthermore, he found their lives imbued
with a system of beliefs, magic and spiritual considerations fully as
complete and resourceful as the hunting strategies on which their lives
depended.

The Naskapi believed that men and animals differed only in their
outward form; inwardly they were identical, sharing a spiritual existence
that transcended physical differences and united them after death. Consequently, animal life was revered no less than human life. Killing an animal

137

was an extremely serious business, to be conducted in a manner that would incur no wrath, according to a set of principles more sensed than expressed. When coming upon animals undetected, a hunter was believed to be the beneficiary of some spiritual communication between himself and his prey. They met so that each might fulfil the other's destiny, and the killing was a devout act that left the hunter deeply indebted to the animal world for the sacrifice it had made. Respect for the animal continued after it had been consumed; certain bones could not be given to the dogs but had to be preserved in a safe place, or consigned to rivers.

'Failure in the hunt, the disappearance of game... with ensuing famine, starvation, weakness, sickness and death, are all attributed to the hunter's ignorance of some hidden principles of behaviour toward the animals, or his wilful disregard of them,' Speck records. Success was largely attributable to a hunter's ability to relate his knowledge and skills to the uncertain nature of the physical world around him, and since that world was believed to derive much of its substance from the spiritual domain, whose edicts were hidden from temporal view, the Naskapi hunter would turn to magic for the clues that might bring him success.

Divination was the principal form of magic that the Naskapi employed. Indeed, Speck describes divination as the Naskapi religion. It took various forms, generally involving the bones of the animal under pursuit. On a bear-hunt, for example, the movement of bear's patella (kneecap) placed round-side-down on a hot stone would indicate the likelihood of success; when hunting beaver, the number of chips made at the point of fracture as a beaver's tibia was broken told the hunter how many beavers he would catch; when fishing, the configuration of cod mandibles tossed onto the ground would suggest strategies that might prove successful.

Most important of all, however, was the Naskapi practice of heating a caribou shoulderblade over a fire until it cracked and burned, and then interpreting the pattern in terms of local geography and caribou concentrations as a means of deciding which direction the hunt should take. The caribou occupied the most vital and conspicuous position in the Naskapi world view – they could not have survived without it. When caribou were scarce and people beginning to starve, hunters would resort to shoulderblade divination every three or four days. First they would sing and drum and induce heavy sweating as a preliminary to sleep and dreams which they hoped would include some premonition of caribou and the hunt. If the dream had seemed auspicious, on waking they would take a clean caribou shoulderblade and hold it over the fire. As cracks and burns appeared on what was essentially a blank chart of the hunting territory, the hunter would read them in terms of local topography, caribou trails, and the actual route that he should follow. Speck records 19 instances of shoulderblade divination, 12 of them successful. Unsuccessful hunts were always attributed to some failure on the part of the hunter. If he did not find the promised caribou it was because he had interpreted topography or distance incorrectly. The bone itself prophesied falsely, the Naskapi believed, only when a hunter was guilty of deception or negligence.

Scapulimancy, as the practice of shoulderblade divination has been termed, is known from many parts of the world and has been the subject of extensive description and discussion, among which Speck's account of Naskapi scapulimancy is but one fairly typical example. Like others before and since, Speck himself merely stressed the capacity for belief that scapulimancy amongst the Naskapi demonstrated, and it was another scholar, Omar Khayyam Moore of Yale University who, in 1957, published a paper showing how Naskapi scapulimancy and magical practices did, after all, serve practical, rather than simply cultural ends.

Moore had been studying the processes by which humans solve problems and, while looking for examples of ineffective problem-solving techniques from which some insights might be gained, he turned to the anthropological literature on magic. Magic, he noted, was generally considered to be a notoriously ineffective way of attaining the ends its practitioners hoped to achieve and therefore, surely, a classic case of poor problem-solving. But instead of confirming the view that magic was an ineffective way of solving problems, Moore's review of the literature produced evidence suggesting that magic could, in fact, serve a practical purpose.

Naskapi scapulimancy, for instance, made the choice of where to hunt a random one, Moore said, and its function was to avoid the danger of hunters regularly returning to places where they previously had been successful and where, accordingly, the animals would become sensitive to human behaviour and would learn to avoid the hunters more effectively. Thus, Moore suggested, the apparently worthless practice of divination could be saving the Naskapi from success-induced failure.

Human beings are creatures of habit, tending to adopt regular patterns of behaviour, they need 'a functional equivalent to a table of random numbers if they are to avoid unwitting regularities in their behaviour which can be utilized by adversaries.' Reading the burnt shoulderblade introduced an unbiased, random element of chance to Naskapi hunting strategy, Moore suggested.

Whether or not the randomising strategy was the whole explanation of scapulimancy, and whether it could be applied to the magical practices of other societies, were questions that only further research could answer, Moore concluded, though in the case of the Naskapi, whose precarious existence depended on the day-to-day success of their hunting, he thought it 'unlikely that grossly defective approaches to hunting would have survival value.' In other words, if reading the shoulderblade had not produced long-term benefits, the practice would not have persisted.

Naskapi scapulimancy is a good example of a magical belief that serves a practical end, and as such it is an example of the human capacity for behavioural innovation. People are capable of formulating any number of strange ideas, not necessarily directed towards any particular end, but if they do have a practical application and are successful, they may persist. And if they persist long enough people will begin to believe in them.

The image of man as a violent and aggressive hunter has featured prominently in many popular accounts of human evolution and origin over

139

the past few decades, promoting the belief that the human capacity for violence is an inherited and therefore unavoidable consequence of the aggressive behaviour that had carried mankind through the evolutionary transition from ape to man. Books like Konrad Lorenz's *On Agression* (1966), Robert Ardrey's *African Genesis* (1961) and *The Hunting Hypothesis* (1976) were major vehicles of dissemination, and their thesis is typified by the fact that readers seeking a reference to *tools* in the index of *African Genesis*, for example, will find the instruction: '*see* Weapons'. The opening sequence of the film *2001*, in which the killer man-apes are seen eliminating their less able brethren, is another example of the way in which the idea of man's aggressive ancestry became established in the popular imagery of postwar western culture.

The origin of the killer man-ape belief can be traced back to Darwin, who wrote that the evolution of an erect stance would have rendered the progenitors of man 'better able to defend themselves with stones and clubs, to attack their prey, or otherwise obtain food', but it found its most forceful expression in the publications of Raymond Dart, the anatomist who in 1925 named a newly found fossil primate *Australopithecus africanus*, and described it as the link between ape and man hitherto missing from the story of human evolution.

During the 1930s, '40s and '50s australopithecine fossils were found at several sites in South Africa (and subsequently in East Africa as well), along with the fossil bones of many other animals. Several of the australopithecine skulls were crushed, as though by a hard blow to the head. The bones of baboons, antelope, pigs, horses, elephants, rhinoceros and other animals found in the cave sites likewise showed signs of violent treatment. Dart derived a theory of mankind's violent ancestry from this accumulating evidence which he set out with colourful eloquence in a paper entitled *The Predatory Transition from Ape to Man*.

The australopithecine ancestors of mankind were not fruit-eating, forest-loving apes, but creatures of sanguinary pursuit and carnivorous habit, Dart declared. They were 'human in their cave life, in their love of flesh, in hunting wild game to secure meat.... These Procrustean proto-human folk... differed from living apes in being confirmed killers: carnivorous creatures, that seized living quarries by violence, battered them to death, tore apart their broken bodies, dismembered them limb from limb, slaking their ravenous thirst with the hot blood of victims and greedily devouring livid writhing flesh.'

Dart believed that the evidence of ancestral violence he had found among the fossil assemblages of the South African cave sites explained what he saw as the predominantly aggressive behaviour of mankind. 'The loathsome cruelty of mankind to man forms one of his inescapable, characteristic and differentiative features; and it is explicable only in terms of his carnivorous, and cannibalistic origin.... The blood-bespattered, slaughter-gutted archives of human history from the earliest Egyptian and Sumerian records to the most recent atrocities of the Second World War accord with universal cannibalism, with animal and human sacrificial practices or their substitutes in formalized religions and with the world-

140

wide scalping, head-hunting, body-mutilating and necrophilic practices of
mankind in proclaiming this common bloodlust differentiator, this pre-
dacious habit, this mark of Cain that separates man dietetically from his
anthropoidal relatives and allies him with the deadliest of Carnivora'.

Not a word of academic support greeted Dart's theory. But as it was
dismissed from academic circles, Dart's killer-ape proposition found a
niche in the popular consciousness, to the extent that Robert Ardrey
described *The Predatory Transition from Ape to Man* as 'a paper that may
some day rank with the *Communist Manifesto* among those documents
which have contributed least to man's ease of mind'.

Since that time, however, further investigations have rather tended to
discredit the Dartian view of human origins bathed in blood. In the first
instance, detailed analyses of the fossil bones found in the caves have
shown that they accumulated naturally, over hundreds of thousands of
years. The bones had fractured under rockfalls and the sheer weight of the
assemblage. Furthermore, they were the remains of animals that had died
in the caves or else had been carried there by leopards or other predators –
or even by porcupines, who make a habit of dragging large bones back to
their dens to gnaw (leaving tell-tale signs). And as regards the australo-
pithecines, a definitive survey of the evidence published by Dr C.K.Brain of
the Transvaal Museum concludes that far from being the bloodthirsty
hunters of Dart's beliefs, these candidates for human ancestry were in fact
the prey of leopards.

Furthermore, close investigation of wild gorilla, chimpanzee and other
primate populations conducted since the 1960s have shown that man's
'anthropoidal relatives' are not such innocent consumers of vegetable food
alone as Dart would have his readers believe. They all eat flesh of some
kind from time to time, and the chimpanzees at Jane Goodall's Gombe
stream research station in Tanzania, for instance, have been observed
hunting in organised bands and eating meat with fair regularity. In the
literature, chimpanzees are described as frugivores – fruit-eaters – but at
Gombe the chimpanzees were seen to kill and consume 162 animals over a
13 year period, including monkeys, baboons, bush pigs and bushbuck.
Doubtless more kills passed unrecorded, but estimates based on available
data conclude that each chimpanzee eats about 10 kg. (22 pounds) of meat
a year on average and devotes about 10 percent of its annual feeding
activities to the pursuit, capture and consumption of other mammals –
which denotes a fairly high level of interest for animals that were believed
to subsist on fruit. In truth, the primates – including the human ancestor –
all probably inclined towards a omnivorous diet, without any exceptionally carnivorous tendencies.

Then there is evidence from contemporary groups of the hunter-
gatherers whose lifestyle is believed to closely approximate that of the
early human ancestor. In Dart's day the most intensively studied hunting
and gathering societies were the eskimos and the Indians of north America
and the Canadian arctic. Among these groups hunting was certainly
predominant, and what was known of hunting activities among the more
elusive Australian aborigines and African bushmen seemed to confirm the

141

belief that early man had been an out-and-out carnivore. Since then, however, intensive research among hunter-gatherers of tropical climes has shown that, where adequate vegetable food is available, these people are more inclined to gather than hunt.

In the far north, for much of the year there is no alternative to a diet of meat, but no one supposes that humanity evolved up there. Since Darwin's day, the equatorial regions of Africa have been deemed the most likely site of man's origin, a contention now well supported by fossil and genetic evidence, and studies of contemporary hunter-gatherer lifestyle and diet strongly suggest that hunting did not constitute a predominant activity for much of mankind's evolution, which implies that it was not bloodlust that carried the human ancestor across the transition from ape to man, as Dart and his advocates had believed.

But *Man the Hunter* is an image so deeply engrained in the popular consciousness that it was chosen as the title for one of the most highly regarded and most frequently quoted books in the anthropological literature, even though the book's contents stress the overwhelming importance of gathering, and of women, in the affairs of pre-agricultural societies. A survey of studies on 58 hunter-gatherer groups from around the world, compiled by Richard Lee, showed that only 11 (18.96 percent) were primarily dependent on hunting for their food, and only two of these – the Copper Eskimoes and the Chipewyan Indians of north America – did no gathering at all; among the other nine, gathering supplied at least 10 percent and up to 80 percent of the subsistence diet.

The survey also showed a direct correlation between the distance a group lived from the equator and their principal subsistence activity. In the arctic regions, above 60 degrees north, hunting (which included the pursuit of sea-mammals, such as seals and whales) was the major source of food; in the cool temperate latitudes, 40 to 59 degrees from the equator, fishing was most important, and in the temperate to tropical latitudes, zero to 39 degrees from the equator, gathering was by far the most common form of subsistence, supplying the staple diet for 25 of the 28 groups that lived in those latitudes.

The degrees of dependence upon hunting that the survey revealed can also be set against the degrees of temperature that people have to contend with. While gathering was the principal source of food among 75 percent of the groups living in mild to hot regions, where the annual average temperature exceeds 10°C (50°F), hunting was the dominant activity employed by 60 percent of the groups occupying very cold regions where the annual average temperature was less than 1°C (33°F). In this scheme of things hunting could well have been a strategy that was principally intended to provide the means of keeping warm, and only an incidental source of protein to begin with, though it subsequently became the strategy that enabled people to inhabit the more extreme climatic regions of the globe.

Nowadays the groups of people that subsist on either hunting, or fishing or gathering, or combinations of the three activities, are confined to those parts of the globe that have proved unsuitable (or uneconomic) for

agricultural endeavours. Before the innovations of planting crops and
domesticating certain animals began to impose a sedentary way of life
upon increasing numbers of people, sometime around 12,000 years ago, all
people were hunters and gatherers and, indeed, always had been. For by far
the greater proportion of the time that humanity, as recognised by over
three million years of fossil evidence, has existed, people survived by the
hunting and gathering lifestyle.

The three individuals who left their footprints across a mudpan 3.6
million years ago, where they became fossilised and were uncovered by
Mary Leakey's expeditions to Laetoli in 1978 and '79, walked upright in a
distinctively human fashion, but no stone tools have been found at Laetoli;
the earliest undisputed evidence of this innovative stage of human
evolution comes from deposits 1.9 million years old at Olduvai Gorge. The
Gorge is just one hundred kilometres (60 mi.) or so across the plain from
Laetoli, but the vast temporal distance separating the two sites suggests
that for about 1.7 million years – 50 percent of the time that people are
presently known to have existed – stone tools were not a feature of their
way of life. They may have used tools of wood or bone which were not
preserved as fossils; it is possible that the oldest stone tools have not yet
been found – nothing is proven. But the evidence provides good reason to
believe that the weapons Dart and Ardrey assumed to be the tools of early
man were lacking from the early stages of human evolution.

Around 12,000 years ago, when the human population of the world was
about ten million, all people were hunters and gatherers. Five hundred
years ago, when 350 million people inhabited the earth, only one percent
of them hunted and gathered their food. By 1987 the world population had
soared to 4.8 billion, of whom no more than 0.0001 percent still followed
the lifestyle that had nurtured humanity through over 99 percent of its
existence.

Since the advent of agriculture, the few people still following the
hunting and gathering lifestyle upon which scientists based most of their
suppositions about the evolution of human behaviour and culture have
been pushed relentlessly into the regions that no other groups wanted. By
the late 1800s, they existed nowhere else and seemed to support Thomas
Hobbes' contention that life in the raw was 'nasty, brutish and short'.

But it is quite illogical to suppose that people have always inhabited the
northern wastes of the Arctic, and that the Kalahari Bushmen had taken to
the desert by choice. When the entire world was available they doubtless
inhabited more congenial environments and, indeed, their survival in
some of the least productive environments that the world has to offer is in
itself testimony to the adaptability and resilience of the lifestyle they had
originally developed. In any case, subsequent research has shown that the
life of the hunters and the gatherers was neither so nasty, so brutish, nor so
short as had been supposed – even in what were judged the least congenial
environments.

The San people, frequently referred to as the Bushmen – a term which
has acquired derogatory connotations – once ranged across the entire

143

savannah region of south and eastern Africa. Since the turn of the century, however, they have been principally confined to the Kalahari desert in Botswana and Namibia, with only very small isolated populations – the Hadza and the Sandawe of Tanzania – surviving elsewhere. In total there are estimated to be about 50,000 San people in the Kalahari region, of whom no more than about 5,000 still follow the hunting and gathering lifestyle exclusively.

The average rainfall of the Kalahari ranges from 100- to 400 mm. (4 to 16 in.) per year, and droughts are frequent. Though the rainfall is sufficient to support a diversity and density of grass, scrub and woodland that quite belies the term 'desert', there is no natural permanent water. Seasonal pans and wells are sufficient to support animals and nomadic San alike throughout the desert, however, for much of the year, but the semi-nomadic groups that constitute most of the contemporary population are based around boreholes the government has sunk in areas such as that inhabited by the !Kung San of the northwest Kalahari, among whom Richard Lee conducted a 15 month study in the 1960s.

Lee's field research spanned the third year of one of the most extreme droughts ever recorded in southern Africa. The crops of Botswana's predominantly agricultural Bantu population had failed for the third successive year; 250,000 head of their cattle had died; and 180,000 people (30 percent of the national population) were being kept alive by a United Nations famine relief programme. And yet, throughout that period, the 466 !Kung San whom Lee was observing consumed on average 2,140 calories and 93.1 gm. (3.28 oz) of protein per person, per day. This intake amounted to 8.3 percent *more* calories and 55 percent *more* protein than Lee's estimate of the Recommended Daily Allowance for people of !Kung stature and activity. Moreover, the !Kung were able to satisfy their needs so plenteously with surprisingly little effort. Individual adults devoted a total of between 12 and 19 hours a week to the task of finding food, Lee's study revealed, and even the most energetic individual, a man who once went hunting on 16 out of 28 days, spent only 32 hours a week at the task.

A 32-hour week begins to approach the workload of a western bread-winner, but 12 to 19 hours is far below it. And yet, with so little effort, the !Kung were able to get more food than they needed from an environment rated among the harshest on Earth, at the height of a severe and prolonged drought. And not only that, the !Kung environment also sustained a number of Herero and Tswana agriculturalists of the surrounding region during that period, whom the famine relief programme did not reach, and whose women took to foraging for wild foods with the !Kung. Thus the area was actually supporting a larger population during the drought than it did in better times, with no adverse effects on the !Kung.

Lee found that vegetable food comprised from 60 to 80 percent of the total !Kung diet by weight, derived from a total of 85 plants species: the fruit, berry, melon or nut of 32 species; the root or bulb of 31 species; the resinous secretions of 16 species of tree; and the leaf, bean or seed of six species. Though all perfectly edible, not all of these vegetable foods were equally tasty or easy to collect, nor were they all available all year round, and this diversity of characterisics imposed its own logic upon the !Kung subsistence strategies. In the flush of growth that followed the summer rains the !Kung selected the tastiest and most easily collected food plants, and would travel some distance in search of them, bypassing the ones they did not like so much and thus leaving some kind of food everywhere. As the dry season advanced they gathered the best of the less attractive varieties they had located on previous foraging expeditions and in severely dry years were obliged to eat the plants they liked least of all (possibly deriving important trace elements from these rarely used items, Lee suggests).

The safety margin that the !Kung food preferences create is well illustrated by the fact that 90 percent of their vegetable diet comes from only 23 of the 85 plant species they know to be edible, leaving the produce of another 62 species (principally roots, bulbs, berries and melons) in store for hard times. Furthermore, one single item – the nut of the mongongo tree – supplies a full 50 percent of all the vegetable food that the !Kung eat, which reduces their dependence on the other 84 species yet again and enhances the subsistence capacity of their environment still more.

The role of the mongongo in !Kung diet matches that of cultivated staple crops such as rice, potatoes and maize in the diets of agricultural societies – though, while dependence on a single crop might be safe enough for a group of sedentary farmers, the strategy seems distinctly inappropriate to the requirements of subsistence hunters and gatherers in the harsh, marginal environment of the Kalahari. But here again, supposition based on common belief would be wrong. The mongongo is an altogether remarkable botanical phenomenon – more productive and more reliable than any comparable cultivated crop. The trees are drought resistant and long-lived. They stand in groves, where each year literally thousands of kilogrammes of nuts may be harvested. Even in exceptionally dry years, when cultivated crops would certainly fail, the mongongo will produce a reliable abundance of nuts. Furthermore, an extremely hard and durable shell protects the kernel from decay, so that the nuts may be harvested up to a year after they have fallen. But not only is the mongongo far more productive and reliable than cultivated crops – it is also far more nutritious.

Weight for weight, Lee reports, the mongongo contains five times the calories and ten times the protein of an equivalent unit of cooked rice or maize. The !Kung each eat about a handful every day – a modest enough portion weighing about 200 gm. (7 oz) which in fact provides a far from modest daily intake of 1,260 calories and 56 gm. (2 oz) of protein – the equivalent of 1.13 kg. (2.49 pounds) of cooked rice and nearly 400 gm. (14 oz) of lean beef. No wonder the !Kung have declined invitations to take up agriculture, Lee remarks. 'Why should we plant,' they ask, 'when there are so many mongongo nuts in the world?'

The nuts and roots, bulbs, leaves and fruit that comprise the greater part of the !Kung diet are gathered almost exclusively by women. Every three or four days the women will go out foraging – 12 to 19 hours per week in all –

145

and will usually bring back enough to feed their camp for the next two or three days. The camp comprises a small group of families, usually totalling between 15 and 25 individuals, Lee found. Available food is shared among all camp members, and when it is finished the women will go to gather more. The men, meanwhile, are no less active in the quest for food. They hunt, and like the women spend from 12 to 19 hours a week at the task. But they are far less successful, contributing only 32.24 percent of the calories and 26.98 percent of the protein that the !Kung consume each day – even though they devote the same amount of time and probably more energy to the task.

In a detailed analysis of effort and production over a period of time Lee found that women brought in 67 percent of the calories and protein that was eaten, while the men provided the other 33 percent. For every hour spent foraging a woman produced 2,000 edible calories; for every hour spent hunting a man produced only 800 calories. Thus the women's gathering activities were 2.5 times more productive than the men's hunting. Furthermore, it was far more reliable. The seven hunters in the camp observed by Lee devoted a total of 78 man-days to hunting during the period of his study and brought back meat on 18 occasions – once every 4.3 man-days, which in this instance means that whenever the men went off hunting there was a 1 in 4.3 *chance* of their bringing back some food. By contrast, whenever the women went out gathering there was a 100 percent *certainty* of their bringing back food.

In these terms it seems that hunting is hardly worth the effort. Indeed, if the women already bring in 67 percent of the food supply without exhausting the available resources, a little more effort (or male assistence) could dispense with the need for meat altogether. So why hunt?

For social reasons, it is often assumed. Hunting is a difficult and arduous undertaking and therefore provides an opportunity for men to prove themselves and establish the hierarchies of authority and respect that societies need. Furthermore, meat is tasty, comes in large packages and has to be prepared – so that a successful hunt provides an opportunity for people to gather together in mutual endeavour, sharing both effort and reward in a festive social occasion that will forge and reinforce bonds of mutual dependence and obligation. There may be some justification in these assumptions. Social factors are evident in the persistence of hunting among people who could get enough food by other means, but they are the consequence rather than the cause of the phenomenon. The cause is nutrition.

The human body requires a regular supply of between 40 and 50 different nutrients for its growth, operation and maintenance – 14 vitamins, 15 minerals, and quantities of protein, fat and carbohydrate – and some of them are best obtained from meat.

Meat is an especially useful source of proteins, some of which cannot be derived so readily from vegetable foods. Proteins themselves are made of amino acids, and combinations of about 22 different amino acids make up all the many thousands of different proteins the human body needs. Twelve of these amino acids can be assembled internally from nutrients in the food that is eaten, but the other ten have to be consumed ready made, as it were, and are therefore known as the 'essential' amino acids. When any one of the essential amino acids is absent from the diet, protein assembly ceases, regardless of how plentiful the others may be, and malnutrition sets in. All ten of the essential amino acids are found in plant foods, but not in the right proportions. In fact, the amino acids most needed by the human body are precisely those that are least abundant in plants. Some adjustment to these deficiencies can be achieved by eating combinations of plant foods. A quantity of cereals and beans eaten together, for example, more than doubles the amount of protein that can be assembled from the same quantity of either food eaten on its own. But this strategy – though common among agriculturalists long before it was scientifically understood – has been available only since people started cultivating crops; before then, and among non-agriculturalists today, meat has always been a better option.

Because the human body assembles exactly the right amounts of precisely the proteins it needs, human flesh would provide the best source of protein that people could eat. Not many do, however, and whatever the moral and ethical objections to cannibalism may be, an important reason for its lack of favour is that eating your own kind is a self-defeating exercise – reproduction could never keep pace with consumption. Fish, birds and animals in general are a more sustainable source of the proteins that people need.

Fat is another good reason to go hunting, and although the fads of western culture seem determined to eliminate it from the diet, fat does perform several important nutritional functions. Fat is essential for the absorption, transport and storage of vitamins A, D, E, and K, which respectively enhance vision, bone strength, fertility and blood coagulation, for instance. Children need two particular kinds of fat for their growth processes. Fat also aids the regulation of oxygen absorption; it accumulates in the body to provide a source of energy for times when sugars and starch are unavailable and, moreover, fat helps the body to metabolize lean meat. The dangers of a meat diet without fat have been described by Vilhjalmur Stefansson, who lived with the eskimoes and maintained excellent health on their diet of raw meat with plenty of blubber, but gives a graphic account of what happens to people obliged to eat only meat with little fat in it, such as rabbit: 'If you are transferred suddenly from a diet normal in fat to one consisting wholly of rabbit you eat bigger and bigger meals for the first few days until at the end of about a week you are eating in pounds three or four times as much as you were at the beginning of the week. By that time you are showing both signs of starvation and of protein poisoning. You eat numerous meals; you feel hungry at the end of each; you are in discomfort through distention of the stomach with much food and you begin to feel a vague restlessness. Diarrhoea will start in from a week to 10 days and will not be relieved unless you secure fat. Death will result after several weeks.'

Pre-agricultural societies were fully aware of the need for fat. Indeed, some north American Indians were known to hunt and eat creatures they would normally shun when particularly short of fat, while Australian aborigine hunters would abandon untouched the carcass of a kangaroo they had laboriously hunted and killed, if there was too little fat on it.

There are fats in plant foods too of course, and, as with proteins, there are feeding strategies that enable people to get the fats their bodies need from vegetarian diets (though such diets often include fish, eggs and dairy fats, it should be noted), but humans are fully equipped to deal with an omnivorous diet and meat is certainly the most convenient source of many of the nutrients they need. As Marvin Harris puts it in his book *Good to Eat* (1986), 'while plants food can sustain life, access to animal foods bestows health and well-being above and beyond mere survival'.

It seems certain that, although hunting and meat-eating were never the obsessive and bloodthirsty occupations that Raymond Dart proposed, the nutritional shortcut that meat provided was recognised at a fairly early stage in human evolution. Need established a taste for meat that has persisted ever since, and the !Kung's attitude to diet is typical of many societies: they 'eat as much vegetable food as they need, and as much meat as they can.' Lee concludes.

All in all, the work of Lee and other researchers has done much to eradicate the image of the life of man in nature as 'nasty, brutish and short'. On the contrary, hunters and gatherers have plenty of food and plenty of leisure time for games and dancing, folklore and other aspects of cultural life. And if the !Kung are anything to go by, many hunters and gatherers lived long enough to enjoy a full measure of all these things. In the total population of 466 men, women and children among whom he conducted his study, Lee established that no fewer than 46 individuals (17 men and 29 women) were over the age of 60, a proportion which, as Lee remarks, 'compares favourably to the percentage of elderly in industralized populations'.

The slightly Utopian image of well-fed, long and leisurely lives that modern studies of hunters and gatherers project does raise a puzzling question, however, to which science has not as yet been able to provide a full and wholly satisfactory answer. The question is this: if hunter gatherers such as the !Kung live in such beneficent circumstances, why are there not more of them? It is to be expected that an adequate food supply and long leisurely lives would combine to produce the largest possible population that the environment could support. But this is not the case. Hunter gatherers in general and the !Kung in particular seem to live in numbers comfortably below the carrying capacity of the environment – insofar as that can be assessed. How do they manage to regulate their population size so effectively?

Lee found that the long term population growth rate among nomadic San was a mere 0.5 percent a year and the birth interval between living children approximately four years, which suggests that caring for one child inhibited the production of another in some way. Lee thought that the burden of carrying one child on foraging excursions would be enough to discourage women from having another before the first could walk, but exactly how the women exercise this birth control is not precisely known. The mechanism could be purely social, a matter of restricting sexual intercourse, aborting unwanted pregnancies, or even killing babies.

Social mechanisms apart, Rose Frisch of Harvard University's Center for Population Studies, has proposed that biology is a significant factor in the maintenance of stable population size among hunter gatherers (and indeed other groups as well). Reduced fertility as a result of prolonged breast-feeding is the mechanism involved. The San, for instance, breast-feed their infants until they can walk, and since producing milk calls for an additional 1,000 calories a day, over and above a mother's own require-ments, such prolonged lactation is likely to depress a woman's nutritional status below that required for ovulation and conception.

The idea that nutrition affects fertility was in fact expressed by Charles Darwin in 1868, when he remarked that 'hard living retards the period at which animals conceive', that fertility is affected by variations in the food supply, and that lactating females do not fatten readily. Darwin was referring to domesticated animals, but Frisch's study shows that the principle is no less applicable to the human animal – and not only in the so-called 'natural' circumstances of the hunter gatherers. Her analysis of historical data shows that industrialized societies can be similarly affec-ted. The unexpectedly low population growth rates of some social groups in mid-19th century England and Scotland, for example, can be explained as being primarily due to low fertility resulting from 'undernutrition and hard living'.

Several thousand kilometres to the north of the Kalahari there is another vast natural environment that is still inhabited by substantial numbers of hunters and gatherers – the equatorial rainforest of the Congo Basin (a formal geographical term still used even though the river and the nation have been renamed Zaire). The forest is as drenched with rain as the desert is bleached by the sun, and, with the help of unvarying high temperatures, produces at least 20 times more vegetation per unit area each year (up to 5,000 gm of dry matter per square metre – about 9 pounds per square yard – in the rainforest, compared with between 10 and 250 gm in the desert), but the people and their lifestyle are essentially the same. San and Pygmy are both of small stature, with deep-golden rather than deep-brown skin colour, they both live in small bands and both subsist on the food they hunt and gather from the environment. But there are important differences too, and just as Lee's study of the !Kung contributed to a revision of knowledge and belief concerning the life and times of hunters and gatherers in general, so recent research has produced facts and figures that overturn several accepted beliefs concerning the Pygmies of the equatorial rainforest.

For a start, the Pygmies are not the remnants of an ancient forest-dwelling group from which humanity sprang, as popular misconception assumes. They are more likely remnants of Africa's widespread hunting and gathering groups which moved into the forest before the advancing herders and agriculturalists, just as the San moved into the Kalahari. It is

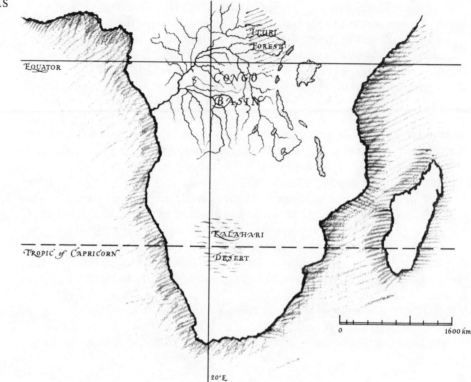

generally believed that the move began sometime before 2,000 years ago, and it is beyond doubt that modern Pygmies are highly dependent upon swidden farmers established in the forest, with whom they regularly trade labour, meat and honey for supplies of cultivated food crops. Furthermore, there is a strong suggestion emerging from the early findings of Harvard University's long term study of the Pygmies in the Ituri forest of northestern Zaire to the effect that humans – Pygmy or otherwise – could not exist in the rainforest without resorting to agriculture.

The rainforest is enormously productive, but most of its biomass is piled up in trees and its edible resources are just too widely distributed to sustain viable groups of people on a continuous basis. Out on the savannah something like 50 percent of the vegetation is immediately available for the nourishment of grazing mammals; in the forest probably not more than 2.5 percent is available. The rainforest therefore supports a relatively small number of game animals – and most of those are the birds, monkeys and other arboreal creatures that occupy the high canopy, where hunting is difficult. Carbohydrates are also scarce in the forest. For all its rain and fecundity the equatorial forest of the Congo Basin is less able to sustain people than the dry Kalahari.

Before agriculture came to the rainforest, suggest Bob Bailey and Nadine

150

Peacock of the Harvard research project, the Pygmies probably were not distributed throughout the Congo Basin, but exploited the more productive forest-savannah ecotone around its rim, where of course they enjoyed access to the produce of two systems, forest and savannah. When herders brought cattle onto the savannah and agriculturalists took over the ecotone, the Pygmies turned increasingly to the forest for subsistence and were, therefore, increasingly obliged to develop links of mutual benefit with the agriculturalists, exchanging labour, meat and honey for the essential foods that the forest could not provide. Of the three items they offered, labour was probably the most important, becoming the basis of a bond between Pygmy hunter gatherer and Bantu agriculturalist that enabled both to move ever deeper into the forest, following rivers and animal trails, clearing stands of primary forest to establish villages and creating a patchwork of secondary habitats significantly more productive than the pristine vegetation. By the time Europeans first visited the region, Pygmy and Bantu were bonded in what seemed a slave and master relationship. Georg Schweinfurth, who explored the Ituri region in 1870, described the Pygmies as the 'remnants of a declining race', the original inhabitants of the forest who once had lived as independent hunters and gatherers, but were now so degenerated that they depended upon the villagers for the means of survival.

Georg Schweinfurth was a botanist. The first visitor of anthropological intent to devote serious attention to the Pygmies was Paul Schebesta who, following an earlier study of the diminutive races of southeast Asia, spent 18 months among the Pygmies of the Ituri forest during 1929 and 1930, under the auspices of the Society for the Furtherance of German Science. Along with *pince-nez*, camera and notebooks, Schebesta took a familiar package of beliefs and attitudes with him into the forest. Having secured official approval for his study and enlisted the help of Bantu assistants, the first Pygmy that Schebesta encountered was dragged shouting and screaming into his presence by a group of Bantu villagers, struggling 'like a fish on a hook', and looking 'exactly like a hobgoblin on the cover of a book of fairy tales... hideously ugly'. Almost all the Pygmies he met 'were indescribably repulsive', he went on. Furthermore, 'the forest dwarf gives out an extraordinary unescapable blend of stenches... more pronounced and even more unpleasant' than the 'extremely offensive' odour of negroes. But European stoicism prevailed where European sensibility failed. 'With a little fortitude one becomes accustomed to anything, no matter how loathsome [and] in the course of eighteen months I grew accustomed to this nuisance and to many other unpleasant habits among the pigmies (*sic*).' Schebesta's observations on these people of loathsome and unpleasant habit convinced him that the Pygmies had long since been unable to support themselves without agricultural foods and had consequently become the 'vassals' of their village 'overlords'.

Martin Johnson, who also spent some time with the Ituri pygmies in the early 1930s, left with somewhat different impressions – but then Martin Johnson had arrived with rather different intentions. Johnson and his wife Osa were film-makers. Their previous films had awakened a popular taste

151

for thrilling stories of adventure and encounter in Africa and now they wanted to show the folks back home two scenes from the wild continent that had never been filmed: the gorilla, 'that hairy ape of which strange tales are told', and the 'joyful pygmies who go through life with a song on their lips and on dancing toes, with never a care or worry'. The song was particularly important because the film was to be the first of its kind to carry a synchronised soundtrack.

First impressions convinced the Johnsons that the Pygmies were the 'unspoiled children of Nature, with the mentality of ten-year-olds... [who] spend their days like youngsters at an endless picnic, always ready to sing, dance and make merry'. The Johnsons spent three months filming the Pygmies, paying for their services with food, salt, matches and small bars of pink soap. When obliged to feed 500 pygmies they had gathered together for some crowd scenes, the Johnsons stripped the region of bananas for 80 km. (50 mi.) around.

The film they made, and the book recounting the adventures of making it (*Congorilla*, 1932), are nothing if not confirmation of first impressions. The Pygmies had no hate, no vanity, no jealousy, reported Martin Johnson. Their lives were not dominated by emotions, like those of the rest of us, and their love was like that of children, he said, ruled more by friendly affection than passion. Parents cared for their young, and played with them as children play with dolls, he added. Johnson saw absolutely no sense of religion or superstition among the pygmies, and learned of no ceremonies or rites that they practised. The Pygmies 'are just simple, primitive animals', he concluded, 'caring nothing about the hereafter, and little about the "here"'.

The Johnsons' impressions of the Pygmies deserve to be dismissed as fanciful confections served up to satisfy popular taste – which indeed is what they were. On the other hand, the fact that they were so confected is in itself a very good indication of what popular western culture of the day wanted to believe about people like the Pygmies. With their film and books, the Johnsons effectively transformed popular belief into common knowledge for large numbers of people. Intellectuals may have dismissed the Johnson productions as trite and superficial, but for the vast majority of western humanity who acquired their knowledge through the medium of entertainment, the Johnsons' films and books confirmed a popular belief that all blacks were inferior though some could be very amusing clowns. A serious indictment. It was from such a pool of common knowledge and belief, for example, that some Belgian settlers drew the conviction that it was all right to cut a hand off the occasional slack worker as an example to the others. This practice, however widespread it may or may not have been, sank into the folklore of the people of the Congo basin as evidence supporting *their* popular belief that all white men are cannibals. Missionaries, for all their good intentions, unwittingly compounded this belief when they told stories of the crucifixion and ritually consumed blood and flesh at the altar. The behaviour of white mercenaries during the Congo rebellions of the 1960s did nothing to dismiss it either, and the fact that cannibalism had been known among the Africans themselves only served to enhance its credibility. African christians are not conspicuously numerous in the Congo basin, and deep in the forest, where little outside influence touches the power of the inherited folklore, the people – Pygmies and villagers alike – still fear that a white visitor may kill and eat them.

Meanwhile, folklore notwithstanding, white anthropologists of the postwar period have been able to add a more comprehensive and realistic assessment of the forest inhabitants to the preliminary and sometimes fanciful observations of Schweinfurth, Schebesta and Johnson.

The word pygmy is derived from an ancient Greek term referring to fabulous dwarfs who were believed to be no taller than the distance between a man's elbow and his knuckles. Nowadays they are more properly called the Bambuti, and their average height is known to be 1.44 m. (4ft 8.6 in.). The Bambuti are the shortest group of people in the world, and as it happens, the tallest people in the world – the Tutsi pastoralists – live almost next door in the savannah environments of Rwanda and Burundi. The average Bambuti is about 32 cm. (12.6 in.) shorter than the average Tutsi. It is not known whether the Bambuti were always small or became small in the forest, but their diminutive stature is an advantage in the tangled and steamy environment of an equatorial rainforest. Small stature not only enables a person to move more easily through the hanging branches and vines that obstruct progress in the forest, it also requires relatively less food, which is a help where food is scarce, and can lose heat more quickly by virtue of its high surface to volume ratio, which is particularly important in a humid forest environment where the temperature often approaches blood heat (37°C; 98°F) and only occasionally falls below 27°C (80°F).

There are thought to be a total of about 140,000 pygmies distributed throughout the forests that cover well over three million square kilometres (1.2 million sq. mi.) of the Congo Basin, but the best known are the Bambuti of the Ituri forest in northeastern Zaire. The Ituri forest is about the size of Virginia (102,835 sq. km.; 39,694 sq. mi.) in the United States, and it is home to approximately 40,000 Bambuti and 60,000 Bantu villagers. The Ituri Bambuti are divided into four distinct population groups, each attached to a distinct tribe of villagers. The most numerous group is known simply as the Mbuti, and occupies the southern and central areas of the forest in association with a tribe of village agriculturalists of Bantu origin called the Babila. The next largest group is the Efe, who are widely spread across the north and eastern regions of the forest where they live in association with villagers of the Mamvu and Walese tribes. In the west there are the Sua Bambuti, who are associated with the Babudu, and in the northwest the few remaining Aka are associated with the Mangbetu.

The Bambuti have no language of their own, but speak primarily the language of the villagers with whom they are associated. Many also speak Kingwana, a dialect of the Kiswahali that is common throughout east and central Africa, but French, the official language of Zaire, is neither much spoken nor understood outside the main urban centres.

153

Apart from the social factors of language and association that separate the various Bambuti of the Ituri, there is a factor of functional significance that divides them into two broad groups. In the north, the Bambuti (principally the Efe) hunt with bow and arrow and spears, and are commonly referred to as 'archers'. In the south they (principally the Mbuti) also use bows and arrows or spears occasionally, but most of the time hunt with nets, driving the game from a wide area into an enclosure of nets strung through the undergrowth (the nets are woven by the Mbuti themselves with string made from the bark of a forest vine). This distinction between archers and net-hunters in the Ituri was noted by Paul Schebesta and has become one of the classic questions in anthropological research. Why should two groups of hunters stemming from the same root, following essentially the same lifestyle in the same kind of environment, employ such totally different methods in pursuit of the same end?

It is generally agreed that bows and arrows, and possibly spears too, must have been the hunting strategy first used in the Ituri, and that net-hunting came later – probably developing from techniques introduced by Bantu agriculturalists as they moved in after the Bambuti. And it has been generally assumed that nets catch more meat than bows and arrows or spears. So why does the old-fashioned, less efficient strategy persist?

Colin Turnbull, whose field research during 1957 and 1958 concluded that the Bambuti were fully able to subsist on forest produce, without the help of the villagers, was inclined to believe that the two hunting strategies persisted among the Bambuti more or less fortuitously, simply because the resources of the environment were sufficiently abundant to supply enough food by either means. Turnbull stressed the ideology of the hunt, and its pervasive influence in Bambuti society and daily life. Following up Turnbull's assertions with a detailed study of the Bambuti hunting economy, a Japanese researcher, Reizo Harako, concluded that the persistence of the two strategies was not fortuitous at all, but the result of historical and linguistic circumstance. Net-hunting was brought into the forest by the Babila, spread among the Mbuti with whom they were associated, but went no further because of language differences.

In 1979, however, another researcher, W.Abruzzi, dismissed Harako's explanation as 'non-ecological'. Abruzzi felt it was more likely that the Mbuti in the south had been obliged to adopt net-hunting simply in order to improve their returns and catch enough meat to trade for the extra quantities of cultivated food their increasing numbers required, while the archers in the north were still able to secure enough meat and crops by traditional means.

A study of food acquisition and village exchanges among three groups of southern net-hunting Mbuti, conducted by John Hart from Harvard over a period of 18 months between 1973 and 1975, appeared to confirm the first part of Abruzzi's contention. Hart found that Mbuti hunting had become a predominantly commercial exercise. Of the 85 hunts he monitored, 61 were stimulated by commercial demand and the catch – 648 kg. (1,428 pounds) – was sold to traders rather than exchanged with villagers in the traditional manner.

154

While these male researchers derived their conclusions from the economics of hunting, collecting data by direct observation and occasionally even sharing the ardour of the hunt itself, in 1985 a female researcher produced a perceptive ecological explanation of the persistence of two hunting strategies among the Bambuti from across the clear distance of the Atlantic. Katharine Milton had studied the ecology of the Maku Indians in the northwestern Amazon forest. Subsistence patterns in the Amazon and the Ituri were similar and, pursuing some interesting parallels, she found data suggesting the simple proposition that the Ituri forest environment was more productive in the north than in the south. The soils were inherently more fertile in the north, the rainfall was more constant, the vegetation more diverse and, therefore, animal life probably more abundant too. Consequently only the more effective (but very tedious) net-hunting would produce enough meat in the impoverished southern forest, while the less dependable success of lone archers would suffice in the more richly endowed northern environment. In other words the Mbuti had no choice but to use nets, while the Efe had no need to get involved with the tedious business of making and using them.

The Harvard Research team's work among the Bambuti of the Ituri forest has been as illuminating as was Lee's among the !Kung San. Concentrating on the Efe archers of the northern forest, they have shown that here too the women provide over 70 percent of the food supply – calories and protein. The Efe regularly consume 26 percent more calories and 138 percent more protein than the World Health Organisation recommends as a minimum for their size and activity patterns. They are generally in a good state of health, but, like the !Kung, their population growth rate is lower than might be expected, although there is some suggestion that the Efe's low infertility might be a consequence of gonorrhea.

But the most provocative suggestion emerging from Harvard's Ituri project is the contention that the Bambuti could not survive in the forest without access to cultivated food. Even at times when the villagers themselves were short of food and reluctant to barter with the Efe, the study has recorded no instance of any Efe group subsisting without cultivated food for more than six days. 'The Efe themselves do not consider moving into the forest to depend exclusively on forest resources as a viable alternative for coping with pronounced shortages of agricultural food... [they] can garner a significant proportion of their diet from the forest, but they do not and probably cannot depend upon the forest habitat for their total subsistence.'

Neither hunter gatherer nor farmer, the Pygmy has found a unique position between the two ways of life. Just as the Indians on the northwest Pacific coast of America occupy the ecotone between marine and terrestrial environments, with access to the resources of both, so the Pygmies occupy what might be called the ecotone between two cultural strategies, with access to the benefits of both. And, in the neglected regions of an under-developed country like Zaire, where 'culture' for most people means simply finding something to eat, that is not a bad place to be.

CHAPTER NINE

THE POTATO GROWERS

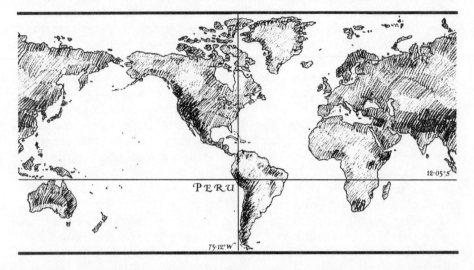

Throughout history, civilisations have been founded upon an ability to keep food production ahead of food demand, and intensive agriculture has been the strategy which performs this role. With the domestication of plants and animals around 10,000-12,000 years ago, numbers of hunters and gatherers adopted a more sedentary way of life – planting crops, building more permanent houses, settling in communities. Once relatively large groups were living in close proximity, all engaged in similar patterns of activity, people could organise their labour to achieve the most productive return on their efforts. In regions of high rainfall, such as the 'fertile crescent' of the Middle East, where wheat and barley are believed to have been domesticated, communal effort enabled people to cultivate and harvest more food than individuals alone could produce. In river valleys, large communities were able to organise the labour force required for the construction of major irrigation schemes which brought huge tracts of land under cultivation, greatly increasing the amount of food produced for every hour of labour. Thus the river valleys of the Indus, the Euphrates, the Nile and the Yellow River in China became the cradles of civilisation, from about 5,000 years ago, and in every instance the staple food that had once sustained small independent groups of people became the fuel of a huge, complex, social and cultural entity.

It is tempting to think of civilisation as an end, rather than a means, of human existence. But that would be wrong. There is no primary law that drives people towards civilisation as a mode of living. Civilisation is a very impressive demonstration of human ingenuity applied to the problems of fulfilling human requirements, but, in the story of human evolution, it is actually a very recent innovation. If the upright stance of human beings is taken to be a first indication of humanity, then the trail of fossil footprints uncovered at Laetoli shows that people have existed for at least 3.6 million years. If the manufacture of stone tools is regarded as a first sign of man's inventive potential then the earliest known stone tools (from Olduvai Gorge) show that people were already on the road to civilisation 1.9 million years ago. Civilisation as a way of life made its first appearance less than 5,000 years ago, however, which means that for 99.86 percent of the time that human-like beings have been walking upright, and for 99.74 percent of the time that has passed since humans first demonstrated a talent for technical innovation, people managed perfectly well without civilisation.

And even in the brief span of time that civilisation has been a feature of human existence, it has not demonstrated any tendency to produce a well-regulated steady state wherein people are well-fed and secure, generation after generation. Civilisation is distinguished more by its erratic cycles of uncontrolled growth and collapse than by any inherent tendency towards stability. Time and again, it has risen dramatically from the field of human endeavour, then collapsed and fallen. Human ingenuity drives the process. Human inability to impose adequate restraint brings it down. Inventions provide the initial impetus, intellect supplies methods of application and solutions to problems that arise as the system swells and grows, but, in every instance so far, the uncontrolled growth of civilisation has ultimately thrown up more problems than human intellect could solve.

The city states of the Indus Valley, for example, were founded about 4,500 years ago on the irrigated cultivation of wheat, but continuous irrigation progressively increased the salinity of the soil to levels at which wheat no longer thrived. The farmers then switched to barley, which is much more tolerant of saline conditions, and wheat disappeared from Indus valley agriculture about 4,000 years ago. Soil conditions continued to deteriorate, however, with adverse effects on the barley crop, and the violent defeats that heralded the total collapse of the Indus Valley civilisation around 3,700 years ago were doubtless due in large measure to its failure to raise and feed armies strong enough to defend the cities and their material wealth.

Archaeologists have found the streets of the ancient Indus city Mohenjo-daro littered with the skeletons of people who had suffered a violent death, and this image could stand as a symbol for the repeated failure of civilisation to regulate its growth. As city states have expanded into nations, kingdoms and empires, civilisation has repeatedly become obsessed with the acquisition and wielding of power; an activity that has left millions of people dead in the streets and dominated the pages of history so much that the significance of the subsistence bases upon which civilisations are founded has been all but ignored.

The cultivation of grain was the subsistence base that underwrote the rise and fall of civilisation in the Middle East and Europe. But the Inca civilisation that dominated the Andean regions of South America at the time of the Spanish Conquest was founded on the humble potato. The Incas grew maize and used the grain to maintain their power, but maize

157

was an introduced crop which supplemented, rather than supplanted, the indigenous potato that had always been the basic subsistence crop of the region. The potato is still the basic subsistence crop of the Andes, and has moved out to become the basic subsistence crop of people in many other parts of the world as well.

When Francisco Pizarro and his small band of men and horses kidnapped the Inca ruler, Atahuallpa, at Cajamarca in 1532, up to nine million people are estimated to have been living under the Incas – 40 percent of the entire population of North and South America. After the death of Atahuallpa, Inca capitulation was swift and absolute, and once the glory of conquest had faded, the Spaniards found themselves faced with the task of ruling an empire 3,500 km. (2,200 mi.) long and 320 km. (190 mi.) wide, covering more than twice the land area of Spain in one of the wildest and most remote regions of the known world, with only the barest idea of how it had been ruled prior to their conquest.

From the Spanish point of view, some degree of administrative continuity might have seemed desirable when they acquired control of the Inca empire, but the Incas had not developed a written language, and therefore had left no written account of their empire and its resources, no documentary record of their administrative organisation and systems of law, land tenure and taxation for the Spanish to draw upon. The Incas had ruled by word of mouth and memory, making one of their original languages, Quechua, the language of administration throughout the multi-lingual territories their empire embraced.

But although the Incas had compiled no history books, they did not lack historians. Throughout their empire and rule, official historians had been obliged to memorise vast amounts of information and repeat it for the benefit of administrators as required. Not surprisingly, the role of historian passed from father to son, and from such sources the Spanish were able to compile several detailed accounts of how the Inca civilisation had functioned. Some of these reports are considered more reliable than others, but within a century of the Spanish conquest – by which time war and disease had reduced the Inca population to no more than 600,000 people, a mere seven percent of its former total – they comprised the only written record of the unique civilisation that the Spanish had utterly destroyed.

The Incas ruled their empire for less than 100 years. Legends tell of their origin among the several small tribal groups of subsistence farmers on the Andean plateau to the north of Lake Titicaca. Sometime after 1200 AD, three of these groups united under Manco Capac, legendary founder of the Inca dynasty, and established themselves on fertile land in the Cuzco valley. Subsequently they captured the town of Cuzco, formed an alliance with the neighbouring Quechua tribe and, in 1438, defeated the powerful Chanca in a series of decisive battles that established the Incas as the strongest group in the southern Andean highlands.

The rise of the Incas stemmed from their determination to retain control of the territories they conquered. Instead of the invasion, plunder and withdrawal that had characterised military exploits until that time, the

Incas installed local administrators and garrisons throughout the territories they conquered, and organised the production and distribution of food. They instigated massive programmes of terracing and irrigation, which intensified agricultural production tremendously, and laid down over 23,000 km. (14,300 mi.) of paved roads along which produce, materials and men could be distributed throughout the empire with a minimum of delay. The empire was controlled from its capital, Cuzco, and without the wheel, without horses, without the written word, it performed wonders of organisation. When 50,000 artisans were employed on construction work in the Cuzco region, for example, they and their families received supplies of maize, dried meat and dried fish every four days.

The Incas worshipped the gods of sun and thunder, of the Earth, the sea, the moon and the stars. The sun was the divine ancestor of the Incas dynasty, they believed, the giver of life in the cold highlands where the Inca people had originated. Thunder was the god of rain. The Earth was *Pacha-mama*, mother Earth, the patroness of agriculture. The sea was *Mama-cocha*, mother sea, provider of fish. The moon regulated the annual round of cultivation, and the Pleiades watched over the grain that was stored in the granaries. In one way or another, food was the dominant feature of the religious and state organisations that comprised the Inca civilisation. Throughout the empire, the agricultural land accessible to each settled community of people was divided into three parts: one for the Gods, one for the State, and one for the community. The farmers were obliged to cultivate all three, but lived principally off the produce of the communal land. The harvests they reaped from the other two categories of land were consigned to the stores of the gods and the State, to be used in ceremonies, to feed the armies of soldiers, masons, miners and craftsmen assigned to work for the greater glory of Inca civilisation, and also for distribution to the needy in times of crop failure.

The masterstroke of the Incas was the diffusion and intensification of maize cultivation, and they were not unaware of the significance of maize in their lives. At the *Coricancha*, the Sun Temple in Cuzco, where 4,000 attendants watched over shrines and treasures including the Incas' golden image of the sun – a great disc of solid gold, with sunbeams radiating from a human face at its centre – there was also a garden dedicated to the sun, where lumps of gold were scattered to resemble clods of earth and golden cobs of maize stood lifesize on stems of silver.

Maize was the lifeblood of the Inca empire. Highly productive, long-keeping and easily transported, it flowed continuously through their arterial network, nourishing their physical, economic, and strategic systems. Land never before cultivated was put under maize production. The steep sides of highland valleys were terraced; canals and aqueducts brought water from distant sources to irrigate dry land; guano and fish remains were brought from the coast to fertilise the soil.

Maize was not indigenous to the high Andean homelands of the Incas, however. It was an introduced crop, native to Mexico, and the fact of its foreign origin probably contributed to the almost sacred status that it was accorded by the Incas. A grain so rare and so rich might have seemed a gift

159

of the gods when it first arrived in the high valleys and plateaux of the central and southern Andes. But the most important aspect of Inca development was that, while maize fuelled an empire, it did not displace the traditional subsistence agriculture that produced it. Terraces and irrigation produced maize on difficult, uncultivated land – never threatening the pattern of mixed agriculture and herding that had supported the Inca's ancestral tribes for at least 2,000 years.

Potatoes were the staple crop of the high Andes, grown in rotation with two indigenous cereals, *quinoa* and *canihua*, on land lengthily fallowed and fertilised by herds of domesticated llama and alpaca. Most of this cultivation took place on high open grassland above 3,000 m. (10,000 ft), where maize will not grow, and extended upward to close on 4,500 m. (15,000 ft). The Incas required people to build terraces and irrigation systems for maize, and tend the crops, but the patterns of organised labour they introduced also increased all-round efficiency, which allowed people to continue cultivating their traditional land and live off its produce even while they were obliged to work regularly on state and religious lands or projects for the benefit of the great Inca empire. People never starved under the Incas, it was said, though they lived at the order of the state.

In the space of little more than 50 years, maize and a tremendous talent for organisation enabled the Incas to bring up to 9 million people and over one million square kilometres (386,000 sq. mi.) of territory under the direct command of a small group of individuals who lived in Cuzco and promoted the idea that they were divine descendents of the sun itself. The achievement is staggering. They cultivated an estimated total of 19,560 sq. km. (7,550 sq. mi.) of land, much of it terraced and irrigated; they constructed stone cities and temples of immense ingenuity. Without the benefit of either draft animals or the wheel, the human effort engaged in these endeavours was vast. Merely to move one particularly large block of dressed granite from quarry to construction site, for example, is estimated to have required the efforts of 20,000 men, of whom 3,000 died in the process. And yet there were hundreds, if not thousands of sites. Most of the stone blocks required for their construction were considerably smaller than the one mentioned above, but each stone on every site was laboriously quarried and dressed by hand. The bronze that Incas smelted was too soft for working stone, so the masons used hammerstones to shape the blocks, and sand and water to smooth the edges for a perfect fit.

The Incas mined gold, silver, copper, tin and platinum – some of it from mines 80 m. (260 ft) deep. Their craftsmen made articles of exquisite beauty – gold and silver work, pottery, textiles. Their surgeons developed the art of trepanning – cutting out a section of the skull to relieve brain pressure and in some instances inserting a plate of gold in its place.

Given the size and strength of the Inca empire in 1532 it seems odd that they should have capitulated so readily to the pilfering Pizarro and his force of just 200 men. But the seeds of their fall had been sown some years before and were already well-rooted by then. Opposition to Inca rule was rife in some parts of the empire following the death of Atahuallpa's father, Inca Huanya Capac, in 1527 (so much so that some factions actually

welcomed the Spanish when they arrived). Huanya Capac died suddenly in
the Inca's Ecuadorean capital, Quito, of smallpox in an epidemic that
spread from Pizarro's exploratory landing on the coast that year, without
declaring which of his sons, Ninan, Huascar or Atahuallpa should succeed
him as absolute ruler. The first born, Ninan, died in the epidemic shortly
after his father, leaving Huascar and Atahuallpa to vie for control. Their
political intrigues culminated in civil war, from which Atahuallpa had
only just emerged victorious, with the defeat and capture of Huascar in
1532, when Pizarro and his men arrived at Cajamarca.

By then the systematic slaughter of Huascar's family and followers was
complete and Atahuallpa was journeying to Cuzco for his installation as
ruling Inca. He paused to meet the Spaniards who were virtually impris-
oned in Cajamarca by encircling Inca armies. An eyewitness, Francisco de
Jerez, records how Atahuallpa entered the town at twilight with a party of
his senior generals, all splendidly dressed and bedecked with gold and
silver regalia. A group of retainers swept the road clean before them,
dancers and singers accompanied them, and Atahuallpa was carried in a
litter lined with red, yellow and blue parrot feathers. In the town square a
cunning ambush awaited them. Atahuallpa was captured and his com-
panions slaughtered before the armies outside the town could be alerted.

With Atahuallpa captive and their leading generals dead, the Inca armies
fell into disarray. Pizarro played one disaffected faction against the next
and eventually gained control of all. Huascar attempted to negotiate
secretly with the Spaniards and was executed by Atahuallpa's men.
Atahuallpa was held hostage while a vast treasure of ransom was collected
against his release, then he was tried on charges of offending the laws of
Spain, found guilty and executed by strangulation.

'The earth refused to devour the Inca's body – rocks trembled, tears
made torrents, the Sun was obscured, the Moon ill', a 16th-century
account laments, and with the death of Atahuallpa, the last divine image
of the Sun on Earth, Inca civilisation shuddered and fell.

The rise and fall of the Inca empire is a remarkable story by any measure –
most remarkable of all, perhaps, for the fact that it rose in one of the
harshest environments on Earth. Even by today's standards, less than three
percent of Peru is arable, for example, compared with 22 percent in the
United States and 30 percent in Europe. The coastal belt is a desert where
rain falls but two or three times in a hundred years and the dense fogs
condensing above the cold Humboldt Current, which flows northward
along the shore, are a more reliable source of moisture for the scant natural
vegetation. The mountains rise sharply from the desert to snow-capped
peaks 6,000 m. (20,000 ft) high, steep valleys are enfolded below glacial
moraines and bare windswept highlands. To the east of the mountains lie
the dense and luxuriant tropical rainforests of the Amazon basin, well-
watered but, in the nature of such places, incapable of supporting large
numbers of people.

Most of the areas that were suitable for permanent human habitation at
the time of the Incas lay in the mountains, more than 3,000 m. (10,000 ft)

161

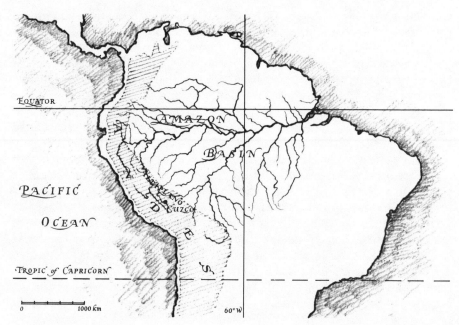

above sea level, where available oxygen is less than 60 percent of that to
which most people are accustomed, where the year round temperature
averages 8°C (46°F), where frosts are common, where plants grow slowly
and stunted, and where animals can survive only by means of the
adaptations they make to the harsh regime.

The Americas were totally uninhabited by people until sometime
between 30,000 and 15,000 years ago, when groups of hunters and
gatherers crossed the Bering Straits from Asia by way of the landbridge
created during climatic troughs, when oceans froze into the polar icecaps
and caused sea levels to fall around the world. By about 12,000 years ago
people had spread from Alaska all the way to southern Chile, probably
migrating down South America through the long highland basins of the
Andes. The river valleys along the coastal belt were extensively cultivated
from about 4,500 years ago, and with the beginnings of agriculture, human
populations expanded rapidly throughout the region. A succession of states
rose and fell during the first millenium AD – Moche, Nazca and Chimu,
Tiahuanaco and Huari – until Andean civilisation found its ultimate
expression in the achievements of the Inca empire during the 15th century,
when up to nine million people owed obesiance to a few residents of Cuzco
who were said to be the divine descendants of the Sun.

The Temple of the Sun in Cuzco, where the Incas had worshipped golden
images of the natural forces regulating their existence, and planted a
garden with golden replicas of the crops that sustained them, was ceded to
the Catholic church once its treasures had been melted down and shipped
back to Spain. A church, Santo Domingo, was built on the site, where
surviving Incas were encouraged to worship the image of a virgin's son

nailed to a cross and left to die with a spear wound in his side and a twisted band of thorns about his head. Santo Domingo was a noted example of Spanish baroque architecture, but a good deal of it collapsed in the earthquake that shook the Cuzco region in 1950. Indeed, a good deal of Cuzco fell in the 1950 earthquake, but everywhere the Inca stonework upon which the city was founded stood firm.

Santo Domingo has been rebuilt along with the rest of Cuzco, and visitors are directed to the small, steeply sloping patch of dark soil where the golden maize stood amid golden clods of earth. Along the streets that lead from the church up to the Plaza de Armas, the old city square, many buildings stand on courses of Inca stonework. The blocks are regularly scraped by trucks on tight corners and polished by shoulders jostling through the narrow thoroughfares, but they cannot fail to catch the eye and the imagination as a burst of sunlight puts a fine lattice of shadows where the hairline joints fit stone to stone. Such precision, such craftsmanship – such a wealth of ingenuity.

The Spanish may have taken the treasure and reduced the Inca population to a sickly 600,000 of its former nine million in little more than 100 years, and the modern world may have suffused the Andes with foreign influences and a taste for tourist dollars, but the relics of Inca civilisation amount to more than shadows – they are potent images that pervade the world of their successors. Such images are to be found in the back wall of a restaurant, for example, where a patch of Inca stonework offers more to admire than the allegedly Italian food on the plate. They issue from the radio, where the modern pop idiom is expressed in the unique breathy sounds of instruments that originated in the Andes. And most compelling of all, they are encountered on the high cold land where the Quechua farmer pauses to lean on the *taclla* and gaze at the visitor, chin raised, mouth slightly open, and a calm steady look in the eye that reflects a long history of watching transient figures pass over the landscape he tills for a living. Incas, Spaniards, Peruvians, blue-rinsed Americans – it's all the same to the people who actually live off the land.

It seems natural in this landscape that a woman should indicate the distance to some Inca ruins with a quick glance overhead and a gesture to a point in the sky some degrees below the sun's present position – answering the question without a word, not in kilometres, not even in time, but in the distance the sun must fall towards the horizon before the journey would be complete. She was a Breughelian figure – short and very round. Her voluminous dark blue wool skirts were hemmed with a bright band of colourful embroidery, and a striped blanket was draped across her shoulders. She wore a flat-topped hat fringed with strands of green wool which was tied under the chin with silver cord. Two children stood beside her, their cheeks a ruddy purple and chapped. The land was boggy, the soil thick and bound with a tight mat of grass that had been heavily grazed by the villagers' llamas and sheep. The village itself lay below the plateau in a broad valley, each house standing apart in its compound and the mountain rising almost vertically behind, with potato fields marking its soaring slopes like brown paper posters plastered on a rough green wall. Human

163

effort and the taclla are the principal means of cultivating those high and precipitious fields – a tractor could never reach them and an ox could never plough them, even for the farmers who could afford to buy such things.

The taclla is a footplough, a spade-like device with a narrow blade and a handle set low down on the pole to ease the job of lifting and turning the heavy ground. The Incas are said to have invented the taclla, and its modern version is indeed very similar to those that appear in drawings of Inca agriculture. The man worked backwards across the field, cutting a furrow and heaping the soil in ridges, and the woman followed close behind, breaking the clods with a hoe. When the field was done she slung a homespun bag of seed potatoes about her shoulders and walked swiftly down each ridge, dropping potatoes ahead of her and deftly treading them into the soil with her heel on each stride. She was barefoot. The potatoes they planted that day were of a variety called *mariva*, one that usually did well on wet ground, the man explained. On higher ground they had planted a field of *ccompis*.

These are just two of several hundred varieties of potato that are grown by the Quechua Indians. The potato originated in the Andes, and during centuries of domestication the Quechua have selected, cultivated and named numerous varieties according to their identified characteristics – taste, resistance to frost, disease, damp or drought, keeping qualities and so forth. New varieties are arising constantly, seeded by the highly variable wild potatoes that still grow profusely in the mountains, so that while the practice of planting tubers keeps the cultivated strains relatively pure (tubers are effectively clones of the parent plant), cross-fertilisation maintains continuous access to the broad genetic base and inherent adaptability of the original wild potato. A wide diversity of characteristics is the result, and the Quechua depend on it today no less than they have since before the Incas told them to grow maize.

Ten million people presently inhabit the Andean highlands that once comprised the heart of the Inca empire, and most of them still follow the ancient patterns of subsistence agriculture that have been sustaining people there since long before the rise of Inca civilisation. It is not easy for people to make a living at high altitudes in the Andes. Indeed it is not easy for any organism to live permanently above the elevation of 3,700 m. (12,000 ft) which characterises the Andean *altiplano*. The terrain is rugged and the soils are poor. Though solar radiation is often intense, temperatures are generally low. Snow and frosts are frequent, but rainfall is erratic, seasonal and not dependable. These physical and climatic factors conspire to restrict high altitude vegetation to tough grasses and herbs, with a few pockets of low shrubs and trees in sheltered places – all of which grow slowly and, with a corresponding shortage of bacterial decomposers, decay slowly. The nutrient cycle therefore turns slowly and the amount of energy stored in the system is always limited. In short, there is never a lot of natural vegetation available for consumption at high altitudes. Furthermore, the shortage of oxygen imposes additional limitations on the human capacity to function and live permanently at high altitude.

The fact that a human population has inhabited such an extreme environment continuously for thousands of years has made the high Andes an area of special interest to scientists studying the adaptive nature of mankind. Why did people choose to live there in the first place? How have they adapted to the rigours of the environment? Has long-standing occupation of a high altitude environment produced adaptations that are now programmed in the genes and pass from generation to generation? The Quechua Indians living on the altiplano today are believed to be the descendants of the hunters and gatherers who first established a human presence in the mountains, perhaps as much as 12,000 years ago. Since 12,000 years covers a span of 500 generations, and since modern theories of population genetics suggest that substantial changes can occur in less than 100 generations (while new species – significantly moulded to specific circumstances of existence – can arise in 2,000 generations), it is not unreasonable to suppose that significant adaptations may have arisen in a human line through 500 generations of existence under the rigours of high altitude in the Andes.

Intensive research on the biological and cultural adaptations of groups of Quechua Indians living on the altiplano began in the 1960s and although an extensive – even exhaustive – literature on the subject has accumulated since then, its general conclusion must be that the adaptations to life on the altiplano manifested by the Quechua are more cultural and behavioural than biological. The possibility of there being some genetically controlled adaptation is not excluded – it is always possible that the behavioural patterns of the Quechua themselves may be genetically controlled – but if they exist throughout the population they have yet to be distinguished.

There are five stress factors that humans must contend with at high altitudes: low oxygen levels; cold; low humidity; high wind flow, and high levels of solar and cosmic radiation. Clothing takes care of the last four, but shortage of oxygen is a factor that cannot be so easily countered.

Oxygen in effect fires the chemical reactions that produce energy in cells, and is therefore crucial to all human activity. On the altiplano, low oxygen pressure soon has new arrivals very short of breath, stricken with headaches, nausea, insomnia, mental disorientation and fatigue. The body reacts by producing more red blood cells, which transport oxygen about the body, so that, after a few weeks, the newcomer is reasonably adapted to the new circumstances. But the degree of adaptation is limited. Even after a period of years, migrants to high altitudes are unable to achieve the work capacities of people who were born and raised there – or even to match their own achievements at sea level. Furthermore, increased red blood cell concentration thickens the blood, increases capillary resistance and therefore makes the heart work harder – with heightened risk of heart strain – so that in the final analysis increased red blood cell production may be a very short term and self-defeating adaptation to the shortage of oxygen at high altitudes.

Meanwhile, the born highlanders remain healthy and work hard. The only apparent adaptation their bodies have made to the low oxygen

165

pressure of their environment is an increase in lung capacity, relative to their body size. Larger lungs capture more of the limited oxygen available at altitude, of course, but they are not exclusive to the people who have been living up there for generations. Anyone born at high altitudes, or who goes to live there before the age of ten, develops equally large lung capacity relative to bodysize, it seems, and is able to work equally effectively.

Similar findings have characterised the analysis of other biological factors that might be conditioned by altitude. The patterns of cold tolerance, fertility, growth and development, nutrition, health and mortality that are found among the Quechua all seem distinctive at first glance, but have subsequently turned out to be the adjustments that individuals make to the environment as they grow, rather than specific adaptations they have inherited from 12,000 years of residence at high altitudes. In other words, anyone raised from infancy as a Quechua would perform just as well as they do.

The bleak environment of the altiplano probably attracted its earliest inhabitants simply because it was largely free of the parasitical diseases that plagued the lowland forests to the east, and had more to offer than the coastal desert to the west, but staying there on a permanent basis called for some considerable cultural adaptation to the rigours of the system. Under cold conditions people use up energy simply to keep warm, and therefore need more food and more clothes. And yet the altiplano is a region where plants grow slowly, where food can never be especially plentiful and where wild animals – and their skins – are numerically limited by the meagre carrying capacity of the vegetation. Clearly, limitations such as these are a compelling incentive to adapt the nomadic strategies of the hunter and gatherer to the less random and more energy-conserving activities of the sedentary farmer. Potatoes are easier to gather when they are planted together, and planting selected tubers eventually gives rise to more productive varieties. Likewise, herding llamas and alpacas for slaughter uses less energy than hunting them, once they have been domesticated (probably achieved with the rearing and breeding of abandoned young), and animals sheared each year will keep more people warm on a continuing basis than would the skins of animals killed in the hunt.

The transition from hunting and gathering to subsistence agriculture on the altiplano was complete by about 4,500 years ago, and its persistence into the 1980s must testify to the benefits and resilience of the system that the Quechua and other Indians have developed – agropastoralism. The crucial effect of agropastoralism is to speed up the nutrient cycle and to concentrate the energy it produces in an accessible and consumable form. Cultivated crops and domestic animals are the basic elements of the economy, but dung is its indispensible currency. The farmer plants potatoes and, where feasible, native cereals, while their children take the llamas and sheep to graze over the rangelands. The animals convert widely dispersed and otherwise useless vegetation into an easily digested and nourishing human food – meat – and in the process bring back to the compound in which they spend the nights a fulsome supply of concentrated and reconstituted energy and nutrients. The dung is used both as

166

manure for the crops and as fuel for the fires, and so, by providing dung, the animals speed up the nutrient cycle and energy flow of a very slow-moving system. Indeed, the Quechua could not have survived on the altiplano into modern times without llama dung, and as though to be as helpful as they can, the animals habitually defecate on a common heap, which facilitates collection considerably.

A carefully integrated pattern of agriculture and herding has evolved on the altiplano. Fields are cultivated for a year or two at a time. Potatoes are planted the first year, with applications of manure at up to two kilogrammes per sq. m. (3.7 pounds per sq. yd) which effectively concentrates the nutrients from an extensive area of grazing land into a very small area of cultivated land. Andean cereals are planted the second year, without manure, and then the field is left fallow for up to 12 years, during which time it receives some manure from grazing animals. Seven years is considered a desirable fallow period, and as it happens, tests have shown that seven years is about the minimum period of time required to reduce the soil pests that attack potatoes to insignificant proportions.

The typical altiplano family must cultivate about 1,000 sq. m. (1,100 sq. yd) of potatoes and grain for its subsistence needs, and there is obviously a crucial relationship between this requirement and the area of land a family's animals must graze in order to produce all the dung they need – both for manure and for fuel. One study has calculated that the manure to fertilize one square metre of the annual potato crop requires 250 sq. m. (300 sq. yd) of grazing land. A typical family needs a minimum of 25 animals to cover all its needs, it was found, and is best off with 38 llamas, 25 sheep and 10 cattle grazing 134 hectares (331 acres) of land.

Dung may seem primarily important as manure for the potato crop, but potatoes have to be cooked before they can be eaten and on the altiplano, where firewood is virtually non-existent and commercial fuels such as coal and paraffin either unobtainable or prohibitively expensive, dung is also an utterly indispensible source of heat. Given the choice, people will choose llama dung for their fires (or better still, cattle dung – but few families have cattle) and sheep droppings for their fields. Llama dung burns hotter and gives off less smoke, they say, while crops grow better with sheep manure. And analysis has shown that these preferences are not mere peasant whim – llama dung does give off more heat (without smoke) and sheep droppings do put more nutrients back into the soil.

In fact there is very little room for peasant whim in the tight cycle of production and consumption that regulates the altiplano subsistence economy. Detailed studies of energy flow by R. Brooke Thomas have shown that the typical family produces only as much energy as it consumes. People must eat all they grow in order to grow all they need to eat. They may kill a few animals each year so long as births maintain numbers, and sales of wool and meat provide a little money for the replacement of worn farm tools, weaving and household equipment and for things like sugar and salt, but the system supplies very little in the way of a regular, dependable surplus. And the lack of a surplus, along with the other stressful aspects of life at high altitudes, directly affects the size and

167

growth of the human population. Men and women on the altiplano are no less fertile than their counterparts elsewhere, and the evidence of relatively larger placentas suggests that Quechua women provide a foetal environment that compensates for some stresses of high altitude, but even so, altiplano babies are substantially lighter at birth than lowland babies.

The Quechua say they would like to have large families – three boys and three girls was the preferred choice that emerged from one survey, but only 60 percent of those born reach maturity and most families have four or fewer children. Like everything else on the altiplano, the cruel facts of infant survival are demonstrably related to the viability of the system. The jobs that children perform are an essential contribution to each family's subsistence and welfare, but of course children are totally unproductive during their early upbringing. In terms of energy investment it costs as much to raise a child to the age of six as it costs to keep an entire family alive for one year. From the age of six they begin herding animals and thus provide some return on the investment, but until then the birth of each child places a large additional demand upon the resources of the family.

Children on the altiplano grow more slowly than their lowland counterparts, and at maturity are substantially smaller. Under the circumstances this is no bad thing – slow-growing children and small adults eat less food. R. Brooke Thomas has estimated that if altiplano children followed the growth patterns of what are termed 'advanced' communities, the typical family would need to cultivate an additional 88 sq. m. (105 sq. yd) of land for every teenager – an increase for which it probably lacks the land, the labour and the manure. And since children and adolescents constitute more than 50 percent of the total altiplano population, Thomas concluded that the overall consequences of an increase in growth rate and mature bodyweight could ultimately disrupt 'the delicate balance that exists between the human population and the energy-flow system of this high-Andean area'.

The need to maintain the delicate balance between people and the resources upon which they depend has also produced a distinctive system of land tenure in the Andes. In Inca times and before, rural people lived in groups of related families called *ayllu* that were most typically ranged along the shoulders of isolated high valleys. Here they exploited a range of ecological zones on the 'vertical archipelago' of land that extended above and below them, cultivating a variety of crops – tropical fruit at the base, hardy potatoes at the top – in just the same way as the Swiss alpine villagers described in Chapter 4.

Under the ayllu system all land was owned by the community. Some fields were cultivated by the community as a whole, others were allocated to individual households. Periodically, land was re-allocated, so that no household could ever acquire permanent rights to the land it worked and none therefore could ever accumulate more land, more produce, more wealth than the community as a whole deemed fit. Re-allocation also allowed the community to help families in need, and to deal with those who neglected their landholding.

The vertical archipelago and the ayllu systems persisted under the Incas, and although both were severely disrupted by the laws of land tenure that the Spanish introduced, examples survive to this day. In many instances, however, the systems no longer allow people access to a full range of environmental zones, and more people than ever before now depend exclusively on the agropastoralism that remains the only viable means of subsistence at the high altitudes of the altiplano.

Andean agropastoralism is a pattern of simple and direct connections between people and their environment which excludes virtually everything that does not offer some positive and tangible contribution to human welfare. The simplicity of the system has enabled researchers to define its components and measure the flow of energy between them with a degree of precision that studies of human ecology rarely attain. Furthermore, the general absence of surplus in the Quechua system means that it is not overlaid with the complexities of surplus disposal which characterise many other societies. On the altiplano, researchers with a functionalist turn of mind can reasonably assume that every activity contributes something to the balance between human population and energy- flow through the system. And it should be possible, therefore, to explain the relevance of some puzzling aspects of human behaviour in strictly functional terms. What does the Quechua's adopted Catholicism contribute to their subsistence system, for example? And what is the role of the fiestas they celebrate? And guinea pigs – why do they eat so many guinea pigs at fiesta time?

The origins of the guinea pig are obscure, but it is assumed to have been first domesticated in the Andes; certainly it has long been a feature of Andean life. Writing on the food resources available to prehistoric man in the region, historian Edward Lanning remarks: 'If we had any way of estimating the number of guinea pigs eaten in ancient times, we might find that they ranked with seafood as the most important sources of protein in the ancient diet, well ahead of the camelids {guanaco, llama etc.} and the Andean deer.'

Guinea pigs are said to have been the only regular meat supply available to rural people during the Inca period, and they featured prominently in the festivals of the Inca calendar: 1,000 guinea pigs were sacrificed at the Temple of the Sun in Cuzco each August. Throughout the empire, large numbers were sacrificed to the sun in February, and at other rituals concentrated between the months of December and June. Sacrifice seems an inappropriate word, however, for nothing was wasted, and the guinea pigs were cooked and eaten with relish after they had been offered to the gods. Furthermore, the timing of these ritual events seems to have ensured that people had the opportunity of consuming large quantities of guinea pigs several times a year. The practice persists to this day. Guinea pigs are still a highly valued food item throughout the Andes, though they are consumed primarily on festive occasions. As anthropologist Ralph Bolton points out, there are no taboos on eating guinea pigs – anyone may do so at any time of year – but generally people restrict consumption to high days and holidays, on a few of which large numbers of people eat large numbers of guinea pigs. In Cuzco, the festival of Corpus Christi without guinea pigs is as improbable as a festival without processions, remarks Bolton, and the same emphasis on the consumption of guinea pigs applies to Christmas, the carnivals that mark the beginning of Lent, and to the fiestas that follow Easter.

A nicely prepared guinea pig is a delicious source of high quality protein, but it comes in very small packages of around 400 gm. (14 oz) each – fiddly to eat and troublesome to rear in large numbers. How has it achieved such exalted status in the subsistence economy of the Quechua?

Guinea pigs are reared in the kitchen. All rural households, and many town households, keep a flock in a hutch near the warmth of the hearth, where they are fed kitchen scraps and such grasses as are available from the surrounding lands. They grow and breed very quickly, reaching sexual maturity and full adult size at about two months of age, with females usually producing their first litter of two or three young ten weeks later. This means that, in less than one year, a single pair of guinea pigs could produce a flock of more than 40 animals. In practice this does not happen, however, for several reasons: the kitchen would be overrun, the household would be pressed to feed and care for the flock, disease might set in, and – most important of all – many of the animals would have been at their maximum weight for several months, consuming food but adding nothing to their bodyweight.

Setting the dynamics of guinea pig reproduction against the patterns of altiplano climate and food production, Bolton found correlations that explain not only the exalted status of the guinea pig in Quechua subsistence, but also the timing of the festivals at which they are consumed in such quantities. His results show that guinea pigs flourish between October and April, when the rains provide a flush of easily gathered forage and the weather is relatively mild. By December they are beginning to get in the way, and a quarter of the flock are killed and eaten. By February they have increased again, and the flock is culled once more. The same pattern of increase and culling occurs again in April and June, but now the dry season has set in, food is short and forage not easy to find. Consequently the flock is cut back more heavily in April and then reduced to two or three breeding animals in June. Thus different quantities of guinea pigs are available and eaten at different times of year.

This pattern of guinea pig production and consumption neatly matches the round of festivals at Christmas (December), Carnival before Lent (February), Easter (April) and Corpus Christi (June), and variable breeding would easily accomodate the moveable feasts, but what gives the correlation its functional significance is the remarkable extent to which the rise and fall of guinea pig consumption through the year is a mirror image of the fall and rise of total food intake among the human population in general.

Bolton found that guinea pigs were eaten in quantity at just those times of year when protein from other sources was in short supply. And a fiesta marked the occasion. However, as Bolton points out, this does not mean that the Quechua had defined their deficiencies and created a sequence of fiestas to promote health and well-being. They did not need to, since the system sprang directly from the dynamics of guinea pig feeding and breeding, and persisted only because it contributed something useful to the subsistence economy. The fiestas were an ecological conclusion, not a social imperative. The fact that today the festivals are Christian is largely immaterial. The records suggest that each Christian festival merely replaces one held in Inca times, and there is every reason to suppose that the ritual consumption of guinea pigs predates even the Incas.

There are obvious parallels with the traditional Christmas goose in northern Europe in past times. Geese multiply prodigiously and grow fast on summer grass, but in a subsistence economy they would present feeding problems by late December, problems most easily solved by serving the goose up as a welcome supplement to a diet that became increasingly meagre as winter set in. Similarly, the Easter lamb provided a quantity of much- needed protein when the rigours of winter were past. Bolton believes that, throughout human society, the practice of holding regular feasts and fiestas arose as a means of regulating the intake of protein so that people derive the maximum possible benefit from the resources at their disposal. The timing of the feasts would be determined by the availability of whatever was the most limiting factor in the diet, he says, and although these deficiencies may no longer be apparent in some societies, the timing of feasts would still reflect the patterns of deficiency and food production that had prevailed in the past.

Although guinea pigs are an indispensible part of the subsistence diet throughout the high Andes, meat of any kind constitutes a very small proportion of the food that people eat there. Between 83 and 94 percent of the typical family diet consists of vegetables, and potatoes make up more than half of it.

The Incas may indeed have discouraged potato production in favour of maize as their empire expanded, but potatoes nonetheless remained the staple diet of many people under their rule. The fact is that no other crop could sustain people at these high altitudes in the Andes. Maize does not grow well at high altitude, and potatoes are increasingly subject to pests and diseases below 3,500 m. (11,500 ft) in the tropics. So maize and potatoes did not compete for land so much as complement one another. Widespread terracing and irrigation increased agricultural production everywhere, and maize became the currency of the Inca civilisation, to be sure, but when that civilisation collapsed, people quite literally fell back onto the roots from which it had grown – the potato.

The potato is a supreme example of Nikolai Ivanovich Vavilov's contention (published in 1926) that domestic food plants originated wherever the greatest diversity of their wild relative is found. Vavilov was a plant geneticist who rose with the tremendous burst of scientific research that followed the Russian revolution, but later fell from Stalin's favour and died in disrepute (in prison, in 1943, reportedly of natural causes). Vavilov was way ahead of the world and his time; if his research

171

and plans had been allowed to develop he doubtless would have exercised considerable influence on the progress of agricultural science. At the peak of his authority, between 1921 and 1934, Vavilov controlled 400 research institutions with a total staff of over 20,000. He sent expeditions to all parts of the world, hunting down food crops and the origins of their domestication. They sent back 26,000 strains of wheat alone, and in the Andes a party led by his student S.M. Bukasov found wild ancestors of the potato growing profusely on the altiplano to the north of Lake Titicaca.

Bukasov subsequently sorted all potatoes into four groups according to the number of complete chromosome sets in their cells. This work laid the foundations of a school of research into the genetics and origins of potato variability that enrolls the active attention of scientists to this day, but to the people living on the altiplano the significance of such genetic diversity, lies in the large number of different varieties of potato that flourish in the potato's cradle of origin.

The profusion of wild potato species and varieties in the Andes arises from the potential for adaptation and diversity that is inherent in all organisms that reproduce sexually. The genetic reshuffling that occurs with each generation is likely to produce offspring with characteristics the parents did not possess – some of which survive and reproduce while others perish. Over the long period of the potato's evolution, this process of natural selection has produced different varieties, adapted to different conditions of soil, altitude and climate, widely dispersed over a wide range of habitats. However, since each plant must be fertilised by another, the plants continue to diversify, hybrids and new varieties with slightly different characteristics are constantly arising. This potential for adaptation and diversity drives the evolutionary process and supplies the resilience that enables species to survive the changing circumstances that may confront succeeding generations.

In the wild state, the natural tendency of a plant species to adapt and diversify is never threatened, and their gene pool broadens. As plants are domesticated, however, and single varieties are selected for their desirable characteristics and cultivated to the exclusion of all others, the gene pool shrinks dramatically and the inherent diversity of the ancestral species is greatly reduced – which may reduce its resilience as well.

The modern domestic cereal foods – maize, rice, wheat, and so forth, are now far removed from their wild ancestral stock, both genetically and spatially, with their natural potential for adaptation and diversity reduced according. But this has never happened to the potato in the Andes. Because potatoes are cultivated for their tubers, and propagated by tuber, the crops produced by one domesticated variety are all effectively the clones of a single plant. But, while these tuber-clones are harvested from underground, the flowers above remain susceptible to cross-fertilisation, seed is formed and dispersed, and new hybrids will still arise in the cultivated fields. Crosses occur between the domestic varieties themselves, between domestic and wild varieties and, of course, they continue to occur among the wild varieties. So, the vigour and resilient dynamics of evolution and natural selection continue to operate on the potato in its original home.

People in the Andes have given over 1,000 names to the different potato varieties they cultivate, each known for some distinctive characteristic. Many of the names are probably synonyms, but it is generally agreed that over 400 distinct varieties of potato are cultivated. They fall into three broad groups that grow best at different altitudes. Between 3,000 and 3,500 m. (10,000 and 11,500 ft), where rainfall and temperature are ideal, the varieties called *papa maway* produce good crops; between 3,500 and 4,000 m. (11,500 and 13,000 ft) the more hardy *papa puna* are grown, and above 4,000 m. only the frost resistant *papa ruki* will thrive.

The three groups of varieties cover a wide range of land types, while planting and harvesting staggered over several months, as amenable conditions advance up the slope with the seasons, maximises production; but they are not all equally palatable. In fact, the alkaloids that give papa ruki varieties the frost resistance they need to grow at all at high altitude, render their tubers bitter to the point of inedibility. But here again, human ingenuity has found a way round the problem. The bitter potatoes are freeze-dried – spread out after harvesting to freeze each night and thaw each day until all the moisture can be squeezed from them and the potatoes become a dry flour called *chuño*. The alkaloids and bitter taste disappear with the water. In a typical region more than 30 percent of the potato crop was made into chuño; the flour is used to thicken soups and serves as a reserve food when fresh potatoes are becoming short. It is reputed to keep for several years.

No one household grows all 400 varieties of potato known in the Andes, but each will customarily plant from among a local selection of 30 or 40, and the selection itself varies with locality. Everyone has an opinion on which varieties can be expected to produce highest yields under specific conditions, which are most resistant to frost and blight, which store best, which are easiest to cook and which taste best. Any family will generally be able to take up to 25 different varieties from the piles of potato stored in the loft, and will readily reel off the name and characteristics of each. A study conducted by anthropologist Stephen Brush and colleagues from the International Potato Centre at Lima, found 46 named varieties planted in a single field at an altitude of 3,820 m. (12,530 ft) near the Inca ruins at Chincero, outside Cuzco. The varieties were planted at random, insuring the farmer against the wide variety of problems that might afflict the field – late spring, hot summer, blight, early frost – and giving the household a wide choice of potatoes to eat at any time.

Since 1536, when the potato was first encountered by Spanish conquistadores in the Andes, it has become the world's fourth largest food crop – ranking just behind wheat, maize and rice – and is grown in at least 128 of the world's 173 nations. In just 450 years, the potato has become part of the staple diet for many people whose ancestors had subsisted perfectly well upon grain crops for anything up to 4,000 years. The reason for this somewhat surprising development is that the potato is the best all-round package of nutrition known to mankind. Its ratio of carbohydrate to protein is such that anyone eating enough potatoes to satisfy their energy requirements will automatically obtain most of the protein they require.

Furthermore, the 'biological value' of potato protein (an index of the nitrogen absorbed from a food and retained by the body for growth and maintenance) is 73, second only to eggs at 96; just ahead of soya beans at 72, but far superior to maize at 54, and wheat at 53. Potatoes also contain significant amounts of essential vitamins (the British, in fact, derive 30 percent of their vitamin C intake from potatoes). Exceptional productivity is another virtue of the potato. A field of potatoes produces more energy per hectare per day than a field of any other crop. Potatoes grow well from sea level to 14,000 ft (4,300 m.) on a wider variety of soils, under a wider range of climatic conditions, than any other staple food. The potato also matures faster – in 90 to 120 days – and will provide small but edible tubers in just 60 days. All in all, the potato is about the world's most efficient means of converting plant, land, water and labour into a palatable and nutritious food.

The potato was grown and eaten in Spain from about 1570 and, after a slow start, it became the staple subsistence food of all Europe by the mid-18th century. The overall effect of the introduction was dramatic. Improved nutrition of the rural and poorer sections of society led to a sharp rise in population throughout the continent; and the greater productivity of the potato crop not only supplied more labour, but also left a greater proportion of Europe's grain crop available to fuel its developing industrial economy. This process reached a tragic extreme in Ireland, where the population soared to over eight million by 1845, and subsisted on potatoes while exporting grain to England. A disease, late blight, struck the potato crop in 1845 and 1846. A million people died from the ensuing famine and its attendant diseases, and another one-and-a-half million people emigrated, most of them to the United States – an infusion of cultural diversity which contrasts starkly with the lack of biological diversity that had caused the famine. One variety dominated the Irish potato crop in 1845 and 1846 – the 'lumper'. It was exceptionally productive but also extremely susceptible to late blight, and since seed potatoes are clones, every plant in every field was genetically identical. None had any resistance to the disease when it struck, and the entire crop was destroyed, just as though it had been a single plant growing over all the fields of Ireland.

The Irish famine was the tragic extreme of a process that has parallels with earlier developments in the Peruvian Andes: the potato in Europe supplemented a grain-based economy, just as maize had supplemented potatoes in the Andes. The process was reversed, but the effect was the same: a new crop supplied the additional manpower and easily transported grain which made empires of Inca and European civilisation.

CHAPTER TEN

INDIA AND CHINA

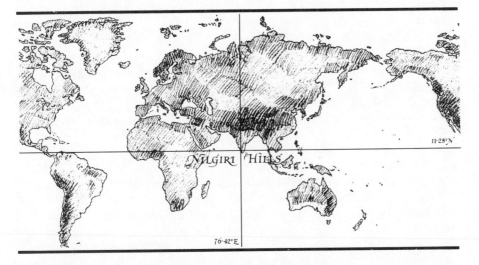

The Toda people live among the high rounded humps of the Nilgiri Hills in southern India, and the buffalo that provide their basic sustenance of milk and butter crop the grass on the open pastureland so short that the heavy morning dew will not even wet the top of a man's foot.

The settlers and administrators of the British colonial era first knew the Nilgiris as the Blue Hills, (blue for the tantalizing hazy outline they saw rising above the plains), and the high hilly plateau – a patchwork of rolling grassland and forest laced with countless streams – offered them a promising realm of agricultural exploitation, a bracing climate for work, and a perfect environment for the rest and recreation of those serving in the Indian outposts of the empire. But it took the British a long time to overcome the difficulties of access through the dense malarial forests which covered the foothills, and it was not until the mid-19th century that a colonial community was finally established in the Nilgiris.

The British also introduced coffee, tea and potatoes to the Nilgiris with considerable success, and attempted to establish orchards that would provide the fruits – apples, pears, plums, and peaches – for which the European palate could find no adequate substitute in tropical India. They dreamed of an orchard paradise in the hills, and built a town on the slopes of a sheltered valley whose local name was translated into English as Ootacamund. A lake graced much of the valley floor, and while the newcomers established their tenancy with a rash of administrative and residential buildings, a club and a church in the style of rural England, they also called upon the local labour force to fill half the length of the lake and make a racecourse of it. Ooty, as the town was soon dubbed by its fans, became a haven for the ill, the jaded, and the merely over-heated colonial

175

administrators and their wives. There was much sport to be had in and
around Ooty. Tigers, elephants, bears, jungle sheep and game birds
attracted those who enjoyed a spot of shooting, and it is said that Neville
Chamberlain perfected the game of snooker in the Ooty club specifically
with the needs of those who had tired of billiards in mind.

The Nilgiris are a massif of ancient rock – far older than the Himalayas –
standing 80 km. (50 mi.) from the shore of the Indian Ocean, 11 to 12
degrees north of the equator. The plateau measures roughly 50 km. (30 mi.)
long and 30 km. (19 mi.) wide, most of it more than 1,800 m. (6,000 ft)
above sea level. Annual rainfall exceeds 10,500 mm (413 in), the second
highest in the sub-continent, but more than 80 percent of the rain falls
during the June-August monsoon. The Toda occupy the upper elevations of
the hills where, in the old days, there were roughly two hectares (five acres)
of pasture for every buffalo, they say; nowadays, however, there are at least
two buffalo on every hectare. Hence the grass is cropped so short. But the
reason for the turnabout lies not with an increase in the number of buffalo,
but with a decrease in the amount of pasture available for them. Confined
to the upper elevations of an already restricted area the Todas have suffered
the encroachment of agricultural settlement from all sides. Furthermore, a
number of dams have been constructed in the high valleys, which have not
only put an appreciable area of pasture and woodland under water, but
have also cut across migration routes to the pasture on the highest slopes,
which the Toda have always reserved for the dry season. Grass grows
sparsely on the Nilgiris in the dry season – even at altitude – so that access
to pasture left untouched on the high ground is crucial to the welfare of the
Toda and their herds.

The Toda were never the only people on the Nilgiri Hills, however. Two
other tribes – the Badaga and the Kota – lived around the rim of the
plateau, and two more – the Irula and the Kurumba – lived in the forest
immediately below. The five groups lived apart and were totally unrelated,
but they were, nonetheless, mutually dependent upon one another. Each
followed a different way of life; the Toda herded buffalo; the Badaga were
agriculturalists; the Kota also grew crops on a small scale but were
principally artisans who made baskets, pots, and iron implements; while
the Irula and Kurumba were nomadic hunters with a fearsome reputation
for magic.

Thus the five distinct tribal groups were ranged around the Nilgiri Hills,
employing a variety of strategies to exploit the available resources of the
Nilgiri Hills in much the same way that the Quechua exploited the
'vertical archipelagoes' of the Andes (see Chapter 9), and the Swiss farmers
exploited the steep valley slopes of the Alps (see Chapter 4) – except, of
course, that the niches on the Nilgiri Hills were social as well as
environmental. Instead of one group exploiting the complete range of
resources, as in the Andes and the Alps, in the Nilgiris a distinct tribe of
people occupied each niche. But although the Nilgiri tribes were socially
independent, economically they were very much dependent upon each
other. Each tribe traded the products of its staple occupation for the
essential goods and products its people needed from the others. The Toda

traded in milk and butter, the Badaga in agricultural produce, the Kota in manufactured goods – the Irula and Kurumba, being nomadic and much fewer in number, were less closely involved in the trade network, but they were a source of forest produce and possibly they traded magic too.

When the British moved into the Nilgiris, the Toda soon became a focus of anthropological attention. A book called simply *The Todas*, published in 1906 by the Cambridge anthropologist William Rivers, nearly 800 pages long, based on field research in the Nilgiris, and packed with facts, figures and genealogy, is a classic of anthropological method and evidence. Rivers' work drew attention to the complicated ritual that evolved round the Toda's dependence on the buffalo. Their relationship with the animals had transcended the simple one of a human need and an animal resource and was, in fact, a religious activity which nurtured the spiritual wellbeing of the Todas no less than buffalo milk and butter nurtured their bodies. Rivers recorded the Toda beliefs and rituals concerning the origin and management of the buffalo herds in scrupulous detail, amply demonstrating the functional relevance of religion in human affairs.

God, for the Todas, existed in the buffalo which provided their milk and butter. The buffalo were born of the hills. Each family kept a herd for its domestic needs, and in addition each clan of related families kept a herd of animals that were deemed to be sacred. There were 14 clans among the Toda; each grazed their herds on a specific patchwork of monsoon and dry season pasture, and migrated with their buffalo between the villages that stood at the centres of the two seasonal locations.

The highest hills in the Nilgiris, to which the Toda took their buffalo in the dry season, were also held to be sacred, and the Toda believed their sacred herds were, in fact, the issue of those hills.

The sacred buffalo grazed with the domestic animals by day, but spent the nights in a separate pen. The task of caring for them moved from family to family within the clan, and the animals stayed longest, it seemed, with the families that most needed the extra milk. The produce of the sacred herd always remained the property of the entire clan, however, to be used or distributed as the clan agreed. The sacred milk was kept apart from the milk of the domestic herd, and churned to butter in a building that the Toda looked upon as a temple, by a man who was accorded the status of a priest.

Thus, very neatly, the Toda's simple dependence on their buffaloes evolved into a complex series of interactions and customs which ensured that the system would go on sustaining the human population for generations to come. The communally-owned sacred herd functioned as a kind of safety net, both to support families in need, and to gather up the surplus produce of exceptional seasons for distribution among the community at large. So, although at first sight religion seemed to be the motivating force of Toda existence, and their lives seemed to be primarily concerned with a complex round of religious obligation and ritual, religion was, in fact, a secondary development that served to formalise the checks and balances on land use and herd ownership upon which the Toda's continued existence depended. The sacred herd was reserve stock and the sacred hills were reserve grazing – both belonged to the community rather than to individual families. The temple was a communal dairy, and the priest was a dairyman whom the clan had put on his honour to perform his tasks for the good of the community.

Despite the encroachments of agriculture, dams, and the destruction of forest on the Nilgiri Hills, the life of the Toda in the 1980s still bears a striking resemblance to that described by William Rivers at the turn of the century. The sacred buffalo still mingle with the domestic herds by day and are kept apart at night. The priest is still appointed, and keeps himself apart from profane activities, wearing only a black loincloth. The men, the women and the children still wear the rough cotton cloak, toga-style, hemmed with geometric patterns of embroidery in black and red wool. On the hill at Morthkedr, where Ponnaye's clan gathered to re-thatch the temple one Sunday morning the people could well have been those who appeared as children in the photographs Rivers had taken for his book.

The heads of the clan arrived together at the village, breaking into a loud deep-throated chant as they appeared suddenly from a grove of trees above, and strode onto the open meadow that sloped down to the temple enclosure. The women standing about the meadow knelt and touched their foreheads to the grass as the men approached.

The temple was constructed like a huge hogshead, laid on its side and sunk into the hill. The roof and sides were a continuous thatch of lemon grass, bound with bundles of split cane; the end walls were slabs of granite, on the central one of which were carved the relief images of a buffalo head with a grand sweep of horns, the sun and moon, flowers, snakes, and the date of the temple's construction: 1976. The only entrance to the temple was set low in the front wall, less than a metre (three feet) high, and as each man arrived he knelt reverentially at the entrance for a few minutes, head and shoulders inside the temple, and offered prayers to the Toda deities – the buffalo – and thanks for their beneficence – milk.

For several hours the men swarmed about the temple enclosure, trimming cane and bundles of grass, lacing on the new thatch from a makeshift scaffold of eucalyptus poles. In the early afternoon they broke off for a meal of rice boiled in milk with butter and jaggery that was served on fresh banana leaves. When the thatching was finished, the priest hammered an abstract carved image into the apex of the thatch. The men formed a circle at the entrance, they linked arms and, pacing their stride, advanced and retreated and circled in time to a chant that had a loud expressed Ha! at the end of every sentence. The unison of the performance was complete and compelling. When it was over the priest, garbed in plain black cloth, took the dairy equipment and a bundle of fresh fern into the newly blessed temple. Then eight young boys were ceremonially taken to stand on the hallowed ground at the temple entrance, close beneath the carved image of the buffalo, for the first time in their lives. Only the priest and his attendants may enter the temple, and only eligible Toda males may enter the temple enclosure. Visitors and Toda women are excluded.

The women of the community took no part in the re-thatching

procedures and ritual, nor did they prepare the rice that was eaten during the course of it. They sat and chatted on the meadow above the temple, and when the thatching was finished started a dance of their own, circling and singing, and ultimately attracting the admiring attention of the men, who collected about the circle, teasing the singers with jokes and ribald comment.

Women hold a position of curiously combined strength and weakness in Toda society. A woman is obliged to acknowledge male authority in general, she is subservient and, for instance, must greet male relatives older than herself by kneeling before them and lifting each of his feet in turn to her forehead. Furthermore, until relatively recent times, there were substantially fewer women than men in the Toda population. An official census conducted by the British in 1871 recorded 140.6 men for every 100 women. In 1881 the ratio was 130.4 men to 100 women; in 1891, 135.9 to 100; and Rivers recorded a ratio of 132.2 men to every 100 women during his period of observation in 1902. The reason for the low proportion of women in the Toda population was female infanticide. Though never readily admitted, the practice was commonplace. Rivers refers to accounts of newborn girls being placed at the gate of the buffalo pen, to be trampled underfoot as the herd left in the morning, and of infants drowned in buffalo milk, but he considered it more likely that unwanted infants were suffocated for a fee by an old woman who then disposed of the child as though it were stillborn.

In a population that probably never much exceeded 1,000, even in pre-colonial times, and hovered about the 800 mark during the latter half of the 19th century, the limited number of women available to produce children at any given time meant that each cohort of mothers was unlikely to do more than replace the existing population. For the Toda as a whole, confined to the upper elevation of the Nigiris by the bands of agricultural activity and forest below, with a severely limited area of pasture on which to graze their buffalo, and no opportunities to expand their territory or intensify their production, this served to keep the human population size under control. For the women in particular, it meant that, despite their social and numerical inferiority to men, they retained a critical amount of control in the matter of who fathered their children.

The control was exercised through polyandry, a form of marriage in which one woman has several husbands, (as opposed to polygyny, where a man has several wives, and monogamy, where there is one of each). Polyandry is common in the animal world, with examples well documented among fleas, fish, birds and elephants, but it is rare among humans, and prevalent only in the Himalayas and the Nilgiri Hills.

Marriage itself is essentially a social strategy which obliges individuals to suspend something of their selfish interests and form a union whose purpose is primarily to ensure the successful rearing of children. In this way marriage furthers the continued existence of the group – though it is a peculiarly human way of doing so. Such alliances are virtually unknown among other mammalian species – most come together only for copulation and very few indeed stay together through gestation and lactation. In

179

human terms, the manner by which female elephants are impregnated would be called rape, for example, and the way a stag abandons his harem after the rutting season would be called desertion.

But no enduring human society lacks a system whereby individual men and women make and generally abide by the formal long-term commitments that marriage implies. No society condones rape. There are none in which all children are the product of casual or impersonal copulation. On the contrary, every society demands that individuals make substantial commitments of time and resources to the raising of their children. And, despite the cost to selfish interests, the vast majority of individuals endeavour to marry and produce children.

Not all individuals are equally successful, however, and the evidence suggests that among humans as in many other animal populations, the female of the species tends to be relatively more successful at finding a mate and producing children than the male. This means that a larger proportion of reproductive females in the population produce children than of reproductive males. Among a group of Yanomamo Indians in the Amazon forest studied by Napoleon Chagnon, for instance, 77.88 percent of all women of reproductive age and above had produced a child, but only 40.69 percent of all adult men.

A suggestion of this male redundancy in human reproduction strategies can be found in modern industrial societies too, although official birth and census statistics are not collated in a way that makes its possible to compare them directly with the Yanomamo figures. However, 29 percent of adult males in Great Britain were unmarried in 1984, for example, but only 22 percent of adult females. Furthermore, 99 percent of all live births in England and Wales were born to women under the age of 40, while the fathers were up to 50 years old. This difference in the reproductive span of the sexes, combined with the fact that pregnant women are effectively absent from the reproductive population for a period of at least nine months, means that, by the very nature of things, there are always likely to be fewer eligible females than males in any society, and an individual male is therefore relatively more unlikely to produce a child than an individual female.

People around the world have developed an impressive number of variations on the basic strategy of marriage, attaching to it so many aspects of property-ownership, prestige and hereditary rights that marriage might be supposed to satisfy a variety of different ends. But the variations are all the product of social adaptation to a variety of prevailing circumstances of environment and population size. The primary function of marriage is always the same: it furthers group continuity by ensuring that the needs of child-caring females are met. And Toda polyandry is a striking example of marriage as strategy that helps to ensure group continuity in an instance where the territory is small, the opportunities for expansion virtually nil, and the options for intensifying food production very limited.

Toda marriage actually begins before the age of three, when children are betrothed by their parents to a cross-cousin. Once adult, however, a wife is free to consort with such additional lovers as her husband approves, and

180

their commitment to her steadily increases as the relationships persist.
Gifts are required. After one year, a man is expected to give a rich shawl;
after two years, gold; after three years, buffalo – and thereafter he is obliged
to share in the responsibility for her upkeep and child-care. When a child is
conceived, its actual paternity is deemed unimportant. Seven months after
conception, the woman declares which of her consorts is to be the social
father of her child and, on the evening before the next full moon, in a
ceremony of touching beauty, she sits before a lamp that the elected father
has set in the bole of tree and accepts from him a small bow and arrow,
whereby he accepts the obligation to care for her and the expected child.
The elected father thus assumes primary responsibility for the child,
whether or not he was its natural father.

By nullifying the significance of actual paternity, Toda polyandry grants
a mother two important choices. When she wants to conceive she can
choose the husband she considers will make the best biological father of
her offspring, and before the child is born she can select the best candidate
for its social welfare. Furthermore, since none of the husbands can be
certain which is the child's true father – regardless of which of them is
selected to be its social father – each is liable to suspect that it might be
his, and each can therefore be encouraged to offer gifts and share
responsibility for the child's welfare throughout its upbringing. And
indeed they do. Though no one in Toda society knows the identity of his or
her father, everyone benefits from the attention of several candidates.

There is of course an aspect of male competition that is being exploited
here, but it serves a very positive function. By leaving actual paternity
undisclosed while consorting with several husbands and encouraging them
all to believe that they might be the father of her child, a wife is able to
bestow the resources, rights, prestige and ambitions of several individuals
onto a single infant. Thus there is a tendency for the assets of many
individuals to concentrate in the hands of a few as they pass from one
generation to the next in Toda polyandry. This contrasts sharply with
marriage systems in which each man has one or more wives, where the
assets of a single individual tend to be divided and dispersed among several
offspring.

Combined with the nasty practice of killing daughters at birth (which is
said to have been done because fathers wanted their firstborn to be males,
but which also limited the number of females available for marriage at any
time), polyandry among the Toda served the function of limiting population growth by making it impossible for a man to establish a family line
which in a few generations might produce more people than the available
resources could support.

But, although polyandry functioned to limit the size of the Toda
population, it also served to create an appreciation of sex as an expression
of love, and as a source of joy and satisfaction. Promiscuity was condoned,
physical attractiveness, desire, and sexual prowess were admired – indeed
they still are. While the women danced above the temple at Morthkedr,
there was more than a suggestion of display in their behaviour, more than a
hint of sexual contemplation in the admiration that the men expressed.

No one knows precisely how long ago the Toda began practising polyandry, but it was certainly well established and controlling Toda population growth satisfactorily when the British arrived on the scene. Once the Toda came into contact with a wider world, however, its tendency to make sex a source of pleasure rather than of children soon destroyed its basic function.

By 1871 venereal disease was rife. A clinic in Ootacamund is reported to have treated four percent of the entire Toda population for syphilis in that year, and it can be assumed that many more sufferers did not apply for treatment. The size of the Toda population declined steadily to the end of the 19th century, then stabilised at around 700 for a decade or so. But then increasing numbers of women proved to be sterile, and numbers again declined steadily until the mid-1950s, when an intensive medical programme obliged every Toda to take a course of penicillin. The effect of the treatment was dramatic and 40 babies were born in the following two years. Meanwhile polyandry was all but abandoned. The fall in the birthrate had also coincided with dramatic changes in the status of the Toda in the Nilgiri Hills. Land allocation had hastened the invasion of agriculture, and the cash economy had drawn the Toda into a wider world. They were still rooted in their traditions, but with a different outlook. And if a polyandrous wife was unlikely to produce a single child, well, that was incentive enough for a man to take another and look to the wider world for the means of support.

So, when Ponnaye proudly ushered his mother forward, and encouraged her to bare the tattoos on the now wrinkled arms that had enchanted and held three husbands, he was accompanied by his second wife, Jeyalakshmie, and their five year old son, Thashtharguttan. In one generation, the marriage strategy of a Toda family had shifted from polyandry to polygny, and while Ponnaye still tended the buffalo and fulfilled his traditional obligations, he also talked enthusiastically of the business dealings to which he was devoting a portion of the resources he had inherited from his three fathers.

All in all, the Toda evidence indicates that what people call 'traditions' are not immutable aspects of society, preserved for their own sake at whatever cost. On the contrary, traditions arise to fulfil specific functions, and disappear when they cease to do so. When they linger on after their usefulness has gone, they are at best harmless and quaint, but at worst they can threaten the stability of the society – as with moka customs in the highlands of Papua New Guinea (see Chapter 2). Traditions, in fact, are merely the tokens of adaptive success that come and go with the changing times, while it is the process of adaptation itself that deserves to be cherished.

India is a stew of tradition, with 761 million people – the world's second largest national population (some way behind China with 1,063 million, but well ahead of the Soviet Union, third largest with 276 million) – packed on 3.28 million sq. km. (1.7 million sq. mi.) of total land area. It has an average population density of 232 people per sq. km. (601 per sq. mi.), though not all of India is equally inhabitable, and the density is considerably higher in some rural areas (and in the cities, of course).

No other country of comparable size supports more than a fraction of India's population density. China, with three times the land area, is less than half as densely populated: 110.8 per sq. km. (287 per sq. mi.). The Soviet Union, the world's largest nation with over 22 million sq. km. (8.5 million sq. mi.) of land area, supports an average of just 12.4 people per sq. km. (32.1 per sq. mi.). By comparison, the United States has an average of just 25.4 people on each of its 9.4 million square kilometres (65.8 per sq. mi.), and Europe's overall population density is 101 per sq. km. (261.7 per sq. mi.)

Why is India able to support such a large population at such high density? There are two main factors involved. Firstly, a full 57 percent of its land area is arable and permanent cropland. Only Barbados with 77 percent, Bangladesh (68 percent), Denmark (62 percent) and Mauritius (58 percent) have higher proportions of productive land, and these are all very small countries with very special circumstances. Among the world's larger nations the United States, for example, cultivates only 22 per cent of its land area, but even that is double the proportion cultivated in China (11 percent), and the Soviet Union (ten percent). And the second factor contributing to the exceptional size and density of India's population is the uniquely fertile and robust character of its soils.

Soils are produced by the interaction of climate and geology over long periods of time. In India this process began relatively recently, in geological terms, so that although it has already generated vast tracts of deep soil throughout the subcontinent (especially on the northern plains where the alluvium of the Himalayas has been accumulating for millions of years), these soils are still rich in nutrients. By contrast, many large areas of Africa, Australia, north and south America, consist of ancient soils so weathered and leached that they are almost devoid of nutrients, unstable and easily reduced to the status of desert.

The intrinsicially fertile soils of India have been supporting agriculture for 5,000 years or more, and together with a warm temperate to tropical climate and a fairly stable pattern of monsoon rainfall, they have become the basis of one of the world's most remarkable farming systems. It all began around 3000 BC with the introduction of cereal crops from their centre of domestication in the Middle East, which was followed by the domestication of native rice, beans and cotton by 2000 BC and the arrival of sorghum and millets from Africa shortly thereafter. Sugarcane, bananas and other tropical fruits were introduced from Southeast Asia during the same period, and in historical times the Europeans introduced maize, groundnuts and potatoes. Along with this wide range of domestic crops, India was also endowed with a wide range of domestic stock. Native cattle and buffalo were domesticated throughout the subcontinent; sheep, goats and camels in the northwest. The pig was indigenous, and the domestic chicken is India's gift to the farmyards of the world.

The climate is temperate enough to support year-round crop growth in most parts of India, though cropping patterns are dependent on water supply. In the north, the river systems of the Ganges plain, and the wells drawing on the great aquifer that lies beneath, provide sources of irrigation that permit virtually continuous cultivation of the most productive crops. In the predominently rain fed regions of the south, however, farmers maintain year-round production by planting alternate crops – sorghum and red gram during the warm months of the summer monsoon on one set of fields; wheat and Bengal gram in the cool season on the others left fallow to soak up and store something of the monsoon rains.

Despite such continuous, increasingly intensive cultivation, the robust and intrinsically fertile Indian soils have maintained relatively consistent and dependable levels of production for centuries. Yields are low, generally no higher than those obtained in Africa, but, as the agriculturalist Sir Joseph Hutchinson points out in his book *Farming & Food Supply*, India's low yields are the result of over 4,000 years of intensive cropping whereas those in Africa are the product of intrinsically poor soils. Maintaining even the low yields of poor African soils calls for frequent and often lengthy periods of fallow; very few could stand even 20 years of intensive continuous cropping, let alone the 40 centuries to which India's soils have been subjected.

India's civilisation – ancient and modern – therefore is founded on the enduring fertility of its soils, and on the exceptional variety of crops and stock that can be raised in the country's diverse range of topography and climate. Soil and produce are the basis of the balance between land and people that has sustained India's large and predominantly rural population for a very long time. But there is more to it than that. The primary demands of exploiting a wide variety of resources, combined with the secondary demands of servicing the dense concentrations of people that India's soil and produce were able to support, has produced a very particular kind of social balance. People have tended to find their own niches – much as the Toda, the Badaga, the Kota, and the forest dwelling Irula and Kurumba have occupied quite distinct ecological zones on the Nilgiri Hills. But while the Nilgiri Hills provide a good introduction to the ecological basis of the stratification that has become so deeply rooted in Indian society, it is among more sedentary concentrations of people that the principle has found its most far-reaching expression.

Across the breadth of India, where even today over 80 percent of the entire national population lives in rural communities of a thousand people or less, the demands of exploiting agricultural potential, and servicing the needs of the masses of people, created an extraordinary variety of occupational niches. Productive members of the community, such as farmers, tinsmiths, tailors, bakers and shoemakers; functionaries such as merchants, tax collectors and priests, and even entertainers such as jugglers, dancers, bear-handlers and snake-charmers, all found distinct niches for themselves from which they might lay claim to a share of the land's resources. Each village community typically contained between ten and 20 such occupational niches, and many nomadic groups regularly visited a string of villages each year or season, dispensing merchandise, or medicine or magic or simple diversions of an entertaining nature.

184

Naturally enough, children followed their parents into the niches they were born into. Families expanded into clans. Marriages were contracted between clans, among villages, but strictly within occupational niches. As these diverse populations grew, India was laced about with a network of strong interconnected social relationships that made institutions of both the ecological diversity upon which the society was founded, and the economic interdependence upon which the full exploitation of that diversity depended.

This division of society into distinct occupational niches is, of course, better known as the caste system; a traditional system that has acquired some unpleasant overtones of social segregation during its long history but which also has functioned as a component of the ecological equilibrium that has sustained India, undisturbed, while waves of conquest and foreign empire ebbed and flowed across the country throughout historical times. Technical innovations, ideas, aspects of religion and art were absorbed or discarded as the case may be, but India's agricultural base and social traditions were largely unaffected, and the ancient equilibrium seemed timeless.

The caste system can be traced back nearly 2,000 years, and probably began long before, since when the number of groups that it incorporates has swelled to 3,000 castes and over 25,000 sub-castes. Some have only a few hundred members, others have several million.

Each caste is a reproductively isolated group of people, but unlike isolated tribes which also marry and produce children only among themselves, the castes have never been geographically isolated one from another. On the contrary, the castes are packed together in the same territories, as the high productivity of the land and the variety of labour requirements demands, and during the centuries of straightforward reproductive isolation they have evolved a complex of cultural differences that separate the castes in the crowded social environment of India no less than rivers or mountain ranges might separate tribes in an empty wilderness. Social barriers can be as difficult to cross as geographical boundaries.

The castes are separated primarily by distinctions of skill and occupation, but centuries of reproductive isolation have also produced secondary practices of diet, dress, language, religious observance and social behaviour that makes each stand out clearly in the crowd. However, like the peacock's tail and the involutions of Balinese culture (see Chapter 2), some of these practices have evolved to lengths that seem some distance ahead of their initial function. The basically functional practices of reserving water and food resources for the caste, and of marrying and sharing food only among one's own kind, for instance, have evolved beyond mere prohibitions and taboos into notions that members of one caste could be physically and even spiritually polluted by contact with the members of another, supposedly inferior caste.

These strictly cultural developments were confirmed in the sanskrit writings of the Hindu religion which formalized – if not sanctified – the ethics of the caste system nearly 2000 years ago. The *Dharma shastras*, Hindu law books compiled between 100 and 500 AD, provide the basic

185

instructions of Hindu life. They define precisely how people of different castes should behave among themselves, and towards other castes, in the full variety of conceivable circumstances. A belief in reincarnation was fundamental, and the faithful performance of caste duties in this life would prepare the soul for higher caste duties in the next. Ultimately, every soul would attain sublime existence in a realm of universal being – heaven – but meanwhile everyone must perform the duties of the caste into which they were born and observe its traditions, rites and practices unquestioningly, no matter how crude or inexplicable they may seem.

To western eyes, the Hindu willingness to accept things as they are, the readiness to spend a lifetime washing other peoples' underwear or in some other form of drudgery, seems like abject resignation – a rejection, by default, of the basic human drive to strive for a better position in life. But the Hindus see things very differently. The blessings or blight of this life are wholly the result of behaviour in a past life, they believe, and only the uncomplaining fulfilment of the tasks ordained for this life will bring an improvement next time round. Numerous reincarnations lie between the status of the *dhobi wallah* and the priest, but each may move a little closer to heaven or further from it according to how he performs in this life.

The law books grouped the castes into four classes, called *varnas*, from the Sanskrit meaning colour, with the Brahmins (priests) at the top, and the Kshatriyas (barons or warriors), Vaisyas (commoners or merchants) and Sudras (artisans and labourers in descending order beneath. Each class was considered to be variously defiled and polluted by their occupations, dietary habits and customs. Pollution and defilement were thought to be contagious, so each class avoided contact with those below and the classes with the most defiling occupations of all were ranked beneath the Sudras, so low that a mere touch could pollute: these were the untouchables.

Although the caste system arose to serve an ecological function and persisted because it furthered the welfare and continuity of all, its traditions have increasingly heaped reward on the few. One observer of the phenomenon has described Hindu social order as 'the most thoroughgoing attempt known in human history to introduce absolute inequality as the guiding principle in social relations'. The system has out-lived its function and the fact was acknowledged some time ago. Government legislation has outlawed the discriminatory social order of caste. Mahatma Gandhi renamed the untouchables *Harijans*, meaning 'children of God'. But the traditions of caste are deeply engrained and, although its divisive character is easily eroded by affluence in urban society, it is, in fact sharpened among the low caste rural communities.

Changes in the laws of land ownership, combined with the spread of the cash economy, have swept aside the security of mutual interdependence on which the caste system was based, without leaving anything serviceable in its place. Life in the villages is actually harder and more uncertain than before. Thrust by circumstance into a wider world, each caste tends to take refuge in its own social identity, seeing others as competitors for the same scant resources – jobs and cash – rather than as contributors to a mutually beneficial system.

The problem dates back to colonial days, when British administrators decided that the iniquities of India's social arrangements might be best adjusted by re-allocating land and offering equal opportunity to all. Among those benefitting most from these changes was the government itself, which assumed ownership of all common land and forest, along with rights to the produce thereof. The intentions were no doubt admirable, but the effects were little short of disastrous. The mutual interests and obligations that had previously encouraged the castes to keep the exploit- ation of common resources, such as grazing and forest, for example, within sustainable limits, were swept aside when the state took possession. The move was intended to preserve the resources, but once the owners became a faceless and mostly absent authority, rather than people of the im- mediate community, they were exposed to the depredations of whoever might think they could get away with it. People find it easier to steal from a state authority than from someone they know.

Among the results of state ownership is the fact that every betelnut palm in Mysore, for instance, is marked on the government survey maps of the district. Every tamarind tree on the road from Srinivaspur to Madana- palle likewise bears a large white-painted number and presumably is listed in some government inventory. The state exploits its resources according to departmental decisions that do not always pay much attention to local opinion – and there are anomalies. The forestry department may fell a tamarind at will, for example, but a householder may not even chop a branch from any sandalwood tree that might stand on his land.

Sandalwood smuggling is one result of the state takeover that has become a highly lucrative activity which ends with exciting tales in the newspapers of police chases and shootouts. For Rajanna, a 26 year old member of the birdcatcher caste who lives on land the state has decided his group should farm near the large village of Rayalpad, the effect is far less colourful, the prospects far more bleak.

Rajanna's people were nomads, travelling a round of villages and forest, catching birds on request for meat and medicine and ornamentation. They still do catch birds, but much of the old forest has been replaced with ranks of eucalyptus now, and the birdcatchers have been told they must become farmers. The 15 families have been allocated 15 hectares (37 acres) of dry sandy ground below the hill that rises to the east of Rayalpad. It is not enough to make them self-sufficient, and their future is utterly dependent on their achieving some success in the cash economy. Education is said to be the route to success. The birdcatchers' children attend the one-room school nearby, but the teacher is frequently absent, and even if they manage to get to a secondary school they are more likely to be among the 70 percent that dropout early than among the 16 percent of the remainder that actually pass the school-leaving exams.

The state offers incentive and advantage to the scheduled tribes (as the lower castes are now designated), but the greater equality of opportunity and achievement that should follow banishment of the caste system advances slowly. If the birdcatchers were the only caste to be caught in the time-lapse that lies between abandoning rural self-sufficiency and achieving some economic independence, success might be more evident. But not a kilometre from the birdcatchers' village lies Mandala, the tax-collectors' village, and across the dam from Mandala lies Dombara-palli, where the combmakers are congregated, and below the dam, beyond a large stand of eucalyptus, is Geljigur, where the Harrijans have been settled – 17 families on ten hectares (25 acres).

All these groups might once have been mutually dependent upon one another; living in a single integrated community, collectively farming a larger area of land. Now they are competitors, living apart, each struggling for a share of the same resource, each identified by the caste labels that legislation supposedly removed. On the face of it, the divisive nature of the caste system seems to constitute a large part of their problem. Progress might come faster if only they would abandon their prejudices and cooperate more. But it is not caste prejudice so much as the breakdown of the system in which caste once made sense that is the problem. Now that the system no longer functions, the traditions of caste have proved to be its most enduring feature – a small haven of cooperative group identity in a very competitive and insecure world.

Sacred cows – that is the label western culture attaches to traditions that have outlived their function, like the caste system, but which persist anyway, often to the detriment of the people who continue to observe them. Sacred cows. The term can be applied to the caste system, to the British monarchy and to the notion of an almighty dollar, but it is derived, of course, from the Hindu tradition of granting the cow such elevated status that it must be revered and never slaughtered. The tradition of the sacred cow has populated India with 237 million cattle, according to a 1982 count: one for every three people. This huge bovine population adds considerably to the pressure on space and resources in an already densely populated and largely underfed country, though with little apparent benefit, it is said.

Cows roam the roads and byways of India with sublime indifference. They cause traffic jams in the towns, accidents on the highways, and leave a good deal of mess underfoot. All India defers to the cow – even the vegetable seller is gentle as he chides and begs her to leave his wares alone. No one troubles them, and no Hindu would ever dream of killing and eating them.

To the beef-eating British, inclined to salivate at the mere thought of a well-roasted joint, generously apportioned, the sacred cow was the ultimate absurdity among a host of ritual customs and traditions that thwarted their attempts to bestow European civilisation on India. Most of the population was half-starved, they reasoned, yet people refused to eat or even control the numbers of cattle that roamed the country.

If people in India could be persuaded to slaughter and consume cattle regularly, the country's problems would be greatly eased, the colonial observers concluded. People would be better nourished, and a large proportion of the resources presently devoted to cattle could be allocated to more productive ends. It all seemed so obvious.

Traditional religious belief seemed the basic reason for the sacred status of the cow in India, and to colonial observers this belief seemed to have acquired excessive importance. Cow and cattle worship are set deep at the heart of the Hindu religion: 330 million gods and goddesses reside in the body of a cow, says Hindu theology; 86 reincarnations are needed to transform the soul of a devil into the soul of a cow. One more, and the soul takes on a human form, but killing a cow sends the soul all the way back to the form of a devil again.

The priests say that to look after a cow is in itself a form of worship. People love their cows and put them in special sanctuaries when they are too old or sick to be kept at home. At the moment of death, devout Hindus themselves are anxious to hold the tail of a cow, in the belief that the animal will guide them safely to the next life.

The Hindu gods are similarly devoted to cows and bulls. Krishna, god of mercy and childhood, is described in the sacred literature as a cowherd, whose wealth lay in the cows he protected. At festivals celebrating Krishna's protective role, priests mould cow dung into images of the god, which calves must trample to dust before mere mortals may remove them. Shiva, the avenging god, rides about the heavens on Nandi, the bull whose image is prominent at the entrance of every temple dedicated to Shiva. Above the city of Mysore, a huge statue of Nandi, gracefully reclined and hewn from the hillside, is regularly decked with flowers and anointed by attendant priests with a holy mixture of milk, curds, butter, urine and dung, a spot of which is also placed on the forehead of visiting worshippers. Not only the body and being, but also every product of the cow and bull is sacred to the Hindu.

The depth and intensity of Hindu devotion to the cow in India has inspired a good deal of frustration among experts charged with the task of developing the country's agriculture and economy. For a century or more, survey after survey has typically written of 'irrational ideologies' maintaining 'vast numbers of useless cattle' that are 'more of a liability than an asset', 'whose utility to the community did not justify economically the fodder which they consumed'. An Indian Select Committee wrote of '20 million uneconomic cattle'. A Royal Commission criticised the Hindu sentiment that preserved animals 'which are quite useless from birth to death'. A National Council of economic research complained of 'old and useless cattle which share scant resources with working and useful cattle'. An International Cooperation report of 1956 declared that '180 million cattle and 87 million sheep and goats are competing with 360 million people for a scant existence', and the UN Food and Agriculture Organisation boldly concluded that 'cattle numbers exceed economic requirements by any standard and a reduction in the number of uneconomic animals would contribute greatly to possibilities of improving the quality and condition of those that remain'.

Indian cattle were small and weak, and the cows yielded on average less than one-tenth of the milk that cows in Europe and the United States provided, it was pointed out. Furthermore, at least 50 percent of all cows over three years old were dry and/or barren, according to one survey.

189

Inferior, uneconomic, useless and a liability – these were the conclusions of numerous enquiries into the status of cattle of India, and many implied that the situation was unlikely to change so long as 'the... Hindu would rather starve to death than eat his cow.' Popular imagery adopted the sacred cow as a symbol of mindless tradition, while anthropologists in general explored the details and ramifications of this seemingly irrational aspect of human behaviour. In 1965, however, one anthropologist in particular was inspired to approach the question from a functional point of view, and the results of his enquiry amount to a very prominent landmark in the progress of anthropological investigation.

Marvin Harris's paper *The Cultural Ecology of India's Sacred Cattle*, was published in February 1966. Among the almost unaminous praise of the reviews that were published with it, one commentator remarked that the paper was likely to stimulate 'much meaningful discussion and research'. He was not wrong. Harris's paper is one of those rare items in academic endeavour – an observation of such startling clarity that it not only throws new light on the subject under discussion, but also illuminates routes by which other subjects may be approached.

The functional approach that Harris adopted began with the assumption that long-persisting cultural practices such as the Hindu taboos on bovine slaughter and eating beef must have arisen in response to ecological pressures of some sort, and can only have persisted because they were successful. Therefore, Hindu attitudes towards cattle must reflect a symbiotic relationship of benefit to both cattle and people, he said, not a state of competition between them, as the experts had concluded. The strength and persistence of the taboos was simply an indication of just how necessary they had become.

To test his functional hypothesis, Harris analysed all major aspects of the Indian cattle complex, and in every case found that people were better off with the cattle than without them. Though the cattle are weak and inefficient, and the Hindu system of management could be improved, 'India's cattle complex is a positive-functioned part of a naturally selected *eco-system*', Harris concluded, 'not a negative-functioned expression of an irrational ideology'.

In the matter of milk production, for instance, Harris found that, although the yield of the average Indian cow is only a fraction of that provided by cows in the United States and Europe, they still supplied a significant 46.7 percent of the nation's dairy production, (with buffalo supplying most of the remainder). And although high caste Hindus would neither slaughter nor eat cattle, the lower castes and scheduled tribes were not subject to such prohibition; nor were the sizeable Christian, Moslem and pagan populations of India. Together, these groups added up to well over 60 million people and they consumed a very large proportion of the 25 million bovines that died each year. And on the way to the cooking pot, these animals contributed their hides to India's leather industry – the largest in the world.

But milk, meat and hides were only the valuable secondary spinoffs of a system that had its roots where every aspect of human existence in India has its roots – in the huge rural economy that the enduring fertility of the country's robust soils had made possible. Bullocks and dung were the indispensible products that made the cow sacred in India, Harris concluded. Bullocks for hauling the plough, dung for cooking the food.

Every previous survey had concluded that India supported more cattle than could be economically justified. Harris, however, concluded that there was in fact a shortage of bullocks. Over 80 percent of the entire population of India lives on the land – 500 million people in 1981 – and 47 percent of that huge number is known to earn less than $100 a year. The vast majority is overwhelmingly dependent on food the people grow themselves. Most of them cultivate holdings of five hectares (12 acres) or less on the 77 percent of India's arable land that is not irrigated. The success of their crops is entirely dependent on rainfall, about 90 percent of which falls in the summer monsoon season. The monsoon tends to begin and end abruptly, and a farmer must therefore plough and sow as soon as the first showers break if he is to take full advantage of the available rainfall.

Over vast areas, therefore, people begin working their land simultaneously. They break the land – packed hard from the dry season – with a tough hand-wrought plough drawn by a pair of oxen. Ideally, each farmer should have his own plough and his own pair of oxen, for if he must borrow or hire those of a neighbour he will certainly have to wait until the neighbour has ploughed and sown his own land, which means that the advantage of the first showers will be lost and late sowing may consequently produce poor crops. There were well over 60 million such farmers at the time of Harris's survey, but only 80 million working animals (including buffalo) – a 40 million shortfall, if each farmer was to have the pair of oxen he needed. Therefore, as much as one-third of India's rural community lacked the minimum tractive assistance it required.

In the modern age it might be thought that a tractor, collectively owned, would be the answer. As Harris points out, a tractor can plough a field almost ten times faster than a pair of oxen, it is true, but the initial investment is 20 times greater and the machine becomes more economical than draught animals only if it is used more than 900 hours a year – which, among a group of small farms, raises problems of allocating its use and maintenance. Tractors make most sense on large holdings, but although their numbers increased ten-fold in the 20 years from 1963, the numbers of draught animals have remained constant.

Ideally, then, every one of the families who derive the major part of their sustenance from India's 60 million plus small farms needs a pair of mature draught oxen. But where are they to get them? The families have insufficient income with which to buy them, and no pasture on which to breed them. The answer is, of course, that they get them from the sacred cows. Every cow that roams about India with no apparent aim or purpose belongs to someone, and is busily converting what nourishment it can find into commodities of great value to its owner – primarily male calves.

The cows wander away from the homestead each morning to crop the roadside vegetation, devour harvest stubble, scavenge in ditches and over

191

rubbish heaps, raid the markets, or perhaps even to receive handouts from people anxious to keep their soul at the 87th incarnation, and now and again they bring home a calf. If the calf is a bullock, the farmer will invest some care in its rearing, if it is female then at least its mother will be converting some of its feed into milk for a time and if the calf survives then it too might one day produce a bullock from scraps. Obviously, the more cows a farmer owns, the more likely he is to secure a pair of working oxen, and while the cost of feeding the cows falls on society at large, rather than on his own small patch of land, the potential reward is well worth the small effort required of him. And calves are not the only reward.

The scrawny scavengers probably bring home a calf only once every three or four years, but every night they bring home a quantity of dung. As with the Quechua of the high Andes, dung is an indispensible element of rural India's economy. Harris found that about 340 million tons of it is deposited as manure when the cattle graze on fallow and newly harvested land; another 160 million tons manures waysides that the cows scavenge, and not less than 300 million tons is collected by the women of the household, moulded into small saucer-size cakes, and stored in neat weather-proof stacks for use as cooking fuel throughout the year. Nine out of ten rural households in India have no other source of cooking fuel. Their firewood resources were long since taken over by the state or depleted, and they have no money to buy coal, kerosene or charcoal. Cow-dung fuel actually provides India with the energy equivalent of 35 million tons of coal or 68 million tons of firewood – an impressive contribution to the country's energy balance which the wholesale introduction of tractors would seriously upset.

Of course, India's wandering population of sacred cows is a very inefficient means of producing dung, milk and bullocks. Their milk production and reproductive rate is absurdly low, and they do not eat enough to produce all the dung they could. Most sacred cows spend their lives in a state of semi-starvation. But, on the other hand, they are the survivors of a line winnowed from centuries of naturally selected breeding and therefore extremely hardy. Most cows that survive to maturity usually produce a calf every three or four years. Of course there are faster and more efficient ways of producing the required numbers of draught oxen. Harris (1986) quotes an agricultural economist who has calculated that India's oxen requirement could be easily maintained by a standing population of just 24 million well-fed breeding stock, rather than the 54 million mature cows that presently roam the country – a strategy that would also make 30 million beasts available annually for consumption or export, were it not for the taboos of the sacred cow. Several facts militate against the over-hasty introduction of modern husbandry methods in rural India, however. Firstly, good modern breeding stock requires a good quality diet, which the small farmer could not provide. Secondly, it is the poorest farmers who own the least productive cows. These skinny scavengers do not amount to much in themselves, but their offspring – though infrequent – do help to keep the farmer independent of his neighbours and the moneylenders who would seize his land on default.

Harris does not deny that the sacred cow and India's general system of cattle management could be improved, or that a better system may not evolve. He says only that the relationship between cattle and people in India is symbiotic, not competitive, and that the present relatively high ratio of cattle to humans is the result of prevailing ecological circumstance, not Hindu ideology. Circumstances may change, new and more efficient food energy systems may evolve, but any peremptory development that simply removed the sacred cow from the landscape, would also threaten to remove more families from the land, leaving them no choice but to join the countless millions already crowded onto India's city streets.

Since the cow fulfils such a crucial role in the rural economy that supports most of the Indian population it is hardly surprising that it should have acquired honoured status – 'the cow is our mother', Hindus say, 'she gives us milk and butter. Her male calves till the land and give us food'.

Culture is the organisation of diversity, not the replication of uniformity, wrote the anthropologist A.F.C. Wallace in a book that attempts to explain the process by which small, quite different groups of people join to become the large national entities and civilisations that leave their mark on world history. Wallace's observation stresses the fact that diversity is the wellspring of human existence and evolution. Diversity can never be swept aside or swamped or ruled out of law by a single uniform system of cultural behaviour.

The two largest and longest sustained civilisations that the world has ever known – India and China – provide classic examples of both the human potential for cultural diversity and the capacity that people have for organising that diversity. At first the two systems appear to be contradictions – India, apparently a mass of rampant, unimpeded cultural diversity; China, apparently conforming to a single uniform strategy. But first appearances can be deceptive. Closer consideration reveals that both civilisations are equally diverse; they appear to be so different only because each employs a different means of organising its diversity. In India, it is religion that has organised diversity to the benefit of group continuity; in China, an equally complex and resilient system of central government has fulfilled that role.

Both systems have been operating for more than 2,000 years. The differences between them derive from the basically different physical attributes of the land upon which their human populations depend. India farms 57 percent of its land area and feeds its 761 million inhabitants on a variety of crops and livestock. China is able to farm only 11 percent, and feeds 1,063 million people predominently on rice and pork. The uniformity that seems to dominate life in China is strictly a matter of food production and distribution; underneath, human diversity flows strongly.

The unchanging uniformity of Chinese civilisation is strictly a figment of Western imagination – or rather of Western observation that paused only long enough for a cursory glance. Chinese civilisation has a tumultuous history of change behind it. The country today embraces 55 acknowledged 'national minorities' whose individual cultural character-istics vary as much of those of distinct nations in other parts of the world. Spoken language and dialect vary so much that people from one part of the country may be totally unable to understand those from another. The Chinese spoken in Canton and the south, for instance, is about as different from the Mandarin of the north as are Portuguese and Italian. In contrast to the diversity of its speech, however, China has only one written language, mutually intelligible to every literate person throughout the country, and indeed throughout over 2,000 years of Chinese civilisation. This single language is probably the most important factor in the organisation of human diversity that created China.

The written language of China has existed for about 4,000 years and has remained essentially unaltered. It is a concept script which uses pictures to signify objects and actions – there is a separate picture for each concept, and abstract ideas are conveyed mainly by a combination of concrete ones. The disadvantage of the system is the huge numbers of signs it needs – over 50,000 altogether, although 'only' about 2,500 are needed to make a daily newspaper intelligible – but the immense advantage of the system is that it does not depend upon the spoken word. Chinese script can be read without any knowledge of the language spoken by its writer. Thus it was the least ambiguous means of communication among people who spoke a wide variety of dialects. Furthermore, being only a written language, it remained consistently the same, even while the spoken languages may have evolved and changed considerably. Thus, modern Chinese readers can understand the scripts of 2,000 years ago to a degree that escapes modern English readers who may want to understand what Chaucer wrote, only 600 years ago.

The Chinese written language played a role similar to that of Latin in the early history of Europe. It was the language of scholars and administrators, but in China it did not require people to speak differently and was backed by very different attitudes to the problems of organising diverse groups of people under one system. The Chinese established a civil service to run the country more than 2,500 years ago. Its principles were set down by Confucius in the 6th century BC. They included benevolence and loyalty, and were intended to maintain harmony among the diverse society of China without the undue use of force (though that intention was not always fulfilled).

Civil servants were recruited and promoted through a series of examin-ations in which excellence in Confucian scholarship featured highly. The examinations were open to everyone and stimulated considerable social mobility. Success could bring privileged status, prestige, a career and wealth to even the most humble-born. There was no hereditary privileged class under the Confucian system. Education, not factors of property or birth, defined the elite of China and over the centuries this single standard has moulded a very large and diverse group of people into a society that shares a remarkably uniform ideological outlook.

The persistence of China as a single national unit – as a civilisation – despite not infrequent external pressure and many rounds of internal calamity, is an indication of how effectively people can organise human diversity, but it is also a measure of the compelling need to do so. Amidst tales of dynastic confrontation and peasant uprising, the history of China is one of continuous adjustment to the problems of population and food supply. Historians have shown a direct correlation between population increase, rising food prices and revolution during the Ming dynasty (1368-1643 AD), for example. Official documents record large and widespread migrations about the country. In the late 14th century, one move resettled 150,000 landless households in the south; another resettled 70,000 in the north. The empty cultivable land of Sichuan province was settled during the 17th century by a general offer of draught animals, seed and five year's tax exemption to immigrants, and immediate promotion for any official who could persuade 300 people to go there. For 200 years Sichuan absorbed the greater part of China's growing population, expanding from eight million in 1776 to over 44 million in 1850; today Sichuan holds 100 million people, China's largest regional population.

The Yangtze highlands, Yunnan province in the southwest, the Han river valleys and the lower Yangtze were all similarly developed and populated by mass migrations during historical times, and in the 20th century Manchuria became the region to which the landless of China's growing population were consigned. Over 2.5 million people were moved to Manchuria in a space of seven years during the 1920s, and the total population of the region leapt from about 15 million in 1907 to over 34 million in 1930.

Since then China has become more concerned with the distribution of food than with the redistribution of people. The communist revolution of 1949 swept aside private land ownership and the gross inequalities that had existed in China until that time, and its success drew very heavily both on peasant support and the Chinese capacity for organisation. During the 20 year struggle that preceded the revolution, Mao Tse Tung and his colleagues laced China into a network of party cadres. Throughout the country, individuals were selected and secretly trained as links in a unified command structure which steadily transformed the rural population from a largely unprotesting peasantry into the conscious agents of change.

After the revolution, the network of command and organisation itself became the agent of transforming agriculture and feeding people. Farming was turned into a collective effort and the state undertook to provide every man, woman and child with a healthy and adequate diet. Mao believed that, given their numbers and capacity for organisation, the Chinese people could solve every problem confronting them – 'revolution plus production' was the catchphrase of a policy that promised to bring prosperity for all. But it failed. Collectivisation did not increase agricultural production. Distribution was a constant problem. People were hungry, some were starving, and even the Cultural Revolution of the 1960s, when every able-bodied person was put to the task of growing food, could not raise production adequately.

With the death of Mao in 1976, the Chinese leadership finally acknowledged that, among many problems, population growth was the main

195

obstacle to the improvement of living standards. With virtually every available square metre of China's arable land under cultivation, the options for intensifying production were limited. Rationing kept people on an adequate if austere diet, and prevented anyone from spending their disposable income on extra food (the theory was that it should be spent on material goods, which would serve to stimulate industrial development), but if the population kept growing, numbers would inevitably race ahead of food production in the not too distant future.

China could never support more than 1,200 million people and must therefore adjust its population growth rate accordingly, the authorities concluded. Resorting once again to the nation's all-pervasive organisational network, they instituted a policy of family planning and birth control. 'Later, Longer, Fewer', the posters urged young adults: marry later in life, wait longer for a child, have fewer of them. In 1979 the One-Child Campaign was put into effect. In 1981 newly married couples were required to sign statements committing them to have only one child, with penalties for those who produced a second, and free vacations for those who had an abortion or were sterilised. In 1982, the year in which a national census reported a total population of 1,063 million, the National People's Congress adopted constitutional provisions that made family planning the duty of all married couples.

The effect has been dramatic. China's birthrate had risen from about 25 per 1000 in the late 1950s to a peak of 44 per 1000 during the Cultural Revolution, but after official restraint began in the mid '70s it fell to 18 per 1000 by 1980. That the world's largest national population has been able to control its growth rate so effectively in such a short space of time is staggering. But the success brings problems that will further engage the organisational capacity of the nation. The government wants the population to stabilise at about 1,200 million by the year 2000 and stay at that level thereafter. To manage that they will have to ensure that the single-child family policy continues through the 1990s and is only slightly relaxed thereafter. Demographers have calculated that a birth rate of 16.7 per 1000 will keep the population constant at 1,200 million once that level is achieved, permitting couples an average of 1.7 children each.

In the immediate term, China's family planning policies have caused a lot of personal distress. Many people want more than one child. Many want a boy, or a girl, rather than whatever arrives first. Female infanticide is far from unknown. In the medium term, the policies have produced a generation of what observers call 'little emperors'; 35 million 'spoiled brats' on whom families lavish most of their disposable income, and who receive all the devoted attention of grandparents, uncles and aunts. The little emperors have acquired such a reputation for selfish and self-indulgent behaviour that the likelihood of their being willing to follow the organising edicts of the state as their parents have done is causing serious concern, and special corrective courses for both parents and children have been introduced.

Then there is the long-term problem of the irregular distribution of age groups that will arise as the population stabilises at 1,200 million. If a

196

stable birth rate of 16.7 per 1000 is achieved, over 30 percent of the population will be past retirement age by the year 2040, compared with less than 10 percent in 1980. Supporting all these non-productive people will put an enormous strain on the available workforce, which is hardly likely to be helped by the fact that many have been raised as little emperors. The problem could be eased by deferring retirement age by five years or so, but old people might be reluctant to work an extra five years, and young people would be deprived of job opportunities.

At this point, maintaining the balance between numbers and food supply swings back to questions of productivity. If fewer people are going to be available to feed the nation, then obviously they must each produce more. Among responses to this problem, the regime of Deng Xiaopeng began encouraging a degree of private enterprise during the 1980s. Farm workers were allowed to cultivate private plots and sell the goods they produced in excess of state established targets. Production increased, and a vigorous small market economy quickly developed throughout the country; tourism brought yet another source of income, and the greater amounts of cash circulating in the economy stimulated industrial development – all with the added advantage of providing more employment prospects for the large numbers of young people born in the 1960s who were now looking for jobs.

The introduction of private enterprise could be rated a great success, and, combined with China's amazing capacity for organisation, it seems to offer the world's largest nation the prospect of a vigorous economy and a well-fed stable population – but it is not as simple as that. Private enterprise in a population that is presently 80 percent rural enhances the economic value of children, people will want to build up their families to make the most of their opportunities, and this could undermine the efforts to control population that private enterprise was intended to support.

CHAPTER ELEVEN

COMMERCIAL FARMERS

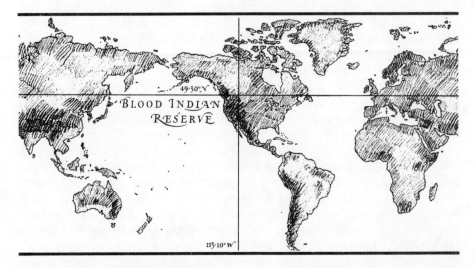

The Blood Indians of north America are the most numerous of three tribes known collectively as the Blackfoot Indians; the others are the Piegan and the Northern Blackfoot. The name, Blackfoot, is said to derive from the belief that their ancestors had lived near a great lake in the east, where cultivating the dark fertile soil had stained their moccasins black. When they moved onto the the Great Plains, where their traditional agriculture was impracticable, the Blackfoot became hunters, subsisting primarily on bison (also known as the north-American buffalo).

The Blackfoot and the bison were virtually exterminated in the late 19th century when white farmers moved onto the Great Plains, and as large-scale commercial farming rapidly replaced a robust subsistence economy, the decline of the Indians and the rise of the white farmers also marked a moment when the production of wealth replaced the production of food as the primary drive of humanity.

The history of the American Indians had already unravelled into over 600 diverse threads of tribe, lifestyle, language, custom and tradition by the time Europeans had penetrated to the heart of the continent during the 17th century. Exploitation of coastal resources supported the largest proportion of the population. Inland, around one million occupied about 20 million sq. km. (7.7 million sq. mi.) of which over four million (1.5 million sq. mi.) were potentially arable – 400 hectares (1,000 acres) per person. In the woodland and the forests of the south and east, and up through the fertile valleys of the Mississippi and the Missouri rivers, native maize, beans and squash were cultivated as the basic subsistence resource of largely sedentary horticulturalists. On the Great Plains of the mid-West, where climate, soils and the open nature of the landscape made horticulture a less feasible option, people were principally hunters, and their principal resource was the American buffalo – the bison.

The Blackfoot speak a dialect of the Algonkian language, like many other North American Indian tribes, but theirs differs more than most from the language spoken by the tribes of the western Great Lakes region, which is believed to be the parent Algonkian tongue. This fact has led linguists to suggest that the Blackfoot were probably the first tribe to move from the timber lands of the east out onto the open prairie. The move occurred in prehistoric times. Whether the Blackfoot were drawn onto the plains by the attraction of plentiful game, or forced out by competition for resources in the timber lands cannot be known. But it is certain that they made the move on foot. The horse did not reach the Blackfoot until 1730 at the earliest, and by then the Blackfoot tribes were already well established across the northern plains to the Rockies.

The Blackfoot homelands were too far north and the climate too harsh for the cultivation of native Indian food crops, but game was plentiful on the vast plains and in the wooded valleys. Wolf, fox, beaver, mink, rabbit, bear, deer, elk, moose and – most plentiful of all – the bison. The vast numbers of bison that once roamed the plains are well documented. Early visitors to the region wrote of 'innumerable herds', 'almost inconceivable' quantities of bison. One told of bison 'in such numbers that there could not have been fewer than 10,000 within a circuit of two miles'; another noted that 'for a distance of forty miles I do not think we were ever out of easy rifle shot of bison'.

The bison was the Blackfoot's 'staff of life', as an Indian Agent of the 1850s put it. By all accounts, three pounds (1.4 kg.) of meat a day may be reckoned a conservative estimate of the average person's consumption. And there was hardly a part of the buffalo's soft tissue that the Indians did not eat. Tongue and rib meat were especially enjoyed; liver, brains, kidneys, blood and bone marrow often were devoured during the butchering process – on the spot, without the benefit of cooking. In an account of a buffalo hunt he joined in 1843, the naturalist John James Audubon records how appalled he had been to hear the refined Blood Indian wife of a white companion ask for the skull of a freshly killed animal to be broken open so that she might eat its brain. Old men ate the testicles raw, claiming they were a source of renewed power. The pasty contents of the intestines of newborn calves were delicacies which informants called 'the Indian's cheese'. Adult intestines were cleaned, filled with blood and boiled to make a sausage. Fat was rendered down and stored in buffalo hide sacks. Large quantities of lean flesh were dried and packed between layers of uncooked back fat, herbs and berries in rawhide envelopes called *parfleches*. In the autumn, dried meat was pounded and mixed to a paste with boiled marrowfat and dried berries. This mixture, called *pemmican*, was stored for winter use in bags made from the whole skins of unborn buffalo calves. In hard winters, when the dried meat and pemmican ran out and there was no other food available, the Indians ate the fat-laden pemmican sacks, and scrapings from softened buffalo hides.

And of course, the bison provided much more than just food. The skins provided clothing of all sorts, footwear, bedding, tipi covers; rope, buckets and shields were made of rawhide, rope was also made of braided hair, and hair was also used as stuffing for pillows. Pounding tools were made of bone, cups and spoon of horn; bowstrings and thread of sinew, paintbrushes of hair. The gall bladder provided yellow paint, and the bull's penis produced a very fine glue when it was cut into small pieces and boiled. Dressed skins were used as winding sheets for the dead, and bison skulls served as a sacred altar in the Sun Dance. The field studies of John Ewer, an authority on the Blackfoot, record 87 specific uses of the bison in Blackfoot culture; a list which serves not only to illustrate their dependence upon the animal, but also their ingenuity in finding uses for its products.

Blackfoot life revolved around the life of the buffalo. Their camps followed the seasonal migrations from the short grass plains where the buffalo calved in the spring, to the open pastures where they grew fat in the summer, to the ranges where forage and berries were abundant in the autumn, and back into the broad river valleys for the winter, where there was timber for fuel, grass and some shelter from the intense cold and heavy snows. People followed the migration on foot, aided only by the strong wolf-like dogs they had trained to haul the A-frame wooden travois on which their possessions were loaded. They probably travelled in relatively large groups of between 20 and 30 families – 100 to 200 people – because that was about the minimum required to surround a small herd of bison for slaughter, which was the most practical method of hunting at the time. In wooded country, they built concealed corrals into which the animals were driven; in hilly country they drove them off cliffs. At a site called Head-Smashed-In, for instance, archaeologists have uncovered accumulations of buffalo bone up to nine metres (30 ft) deep – dating back 5,000 years – at the foot of a cliff face 300 m. (1,000 ft) long.

Hunting the bison always called for a good deal of cooperative effort, but most especially so in the summer, when the herds ranged widest over the open plains. Then many bands would gather and the communal hunt would become an occasion for meeting and feasting which ultimately found its fullest expression in the great tribal ceremonies of the Sun Dance.

When the Blackfoot first took to the plains they retained contact with the tribes in the timberland to the east and inevitably made contact with others to the south. They traded meat and skins for horticultural produce and other useful items, and in due course acquired the two artifacts of European influence that would bring the Blackfoot first glory then despair in less than 150 years: the horse and the gun.

The horse arrived on the plains from the southeast, traded up through the tribes from Spanish breeders at Sante Fe and San Antonio, and reached the Blackfoot sometime after 1730. It was welcomed as a kind of 'big dog', capable of hauling a heavier travois and thereby easing the burdens of following the buffalo, but it soon, quite literally 'lifted the Indian off his feet', as John Ewer puts it, broadening concepts of space and distance, shortening concepts of time, easing the difficulties of hunting, and quickening the whole tempo of life. By 1800, the glorious horse culture of the Plains was fully established.

Men hunted the buffalo by riding into the herds, selecting their prey and shooting arrows into a fatal spot immediately behind the foreleg. Great skill on the part of both horse and rider was required, but two competent Blackfoot hunters 'could kill enough buffalo to provide over a ton of meat in a matter of minutes on a single chase', it was reported. During those brief halcyon years, when the horse brought the Indians heightened access to an immense resource, their basic food supply was limited only by the number of women available to butcher the carcase, and the number of horses available to haul away the skins and meat. An average family of eight (five adults and three children) needed ten horses to hunt and move efficiently. A large family, with five adults or more would need 15 to 20 or more.

Not surprisingly, horses became items of wealth, and as the ease of hunting from the back of a horse left more men with more time and energy for other activities, the acquisition of horses became the primary ambition of active young Blackfoot males. Before long, raiding replaced trading as the customary means of acquiring horses, and the Blackfoot slipped readily into a culture that praised bravery, encouraged theft and approved manslaughter. Young men took scalps as well as horses; they killed and died, and among the most extraordinary cultural perversions to which sudden splurges of excess resources have excited mankind, they developed the bizarre and excruciating techniques of self-torture by which young men were invited to demonstrate their bravery before the tribe at the annual Sun Dance. The torture involved piercing the pectoral (breast) muscles with short wooden skewers, to which rawhide ropes were then attached. The ropes were in turn attached to the centre pole, a stripped cottonwood treetrunk that had been set in a sacred circle representing the Sun, and the candidate was required to dance and pull against the ropes until the skewers tore free through the flesh.

The custom was known to all the Blackfoot tribes but it was most prevalent among the Blood Indians. Heavy Head, one of the last Indians to undergo the ordeal described his experience to John Ewer in 1947.

'I was the last and youngest of the three Blood Indians to undergo torture that day. Inside the medicine lodge... I was laid on my back with my head pointed north. I was barefoot and wore only a breechclout of red trade cloth.... The three old men painted four black dots, one below the other, under each of my eyes. This was called 'tear paint'. If I cried, the tears would run down there. Then they painted a double row of six black dots on each arm. They painted the symbol of the moon, points up, on my forehead in black. On the outside of each leg they painted a double row of six black dots. The rest of my body and my face were painted white. They took some broadleafed sagebrush from the ground inside the sweat lodge and bound it together, placing a wreath of it around my head and bands of it around each wrist and ankle.

I was taken from the shelter and laid upon a blanket on the ground at the north

201

side of the centre pole. Other men were told to keep back away from me. Then an old man named Low Horn was brought forward. He counted four war honours. While Little Bear and Green Grass Bull held my arms, Red Bead took a sharp, iron arrowhead in his hand and asked me, "How do you want me to cut them, thick or thin?" I said "Thin". (I learned later that the man doing the cutting always did the opposite of the young man's request. So when I told him "thin", Red Bead knew to make his incisions deep.) Red Bead recited four war honours. Then he pierced my breasts with the sharp arrowhead and inserted a sarvis berry stick through each breast. The sticks were not sharp but flattened at the ends. Blood flowed down my chest and legs over the white paint. Then Red Bead pressed the sticks against my body. They turned me around to face the sun and pierced my back. To the skewers through my back they hung a miniature shield with feathers on it.

Rawhide ropes were brought out from the centre pole and tied to the skewers in my breast – right side first, then left side. Red Bead grabbed the ropes and jerked them hard twice. Then he told me, "Now, go to the centre pole and pray for your vow to come true." I walked up there. I knew I was supposed to pretend to cry. But oh! I really cried. It hurt so much. Coming back from the centre pole, I was shouting. Then, before I started to dance, I jerked the shield off my back.

I leaned back and began dancing, facing the centre pole. It felt just like the pole was pulling me toward it. I danced from the west toward the doorway of the lodge and back. Then, when the skewers didn't break loose, the old men realized that the incisions had been made too deep. Red Bead cut the outside of the incisions so they would break loose. As I started dancing again the left side gave way and I continued dancing with only my right side holding. Then an old man, Strangling Wolf, got up from the crowd and called out four war honours, then jumped upon me. The second rope gave way and I fell to the ground.

The three old men cut off the rough pieces of flesh hanging from my breasts. They told me to take these trimmings and the sagebrush from my wrists, ankles, and head and place them at the base of the centre pole as my offering to the sun. This I did.

Then I took my robe and walked out of the medicine lodge alone. I went to a lonely place and fasted for a night. I wanted to dream. But I couldn't sleep at all because of the pain. At sunrise I prayed to the sun.'

A tenuous balance between numbers of people, horses and buffalo on the Great Plains had been reached by the early decades of the 19th century. The human population remained small (not least because of an epidemic of smallpox that swept across the plains in 1781) and its growth was restrained by constant warfare.

In the south, the horticultural tribes on the upper Missouri had dwindled away before the advance of white settlement, and the powerful Cheyenne, Comanche and their allies were preparing to resist white invasion of the plains. In the north, the aggressive Blackfoot had swept a number of minor tribes off the Plains with the aid of muzzle-loading muskets acquired during the mid-18th century from friendly tribes to the east who were trading furs with the Hudson Bay Company, and by the turn of the century they were the most powerful tribe on the Great Plains, ranged over an area of more than 80,000 sq. mi. (213,000 sq. km.) – from the north Saskatchewan River down to the upper tributaries of the Missouri, and from the Battle River in the east to the Rockies in the west.

Blackfoot numbers remained low, however. Estimates made by fur traders in 1809 suggest a total population of 5,200. So many men died in warfare and hunting accidents that women out-numbered men by a ratio of two or three to one. Men customarily had several wives, though few men were considered eligible for marriage before they had proved themselves as brave and successful warriors. Consequently, many died before they had produced children. Unmarried girls were expected to be chaste, and adulterous women were liable to have their noses cut off as both punishment and example. All these factors tended to restrain population growth and there was never much likelihood of human numbers over-exploiting the staple resources of the northern plains – the buffalo. Until 1870, that is, when the Blackfoot first acquired the repeating rifle.

The old muzzle-loading musket had served the Blackfoot principally as a means of killing other Indians. It was too cumbersome and difficult to load in the saddle to be of much use as a means of killing buffalo, and the bow and arrow remained the preferred hunting weapon. The new repeating rifle was so easy to fire and reload from a running horse, however, that it soon displaced the bow and arrow and sealed the fate of the buffalo. In 1870, the new weapons were trading for ten or so buffalo skins apiece, and a man with a rifle, good horses and two or three wives to skin carcases could soon amass hundreds of skins.

In 1874, a party surveying the boundary between the United States and Canada found the Sweet Grass Hills in the southeast of the region still 'literally black with the creatures', and the total northern herd was estimated to be four million strong. By 1879, barely five years later, most of them were dead and the Indians were starving.

The Blackfoot were the last of the tribes to be swamped by the waves of white influence that swept onto the Plains during the 19th century. They were protected to some extent by the international boundary which allowed them refuge in Canada, safe from the Indian policies aggressively pursued by the United States south of the border. The United States acted under the principles of what it declared to be 'manifest destiny', namely that the Indians were destined by fate to be overwhelmed by the more powerful white races. 'The Indian had to go,' a US government summary reported in 1935. 'Unable, unwilling to use more than one per cent of the continental resources, he had to yield to the race which was willing and able to exploit, consume, waste or dissipate in 200 years the accretion of the historic and geologic past...'. The shameful and well-documented sequence of broken promises, wanton lies, deceit and massacre by which this displacement was achieved seems at first arbitrary, even mindless, in its progress, but in fact there was calculated direction behind it. 'Beginning about 1870, a leading aim of the United States was to destroy the Plains Indians' societies through destroying their religions; and it may be that the world has never witnessed a religious persecution so implacable and so variously implemented,' writes one commentator.

The prohibition of religion and tribal customs, along with the imposition of concepts of property and ownership quite foreign to the Indians, were the main strategies by which 'manifest destiny' took its effect, but

there was another, yet more sinister aspect of the white invasion –
whisky.

Though the Indians smoked tobacco and knew something of hallucino-
genic plant substances, they had no experience of alcohol until the whites
arrived, and the effects of its introduction were so immediate and
calamitous that, in 1834, even the government felt obliged to prohibit the
trading of intoxicating liquors to Indians. This might seem commendable,
but in fact the law was only enforced where the white presence was already
well established. On the frontiers of the white advance, the whisky trade
was unimpeded. Very little effort was made to control the whisky trade in
the United States portion of Blackfoot territory, for instance, until 1868;
and then it precipitated disaster among the Blood Indian section of the
Blackfoot, whose homeland lay in Canada, just across the border.

In 1869, the Hudson Bay Company ceded their rights north of the
international boundary to Canada, leaving the region effectively devoid of
law and authority. With trading restricted south of the border, two
Americans named John Healy and Alfred Hamilton trespassed north into
the unguarded country and established a trading post at the junction of the
St. Mary and Oldman rivers – in the very heart of Blood Indian territory.
They took in trade goods, including repeating rifles and 50 gallons (230
litres) of alcohol, and brought out skins worth $50,000. Over the next few
years a dozen American posts were established among the Blood and
Piegan Indians. Whisky was a prominent item of trade. About 2,000
gallons (9000 litres) were traded in 1873 alone. Twenty cupfuls were
enough to buy a first quality buffalo skin. Three gallons (14 litres)
purchased a horse.

The effect on the Indians was disastrous. The Healy-Hamilton establishment became known as Fort Whoop-Up. Eyewitness reports claim that,
between 1871 and 1874, at least 162 Indians lost their lives in brawls, or by
freezing to death after bouts of drinking. The American authorities made
some attempts to bring the whisky traders to law – Standoff, site of the
Blood Indian Reserve administration centre, commemorates no Indian
exploit, but actually marks the spot at which US Marshall Charles Hard
stood off and abandoned his pursuit of trader Joe Kipp's whisky train – but
ultimately it was a Canadian responsibility, though slow in fulfilment.

Finally, in 1873, a uniformed civil police force was established
specifically to bring law and order to the north and west of Canada, and in
the summer of 1874, a contingent of the North-West Mounted Police – the
Mounties, as they became known – rode into Blood Indian territory.

Most of the whisky traders either cleaned up their operations or cleared
out when they heard of the Mounties' imminent arrival, but the havoc that
whisky had wrought among Blackfoot society was irreparable. There could
be no returning to the old ways, roaming freely over even the 50,000 sq. mi.
(130,000 sq. km.) of Blackfoot territory that lay within Canada. That time
was finished forever. The buffalo was nearly finished too, but hunting
continued even so. One US firm alone shipped out 75,000 skins in 1876. In
1877, 30,000 skins passed through Fort Macleod, the post established by
the Mounties on the banks of the Oldman River, and the authorities

became seriously concerned. Closed seasons were prescribed, and the killing of animals under two years old was prohibited, but the herds had already declined to such low numbers that the restrictions had to be withdrawn the following year in order to feed the surviving Indians – with inevitable results.

By the summer of 1879, the Blackfoot were starving. Many died, survivors were reduced to eating dogs, horses, and even soup made from the old dried carcasses that littered the plains, contemporary accounts report. In the autumn, over 3,000 Indians gathered around Fort Macleod, pleading for food. Some were persuaded to travel south and join the Blackfoot in Montana, where the buffalo were still less seriously depleted, and the remainder were sustained only by a feeding programme set up by the Canadian Government.

Meanwhile, white settlers had been moving onto Canadian Blackfoot land, establishing farms and ranches where the Bloods and Peigans had reigned supreme less than a decade before. Anxious to avoid the bloody conflicts that had marked the course of white settlement south of the border, the Canadians negotiated a treaty with the Blackfoot. Tribal chiefs and government officials met in council on a bend of the Bow River in September 1877. The Indians were destitute and welcomed the opportunity to salvage at least a remnant of their former status and glory from the wreckage of the past few years. 'If the police had not come to this country, where would we be now?' Chief Crowfoot asked when he addressed the council. 'Bad men and whisky were killing us so fast that very few of us would have been left today. The police have protected us as the feathers of the bird protect it from the frosts of winter.'

The treaty negotiated at Bow River was honest and openly agreed. Good intentions were apparent. The Indians surrendered all their lands to the Crown, but retained the right to hunt throughout the 50,000 sq. mi. region. Reservations would be established for their exclusive use, the size to be calculated at a minimum rate of one square mile for each family of five. Each head chief would receive an annual salary of $25.00, and every individual Indian would receive $12.00 when the treaty was signed, and a further payment of $5.00 per year thereafter. Amid its various social undertakings the government agreed to provide two thousand dollar's worth of ammunition each year for such hunting as was available, and undertook to supply the cattle, agricultural tools and seed that those who wished to take up ranching and farming would require. As they came forward to put their marks on the treaty, each chief was given a medal, a suit of clothes, and a flag, while the North-West Mounted Police band played 'God Save the Queen'. Presumably it was now felt that the Blackfoot Indians themselves were already saved.

The Blackfoot tribes were settled initially on one large reserve, but in 1883 the tribes were given separate reserves, allegedly because they could not get along together, though the Prime Minister subsequently told parliament of a more pressing incentive. The reserve 'was a barrier to settlement', he said, 'and the Indians have been induced to surrender that very large section and take up separate reserves.'

The inducement of which the Prime Minister spoke consisted of little more than allowing the tribes an opportunity to select their reserves from among the available areas on offer.

The Blood Indians chose the high rolling land that lies between the Belly and the St Mary rivers, where they made a rapid and highly successful adjustment to the strange ways of a commercial farming economy. Sustained success was thwarted however, largely by the connivance of a few avaricious whites, who manipulated treaties and landholding rights to the Indians disadvantage. Today the Bloods number some 6,000 people and are struggling to re-establish their rights and identity.

'Canada never cared much for the Indians', says Wilton, a Blood Indian who has made a small success of raising horses on the Reserve, 'and every time Canadians wave their flag we are reminded of just how little they cared. Our old people told them that the maple leaf is a bad omen in Indian belief, and told them not to put it on the flag. The maple leaf is the worst possible symbol for this nation. It turns red before it dies.'

'They chose good,' says the Reverend Jacob Waldner, who farms 4,000 acres of land close by the original Blackfoot reserve. 'That's good land up there on the Blood Indian Reserve. Real good land.'

The Great Plains of which the Blood Indians had chosen a reserved fragment for themselves are indeed good land. In fact they carry the richest agricultural potential of any region on earth. The soils have been described as 'nature's masterpiece of fertility', rich with mineral nutrients eroded from mountain uprisings in geological time, dense with the accumulated humus of biological time. For thousands of years the inherent wealth of the prairies had been continuously recycled through the grasslands, the buffalo, and small numbers of people, in a self-sustaining cycle of feeding and fertilising that served only to enrich the land.

This cycle was broken towards the end of the 19th century, however, when the disappearance of the bison coincided with the arrival of the steel plough. Steel cut the deep interlocking roots of the bluestem grasses and turned the continuous sward of the prairies as no earlier plough had been able to, unlocking the chemical wealth of the soils and hastening its conversion into the monetary wealth of the largest grain harvests in agricultural history.

The Reverend Waldner's knowledge of the prairie lands stems from a lifetime of farming experience. He is an elder and manager of the Hutterite colony at Plainview, and his slow plain English bears a heavy intonation of the old German that is still the everyday language of the 247 Hutterite colonies presently clustered about the Great Plains region of North America. The Hutterites are a strict Protestant sect who follow a communal way of life. Their basic religious beliefs are essentially the same as those of the better-known Amish in the United States, except that, while the Amish feel bound to use only the power of God-given muscle on the land and in their lives, the Hutterites do not believe that the word of God in any way prohibits the use of machines and the latest modern technology. Thus, the Hutterites run their colonies not only as devout

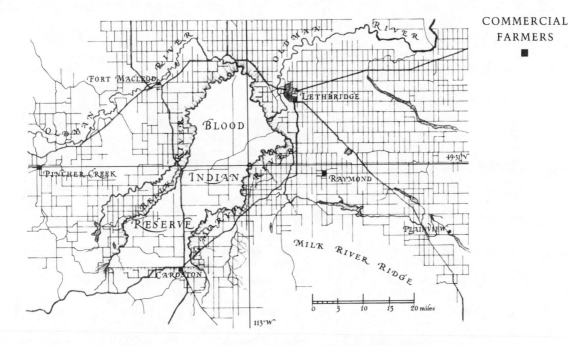

German-speaking religious enclaves, but also as highly efficient and – in the main – highly successful corporate farming enterprises. Waldner's Plainview colony had a gross turnover well in excess of $2 million in 1984, for instance, and the colony paid a total of $370,000 in personal income tax on behalf of its 20 families – 89 men, women and children. Five girls, just turned 18 years old, were taxed $25,000 each.

The Hutterites are pacifists and the notion of personal income tax is part of a formula negotiated with the Inland Revenue which manages to accommodate the Hutterite's reluctance to see their tax money used to maintain Canada's armed forces. But the notion of personal income is almost as abhorrent to them as the notion of warfare. Though they are ostensibly among the nation's highest earners, no individual Hutterite is paid a wage, or even allowed to own anything more than his or her clothing, a wooden chest and some small personal possessions. There is neither poverty, nor wealth, nor any incentive to private profit among the Hutterites. The colony provides food, clothing and shelter; education for the young, care for the old, and a life of ordered security for everyone. All that is asked by way of return is absolute devotion to the beliefs and the pattern of communal living established by the founder of the sect, Jakob Hutter, and his followers during the upheavals of the religious Reformation that convulsed Europe over 400 years ago.

The first Hutterites migrated to north America during the 1870s, and their success in the new continent owes a good deal to their experiences in Europe during the preceding centuries, when their very existence depended upon their maintaining self-sufficiency and communal resilience in the face of unconscionable opposition. The Hutterites were persecuted for

207

their beliefs no less implacably than the Plains Indians had been harassed for theirs. Thousands were executed, and Jakob Hutter himself suffered a horrible death by prolonged torture and burning in the pretty town of Innsbruck on February 25, 1536.

Though variously mistreated, banished and dispersed, the Hutterites maintained their identity through the centuries in a series of moves from present-day Austria and Switzerland to Czechoslovakia, across Hungary to Romania, and finally to Russia in the 1770s. There, for close on 100 years, their religious beliefs were tolerated, and they multiplied from 120 destitute refugees to a vigorous population of 1,265 distributed among a number of colonies which had achieved self-sufficiency in a communal way of life based on dairy and cattle, grain and vegetable farming. Then, in 1871, the Russian government revoked longstanding privileges excusing the Hutterites from compulsory military service. The Hutterites offered to move and open up undeveloped territories in exchange for continued religious freedom, but to no avail. They looked further afield, and having received an assurance from the office of President Grant that 'for the next fifty years we [the United States] will not be entangled in another war in which military service will be necessary', they migrated to America.

During the 1870s, as white settlement swept the Indians into confined reservations, 443 Hutterites moved onto the great plains of South Dakota. They settled in a handful of colonies, where their austere code of self-sufficiency, and their recent practical experience of farming in the Ukraine, were particularly well-suited to the requirements of pioneer living on the western frontiers of the United States. The Hutterites prospered and proliferated. The First World War soon made a lie of President Grant's assurance concerning military entanglements, however, and when the Hutterites found themselves unable to avoid conscription, a majority moved to Canada (where they made an agreement to relinquish voting rights in exchange for the right not to bear arms). Fifteen colonies were established on the Great Plains region of Canada during 1918, nine in Alberta, six in Manitoba.

By the 1970s, the Hutterites in North America had achieved notable success. A study of colony economies in Manitoba found that, although the Hutterites constituted only 6.1 percent of the farming population and worked only 1.6 percent of the land, their grain yields per hectare were substantially higher; they produced a quarter of the province's eggs, pigs and turkeys, and were significantly more productive in every major agricultural enterprise they undertook. Furthermore, they used the land more efficiently − an average of 36 acres (14.6 hectares) per person, compared with 118 acres (47.75 hectares) per person for the rest of Manitoba's farming population. And, in Alberta, a study of farm incomes revealed that the average Hutterite revenue per acre exceeded expenditure by 43 percent, while other farms achieved an average of only 30 percent.

While prospering the Hutterites proliferated too. By the 1980s, the original 443 who had migrated from the Ukraine to settle in North America had multiplied to over 27,000, which makes them the fastest growing human population known. The Hutterite population doubled nearly six times in 100 years, an outstanding achievement that, in the total absence of any recruitment from outside the sect, can be entirely attributed to the exceptional fecundity of the people within it. A report published in 1953 showed that Hutterite women had an average of 10.4 live births each during the preceding 70 years, with those between the ages of 35 and 39 achieving the highest fertility rate known for any society on record, and even Hutterite women aged between 40 and 44 produced more children than the average American woman during her 20s – a woman's most fertile years.

The Hutterites are an extraordinary phenomenon in the modern world. They thrive economically and grow in numbers at a geometric rate, while the rural population of North America drops and its economy stagnates. They sustain above-average standards of living while substantial numbers of North Americans live in poverty, and they remain pacifists while violence increases around them. But success, prosperity and proliferation have done nothing to change the Hutterites, or to integrate them into North American society at large. They have retained the language, the dress, the lifestyle and the beliefs that sustained them through the centuries of persecution in Europe.

Such adjustments as the Hutterites have made to modern western life have been purely pragmatic. They make use of the telephone, but not television. They read farming journals and newspapers but no other non-biblical literature. They allow their children to follow a national education curriculum, but only in the schools they have built on the colonies, and then only to age 15, with a parallel course of instruction in German given by themselves according to stipulations made by the founders of the sect in 1568. In short, the Hutterites have deliberately rejected the option of fully integrating with the larger national community in favour of preserving their own identity. This has contributed to their success, but has also aroused considerable resentment among their neighbours, many of whom see Hutterite prosperity and proliferation as a threat to a shrinking rural economy and population.

The Hutterites buy up land, their critics say, forcing others out of the farming business. As cooperative enterprises, the Hutterites can negotiate preferential prices for equipment and materials, it is alleged. In 1944, when there were widespread complaints that the Hutterites were taking unfair advantage of their pacifist status to buy up the land of men who were fighting and dying in the Second World War, Alberta passed a Communal Property Act restricting Hutterite land purchases and forbidding them to buy any land within 40 mi. (65 km.) of an existing colony. The Act was repealed in 1972, but increasingly vehement calls for its re-introduction were heard in the early 1980s as the agricultural recession began to take its toll among less successful members of the non-Hutterite farming community. Hutterites complained of being shouldered from the sidewalks, and spat upon on their regular shopping excursions. In one particularly ugly incident, several hundred protesters gathered to witness the symbolic hanging of a Hutterite effigy in the small town of Morrin.

At best the Hutterites are tolerated or grudgingly admired by their

209

neighbours while, within the colonies, external hostility merely serves to harden Hutterite conviction and faith in their resolve. 'We do best when things are against us', says the Reverend Waldner, 'good times, and too much freedom make people soft'.

The Hutterites thus constitute a substantial fraction of the white influence presently surrounding the Blood Indians on their reserve, and there is more than a touch of poignancy in the conjunction of their fortunes on the plains of southern Alberta in the late-20th century. Though born of such different environments they have a lot in common. Both have histories of persecution and oppression, and although their fortunes may seem opposed at the moment, it may be more accurate to look upon them as counterpoised in the mainstream of human diversity, both buoyed up by the human capacity for cooperative endeavour. In recent years, the Blood Indians have drawn a unifying faith in themselves from the painful history of deceit and oppression which confined them to a reservation, just as the Hutterites did, 400 years ago.

Jakob Hutter promoted communal living as a means of salvation and survival in an uncertain world, and established the *bruderhof*, wherein a community of married couples and their offspring lived together, worked together and ate together – all in comparative safety. The bruderhof was in fact a self-sufficient economic entity, requiring all to 'work together to a common end, the one doing this and the other that, not for their own needs but for the good of all', as well as a spiritual sanctuary. At an early stage, the elders of the sect adopted the practice of writing down every detail of their history and doctrine, building up a body of precisely defined instruction concerning the regulation and management of Hutterite communal life – work and religious duties, housing and eating arrangements, medical matters, education of the young and care of the old. The manuscripts were copied and bound into books for distribution among the colonies, where they provided a consistent source of reference for dealing with every conceivable aspect of individual and social behaviour.

The elders who began the practice of recording Hutterite history and doctrine in unequivocal form perhaps knew that the future existence of Hutterites would depend upon a means of inculcating convictions resolute enough to sustain community and pacifism in a violent world. The books provided that means. During subsequent centuries of oppression, the books attained the status of sacred documents, zealously preserved along with bibles, always providing a source of unity and direction. They still serve that function today. Whether confronted by dissension within the colony, or by pressure from without, by accidents of fate or by the devilish whims of human nature, the elders can turn to the Bible and the books for an answer to their problems. It is all there – faith, history, Hutterite identity. The Word.

The Hutterites compare their colonies to the ark that Noah built – a refuge of sanctity in a sinful world. 'If you don't get into the ark, you're lost', they tell their visitors, with just a touch of gleeful condemnation. The colony is rigorously ordered, both in its spatial and temporal patterns. The buildings are set about a rectangle, with the kitchen and eating complex at one end, the school buildings at the other, and living quarters spaced along the two sides. In every colony the length of the rectangle lies due north to south – 'squared to the compass', as one elder put it. 'You don't walk crooked to the earth,' he explained, 'you walk straight, that is how our buildings should be, straight with the compass and not askew'.

The men wear beards, black felt hats, black suits with braces holding the trousers high in the crotch. Trainers are favoured footwear on many colonies these days, but the men still walk with a distinctive rocking gait that sets the heel firmly on the ground and brings head and shoulders forward with each stride. The women wear long pinafore dresses which button to the neck, and dark-blue or black and white polka-dot scarves over the head. Their hair is worn long, parted down the middle and neatly braided from the forehead and back over the ears in a prescribed manner that must be mastered in childhood and teaches the girls patience, they say. All clothing is made by the women on the colony (with the aid of sewing machines and steam irons, these days), and each person receives a regular new issue.

When the Hutterites first came to North America, they settled in three colonies and from that time have divided into three groups – *leut*, they call them, from the German, meaning people – the Schmeideleut, the Darius-leut, the Lehrerleut. The Schmeideleut are the most numerous, with about 100 colonies, while the Dariusleut and the Lehrerleut have about 90 and 80 respectively. Differences in colony management and discipline distinguish the groups among themselves; there is no intermarriage between the groups, and they tend to speak rather disparagingly of one another, though to outsiders the only identifiable key to the differences that keep the three groups apart are certain aspects of dress: Schmeideleut women always wear long sleeves, the Dariusleut fasten their coats exclusively with hooks and eyes, and the Lehrerleut use buttons.

Daily life on the colony is ordered into regular patterns of activity according to the time of year, its divisions marked by the pealing of the colony bell. The community assembles for meals in the dining room – fulsome meals eaten rapidly from plain tables with a prayer before and after and little conversation in between. The men hang their hats at the door, but nothing else decorates the room. The womenfolk, as they are called, eat together on one side, the menfolk together on the other. Children eat in a separate room until the age of 15, when they are formally received into the adult community.

In spring the rising bell rings at 6 o'clock, breakfast is at 6.30 and by 7 o'clock the colony is at work. There is a lot of activity. Two shifts of menfolk are working round the clock sowing 3,000 acres (1,200 ha) of cereals; one team of women is on kitchen duty, which began before dawn, while another is set to pluck a handful of down feathers from the breasts of each of their 200-strong flock of geese immediately after breakfast. They herd the birds into a barn, and each cutting out small gaggles by turn they fill a dozen sacks in barely 30 minutes.

A day or two earlier the entire Pincher Creek colony drove up into the hills southwest of the Head-Smashed-In buffalo jump to help the Spring Point folk brand the new calves among the cattle that had been rounded-up the previous day. It was hard work, but an outing too – the boys testing their riding and roping skills, the girls handing round cold drinks and sandwiches during a lunch break but sitting on the fences much of the time, assessing the talent on display in the ring with more than just the boys' cattle-handling skills in mind. The young folk are expected to meet up and plan visits between the colonies – courting is considered a proper activity of young people, though its intentions must be directed solely towards marriage – what else is courting for? they ask. Pre-marital sex is absolutely taboo, and the Hutterites guard against allowing their young-folk any opportunities for it so successfully that illegitimacy is virtually unknown on the colonies. Only ten illegitimate births were recorded in the 75 years between 1875 and 1950.

Sex, the enchanting goad of all fertile young people, is permitted to Hutterites only in marriage, but marriage is permitted only after baptism, and baptism can be given only when the young folk have convinced the elders of their absolute commitment to the Hutterite faith and way of life. Baptism is a very serious matter indeed – there can be no turning back – and by making marriage dependent upon such an abiding pledge to follow colony life, the Hutterites have neatly harnessed the biological drive of the individual to the social continuity of the group. Hutterite couples marry later than might be expected in such a confined and secure social environment (22 is the average age for women, 23.5 for men), but very few remain unmarried and only in very rare instances is the marriage bond broken, for divorce effectively means abandoning the security of colony life, something Hutterites are not well-prepared for. Only one divorce and four desertions occurred between 1875 and 1950, and while married women produced an average of 10.4 children each during the same period, some had 16.

'Be fruitful and multiply', the Lord instructed Noah when the ark fetched up on Mount Ararat, and the Hutterites regard procreation as their holy duty too. Birth control of any kind is considered to be a sin, and in the small closed community of the colony, any recently married couple that did not show signs of producing children within an appropriate space of time would soon become a subject of discussion. Among the Hutterites, there is no physical or economic reason for any couple not to produce children. The colony keeps everyone at a more than adequate standard of nutrition, and the arrival of another child cannot affect anyone's standard of living; there are plenty of willing hands to help care for it; the carpenter will readily make another bed, and the family can move to a larger apartment if need be.

Children, then, are the ultimate expression of the Hutterite success in managing their social and economic welfare. The charts that demographers produce to illustrate the age structure of a population show a pleasing smooth curve in the case of the Hutterites, with children under five comprising the largest proportion (ten percent) of the population, and the size of each age-group steadily declining with advancing years. This is

quite different to the irregular profiles of third-world populations, wherein
similar high birth rates are countered by high infant mortality and short
life expectancy, and of western industrial society, wherein birth rates are
low and life expectancy long. In effect, the Hutterite population combines
the high fertility of subsistence cultures with the low mortality of modern
industrial culture. They bridge the gap, as it were, between subsistence and
civilisation.

The Hutterites are efficient food producers, healthy and fertile, and net
contributors to the broader national communities in which they live. They
pay taxes but accept no welfare payments, child benefits, health-care or old
age pensions from the state. Their success as communities springs directly
from the extent to which individual Hutterites are obliged to commit
themselves to the rules of communal beliefs. 'Individual will must be
broken and fused with the will of the community', they say. 'Just as the
grain of wheat loses it identity in the loaf of bread and the grape is lost in
the wine, so the individual must lose his identity in one corporate body.
Self-surrender, not self-development, is the divine order.'

The process of breaking individual will begins the moment self-
awareness appears in each miraculous bundle that biology and social order
deposit in the arms of Hutterite mothers. Human nature is inherently
selfish and sinful, they say, and the pursuit of selfish individual interests
will lead inevitably to evil. Hutterites, therefore, are taught self-denial,
humility and submission from infancy, and after 20 years or so of such
unremitting indoctrination, they are usually ready to renounce their
selfish interests and receive baptism, in order to marry and produce the
raw material for another generation of communal existence – children.

The colony gathers for prayer at the end of the working day – in the
schoolhouse or the dining room, or in some other place according to colony
practice. There is no 'church', as such, for it is believed that the entire
colony is a sacred space – the ark – in which God's order prevails. During
the service, however, the hierarchical order of the colony prevails. The
senior preacher leads the prayers and delivers a set sermon. Families are
separated, men one side and women the other, ranked according to age.
The absence of any member is made conspicuous to all by the gaps that are
left where the absentees would have sat. No one else can take their place,
each person is an indispensable part of the community. When the service is
over the oldest man leads out the congregation in order of rank, with the
oldest woman leaving behind the youngest boy. The evening meal is taken
after the service, and a relaxed period follows, when people sit outside and
chat if the weather is warm. One evening a woman planted out petunias in
a flowerbed of circular configuration – a rare deviation from the square, the
straight and regular – and elsewhere a child screamed above the sound of a
beating, and an adult shouted at the child in a voice so harsh that it was
impossible to tell whether it came from a man or a woman.

'We believe in using the strap', the Reverend Elias Wipf told a Provincial
Committee on Tolerance and Understanding convened in 1984 to consider
complaints about Hutterite expansion and their attitudes towards state

schooling in southern Alberta. 'The strap plays a vital role in Hutterite [education]', the Reverend said.

Local school trustee Stan Richmond had protested that, while Hutterites insisted on their children attending specially built colony schools, state schools in the area were forced to close for lack of pupils, obliging the handful of children still living in country areas to take long bus rides each day to town schools, and the Reverend Wipf was explaining why the Hutterites did not want their children educated in state schools. The fundamental reason was a resolute determination to shield Hutterite children from the influences of the world outside the colonies, and the strap was a key point in the Reverend Wipf's argument. 'If the strap was used more widely, Canada would be greater for it', he said.

Hopes of tolerance and understanding were expressed at the hearing, but the exchange of views did little, if anything, to change basic attitudes. The president of a local Chamber of Commerce summed up local feeling with the bald statement that the Hutterites were not welcome in the region, while on the colonies the Hutterites were more convinced than ever that the education of their children must never be fully integrated with the state system.

A long battle has been waged on the question of Hutterite education. A compromise reached with the Department of Education allows compulsory state education to be conducted on colony premises, on the understanding that the colonies must provide buildings of an approved design for the schools and teachers' residences, while the authorities will select the teachers and pay their salaries. The children still finish schooling at 15, when they become adults in Hutterite terms, however, and legal action to enforce two years of further education, as required by law, has never been successful. A truce prevails, though the Hutterites have remained suspicious of government intentions ever since becoming aware of a 1959 report that defined the problems of integrating Hutterite pupils into the public school system, and suggested that 'a more subtle approach, aimed at ultimate integration, might be more effective'. The Department of Education could offer salary bonuses to teachers willing to run schools on the colonies, it was suggested. 'Indoctrination is not recommended but it is felt that Hutterite children would respond well to stimulating teachers with plenty of personality', the report concluded.

At stake in the question of Hutterite education is nothing less than the continued existence of the Hutterites as a separate social entity in Canada. The continuity of Hutterite communal life depends not on God or religious belief but on their retaining control of the children's education. 'We could never hold them if they went to school out there', an elder confessed.

The problem is actually a head-on confrontation between the basic principles of two fundamentally different systems. Mainstream western education seeks to nurture the natural diversity that arises among the individual members of every human population, on the assumption that developing the potential of individual talent is the best way of maintaining the flow of creative ideas and innovations which sustains the modern industrial state. By contrast, Hutterite education seeks to impose uniformity, vigorously suppressing the expression of individual diversity and talent in any form not actually designed to maintain the existing system. There is a certain anarchy in the western attitude which leaves the unknown world of tomorrow to be created by the unspecified individual talent that it nurtures today. Western education presumes to create the future, no less, while the Hutterite system prepares only to enmesh it in a web of historic conviction and belief.

The Hutterites actually introduced a system of compulsory education for their children 300 years before it was universal in Europe and North America. Rules defining the purpose and practice of Hutterite education were written down in 1568 and have remained essentially the same to this day.

Education begins in the little school, where children join their peers as soon as they are weaned and begin to learn about the fear of God, self-discipline, diligence, and the fear of the strap. At age six they move on to the big school, where the religious education is increasingly supplemented by the teaching of practical skills that will be useful to the colony. A child's aptitude for one occupation rather than another is encouraged; a boy who shows an interest in cows and calves, for instance, will find himself invited to accompany the dairyman after school, and a mechanically minded child will be encouraged to spend spare time in the colony workshops.

By the age of 15, the combination of strict religious instruction and subtle streaming has produced a set of young adults ready and very keen to apply their developing skills and play a full-time active role in the economy of the colony. Each young man becomes an apprentice and learns a trade, be it that of motor mechanic, welder, carpenter, electrician, shoe-maker or plumber, as well as becoming skilled in some agricultural aspect of the colony enterprise. Young women are all trained in the full range of domestic work on the colony.

Compulsory state education has been more or less tagged on to the Hutterites' pre-existing school system, largely because it follows several years of strict education in the mother tongue of the colony – German.

Ever since the founding of their sect over four centuries ago, the Hutterite colonies have been small enclaves of German-speaking people in foreign lands, locked, as it were, in the language and intellectual perspective of medieval Europe. The children learn to speak a 'Huttrish' dialect at home, and at little school they are introduced to high German, in which they achieve proficiency by reading and writing from the Bible and Hutterite texts. As a result, they move on to the English school as foreigners in their own land, with little or no knowledge of English, and very little of the experience that prepares most western children for school.

Toys are not common among children on Hutterite colonies; sports and competitive play are likewise discouraged because they might awaken a desire for individual possession, achievement and superiority over others. 'Very few know any English at all when they start school', said one state

215

teacher, 'they have no experience of relating figures to words, they don't know the colours, have no habit of drawing or of expressing themselves in words. Getting them to the stage of writing an essay is not easy.'

The elders expect the English school teacher to control the children by the same means that they employ themselves, and the fact that few of them, if any, resort to the strap certainly accounts for the different attitudes that the children hold towards German and English schooling. When asked why they wrote so much more neatly in German than in English, a class with one accord replied: 'because the German teacher uses the strap on us if we don't write good'.

The German and English education that Hutterite children receive consists, in fact, of two quite separate entities. There is little conflict between the two, however, for the style of colony life ensures that German education has a more penetrating influence on the children. The German school has always been part and parcel of Hutterite life, it teaches the children to read and write and count to ten thousand, but it is primarily concerned with preparing them for a lifetime of passive assent to the authority of the colony. The English school, on the other hand, is something imposed upon the Hutterites by the outside world. It offers worldly knowledge, and therefore its influence is strictly controlled. Television, radio, audio-visual aids, tape-recorders and record players are banned from the Hutterite classroom. No pictures can be left on the walls and the blackboard must be wiped clean at the end of lessons if the school is also used for evening prayer (as is usually the case).

The Hutterites adopt a pragmatic view of compulsory state education: they take what the colonies need and reject the rest. Learning English enables them to deal effectively with the people in the surrounding community and to read the farming press, but it does not oblige them to read publications deemed less desirable; learning maths and some science can be useful in dealing with modern farming technology, but higher education is reckoned to be counter-productive. 'The farther the child goes in English school, the less he learns', they say.

The success with which the Hutterites have exploited the two educational strategies to which they are exposed is self-evident. The people are well- nourished, healthy, and appear well-adapted to the constraints of their social environment. The physical environment is also well catered for. 'I don't believe we've had a more golden period than right now', says Jacob Waldner. The colonies earn enough to buy good materials and sound modern equipment, and among them have skills and labour enough to make and maintain virtually everything they need. Building, carpentry, plumbing, central heating, electrical installations, motor repairs – none requires the assistance of outside service. They make the large welded stainless steel baking ovens, washing machines, sinks and other equipment that ease the work of women in the colonies. On the land they have adapted standard cultivators to the particular needs of dryland farming. The Noble Blade, a widely used alternative to disc ploughing, which reduces wind erosion on the open plains, was invented on a Hutterite colony.

The 21 families on Plainview colony subsist on the produce of the 11 acres (4.5 ha) of garden they cultivate, milk from their dairy operation, pork, bacon and sausage from the pigs, cracked eggs and laying birds past their prime from the hen-house. They feed into the national agricultural economy 125,000 bushels of wheat, oats and barley from the 5,000 acres (2,000 ha) they sow each year, 100 pigs each week, 9,000 eggs each day, plus a quantity of milk the Reverend Waldner is reluctant to specify. 'It's on quota', he says gloomily, though the herd is on a computerised system that allocates, mixes and delivers feed to each cow in its stall according to weight and output, and is probably producing more milk than the colony can dispose of.

'We work good', the Reverend announces, returning to a more positive note. 'We're a multi-million dollar operation. We're good producers and with the new technology we're more efficient producers. We can handle it. Give us nuclear – we can handle it!'

There is never any doubt, however, that the drive behind Hutterite efficiency and economic success is primarily directed towards preserving the independent identity of the Hutterites. The goods they produce help to feed the world outside the colonies, but the income feeds the communal ideal that is pursued within them. It is a very simple equation. The economic success of the colonies keeps the majority of their members so healthy and fertile that numbers double every 16 years or so, and then yet more success is required to finance their expansion.

One might imagine that the colonies would accomodate their growing numbers by simply building a few more housing units on the ample spare ground that is available to most of them. But this simple strategy for dealing with expansion does not work for the Hutterites. Expanding populations within the restricted social environment of a colony create problems peculiar to themselves, no matter how extensive the total landholding may be. Human behaviour imposes its own limits on the number of people that can live harmoniously together, it seems, regardless of religious edict and economic preference. As individual workloads decrease with rising numbers in the colony, friction between members tends to increase sharply. People just get too close and see too much of one another, they say.

The Hutterites have found that 150 people is about the most a single colony can accomodate before stress and arguments between members become unmanageable. A founding group of 70 or so individuals must expect to grow to that number within 16 years, and will begin making plans to split and form a second colony well beforehand. 'Branching out', they call it.

Branching out is an upheaval for the members of both parent and daughter colony. The burden falls heaviest on those who must start afresh, but both are thrown back on their basic resources. With a bare minimum of labour and capital at their disposal, both colonies must begin striving for the economic success that will enable them to finance the yet further expansion that each must anticipate. As the split becomes imminent, the heads of every family formally pledge themselves and their families to one

217

or other of the two senior preachers, who then draw lots to decide which will take his followers to start the new colony.

The matter of finding suitable land for the new colony is rather less easily resolved, and promises to become ever more difficult. Hutterite expansion is of course geometric – the original colony founded at Standoff in 1918, for instance, had spawned another six by 1960. The Plainview colony is the fourth on which Jacob Waldner has lived and plans for its next branching out are already in hand. Meanwhile land values have risen even faster than Hutterite numbers. Land that cost $375 per hectare ($150 per acre) when the Plainview colony was established in 1973 was selling for $2,500 per hectare ($1,000 per acre) in 1984, and the total budget for the branching out is set at six million dollars. 'It will take all of that to buy land and get a colony going', says Waldner.

Thus, the Hutterites are something of a paradox, as well as a biological and sociological phenomenon. Simply to sustain their ancient communistic way of life they must achieve outstanding success in a modern capitalistic economy. Self-sufficient farming and separate identity kept the Hutterites and their ideals alive for several centuries, but now the biological success that has flowed from those strategies demands ever greater involvement with commerce and the social system around them.

The Hutterites have shown how effectively religious stipulations can enhance the productivity and expansion of a human population, but the paradox of their involvement in modern commercial farming also demonstrates how the simple biology of human reproduction can outstrip the validity of cultural ideologies.

CHAPTER TWELVE

THE CITY

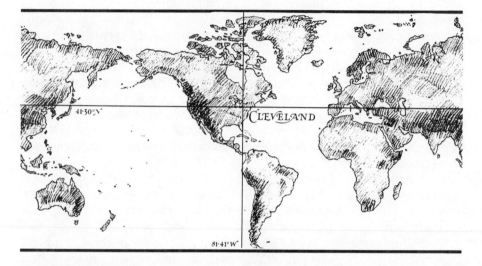

The fall of the Blood Indians and the rise of the Hutterites were part of a changing pattern of land use on the Great Plains of North America that has been described as 'the most important revolution in world agriculture that has ever taken place'. The revolution began with when the first steel plough cut the dense mat of prairie grasses to expose the fertile potential of the soil beneath, and gained immense impetus towards the end of the 19th century as return on investment, rather than the production of food, became the driving force of agricultural endeavour on the Great Plains.

A unique combination of huge potential returns and very particular production demands effectively made a manufacturing industry of farming on the Great Plains – an industry that employed land, labour and capital to produce grain on a vast scale, and quickened the pace of development across the entire face of North America.

Wheat is a grass that evolved in the semi-arid regions of the Middle East, where it was adapted to grow rapidly in a brief period of seasonal rain, and to mature and ripen in the dry season that followed – characteristics that made the potential of the Great Plains as a wheat producing region abundantly clear. The climate was ideally suited to wheat cultivation, and the grassland soils were rich and deep enough to excite expectations of sustained high yields far into the future. There were no forests to be cleared, and the landscape was flat enough to evoke visions of farming on an unprecedented scale. Furthermore, the region was to all intents and purposes virgin territory, hitherto used solely by grazing buffalo and a sparse population of nomadic Indians.

But substantial amounts of capital investment were needed before wheat production could begin to exceed the pioneer settlers' simple wish to make a living from the land. Large-scale farming would become economic only when agricultural machinery was available and efficient enough to replace the large labour force required; and the price of grain produced on the Great Plains would be low enough to compete on world markets only when high volume transport systems were available to carry the grain to distant cities and ports. The profit motive was the single most important factor in meeting these demands, and as soon as financiers became aware of the rewards likely to flow from a mechanised farming industry they were not slow to put up the capital and create the necessary infrastructure.

The promise of the Great Plains hastened development of the agricultural machinery industry, at a moment when the internal combustion engine was virtually waiting to be installed in the tractors, ploughs, seeders and harvesters that would increase production and reduce labour costs at a stroke. American oil would fuel the machines; railways laid across the breadth of the continent would carry the grain in bulk, cheaply, from farm to market and port.

It would be difficult to exaggerate the boost that the advent of industrial farming on the Great Plains gave to the developing economy of North America. The mechanisation of farming helped create an automotive industry and, along with railroad construction, produced a sustained demand for the raw materials of industry – iron ore, coal, and oil. Industrialisation in turn fuelled the growth of cities, drawing in wave after wave of migrant workers from Europe, swelling the numbers of people in America for whom the Great Plains were a source of daily bread.

Before long, the effects of industrial farming on the Great Plains spilled beyond the national boundaries of North America and into the world political arena. The United States was a net exporter of wheat by the first decades of the 20th century, and during the 1920s the concern of its economists moved from the question of how to feed a growing population to the problem of securing profitable markets for the country's immense annual surplus of wheat. They were particularly concerned about developments in Russia, where the communists who seized control of the country in the revolution of 1918, were now planning an agricultural revolution that threatened to undermine the grain economy of North America. The concern was not unjustified.

The Russian grain lands, of which the Hutterites had farmed a portion before leaving for North America (see Chapter 11), lay 200 mi. (320 km.) deep and stretched more than 3,000 mi. (5,000 km.) east to west. According to a review published by a United States analyst in 1931, there were over 1,300,000 sq. mi. (3,367,000 sq. km.) of land suitable for growing wheat in Russia, compared with about 350,000 (900,000 sq. km.) in the United States. Furthermore, the Russian wheatbelt lay from east to west across the country, with largely the same climate throughout, while the North American belt ran north to south and was thus subject to climatic variation down its length. In addition, the most productive parts of the North American wheatbelt lay 500 mi. (800 km.) from the nearest navigable river and more than 600 mi. (1,000 km.) from the nearest tidewater, while the western end of the Russian belt lay on the very shores of the Black Sea and the broadest part of its most productive region was transected by three large navigable rivers.

Then, in 1928, Stalin's government announced a Five Year Plan which would establish a string of huge mechanised state farms and, if successful, thereby give the Soviet Union the capacity to swamp the world grain market.

Before the First World War, Russia had been a significant exporter of wheat, virtually all of which came from the great landed estates, where the feudal manner of its production by the many, and the disproportionate amounts of wealth it put in the pockets of the few, contributed to the widespread social dissatisfaction from which the communist revolution drew its strength. The estates were broken up after the revolution, agriculture collapsed to subsistence levels, and Russian grain exports ceased – almost precisely at the moment when North America's farming enterprise was poised to supply grain in their place. By the early 1930s, the prospect of the Soviet Union re-entering the world grain market on any substantial scale was viewed with concern – 'In this matter Russia has a potential advantage that cannot be ignored by the United States', remarked one analyst.

The Five Year Plan was intended to revitalise Soviet farming and turn the country's most negotiable asset – wheat – into the hard currency needed to finance the Soviet Union's ambitious programme of social and industrial reform. Large collective farms were an integral part of the Plan and some 75 million acres (30 million ha) were allocated to that purpose.

In the aftermath of the revolution there was a good deal of Soviet agriculture that urgently needed revitalising – even as late as 1928, the British economist Alec Nove reports, for instance, 40 percent of the grain crop was still reaped with sickle or scythe and threshed with flails – but the results of Russia's grand collectivisation programme were little short of disastrous. Small quantities of grain were exported during the first flush of the Five Year Plan, but thereafter the Soviet Union has been a net importer, struggling even to achieve self-sufficiency. Successive Five Year Plans grappled with the problems of Soviet agriculture, but it was not until the 1950s that output reached even the levels of the pre-revolution era, and while agricultural productivity has increased around the world, the general trend in the Soviet Union has gone from bad to worse. In fact, the only bright spot in Soviet agriculture is the private sector, which in theory ought not to exist at all.

A United Nations publication has noted that, even in 1955, up to 80 percent of fruit and vegetable, over 50 percent of meat and 30 percent of dairy consumer purchases in the Soviet Union were the product of private plots and enterprise. More recently it has been reported that the small-holdings of private individuals account for fully one-third of the Soviet Union's total agricultural output, though they occupy less than five percent of the country's total cropland, and where officials previously turned a pragmatic blind eye towards this blatant contravention of the communist ideal there is now tacit approval and encouragement – in the

221

three years to 1985, for instance, the Politburo authorised 5,000 Soviet shops to stock seed and gardening equipment.

The collectivisation of Soviet agriculture was the world's first major attempt to put Marxist theory into practice, and its failure seems to suggest that the social theories Marx developed amid the economic exploitation of people living in the cities of vigorously competitive industrial nations, were not directly applicable to a rural agricultural economy. Principles that might work for a community cannot be applied to an economy. Certainly, the failure of Russian farming under communism stands in vivid contrast to the success of communal farming endeavour in many other parts of the world, and throws the paradox of the Hutterites into particularly high relief. The Hutterites developed their communal ways on the wheatlands of the Soviet Union, and today they are among the most successful farmers in North America – still following their communal ideal in the world's most powerful capitalist nation. Meanwhile, the Soviet Union was obliged to import 36.5 million tons of grain on average each year between 1980 and 1982, while North America fulfilled its own needs and exported 132.8 million tons – which amounted to an astonishing 87 percent of the world's total export trade in grain.

The United States and the Soviet Union have more cropland per capita within their national boundaries than any other major country – 0.95 hectares (2.35 acres) per capita in the United States, 0.93 (2.3 acres) in the Soviet Union, compared with 0.26 hectares (0.64 acres) per capita in Western Europe, 0.16 (0.4 acres) in China and just 0.05 (0.12 acres) in Japan. Abundant agricultural resources obviously have considerable bearing on the status of the United States and the Soviet Union in world affairs, and the use each makes of those resources must affect their relative standing. The awesome mutual antagonism that sparks between the two nations has not been generated solely by the urgency of the Soviet post-revolution food problem, nor by the foreboding with which capitalists once viewed the prospect of Soviet success in revitalising their farming industry, but secure grain supplies are a fundamentally important weapon in the armoury of the Cold War – lacked by one, wielded by the other. There is nothing new in this. Grain has been at the centre of major human interactions ever since people began living in cities over 5,000 years ago.

The phenomenon of the city first appeared on the face of the earth in Mesopotamia sometime between 4000 BC and 3000 BC, marking a significant moment in a trend whose origins the American botanist Jack Harlan re-enacted one afternoon in the early 1970s, when he used a flint-bladed sickle of the early stone age period to harvest four pounds (1.8 kg.) of wild wheat in the space of one hour from the foothills of the mountains that surround the Tigris-Euphrates basin.

The earliest known cities were built on the plains of Mesopotamia, close by the Euphrates and the Tigris rivers, between 4000 BC and 3000 BC. The city of Ur, with canals, harbours and temples, housed about 24,000 people within the bounds of its 240 acres (97 ha). Cities established during the third millenium BC have been excavated at Memphis and Thebes along the Nile, at Mohenjo-dara in the valley of the Indus river in Pakistan, and along the Yellow River valley in northern China. All these and many other cities were built – both physically and economically – on fertile alluvial plains that were easily irrigated and, in their prime, highly productive.

The advent of the city as a centre of human endeavour freed ever-increasing numbers of people from the burden of finding food for themselves. Human ingenuity, tied for thousands of generations to the problems of feeding and managing small groups of people, was suddenly freed to pursue its seemingly infinite potential. Cities provided the fertile environment that left the likes of Michelangelo free to paint, Newton free to ponder the working of the universe, and Hitler free to scheme. Trade, crafts, and the arts proliferated; methods of transportation and communication were refined; patterns of economic control, social administration, intellectual activity and religious obligation emerged.

And the influence of the city has been pervasive, reaching beyond its last houses to the most distant sources of energy upon which it depends – food, fuel, raw materials or wealth. Cities derive their energy from the resources they control and, as anthropologist Bernard Campbell remarks, 'the city's greed for energy was, and is, remorseless'.

The city was the cradle of civilisation, but this great artifact of human ingenuity could never have come into being without the readiness of some people to assume absolute authority, and often inhuman powers of life and death, over large numbers of other people. Classical Greece, for example, though a civilisation which has endowed humanity with so many pleasing images of the ideal city and civilised living, was itself nothing short of a slave economy.

The word 'democracy' comes from the Greek *demos*, meaning common people, but the people enjoying the privileges of democracy in Athens at the height of its development in the 5th century BC, were exclusively male, outnumbered by women and other free residents of the city, and owned an average of 2.5 slaves each, as Lewis Mumford notes in his book *The City in History*. Their free and civilised activities were utterly dependent on the economic surplus produced by a captive majority.

Aristotle, whose reflections on the form of the ideal city and the behaviour of ideal citizens are a founding component of western philosophy, thought it entirely in order for one group of people to subjugate another and in his discourse on politics suggested that automation was the only conceivable alternative to slavery in the civilised world. 'The slave is a living possession', he said, '... an instrument of instruments. If every instrument could accomplish its own work, obeying or anticipating the will of others... if... the shuttle would weave and the plectrum touch the lyre, chief workmen would not want servants, nor masters slaves.'

Slaves in classical Greece were very cheap. In the late 5th century BC, for example, two could be bought outright for little more than the cost of hiring one artisan for a year, whereas in mid-19th century America one slave generally cost at least four times an artisan's annual wage. Most of the slaves were barbarians – barbarian being the Greek term for anyone

223

who did not speak Greek – brought back by the boatload from plundering expeditions around the eastern Mediterranean. 30,000 are said to have been sold in bulk to slave-dealers following the sack of Thebes by Alexander in 335 BC. One source writes of large scale expeditions that captured 50,000 slaves in 240 BC, and another reports that the price of Jews to be captured on an expedition in 165 BC was fixed even before the campaign had begun.

Human beings featured prominently in the trading economy of classical Greece, but the greater part of what is known of Greek trading concerns a far more crucial commodity – namely the fuel required to operate both slaves and the society they sustained: grain. As the settled populations scattered about the Aegean Sea coalesced during the 8th century BC into the numerous city states of the classical Greek era, they soon strained the agricultural resources of their immediate environment. The soils were generally shallow and light, and widespread irrigation was not feasible. The islands and peninsulas of ancient Greece produced good crops of fruit and olives, and supported ample flocks of sheep and goats, but only limited amounts of the staple food – corn – and, as populations grew, the city states were obliged to look further afield for their corn supply. Those with limited wealth, or situated inland, had precious little opportunity to alleviate their plight and succumbed to more powerful states, but those on the coast, with access to timber and shipbuilding technology, looked across the sea for alternative supplies, and the interacting agencies of need, ingenuity and initative soon created a network of trade routes across the Aegean and beyond.

During the 5th century BC, Athens was bringing corn from the shores of the Black Sea, tapping the western end of Russia's great wheat lands; by the 4th century, the city controlled the corn trade of the entire eastern Mediterranean; and during the 3rd century, Alexander the Great extended the power of Greece down the Nile and through southern Asia to India.

Grain supply ranked with matters of defence at the meetings of the Assembly in Athens and inspired the construction and maintenance of a substantial naval force to keep open the vital routes, but the trade itself was left in the hands of private merchants, where it inspired a trade in goods for export and thus became the basis of a vigorous economy within the city. Landowners traded fruit, olives, oil and wine; manufacturers developed new lines in pottery, cloth, and metal goods – all of which featured prominently in the export trade and contributed to the cultural development of the city.

'So deep is their love of corn', said Xenophon around 400 BC, 'that on receiving report that it is abundant anywhere, merchants will voyage in quest of it; they will cross the Aegean, the Euxine [the Black Sea], the Sicilian Sea; and when they have got as much as possible, they will carry it over the sea, and they will actually stow it in the very ship in which they sail themselves. And when they want money, they don't throw the corn away anywhere haphazardly, but they carry it to the place where they hear that corn is most valued and the people prize it most highly...'

By the 2nd century BC, the flower of Greek civilisation was fading, and

Rome succeeded Athens as the greatest power in the Mediterranean. The influence of Rome in western civilisation is founded on the cultural heritage of Greece, but, while ancient Greek has endowed western languages with the words for abstract concepts like aesthetics, philosophy and the terms describing aspects of social organisation – democracy from *demos*, politics, policy, even politeness, from *polis* – it is Latin that has supplied words for the realities of civilised living and its administration – city, and civilisation itself from *civilis*, people from *populus*, grain from *granum*.

Rome is located on an extensive plain of fertile volcanic soils well suited to the cultivation of grain crops, and was thus inherently better able than its Greek counterparts to support large numbers of people. Indeed, the construction of aqueducts towards the end of the 4th century BC suggests that water rather than food was the most pressing of the city's supply problems during the early stages of its development. Inevitably, however, the problems of food supply increased with the growing population, and the city's location then proved to be less advantageous than it had first seemed. It is estimated that at least half a million people were living in Rome by the middle of the 2nd century BC, and keeping them fed was a problem of such scale and consequence that it can truly to said to have been the stone that honed the cutting edge of Roman civilisation.

In 123 BC, Rome assumed the responsibility of distributing a monthly ration of corn – free – to every eligible citizen, while private merchants continued to supply the needs of non-eligible residents and the city's substantial slave population. The ration was sufficient to provide an adult male with between 3,000 and 3,500 calories a day, which gives some indication of the pre-eminence of grain in the Roman diet. An indication of the total Roman grain requirement is given by historian Geoffrey Rickman in his study of the corn supply of ancient Rome. Some 320,000 eligible citizens are known to have been receiving free distributions of grain in 5 BC, and the total population of the city must then have been close to one million, including 200,000 slaves and 480,000 women, children and other residents not eligible for free grain. Assuming that non-eligible residents bought slightly less per person than was distributed free, and that slaves received the same amount as was detailed in accounts from other periods, Rickman concludes that Rome was consuming about 320,000 tons of corn a year at that time – over 6,000 tons a week.

With one million inhabitants, Rome of 5 BC was about the size of, say, Cleveland Ohio and its immediate environs in the 1920s, when Cleveland was a flourishing industrial city, producing steel and oil and much else besides for the burgeoning grain-based economy of North America. Six thousand tons of grain would fill a good number of railway wagons, but they could be shunted into Cleveland from the not too distant wheatlands of the Great Plains with comparative ease each week. Feeding Rome was another matter altogether. One might imagine that grain requirements had inspired construction of all the roads leading to Rome, and that they were constantly busy with the traffic of ox-wagon trains carrying grain to the

225

city, but although local corn and other produce doubtless did reach the city by road, feeding Rome by that means in the long term was impracticable. The heavy four-wheeled Roman wagon carried only about half a ton of grain and travelled at less than five kilometres (3 mi.) an hour. Each wagon required two oxen to pull it, a man to drive it, daily supplies of food and water for men and beasts, overnight lodgings along the route and, since Rome would have required a minimum of 12,000 wagonloads a week, the amount of labour involved in such an undertaking might well have consumed the larger share of the corn it brought to the city. And in any case, there were no corn-growing regions of sufficient size within reasonable overland reach of Rome.

Water was the only practicable means of transporting sufficient quantities of grain to Rome. The Tiber helped to some degree, and barges served the city from upstream but, to all intents and purposes, Rome was fed from abroad. Carthage was conquered by Roman forces in 146 BC, giving Rome access to the developed agriculture not only of the north African territories, but also of lands previously controlled by Carthage in Sicily, Sardinia and Spain. Six thousand Roman citizens were settled on generous allotments of farmland in north Africa in 123 BC. The rich cornfields of the Nile came under the control of Rome with the conquest of Egypt in 30 BC, and supplied the city with over 100,000 tons of grain a year in the decades immediately before the birth of Christ, it is recorded, when Rome's African colonies were supplying at least another 200,000 tons each year.

The production of such vast quantities of corn in foreign lands, regularly and reliably, year after year, called for a massive administrative organisation. Simply arranging for the cultivation and harvesting of the grain was challenge enough, and transporting it to the harbours by wagon, donkey and camel train was also a formidable task, but the ultimate achievement lay in the fleets of vessels that carried the corn to Rome.

Some ships are known to have had capacities of over 1,000 tons, many carried only up to 80 tons, but Rickman puts the average at between 340 and 400 tons, which means that a minimum of 800 shiploads would have been required to feed Rome in 5 BC, though the actual number is likely to have been considerably higher. Shipwreck, pirates and spoilage all took their toll. Simply keeping the grain dry during the voyage, in wooden ships without the benefit of plastic, was a challenging proposition, and the voyage itself, without the benefit of engines, was not the kind of Mediterranean cruise that people enjoy these days.

The Egyptian port, Alexandria, was over 1,500 km. (930 mi.) from Rome and, although sailing down on the Mediterranean's prevailing north to north-westerly winds could be a relatively easy week's journey, tacking back against the wind, heavily loaded, in square-rigged ships that could head within no more than seven points of the wind, was an arduous and frequently dangerous exercise which could take up to 70 days. The north African ports were less than half the distance away, and a report of fresh figs arriving in Rome three days after they were picked in Carthage does indicate that grain from north Africa could reach Rome in a fraction of the time it took to travel from Egypt, but even north African imports were

subject to the seasonal constraints that affected the movement of corn
throughout the Mediterranean.

Winter bad weather, with cloudy skies hindering navigation by sun and stars, restricted sailings across the Mediterranean to the summer season for the cautious, and to the months from spring to autumn for the adventurous, so that, at the very most, there were only eight months of the year (early March to early November) in which sailings were feasible, and only four (late May to September) in which prospects of a safe voyage were good. Furthermore, the corn ripened only in the late summer, so that, no matter how efficiently the crop was harvested and transported to the ports, only a fraction could be shipped out in the same year, leaving the greater part of the crop to be stored over winter for export the following year.

Storing grain in bulk raises its own problems. Quite apart from the obvious need to guard it against the depredations of rodents and thieves, in containers big enough to hold the volume, and stout enough to withstand the considerable pressure that bulk grain exerts in all directions, temperature and humidity are critical. Much above 15°C (59°F) and there is a risk of weevil and beetle infestation; more than about 15 percent moisture and the grain is likely to germinate and rot.

All the problems of handling and storage that confronted exporters were multiplied several times over in Rome, where shipments of various origin were all likely to arrive in the same brief period of time, in various states of disarray, at the mouth of the Tiber 35 km. (22 mi.) downstream. Some ships unloaded at riverside quays, others sailed to safe harbours further along the coast, from which their cargoes were transhipped to barges. A large harbour was constructed in the proximity of the river mouth, but it silted easily and appears to have afforded but limited protection – in 62 AD a storm sank nearly 200 ships moored in the harbour with grain for Rome. Not until the 2nd century AD was a fully safe harbour available at Ostia, and even then the grain still had to be transferred to barges for shipment upstream to Rome. Barges were towed up the meandering river by teams of men or oxen. The journey took three days, and with a minimum of 4,500 bargeloads required to shift Rome's annual corn supply alone in Rickman's estimation, plus all the other produce and materials flowing into a city of one million inhabitants, the amount of traffic on the river must have been considerable. No less impressive were the arrangements required to offload and store the corn for distribution in the city itself. Porters carried at least six million individual loads down the gangplanks from ship to shore each year during the height of Rome's development.

While marvelling at the dimensions of the permanent mark that Rome has left on western civilisation, it is easy to overlook the instability of the city's year-to-year existence. The survival of Rome depended utterly on its inhabitants' ability to secure and store enough of one year's corn harvest to satisfy its needs until the arrival of the next, and the talents that this problem exercised were fundamental to the rise and success of the entire empire. From the time that free grain was distributed to eligible citizens in 123 BC, the state played an increasingly important role in civic and social life. The annual grain supply was too unpredictable, and demands on it too unremitting, for the market to be left entirely to private merchants, and many of the most admirable facets of Roman administration and justice probably derive from the problems of balancing the positive values of individual ambition against the negative effects of excessive exploitation. As Geoffrey Rickman points out, the corn market was the subject of a 'fundamental change in the relationship of the state to the individual, whether he was a farmer, a shipper, a baker, or metropolitan corn recipient. The feeding of Rome was always a political as well as an economic problem and it involved much more than simply putting food into the stomachs of the inhabitants.'

The importance of grain in the Roman economy is emphasized by the ears of corn often depicted on its coinage. In 58 BC the distribution of free grain is said to have cost Rome more than one-fifth of all its revenues, and there is evidence that country people moved permanently to the city to take advantage of the distribution, and that wealthy citizens made free men of their slaves simply in order to gain access to further amounts of free corn. Such developments put increasing demands on the system, and provoked trouble for the government when the distribution failed or faltered. In 22 AD, Tiberius told the Senate that 'the utter ruin of the state will follow' any failure to fulfil its duty of feeding Rome, and the corn distribution was always a potent factor in the political machinations of the city. Caesar vainly attempted to limit the number of eligible recipients, but Septimius gave out free oil along with the free grain, and Aurelian added regular supplies of pork and wine to the distribution. And in the 2nd century AD, freshly baked bread replaced grain in the distribution, bringing one more aspect of the city's food supply under state control.

At its height, the Roman Empire controlled the entire Mediterranean and the rest of the known world, from Hadrian's Wall to the Euphrates. An army of over 600,000 men was stationed among its 119 provinces; 30,000 civil servants administered affairs abroad, and Rome was but one of many capital cities in the Empire. Then Rome declined, leaving history to note the excellence and decadence that marked its rise and fall, but generally without according proper importance to one of the most crucial factors in the process – the food supply.

Not until 1800, when a census recorded 959,310 people living in London, did another city approach the size of Rome at its zenith. Meanwhile, though the physical evidence of Rome's glory – its cities, roads, aqueducts, and artifacts – crumbled to the status of antique curiosities after the fall of the last Emperor in 476 AD, the influence of Roman civilisation was preserved in its language – Latin – whose clarity and lack of equivocation were doubtless forged by the necessities of administering a huge city and a vast and sprawling empire. And as the influence of Christianity spread through Europe, Rome remained the administrative capital, and Latin the language of authority.

Europe assumed its feudal character, with most of its population working on the land and such surpluses as they produced turning to wealth in the hands of the landowners. Merchants traded produce and basic commodities between local markets, and luxury goods from the ports and centres of specialised manufacture. The church sanctioned the hierarchical structure of the developing economy – aristocrat, prelate, merchant, manufacturer and peasant – and, as towns became centres of trade, the Roman Catholic Church itself became the most important component in a new kind of economy – one that approved of the accumulation of wealth for its own sake.

This development was the key to a critical transformation from market town to merchant city which occurred during the first millienium AD, by the end of which raw materials, craft, talent and invention were the most precious items of trade, while gold and silver had become the most consistently valuable media of exchange. Accumulated money became capital, capable of investment, leading to the even greater accumulation of wealth. The church grew very rich indeed, and the marvels of ecclesiastical architecture that grace every major medieval city are as much monuments to money as expressions of Christian faith. 'Not Caesar now, but money, is all', wrote Alain of Lille in the 12th century.

Cities themselves, then, tended to rise and fall on the threads of trade, rather than upon their direct control of an adequate agricultural resource. Even exploration and conquest were essentially trading adventures. Africa, India, the Far East, the Americas. Sugar, tea, furs, timber, china, ivory, precious stones and metals... the economic history of medieval Europe evokes images of a relentless scramble for the material wealth of the world, quite beyond individual need and only tenuously related to the sustained well-being and continuity of any particular group.

The huge quantities of South American gold and silver that the Spanish plunderers introduced to the scramble fused the links between Church and trade, ultimately producing the social climate that drove the Hutterites into a communal way of life and persuaded the Pilgrim Fathers that a better life might be possible in the New World of North America.

Though the Pilgrim Fathers and other early settlers from Europe experienced shortages and hardship, they succeeded in founding settlements and a pattern of social endeavour in New England for which there was ample prospect of future growth and expansion across the uncharted and seemingly infinite territory to the west – a prospect in which ambition might be either sharpened or tempered, according to disposition, by any objections raised by the Indians already occupying the territory. The size of the Indian population never again attained its pre-contact level, but the white population expanded steadily as more settlers were attracted to the colony and families raised their children. When the first census was conducted in 1790 there were 3,929,214 people settled in North America, and Britain's continuing exploitation and taxation of the colony provoked them to rebellion and the American War of Independence.

The War of Independence was more about who had the right to exploit the resources of America, colonist or colonial power, than about the actual occupation of the country, and with the defeat of the British, the more adventurous of those on the eastern seaboard of the continent could turn their backs on Europe and look to the hinterland: not for food alone, nor even simply for somewhere to live, but primarily in search of a fortune. Cleveland is a product of the fortune-seeking tendency.

The land on which Cleveland stands, 700 km. (435 mi.) to the west of the Atlantic, had been granted – sight unseen – to the state of Connecticut by Charles II in 1662, under the terms of a charter which defined the New England colony as extending from its known limits on the Atlantic coast, across the full extent of the then still unknown continent, to the shores and islands of what the charter called 'the south sea on the west'. Subsequently, the eastern portions of this generous but decidedly untenable grant were occupied by the colonists of New York and Pennsylvania, and in 1786 Connecticut was obliged to cede the remainder to the newly constituted United States – but not without compensation. Because of its small size, and in return for abandoning further claims on any of the vast swathe of land that Charles II had granted the colony, a 120-mile (193 km.) strip of the original claim lying along the shores of Lake Erie immediately to the west of Pennsylvania was reserved for possession by the residents of Connecticut.

This expanse of 3.5 million acres (1.2 million ha) became known as the Connecticut Western Reserve, but development and exploitation by its new owners were not able to proceed until the resistance of its current occupants, the Indians, was overcome by General Wayne at the battle of Fallen Timbers in 1794, and by a Treaty of 1795, which obliged the Indians to retreat west of the Cuyahoga River and stay there.

In the autumn of 1795, within months of the Indians' capitulation, a group of 35 wealthy citizens, who had pooled their resources to form the Connecticut Land Company, bought three million acres of the Western Reserve for $1,200,000. In the spring of 1796 they despatched a party of 45 men to survey the property, lay out township boundaries and establish the site of a principal town. Moses Cleaveland, a director and shareholder in the company, was appointed leader of the surveying expedition.

During their arduous and occasionally hazardous journey through the forests and back trails from Connecticut to the Cuyahoga, the surveyors celebrated the 20th anniversary of the Declaration of Independence and encountered several groups of Indians. 'I am the head man from the East and now with my brethren am going to the west to settle lands on the south side of Lake Erie... we mean to treat you as friends and brothers and to act honestly and honorably with you...', Cleaveland assured one group, while his 'shrewd bargaining' persuaded the Mohawk and Seneca Indians to relinquish their claims to the land east of the Cuyahoga 'in exchange for 500 pounds New York currency, two beef cattle, and 100 gallons of whisky'.

A noble race!
But they are gone,
With their old forests wide and deep,
And we have built our houses upon
Fields where their generations sleep.
William Cullen Bryant

The town that Cleaveland and his party laid out on the bluff above the eastern bank of the Cuyahoga, close by the lake shore, was neat, regular and precisely measured – as might be expected of speculators principally concerned with facilitating the sale, rather than the use, of land – but settlers were slow to arrive. Not least, perhaps, because prospective settlers knew full well that, although the map showed a neat plan of 222 two and four acre (0.8 and 1.6 ha) plots laid out like a New England town in a squared-off grid of streets with an expansive ten-acre (4 ha) Public Square at its centre, the reality was a pattern of surveying pegs linking some rough clearings in the midst of a dense hardwood forest. 'The soil is pretty good and the water extraordinarily good and plenty', reported one of the surveyors encouragingly, 'The timber is beech, elm, ash, maple, walnut, chestnut, oak, whitewood, butternut... There are grapevines at this place loaded with their first fruit and that is extraordinary good of the kind.'

Two traders and their families set up shop in a two-storey log cabin on the river bank in 1797, offering 'a meal, a bed, and a drink of New England rum' to travellers, and operating a ferry service to facilitate trade with the Indians across the river. In 1798, a blacksmith joined them, encouraged by an offer of ten acres additional land, free, in return for a commitment to stay at least one year, and when the Connecticut Land Company reduced its prices to $25 a plot and offered extended terms, other settlers followed. A primitive distillery was the first manufacturing business to be established in the settlement, producing raw spirit ostensibly intended for medicinal purposes but principally a trading item valued for its 'calming influence on unruly Indians'.

Thirty-two Cleveland residents – 12 women and 20 men – gathered in the trader's riverfront cabin to celebrate America's 25th Independence Day on July 4 1801, and although the population of the Western Reserve had swollen to 1500 in time for the 35th anniversary, ten years later, there were then still only 57 people living in the town. And the town hardly merited that description. '... when I rode behind my father on horseback to Cleveland... there were many large stumps in the Square, and clumps of bushes which extended to the lake, and all along the bank of the lake, from the summit to the beach, the trees were all standing,' one early settler later recalled. '... from the Square... was woods, except some four or five spaces adjoining the street for as many houses and gardens... west, south and east, the forest stood in its native grandeur. Only a narrow strip had been cut out for a road where Ontario Street is'.

By 1815, tree stumps still hindered passage along the only two streets that had been cleared, and bushes still flourished in undisturbed clearings, but Cleveland was beginning to prosper. Just 150 people were living in the town at the time, and most of the 34 houses then standing were of unsawn log cabin construction, with earthern floors and windowless, but three frame-built houses stood on prominent corner sites amongst them, and a two-storey courthouse (with jail) had been erected on the Public Square. A judge had been appointed (and an Indian publicly executed for the murder of two fur-trappers), the town's first lawyer had hung up his shingle, and several more traders and craftsmen had been attracted to the location.

Cleveland prospered on the American fortune-seeking frontier then advancing remorsely westward across the continent, and its economy received a sizeable boost from the war of 1812, when the city became a base for the naval operations that repulsed Britain's attempts to extend her Canadian territories across Lake Erie.

The defeat of the British on Lake Erie cleared American access through the Great Lakes and overland to the Great Plains and the huge potential wealth of the northwestern United States. Cleveland flourished on the development, its location at a critical point on the trade route suddenly enhanced. The population rose to 500 in 1825, and in 1827 more than 1,000 Cleveland residents saw the first vessel complete her journey through a 38-mile (61 km.) canal that had been dug (mainly by German and Irish immigrants) to link Cleveland and the lakes to the Ohio River, Pittsburgh and beyond.

In 1828, an enterprising farmer shipped a bargeload of native coal down the canal to Cleveland and, although wood remained the preferred domestic fuel, coal soon fired steamboats on Lake Erie and – no less significantly – a growing number of iron foundries down on the flat estuary of the Cuyahoga River. Cleveland's iron industry began in a small way, casting pillars, plates and decorative iron-work for the construction trade from a local low-grade ore, but with the discovery of vast reserves of high-grade ore in upper Michigan state during the 1840s, and the construction of canals and facilities to ship ore through the lakes in the 1850s, Cleveland's iron and steel industry became the most advantageously situated in north America.

The frontier had moved on, but Cleveland now found itself fortuitously situated halfway between the resources and the market, ideally placed to buy in the raw materials cheaply and convert them into products that could be sold profitably. Meanwhile, the unbridled development of the industrial revolution in Europe was adding to the benefits of the city's situation.

The opening up of the mid-western United States during the early part of the 19th century was a very important factor in the early development of industrial expertise and capacity in Europe. Britain's manufacturing industry was fuelled by coal, made of iron. Vast numbers of workers were involved at all stages, for whom a source of cheap food was required. At the same time, the iron industry needed large markets to develop largescale production economically. America served both requirements – and the development of railways as a viable means of transportation during the 19th century stands out as a notable result of this appealing economic equation. The manufacture of locomotives, rolling stock, and railway lines in Britain received considerable impetus from the American drive to push back the western frontier, while the development of America's agricultural base was considerably advanced by the railway system that Britain supplied, and in turn supplied the grain that Britain needed. For financiers, the trade offered prospects of huge profits in both directions – supplying equipment to extend the frontiers, shipping out frontier produce.

American profits would be greatest, of course, if the rails required to

232

advance the frontier and carry out its produce could be manufactured in America, rather than bought from Europe, and this observation must have become very vexing indeed as 4,185 mi. (6,735 km.) of British-made track were laid before America produced even its first cast iron rail in 1826. 'If we had more of poverty, more of misery, and something of servitude, if we had an ignorant, idle, starving population, we might set up for ironmakers against the world', the United States Congress was told in 1824. The slaves of the southern states already constituted such a population, of course, but they were working on the plantations at the time, where their relatively high cost (see p. 223) gives some idea of their value in the highly profitable enterprise of producing cotton for the 'black satanic mills' then drawing another kind of slave-labour into the cities of northern England. Within a few decades, though, the mighty flood of European migrants into the United States began. First the Irish refugees from the potato famine, then wave upon wave of Germans, Lithuanians, Czechs, Poles, Swedes, Italians, Hungarians – providing just the impoverished, servile and hungry work-force that Congress had been told was needed.

Meanwhile, one agent alone bought 40,000 tons of rails from Britain in 1836, and although eight companies had been established to produce rails in the eastern United States by 1846, they struggled to match the import price of $55 a ton, and by the early 1850s still only one quarter of the 400,000 ton annual consumption was made in the United States.

The scale of the financial enterprise, the quantities of material and labour involved, and the lengths of railway laid during this period of incredibly rapid development in the United States was phenomenal. By 1850, a total of 8,350 mi. (13,440 km.) of track had been laid through the east and south- eastern states, and the demand for rails was unremitting – both for new track and to replace worn rails. By 1860, a total of 25,211 mi. (40,572 km.) had been laid as the railways reached out towards the west, and in the decade to 1870, 12,476 mi. (20,072 km.) of new track were laid in the west and mid-west alone.

The railway reached Cleveland in 1851, securing the city's share of the massive investment in the iron industry that was to lift United States production of rails from 141,000 tons in 1856 to over 335,000 tons a year by 1864, and again to more than 775,000 tons by 1871. And rails were not only product that Cleveland's expanding iron and steel industry was supplying to a relentlessly expanding nation. Steel plate, castings, locomotives and shipbuilding, wheel-barrows, shovels, sewer and drain pipes, barbed wire and nails – the demand for steel products mounted annually and each decade brought further innovations and inventions which opened new markets and provoked still more demand. The introduction of the telegraph, for example, boosted cable output from 250,000 tons in 1875, the year before Bell's invention was publicly demonstrated, to 1,200,000 tons in 1898, when it had become the indispensible medium of business communications. The electrically operated elevator followed the innovation of travelling cranes and in turn facilitated the construction of the first skyscraper – a ten-storey insurance office building erected in Chicago in 1885. Skyscrapers of course are built around frames of steel. They house people working with machines made of steel – typewriters, accounting machines, printing presses...

Once in motion, the steel-based industrial economy quickly became, one might say, self-generating – each new invention inspiring some new demand which in turn inspired the search for further invention, each turn adding momentum to a wildly accelerating economy. But, as industry sought the finance to expand its operations, the emphasis of production management shifted from the factory floor to the boardroom and the bank. Production decisions – what to make, how much of it, and for which markets – became more and more the prerogative of financiers, people based in the cities and motivated primarily by the search for a maximum rate of return on the money available for investment.

Financiers tended to congregate in national and regional capital cities where they might have ready access to the government administrations that were beginning to assume an increasingly important role in social and economic affairs. The headquarters of large companies, railways and public utilities were established close by; marketing agencies sprang up alongside, and insurance companies arose to cover the risk. Banking, accounting, management, law, advertising – a new realm of specialised human activity had emerged: the realm of the white-collar office worker.

By 1900, office workers constituted 17 percent of the total United States labour force, and a sizeable industry was arising around their needs – the consumer industry. City dwellers rented housing, bought their food and clothing and generally had money to spare for a little entertainment and an occasional luxury. In the modern commercial city, style and fashion acquired popular significance for the first time in history, and as goods were sold less on their lasting value and more on their immediate appeal, the accompanying development of mass-production manufacturing techniques enshrined the concept of obsolescence and made a virtue of persuasive marketing. Increasingly, the financiers' demands for a profitable return on capital investment encouraged manufacturers to produce what people might want, rather than what they were known to need. Goods were produced speculatively in advance of demand, and advertising was expected to *create* a demand. And because financiers demanded a continuous return on their investments, the consumer market had to expand continuously, new demands had to be created and exploited. The market had to grow.

The transformation of the city from a focus of industrial activity to a centre of political and financial influence, with a massive consumer industry growing around it to serve the needs of expanding urban populations, is a feature of every industrial nation, but it is particularly evident in the United States, where no large city is more than two centuries old and all are therefore uncluttered by the relics of earlier stages of civilisation. Modern America is very evidently a product of the drive to accumulate and manipulate wealth. The amazingly regular grid network that distinguishes road maps of the United States is itself an indication of how large chunks of the nation – the Connecticut Western Reserve, for

234

instance – were bought by speculators and then parcelled up for sale. A grid pattern of streets reduces variety, but it simplifies the business of selling plots – as was the case with Cleveland.

Few cities can have been better located than Cleveland to capitalise on the economic developments of the industrial revolution in north America. Iron ore, timber and coal; river, canal, lake and rail transportation – all had helped to make Cleveland wealthy by the early 1860s, when the city became a centre for what has become one of the prime sources of wealth in the modern world – oil.

In the Allegheny mountains to the east of Cleveland, petroleum could be found seeping from the rocks and floating out on the surface of streams. This mineral oil had its uses locally, but only after Edwin Drake had drilled the world's first oil well in the Alleghenies in 1859, and begun producing crude oil in quantity, was its wider economic potential appreciated. Petroleum offered an alternative source of kerosene, till then only obtainable from coal by a tedious and expensive extraction process. In 1860, three Cleveland entrepreneurs bought ten barrels of crude oil and, convinced that kerosene would replace whale oil as a universal lamp fuel once it was cheap enough, eventually succeeded in producing a barrel of kerosene at a fraction of the cost of extracting it from coal.

The oil refining and supply industry that sprang from the first production of kerosene in Cleveland had an impetus of its own, while the finance, technology, and steel requirements that the oil exploration and drilling industry called into being, gave yet another boost to the growth of Cleveland. The city's population had risen steadily from 1,075 in 1830 to 6,071 in 1840, to 17,034 in 1850, but with the impetus of new industry leapt to over 40,000 by 1860. Foreign immigrant workers constituted most of the influx, but it also included bankers, builders, hoteliers, traders and large numbers of independent souls in search of a fortune. Among the most determined of this latter category was a young man who, having invested $40 in a course of business studies at a Cleveland commercial college in the summer of 1855, launched himself onto the city's job market in the autumn of that year at the age of 17, and went on to be rated the world's wealthiest man: John D. Rockefeller.

Rockefeller's father, William A., was a travelling gent from New York State who peddled a line of patent medicines, including an alleged cure for cancer, but who, according to one biographer, made a more comfortable living in the land and usury business. He bought and sold land, and loaned money at 12 percent, always keen to lend to farmers likely to default on their repayments so that he could foreclose on them and take the farms. William A. moved his wife and family close to Cleveland in 1853, primarily to facilitate pursuit of a lady with whom he entered into a bigamous marriage as Dr Levingston in 1855, it is presumed, and in 1859, when John D. sought the capital with which to join a commission agency partnership at the age of 19, William A. graciously advanced $1,000 against his son's 21st birthday gift at a preferential rate of just ten percent.

In its first year, the agency handled nearly half a million dollars of business and earned $4,400 profit for its partners. In the second year they earned over $17,000 and, with the outbreak of the Civil War in 1861, found the success of their enterprise confirmed, as they took percentages on the demand for produce and goods that the war effort inspired. In 1863, they extended their interests to include the kerosene business, founding the Excelsior Works refinery in a series of shacks on three acres (1.2 ha) of land conveniently close to the rail terminal down on the Cuyahoga flats. John D. Rockefeller bought out his partner's interest in the oil business in 1865 for $72,500 cash and his share of the commission agency. By that time, crude oil was flowing from the Allegheny wells at a rate of 10,000 barrels a day, and Rockefeller saw his future in oil. A large part of Cleveland's future was tied up with Rockefeller's vision too, as it turned out, along with a good part of the economic future of New York, North America, and the world, for Rockefeller turned the Excelsior Works into Standard Oil – Esso – the first of the world's huge multinational oil companies.

Rockefeller's success was based on eradicating inefficient practices, gaining control of ancillary aspects of his business, and buying out competitors. He was also among the first of the major industrialists to use debit financing, and would borrow heavily in order to buy at an advantageous price. Rockefeller avoided trading commissions by buying crude oil direct from the wells, and eliminated the uncertainties of freight charges and delivery by establishing his own railroad to transport the oil to his refineries on the Cuyahoga flats.

By 1872, Cleveland was the oil centre of the nation. Kerosene, for lighting, heating and cooking, was the mainstay of the business, but by-products such as petroleum jelly, lubricants, paraffin waxes and gas – everything from chewing gum to Vaseline, Rockefeller once boasted – produced substantial profits, while control of freight services, railroads and a near-monopoly of pipeline and storage facilities, poured yet more money into the Standard coffers. And of course, with the development of the petrol engine, automotive power and aeroplanes, the prospects of profit for Rockefeller were virtually limitless.

Standard Oil achieved such size and domination of the oil business under Rockefeller that, in 1911, the United States Supreme Court ordered it dissolved, and the company was split into no less than 34 separate entities, each with a different name, each competing one against the other. John D. Rockefeller's income was approximately $55,000 a day at the time, and the bottom line of his personal ledger recorded a net worth of $302,713,419 and 83 cents in 1912. In the words of the popular song: 'Rockefeller, rich as Rockefeller...'

In 1900 the population of Cleveland stood at 381,768, of whom over 75 percent were either foreign-born or the children of foreign parents. By 1910, the continuing flood of immigrants had swollen the population to 560,663, making Cleveland the sixth largest city in the United States. Foreign immigrants flocked to Cleveland in search of the 'American Dream', but found a city wallowing in filth and riches under a cloud of coal smoke. Caring citizens had begun to complain about the deteriorating state of the Cleveland environment decades earlier. 'It is yearly becoming a

thing more necessary to the comforts of our citizens, that the smoke
rolling in such volume out of the chimneys of our large manufactories
should be entirely consumed', suggested a newspaper editorial in 1855.
'We have now in and about our city scores of chimney stacks, that pour out
clouds of smoke and soot, producing a great amount of discomfort.' Some
legislation to control pollution was passed, but never achieved much effect
against the fulminations of the industrialists. The indictment of a railroad
iron mill company for smoke nuisance in 1860 produced a typical
response: '... The idea of striking a blow at the industry and prosperity of
the infant iron manufactories of Cleveland... is an act that should and will
be reprobated by the whole community.' Even attempts to control the flow
of industrial wastes, 'slops, filth etc., into the Cuyahoga River within the
city limits' were opposed on the grounds that the river's current was strong
enough to wash away evil effects, and that such a move would retard the
growth and prosperity of the city. Stinking air and river were simply the
inconveniences of successful industry which had to be endured. Prosperity
was far more important than a congenial environment.

The immigrants endured the smoke and grime as they struggled for a
share of the new prosperity but, needless to say, the industrialists and
businessmen enjoyed both prosperity *and* a congenial environment.
Wealth enabled them to build and occupy successive waves of large
splendid houses as industry and commercial activity advanced steadily
outward from the city centre. Down the length of Euclid Avenue, its very
name a memorial to the geometry of classical civilisation, they built
mansions of such opulence that John D. Rockefeller's house, three floors
with mansard roof and arched windows in ecclesiastical style, and one of
the first on the avenue, eventually seemed restrained and conservative by
comparison. Brick, stone and ironwork, French style, Oriental, Italian,
Palladian, Grecian, all that money could buy – even cupola and turnip
dome, lavishly ornamented, sumptuously appointed... they stood, these
piles of domestic ostentation, as symbols of individual wealth, to be
measured one against the other.

Before long, however, the prevailing southwest winds carried the stink
of prosperous industry from the Cuyahoga flats down the length of Euclid
Avenue, and the wealthy folk moved further afield to Wade Park, Cedar
Heights, Lakewood, Bratenahl, Shaker Heights – the pattern of their
dispersal broadened by their increasing numbers, serviced by enterprising
land and building speculations, facilitated by the provision of municipal
transportation and, ultimately, furthered by the private motor car. They
left what they are pleased to call an 'emerald necklace' of public parks
around the decaying industrial core of the city.

Cleveland achieved a memorable apotheosis on June 22 1969, when the
Cuyahoga River caught fire, flammable industrial wastes and debris
floating on the water having accumulated to the point of spontaneous
combustion. The extraordinary blaze attracted fierce attention from the
United States Environment Protection Agency and a major effort to clean
up the river was instigated. The city set about the long-overdue task of
doubling its sewage treatment capacity; steel plants were obliged to spend

237

millions on water treatment facilities and the chemical giant, Du Pont, established controls which, by 1980, were removing 950 pounds (430 kg.) of heavy metals each day from the waters of the Cuyahoga River.

In a sense, however, heightened concern for the environment was also a reflection of shifting priorities. By the 1980s, industry had all but abandoned Cleveland. The oil refinery closed down and the last steel plant was barely viable. Cleveland shares the plight of cities throughout America and beyond, as the latest twist in human economic organisation carries people ever further from direct involvement with their sources of sustenance and shelter. In 1984, just 3.2 percent of the United States workforce was engaged in agriculture, 8.1 percent were unemployed, while 23.8 percent were involved with the production of raw material and consumer goods, and a massive 64.9 percent were employed in the service industry (15.13 percent in government alone).

With agriculture having achieved levels of such efficiency that 3.2 percent of the workforce can feed a nation of over 238 million *and* produce a substantial surplus for export, while 23.8 percent is sufficient to produce all the goods they need, it seems clear that the service industries will dominate the United States' economy as the 20th century draws to a close. Finance, insurance, health care, management, real estate, advertising, entertainment – these are the activities that offer the best options of revival for the declining fortunes of Cleveland, and they have packed the city offices with a new wave of aspirants energetically committed to the wealth motive. They live in lush suburbs – Hunting Valley, Chagrin Falls, down Pepper Pike, some in houses as opulent in the modern idiom as any that once stood on Euclid Avenue. The style is informal but the codes of membership are as distinctively drawn as those of the merchant and craft guilds of old Europe. Golf course and club are exclusive venues at which a uniform of lime-green jacket and lemon-yellow trousers seems obligatory for the Saturday evening clambake (dark-blue trousers sprinkled with little white whales for the trendsetters), but genial hospitality cannot hide the nervous discomfort of a host whose guest arrives without a tie.

There is a brittle quality to the wealth that surrounds Cleveland in the late 1980s. It is riven with fears of the impoverished, jealous and disorderly factions that have arisen among the people in the city, and elsewhere in the United States, who are without a job now that industry has moved on. The residents of the suburbs spend thousands of dollars each year on the lawns that run smooth and unfenced down to the roadside. They raise the national flag from balconies over the pillared portico, and luxuriate around cool pools during the sweltering days of August. But they fear for their wealth and personal safety to the extent that security agencies are one of the booming service industries of Cleveland. People decline to be interviewed (or photographed for books like this) for fear that they may be identified, robbed, or attacked, by 'some loony crank'. Even publishing the details of a will excites fear of attracting the attention of industrious thieves, and the funerals of wealthy citizens have become more private affairs since public announcements were seen to invite burglary while the principal mourners were at the cemetery.

Each day, the custodians of Cleveland's economic future drive speedily through a three-mile (5 km.) band of derelict and decaying residential properties lying north and south of Euclid Avenue. The area is now the home of blacks, the unemployed and the impoverished, for whom the once exclusive inner city is a cheap place to live. So cheap, in fact, that in 1984 one private charity was able to buy four entire blocks of land in the proximity of Euclid Avenue for $12,000. Riots swept the inner city area during the 1960s and '70s, reducing substantial tracts of it to rubble. It is a depressed and depressing place, undeniably, and Cleveland's new office work-force are more likely to be tuned in to early market reports on the radio than to the plight of the inner city residents as they drive through. It is physically dangerous to stop there or venture down the side roads, they say, for casual visitors are likely to be attacked and robbed. The people there are washed up, they say.

The Cleveland Museum of Art is set back among the beautifully tended lawns, trees, cycle-ways and jogging tracks of the 'emerald necklace' which the city managed to preserve from the depredations of land speculators. It is within easy walking distance of Euclid Avenue, where its benefactors once congregated.

The Museum was established in 1913 around an assortment of artifacts, sculpture and paintings collected by a number of the city's wealthy residents, with the help of substantial private bequests. The building initially constructed to house the Museum is of classical inspiration, and the early collections reflected a similar affection for images of ancient civilisation. With their own fortunes secure, Cleveland industrialists turned to cultural philanthropy, a commentator notes, foreign travel having made them acutely aware of a manifest lack of culture in the United States. They used their wealth to acquire culture in the form of artifacts from ancient Egypt, Greece, Rome and medieval Europe and displayed them with the explicit intention of evoking an appreciation for the finer things in life. 'May this museum reveal to those who enter its portals the universal beauty of all about us,' a speaker implored at the opening ceremony, 'and inspire us all in the Art of Arts – the Art of Living'.

The endowments of which the Cleveland Museum of Art is sole beneficiary presently total over $150 million dollars, and the income from this steadily increasing sum of money has enabled the museum to assemble one of the world's foremost collections of art, with outstanding examples from every age, every field, every school – from Africa to Oceania, from Classical to Byzantine and Impressionist. A permanent feature of the museum – and one that makes it a *museum* of art, rather than simply a gallery – is a winding tour that takes the visitor through the entire history of western civilisation, each stage illustrated by some exquisite artifact. A headless, but very dignified sculpture of a robed figure from the early Mesopotamian city of Lagash begins the tour, followed by an Assyrian relief sculpture of a winged figure pollinating the earth, artifacts from ancient Egypt, Greece and Rome, early Christian paintings,

239

Romanesque, Gothic, Medieval, Renaissance, Baroque, 18th-century Dutch, French, Spanish; 19th century, Impressionist, Early American and so on... to the modern day.

This unequalled display of art and civilisation is a powerful image of the cultural heights that mankind has attained over the last five thousand years but, viewed in the context of the unbridled industrial exploitation that funded its assembly, the collection also casts a shadow over the gracious Art of Living that it was intended to inspire.

A tragic conflict between aspiration and exploitation flaws the history of civilisation — the commonality of man always divided by individual interests; the inspired ideals of humanity always compromised by the pragmatism of human behaviour. Time and again the human capacity for ingenious adaptation has lifted people above the determining bounds of the environment into realms of civilisation where culture seems an end in itself, and mankind truly the paragon of animals. Then, time and again, human ambition has reached beyond prudence and civilisation has foundered. Mankind seems on the brink of such a crisis now, with the relentless exploitation of resources, and the reckless pollution of the global environment consorting to threaten disaster on an unprecedented scale. But this time mankind has all the knowledge which is needed to understand the effect of human excesses on the Earth and its tender living mantle, and all the technical skill with which to monitor and control them. That knowledge and skill, combined with the seemingly infinite talent for social and cultural adaptation that this book has sought to demonstrate, are a wellspring of hope.

'What a piece of work is a man! How noble in reason! how infinite in faculty! in form, in moving, how express and admirable! in action how like an angel! in apprehension how like a god! the beauty of the world! the paragon of animals!'
William Shakespeare

Photographs taken by the author: a pictorial summary of
Man on Earth.

1

Quechua Indian family, planting potatoes on the Andean
altiplano, 4,000 m. (13,000 ft.) above sea level.

A family on Yap (3), a 39 sq. mi. (100 sq. km.) island in the western Pacific. Prior to the arrival of Europeans the island is believed to have supported up to 34,000 people. The corms of taro (2) are an important source of carbohydrate for Pacific islanders.

2

A coral reef surrounds Yap, and mangroves take root in the shallows of the enclosed lagoons (5), steadily extending the cultivable land area of the island as they convert seashore to mangrove swamp. Fish provided protein for the early colonisers, but the Pacific islands were virtually devoid of vegetable foods. Breadfruit,

banana and coconut (6) are all introduced crops (as is taro). Yap is renowned for its stone money (4), wheels of aragonite which were quarried from limestone caves on Palau, 400 km. (250 mi.) away, and transported to Yap by sailing canoe. The stone money is still used in property transactions on Yap.

A family on the Nembi plateau in the eastern highlands.

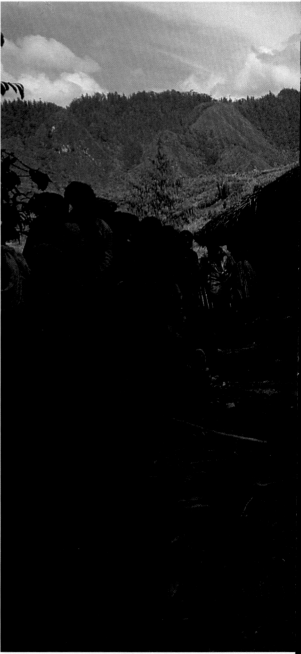

7

*The sweet potato – planted in mounds on newly
cleared land (7) – is the staple crop of the highlanders,
feeding both people and the pigs that constitute the
currency of the* moka *ceremonies, for which the men
adorn themselves with paint, don bird of paradise
feather headdresses, and brandish weapons still
occasionally used in inter-tribal warfare.*

On the Nembi Plateau in the Eastern Highlands (9), as elsewhere in Papua New Guinea, women do most of the work in the gardens. Though productivity is low in highland agriculture, the increasing demands of the cash economy in modern times have encouraged many women to grow crops for sale as well as to feed their families.

A woman from the Nembi Plateau, wearing paint and pearlshell necklaces, carries produce to market in her *bilum*, a string bag suspended from her head (10).

Ash-grey body paint and necklaces of the seeds known as Job's tears are the dress of a recently widowed market-seller (11). She will take off one string of seeds each day and her period of mourning will be complete when the last is removed.

10

Pearlshell, smeared with ochre (13), is a traditional form of exchange in New Guinea highland culture. In pre-colonial times, aggressive display (14), violence and warfare among men in the highlands were largely a matter of defending tribal territory and resources to ensure the continued well-being of its inhabitants. Nowadays it is more a matter of personal aggrandisement that preoccupies the men (12) and consumes an inordinate proportion of available resources.

13

14

Rice subak *leader and family, Bali, Indonesia. Rice is mankind's most important food crop, supporting 60 percent of the world population, though most of the crop is eaten within walking distance of the field in which it was grown.*

17

1

19

Rice is grown all year round in Bali, and maximum production is maintained by ensuring that each terrace is cleared (20), flooded and planted (19), drained, ripened and harvested (18), in sequence down the slope. with the result that all stages of rice cultivation can often be seen simultaneously, on the same hillside (17).

Rice production throughout Bali is ordered by a calendar of religious events. Offerings to the Rice Goddess are erected on the terraces (23) on specified occasions, and religion pervades every aspect of Balinese life – from dance (24) to funeral (21) – and carved images of demons (22), are an ever-present reminder of the dangers of non-conformity.

Three generations of the Seematter family (26) are the present-day representatives of one of 12 family lines that have lived at Törbel (25), in the Swiss Alps, continuously for at least 500 years.

The Törbel lands extend over 800 ha (2,000 acres) of south-facing alpine slope, at altitudes ranging from 900 m. to 1,900 m. (3,000 ft to 6,250 ft). The vineyards, hay meadows and arable land that range up the slope are divided into parcels of privately owned land, some very small, like the hay meadows around the satellite hamlet of Feld (27). Most men have jobs out of the village these days, but cows, milk, hay and cheese remain a significant component of the village economy. The land is still worked according to the strict rules of land use, landholding, water rights and inheritance that were set down in a series of vellum documents dating back to 1224 (29). The old wine jugs and wooden beakers are still used at council meetings, though the tessels – slips of wood registering bundles of firewood delivered to the village priest – have become redundant.

27

28

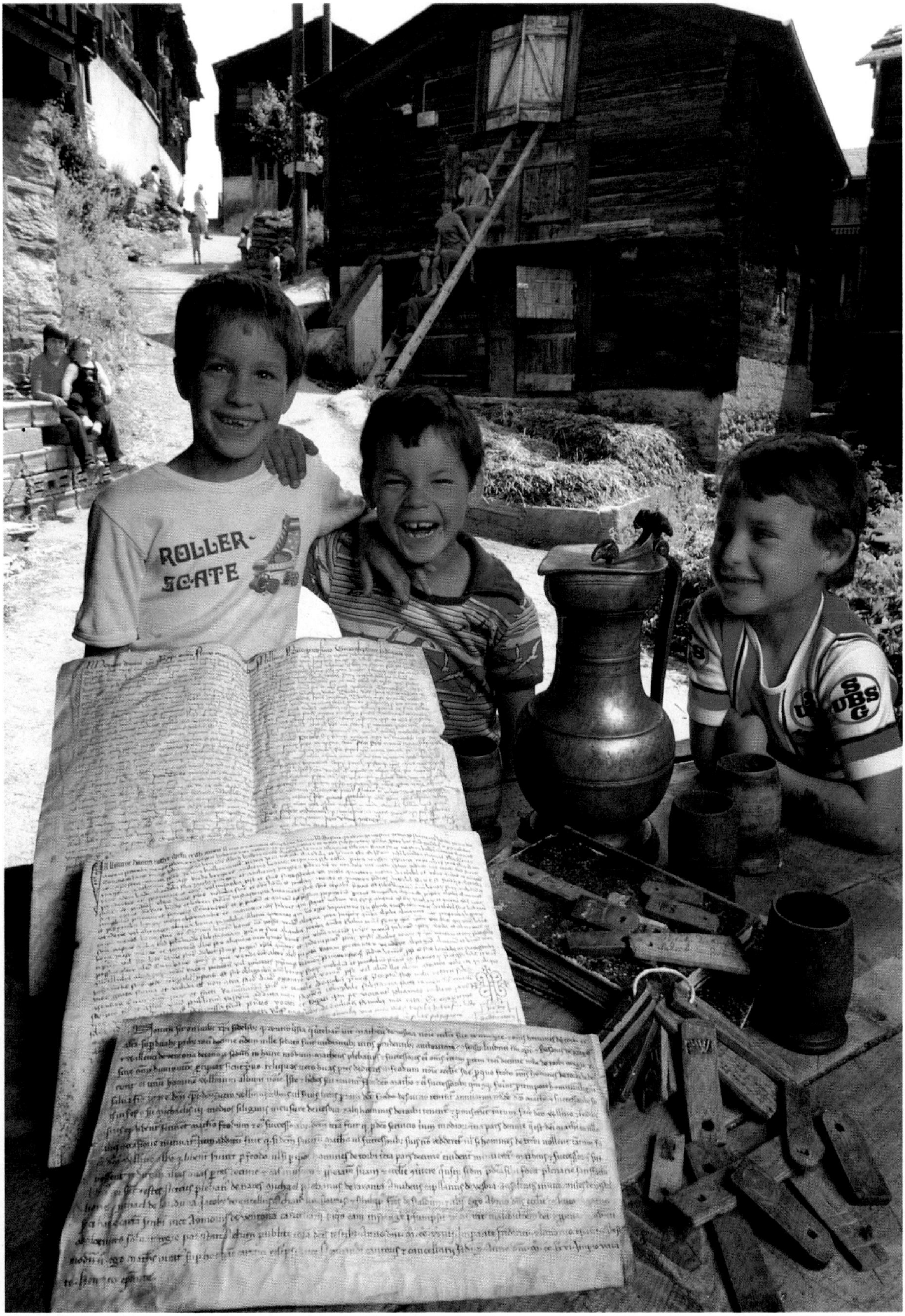
ROLLER-
SCATE
UBS

A subsistence storage economy based upon the cow sustained Törbel through the centuries. Ideally, each household kept at least two or three cows, and made enough hay and cheese each summer to sustain both cows and people through the following winter. The village herd spends ten or 12 weeks of the summer months grazing the communally owned high alpine pastures in the care of an appointed herdsman (32) and his assistants, while their owners attend to the laborious task of mowing and storing hay for the

winter. The first day on the alp, when the cows are brought up the winding road from distant barns around the village (31) and assemble in a fenced meadow to establish their herd hierarchy (30), is a day out for the villagers.

Nomadic pastoralism is a strategy by which people sustain themselves, generation after generation, on the resources of tropical semi-arid lands.

33

Rain is essential if sufficient cows or other stock are to be kept in milk at all times, but rainfall is often erratic, limited or localised (33), and in the language of the Samburu people in northern Kenya (34) its importance is denoted by the fact that the word for rain and the word for god are the same: Nkai.

The Samburu live in family units, and during dry seasons the major part of the herd ranges widely, spending the nights in temporary camps (37) and defended by moran *(warriors 35), while a nucleus of milch stock sustains women, children and old men in semi-permanent home settlements.*

35

36

The Samburu believe that Nkai resides on Mount
Nyiru, a massif which rises sharply to 3,000 m. (10,000
ft) from the northern portion of their rangelands.
Samburu cattle are taken up to Nyiru's lush high
meadows (39) in severe droughts (40), and the
significance of the mountain is acknowledged in many
aspects of Samburu life. After a meat feast (38), the
participants will make a respectful salutation to Nyiru.

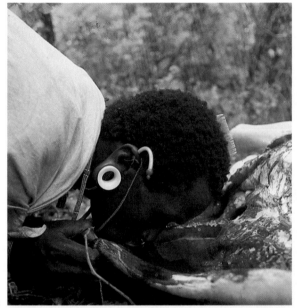

38

39

Several different groups of nomadic pastoralists utilise the rangelands of northern Kenya, separated primarily by ecological constraints, and kept apart by cultural characteristics.

41

The Samburu are able to keep cattle, but only camels can sustain the Rendille (41, 42) in their drier territories to the north and east. The Turkana (43) occupy an even harsher region to the west, where they keep goats as the basis of an opportunistic lifestyle that includes the theft of cattle and camels from the other groups.

The reindeer was the basis of the nomadic pastoralism which enabled
the Lapps to utilise the tundra regions of northern Scandinavia, but the herds – though
owned – were never tamed. The Lapps tracked and hunted their reindeer along
the animals' seasonal migration routes, depending more upon meat than upon
milk for their sustenance.

The system began to break down when land settlement and national boundaries
disrupted the migrations. The boundary between Finland and Norway, which
follows the course of the Tana River (44), was closed in 1852, denying herders the
right to follow the reindeer as they moved between upland summer pastures and
coastal winter retreats. Reindeer herding continues on both sides of the border, but it
has become a commercial, rather than a subsistence, enterprise, and is little more
than a folk memory for most Lapps still living in the region (45).

The natural resources of the circumpolar regions are surprisingly prolific. Coastal waters and rivers are well stocked with fish, the land is always moist and vegetation grows prodigiously in the relatively high temperatures and continuous daylight of the summer months.

As the Lapps were enclosed by national boundaries and drawn into national economies, the resources that once sustained their nomadic way of life were subtly transformed into luxury items for consumption by the population at large. Berries, salmon, reindeer meat and furs all fetch very high prices. The resources are reserved for Lapps, but not all are involved and the profits made by the few cause some resentment among the many.

48

49

■ OMAN: DESERT NOMADS ■

The religious conviction that still inspires men to turn and pray to Mecca (50),
wherever they may be, was an important element of the strategies that enabled
nomads to survive in the deserts of the Arabian Peninsula. Oases, and the places
where fresh water rose from the base of the mountains (51), were indispensible sources
of water, dates and other produce and were fortified against attack (52).

51

52

50

Oil has brought wealth to the Bedu, but it has not persuaded all of them to leave the desert. On the contrary, many of the Harasiis Bedu, for instance, now occupy their territory along the fringes of the Empty Quarter in Oman all year round (53), though formerly they lived there only during the months when dense mists left copious supplies of dew for collection on blankets hung out overnight. Nowadays, the Harasiis regularly drive in supplies of water to their desert camps, and transport their camels long distance by truck (54), while their goats receive a supplementary diet of dried sardines (55) when browsing is sparse. The sardines are brought in from the coast at considerable cost.

54

55

*The Maine lobster fishery is controlled by 'harbour gangs' who operate from the
limited number of sheltered anchorages along the rocky coast.*

*Maine supplied nearly 50 percent of the 34 million lobsters eaten in the United States
during 1986. Dan (left 57, with his stern-man, Seth) has created a tidal pond beside his
tackle-shed (56), in which he holds his catch for sale at optimum prices.*

The bays and offshore waters of New England are littered with marker buoys during the season (60) – up to 10,000 pots may be set in an area of little more than 30 sq mi. (78 sq. km.) – but although lobster fishing is, by law, open to anyone who takes out a licence, in effect it is reserved for those already established in the

business. Along the coast of Maine, the men fishing from each harbour control a clearly identified stretch of water; strange pots are recognised by their licence colours (59), and their owners warned off. Persistent trespassers from other harbours (and even innocent vacationers) are likely to find their pots cut loose.

*Stylized images of animals, birds and fish carved on totem poles by
Haida Indians are symbols of a unique culture, recreated in the work of the Haida
artist, Alfred Collinson (62).*

The huge softwood forests of the Queen Charlotte
Islands, which supplied the basic materials of the
Haida Indian culture for thousands of years, are now
exploited by the woodpulp and paper industry – with
devastating effect (63). Natural regeneration involves
three or four cycles of colonisation by different tree
species (64), and a century or more will pass before the
original forest is replaced. The Haida protest that they –
not external business interests – should control the
resources of the islands.

All signs of human habitation have disappeared from most of the sites that the Haida once occupied around the shores of the islands, but a few decaying totem poles still stand at Skedans (65), and a moss-covered skull (66) lies beside a fallen mortuary pole.

Minimal rainfall produces a wealth of edible vegetation in the Kalahari desert, and San Bushmen (68), on average, each spend less than 20 hours a week looking for food. The tscha *melon (67) ripens at the height of the dry season, when it is an important source of fluid.*

Vegetable foods comprise up to 80 percent of the San diet, harvested as required from the wide variety of plants that are available at different times of year. Women gather most of the food that the San consume, foraging every three or four days, venturing some distance from the camp in search of the most palatable plants, leaving less palatable items found close by for easy collection in times of hardship. The men hunt, and thus supply essential proteins, but studies have shown that their hunting expeditions have only a one-in-four chance of success, while the womens' foraging offers a 100 percent certainty of providing food.

70

71

72

73

The equatorial rainforests of west and central Africa produce at least 20 times more vegetation per unit area than the Kalahari each year, but most of it is piled up in trees and only about 2.5 percent of the biomass is actually available to feed the people and the animals they hunt.

Essential carbohydrates are very scarce in the rainforest, and the Bambuti acquire a substantial proportion of their requirements from villagers who have settled along roads through the forest. The villagers exchange their garden produce for a share of the game meat that the Bambuti catch – essential protein the villagers otherwise would be unable to obtain. The two groups distrust one another but both depend upon the strong symbiotic relationship which has developed between them, suggesting that neither the villagers nor the Bambuti could live permanently in the forest without the other.

Some Bambuti children attend school (79) at Nduye in the Ituri forest, Zaire. The village (78) is located along a track that crosses the Nduye river (77), far from business and administrative centres, and the prospects of education freeing either villagers (80) or Bambuti from their mutual dependence on the forest are very slight.

78

79

77

80

The potato originated on the Andean altiplano, where it was first domesticated about 4,500 years ago and is still an integral part of the agricultural system that sustains the indigenous Quechua Indians (82).

81

The potato thrives at altitudes of 3,000 m. (10,000 ft) and more – where no other crop can match its productivity. Patches of the poor, heavy soil are cultivated in rotation with the aid of the taccla (81), a foot-plough which pre-dates the Incas and is the only practical implement on steep slopes.

83

6
Potato fields behind San Juan de Jarpa (84), in the central Andes near Huancayo, rise to over 4,000 m. (13,000 ft). Several hundred varieties of potato have been developed from the indigenous wild stock in the Andes, each with distinctive characteristics of productivity, frost and drought resistance, susceptibility to disease, taste and storage qualities. Farmers plant (83) the variety best suited to the land and their requirements.

86

87

The Incas ruled the Andes for less than 100 years before they were overwhelmed by the Spanish conquistadores in the 1530s. They arose from among the Quechua tribes of the altiplano north of Lake Titicaca and built their empire upon the cultivation of maize, an easily stored and transported crop they introduced from central America. Maize was grown on irrigated terraces along the valleys, but could not survive at high altitudes, so never supplanted the potato, which remained the peasants' subsistence crop. The same pattern still exists in the Andes, among the Inca ruins at Chinchero (85) and along the Urubamba River (87).

*The Toda people herd buffalo on the high plateau of the Nilgiri Hills
in southern India.*

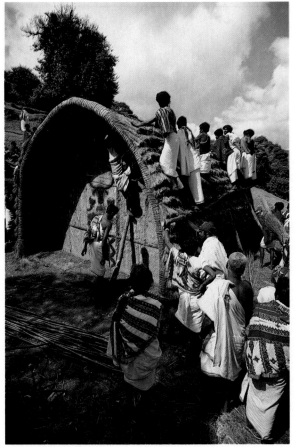

88

*Toda religion deifies the buffalo, but in a very practical
way. The temples built and maintained (88) by each of
the 14 clans are, in effect, dairies where the milk of a
sacred, communally owned herd is collected and butter
churned for equitable distribution among the
community, and especially to those in need.*

*The Toda practice polyandry – the system of marriage
in which a woman takes several husbands. In the
confined, relatively small, high altitude environment
of the Nilgiri plateau, polyandry serves the important
functions of limiting Toda population growth,
restraining the establishment of new male lines and
concentrating wealth as it passes from one generation
to the next.*

Sinthothy (90, in doorway), had three husbands, all of whom assumed paternal responsibility for Ponnaye (90 standing) and made him their heir. During the past 50 years, however, social and economic developments have drastically altered the priorities of Toda life, and their marriage strategy has moved from polyandry to polygyny – one man, several wives. Ponnaye has two wives and his son Thashtharguttan (91) will inherit only a share of just one man's wealth.

■ INDIA: DIVERSE AGRICULTURE ■

Fifty-seven percent of India's land surface is arable and permanent cropland (compared with 22 percent of the United States and just 11 percent of China). Indian soils are inherently fertile and robust, the climate is congenial, and rainfall or ground water generally adequate. These factors have combined to make India the most densely populated large nation on Earth, with 80 percent of its inhabitants living directly from the land or in the service of small rural communities.

Indian agriculture has been conducted by human labour throughout most of its 4,000 year history, with the indispensible help of the cow – which supplies milk, bullocks for the plough and dung for fuel (94). Exploiting the land's capacity to produce a variety of crops and to support large numbers of people from relatively small areas, imposed a continuous demand for labour, artisan skills and service on the community, which in turn created societies that were split into a series of occupational niches. These niches became the basis of the caste system. The castes were mutually dependent, but they lived apart – the birdcatcher (95) a short distance from the combmakers (top 96) and the tax collectors (bottom 96). The caste system has been outlawed, and its basis of mutual dependence has virtually disappeared, but it persists as a divisive element of rural Indian society.

The fundamentals of Indian agriculture are also the most sacred aspects of India's Hindu religion. The River Ganges feeds the aquifers and irrigates the fields of northern India, and its headwaters at Rishikesh are a place of pilgrimage for Hindus, where wandering holy men, the sahdu *(98), congregate. The cow is sacred, and the statue of Nandi (97), Shiva's Bull, carved from solid basalt on a hill above Mysore, is attended by a priest who assists pilgrims with the rituals and offerings which acknowledge the significance of the cow in Indian life and religion.*

*Only 11 percent of China's land area is suitable for cultivation, and its history is
one of continuous adjustment to the problems of food supply and population growth.*

100

101

*Intensive rice production (100, 101 – at Dali on the road
to Tibet, Yunnan Province) enables China to support
the world's largest national population (1,063 million
in the 1982 census). Projections indicating that the
country can never support more than 1,200 million
people have inspired the government to introduce laws
restricting parents to one child each (99). The
subsequent drop in population growth rates has been
dramatic. But the policy has begun to produce a
generation of 'little emperors', children whose capacity
to work as hard and submissively as their parents is
seriously doubted.*

102

103

Participants in China's new free enterprise economy: market-sellers at Shapin (102, 105); hairdresser at Kunming (103); factory workers and 'little emperors', Kunming (104)

104

105

■ THE GREAT PLAINS: BLOOD INDIANS ■

While the nomadic Blood Indians still ruled the northern Great Plains of the United States and Canada, they made their winter camps in valleys such as that of the Milk River (106), in southern Alberta. During the late-19th century, the Blood Indians were virtually exterminated along with the bison on which they had subsisted, and the few hundred destitute survivors were settled on the Blood Indian reserve near Fort MacLeod, where their descendents still reside. Social and economic pressures provoked a consolidation of ethnic identity during the 1970s and 1980s, expressed in the new assertiveness of their young people (107).

106

Natural processes had made the Great Plains exceptionally fertile, and once the advent of the steel plough had enabled farmers to penetrate the dense sward, and mechanisation had enabled them to cultivate huge expanses of land (108), the plains rapidly became the most productive grainfields on Earth.

The agricultural potential of the region attracted many settlers, among them the Hutterites, a strict anabaptist group who emigrated to America from the Ukraine in the 1880s, and whose families (109) still follow the communal way of life that had sustained their forebears during centuries of religious persecution in Europe.

Communal life and an austere code of individual behaviour supplies the Hutterites with a dedicated and hard-working labour force. With grain, cattle (111), poultry (110) and arable farming, the elders (112) manage their affairs to achieve returns which often cause resentment among their less successful neighbours.

110

111

112

The lifestyle and farming skills developed by the Hutterites in the Ukraine were particularly suited to conditions on the Great Plains, and their success on the land has been matched by a spectacular increase in numbers. Hutterite women (113) produced an average of 10.4 live births each during the group's first 70 years in north America, and the original 443 immigrants who arrived in the 1880s multiplied to over 27,000 by the 1980s – a 60 fold increase which makes them the fastest growing human population known in the world. The Hutterites speak German among themselves, and although the law obliges them to accept state education for their children, they do not allow this to over-shadow either their German language or the

formal Hutterite schooling (114 top) which every Hutterite child receives. Each colony provides a classroom for state education, and the state supplies the teachers, but only Hutterite children attend (115), and the education they receive is seen as a supplement to the classes which each colony still runs according to the form laid down by the sect's founders.

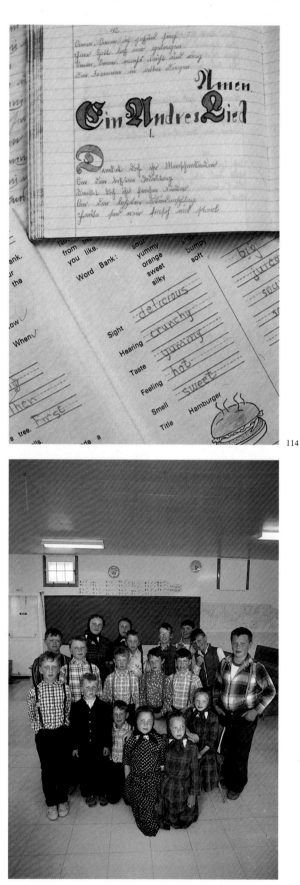

114

Former auto-plant worker and his wife with some immediate family: they still remember grandparents who were born in slavery.

116

Residents of Cleveland's public housing where, in 1984, 41 percent of families lived below the poverty line, and 39 percent were single parent families.

Pediatrician from the world-renowned Cleveland Clinic: resident in Cleveland since 1981.

117

118

119

City landscapes reflect the economic circumstances that led to their formation. Jodhpur (120), in India, is a market city which grew around the fortified palace from which the Jodhpur Maraharajas ruled their territories. The suburbs of Cleveland (121) were designed and built to provide middle-class housing during the city's post-war phase of rapid economic expansion. The success of Hong Kong's (119) trading and financial enterprises has obliged the city to expand vertically on its severely limited land area.

Modes of urban transportation, such as the bicycle in Jaipur (122), 'jeepneys' in Manila (123), trams in Hong Kong (124), and private cars in Cleveland (125), reflect aspects of convenience in a city but are primarily a reflection of its inhabitants' economic status.

122

123

124

125

126

Classical sculpture on display in the Cleveland Museum of Art.

▪ ACKNOWLEDGEMENTS ▪

The influence, help and encouragement of very many people lies behind this book, but its greatest impetus has stemmed from the experiences and conversations I have shared with Michael and Judy Rainy over the past 15 years. Michael has lived and worked among the Samburu people of northern Kenya since 1965. His study of the ecology of cattle pastoralism among the Samburu forms a major part of chapter 5, and his insights into the relationship between the environment and the social and cultural practices of the people inhabiting it, have stimulated my enquiries in other chapters too. He has alway been generous with his knowledge and his ideas, and I am deeply grateful.

And I owe a very special debt of gratitude to Brigitte.

In practical terms, the book owes its origin to Robert MacDonald and a series of spirited conversations we enjoyed under the refereeship of Hilary Davies. Adrian House and Pat Kavanagh put the project into a formal context, and Crispin Fisher has steered it through the machinations of publication with cool aplomb. Robert edited the text, Chris Lovell drew the maps, and Peter Campbell designed the book – their care and attention has been invaluable. My thanks to all.

The preliminary research for the book was advanced considerably by conversations with: Jonathan Benthall, G.A. Harrison, David Harris, David Pilbeam, Maryellen Ruvalo, Edward Wilson, Irven deVore, Bob Bailey, Nadine Peacock, Andrew Hill, Richard Wrangham, Matthew Spriggs, Tim Ingold, Roy Ellen, Tim Bayliss-Smith, Sally McBreaty, Jeremy Cherfas and Theya Molleson, to all of whom I offer my sincere thanks. And I am particularly grateful for the assistence I received from the staff at the London Library, and the libraries of the Royal Anthropological Institute and the Royal Geographical Society.

On my travels, Gerry Perrin, Henry Worswick, Sam and Margie Falanuw, John Tamag, Moolong and his family, Kurt Reddoch and Tim Thornburgh were extremely helpful on Yap; in Papua New Guinea, Andrew Strathern, David Lockwood, Lance Hill and Dominic Dia gave me invaluable preliminary advice; Robert Crittenden, Janis Baines and Michael Bourke were generous with assistence and the results of their studies on the Nembi plateau; Gretta and Michael Todurawai, Ian and Enese Bagley also gave me valuable advice and much valued hospitality; I am grateful to all. In Bali, special thanks are due to Oka Wati, Madi Dendi and Steve Lansing in Ubud, and Made Jaya and his family in Tatag. Father Markus Jossen kindly provided introductions to villagers in Törbel and made it possible for me to examine and photograph items from the village archives. I also owe a very special debt of gratitude to Roman Wyss, and to Oswald Seematter and his family. Michael Rainy provided a good deal of information on the Samburu for chapter 5, while Paul Robinson kindly introduced me to his study of the Gabbra. Matti Sulkinoja made it possible for me to visit the University of Turku's Subarctic Research Station at Kevo, northern Finland, where Saini Heino and her colleagues made my stay a very pleasant and productive one. I am also indebted to Samuli Aikio, Sophia Aikio, Hans Vuopio, Leif Halonen, Ula and Siri Dikkanen for their help and hospitality. I visited Oman under the auspices of Anthony Ashworth and the Ministry of Information and am grateful for the facilities they provided, but I am especially indebted to Ralph Daly, Adviser for Conservation of the Environment, for the opportunity to visit Al Yalooni, to Mark and Karen Stanley-Price for their assistence and hospitality, and to Dawn Chatty for her insights into the Harasiis.

Jim Acheson and his family made me very welcome at Pemaquid, with fulsome amounts of lobster as well as information on lobstering. Dan Cheney kindly allowed me to join him hauling traps and Seth agreed to be photographed – I am grateful to all.

My visit to British Columbia for chapter 7 was aided by the advice and hospitality of Art Roberts in Vancouver; Paul and Maureen Koroscil made my visit to Nara Mata very pleasant indeed, and gave me a wealth of information on the Okanagan valley that I have unable to find space for – I hope they will understand. Patricia Marchak provided much useful information on the forest resources of British Columbia, and in the Queen Charlotte Islands, Miles Richardson, Ernie Collison, Nick Gessler, Mel Hutchinson and Alfred Collinson provided insights into the present-day status and preoccupations of the Haida Indians. I am especially grateful to Frank Beban, who made it possible for me to visit Skedans.

Bob Bailey gave me invaluable advice on travelling to the Ituri forest in Zaire for chapter 8, which Andrew Galloway and Billy MacAleister helped me put it into effect. I should also like to thank Don Dix and Jim Given of the Africa Inland Mission, and the director of the Missionary Aviation Fellowship, but they were more of a hindrance than a help – though even their hindrance was advantageous in the end. I am more positively indebted to Commissaire

241

Mendela Kikola Batangwe, Tchame Nyonge, Suditau Augustin and Mukesh Visani, and most especially to Father Carlo, of the Catholic Mission in Mambasa, and to Fathers Gerard and Duilo in Nduye.

My reporting in Peru for chapter 9 was facilitated in part by the International Potato Center, through its director, Richard Sawyer. Robert Rhoades, Carlos Ochoas, Norio Yamamoto and Deborah Rabinovitz kindly spared time for my enquiries in Lima, and I am especially grateful to Gordon Prain, who took me to Huancayo and showed me around his study area. It was an invaluable experience. In Cuzco, Wilbert Salas Atasi was extremely helpful. The late David Horsburgh and his family welcomed my son and I to Rayalpad, in southern India; our stay there provided a foundation of observations for chapter 10, and left us with fond memories of an admirable man. Conversations with Anil Agarwal in New Delhi, Madhav Gadgil in Bangalore, Promodh Misra in Ootacamund, Dr S.P. Malhotra in Jodphur and Swami Amarnath in Rishikesh were very helpful, and I am especially indebted to Yvem Pilgian for her invaluable help and advice in the Nilgiri Hills. Daljit Singh was similarly helpful in Jodphur, and the trip through India was greatly eased and enhanced by the company of Mark Reader. In Ootacamund we met Fleming and Edna Allison and their home in Hong Kong subsequently became the starting point for my excursion into China – I am very grateful for their kind help and hospitality.

Wayne Wells, Leslie Tailfeathers, Steve Mistaken-Chief, Kathy Wells and Marie Marule provided much helpful information on the Blood Indians of British Columbia for chapter 11; Sophie Allison and Brad Taylor helped with the broader context, my thanks to all. Among the Hutterites of British Columbia, I am pleased to acknowledge with gratitude the help and hospitality of all at the Pincher Creek colony, and the courteous and helpful manner with which my enquiries were answered by Jacob Waldner at the Plainview colony, Martin Walters at Spring Point, John Wurz at Wilson Siding and Sam Entz at Ponderosa. I am also grateful to Ken Hoeppner for an initial briefing, and to John Davies for providing an opportunity to fly over the colonies.

I owe a very special debt of gratitude to Bill, Loulou and Bobbie Brown for their help and hospitality in Cleveland, Ohio, and to the many other residents of the city who assisted my research and reporting for chapter 12 – especially John and Diane Grabowski, Adele Silver, Bill Kimbel, Ceola King, Martha Bolden, Marie Childress, Robert and Shirley Cunningham, Chris and Paula Jagelewski, Norm Krumholz, Matthew Browarek and Fred Stevenson.

▪ BIBLIOGRAPHY ▪

The source material for *Man on Earth* was drawn primarily from among published studies of the social and cultural adaptations that have enabled people to inhabit the wide range of environments that the Earth has to offer. The following books provided a good deal of basic information on the subject, much fascinating reading and numerous references to the greater detail of mankind's relationship with the global environment.

Bayliss-Smith, T.P. 1982. *The Ecology of Agricultural Systems.* Cambridge University Press
Blaxter, K. 1986. *People, Food and Resources.* Cambridge University Press
Broek, J.O.M. and Webb, J.W. 1978. *A Geography of Mankind.* New York, McGraw Hill
Campbell, B. 1983. *Human Ecology.* London, Heinemann
Chagnon, N.A. and Irons, W. (eds) 1979. *Evolutionary Biology and Human Social Behavior.* North Scituate, Mass., Duxbury Press
Colinvaux, P. 1973. *Introduction to Ecology.* New York, John Wiley & Sons
Forde, C.D. 1934 (and reprints to 1979). *Habitat, Economy and Society.* London, Methuen
Harris, M. 1986. *Good to Eat.* London, Allen & Unwin
Harrison, G.A. and Boyce, A.J. (eds) 1972. *World Population and Settlement: the structure of human populations.* Oxford, Clarendon Press
Harrison, G.A., Weiner, J.S., Tanner, J.M. and Barnicot, N.A. 1982. *Human Biology* (2nd edition). Oxford University Press
Hutchinson, J. 1972. *Farming and Food Supply: the interdependence of countryside and town.* Cambridge University Press
Jochim, M.A. 1981. *Strategies for Survival: cultural behavior in an ecological context.* New York, Academic Press
Klee, G.A. (ed) 1980. *World Systems of Traditional Resource Management.* London, Edward Arnold
Lee, R.B. and Devore, I. (eds) 1968. *Man the Hunter.* New York, Aldine
Netting, R. 1977. *Cultural Ecology.* Menlo Park, Calif., Cummings Publishing Co. Inc.
Steward, J. 1977. *Evolution and Ecology.* University of Illinois Press
Ucko, P.J. and Dimbleby, G.W. (eds) 1969. *The Domestication and Exploitation of Plants and Animals.* London, Duckworth
Vayda, A. (ed) 1968. *Environment and Cultural Behavior: ecological studies in cultural anthropology.* Garden City, New York, Natural History Press
Wilson, E.O. 1975. *Sociobiology.* Harvard University Press
World Resources 1986. *World Resources: an assessment of the resource base that supports the global economy.* New York, Basic Books Inc.

The principal sources from which I have drawn material for the introduction and the specific themes of each chapter are:

INTRODUCTION

Cann, R.L., Stoneking, M. and Wilson, A.C. 1987. Mitochondrial DNA and human evolution. *Nature* 325: 31-36
Jones, J.S. and Rouhani, S. 1986. How small was the bottleneck? *Nature* 319: 449-50
Wainscoat J.S. et al 1986. Evolutionary relationships of human populations from an analysis of nuclear DNA polymorphisms. *Nature* 319: 491-93

CHAPTER 1: ISLANDERS pages 9-30

BOOKS
Bayliss-Smith, T.P. 1982. *The Ecology of Agricultural Systems.* Cambridge University Press
Bayliss-Smith, T.P. and Feachem, R. (eds) 1977. *Subsistence and Survival: rural ecology in the Pacific.* London, Academic Press
Brower, K. 1983. *A Song for Satawal.* London, Andre Deutsch
Carroll, V. (ed) 1975. *Pacific Atoll Populations.* Honolulu, University of Hawaii Press

BIBLIOGRAPHY   Chagnon, N.A. and Irons, W. (eds) 1979. *Evolutionary Biology and Human Social Behavior.*
    ■   North Scituate, Mass., Duxbury Press
              Christian, F.W. 1899/1967. *The Caroline Islands – travel in the seas of the little islands.*
                    London, Frank Cass
              Einzig, P. 1949/1966. *Primitive Money: in its ethnological, historical and economic aspects.*
                    Oxford and London, Pergamon Press
              Firth, R. 1936. *We, the Tikopia.* London, Allen & Unwin
              Fosberg, F.R. 1963. *Man's Place in the Island Ecosystem.* Honolulu, Bishop Museum Press
              Furness, W.H. 1910. *The Island of Stone Money, Uap of the Carolines.* Philadelphia,
                    J.B.Lippencott
              Gillilland, C.L.C. 1975. *The Stone Money of Yap.* Washington DC, Smithsonian Institution
                    Press
              Gladwin, T. 1970. *East is a Big Bird: navigation and logic on Puluwat atoll.* Cambridge,
                    Mass., Harvard University Press
              Gunson, N. (ed) 1978. *The Changing Pacific.* Melbourne, Oxford University Press
              Jochim, M.A. 1981. *Strategies for Survival: cultural behavior in an ecological context.* New
                    York, Academic Press
              Klee, G.A. (ed) 1980. *World Systems of Traditonal Resource Management.* London, Edward
                    Arnold
              Labby, D. 1976. *The Demystification of Yap.* University of Chicago Press
              Lewis, D. 1972. *We the Navigators.* Canberra, Australian National University Press
              Tetens, A.F. 1862/1958. *Among the Savages of the South Seas.* London, Oxford University
                    Press
              Vayda, A. (ed) 1968. *Peoples and Cultures of the Pacific.* Garden City, New York, Natural
                    History Press
              Ward, R.G. (ed) 1972. *Man in the Pacific Islands: essays on geographical change in the
                    Pacific.* Oxford, Clarendon Press
              Wiens, H.J. 1962. *Atoll Environment and Ecology.* New Haven & London, Yale University
                    Press

              PAPERS
              Alkire, W.H. 1969. Cultural adaptation in the Caroline Islands. *J. Polynesian Soc.* 69:
                    123-150
              Beauclair, I. de 1963. Stone money of Yap. *Bull. Inst. Ethnology. Academica Sinica* 16:
                    147-160
              Beauclair, I. de 1968. Social stratification in Micronesia: the low-caste people of Yap. *Bull.
                    Inst. Ethnology. Academica Sinica* 25: 45-52
              Bellwood, P.S. 1980. The peopling of the Pacific. *Scientific American* 243: Nov. 80,
                    174-185
              Falanruw, M.V.C. 1982. People pressure: management of limited resources on Yap. *Paper
                    presented at World National Parks Congress,* Bali 1982
              Ghyben-Herzberg law, in Cox, C.D. 1951. Hydrology of Arno atoll, Marshall Islands. Atoll
                    Res. Bull. No. 8. Dec 15
              Gifford, E.W. and D.S. 1959. Archeological excavations in Yap. *Anthrop. Records* 18 (2):
                    162-195. Berkeley, University of California Press
              Harvard University Peabody Museum, 1952. Micronesians of Yap and depopulation. *1947-48
                    Expedition Reports.* CIMA report 24
              Hunt, E.E., Kidder, N. and Schneider, D.M. 1954. The depopulation of Yap. *Human Biology*
                    26: 21-51
              McGrath, W.A. and Wilson, W.S. 1971. The Marshall, Caroline and Mariana Islands, in
                    Crocombe R. (ed) 1971. *Land Tenure in the Pacific.* Melbourne, Oxford University
                    Press
              Rubinstein, D. and White, G. 1983. Bibliography on culture and mental health in Pacific
                    islands. *Micronesia.* 190 (1-2): 183-245
              Schneider, D.M. 1955. Abortion and depopulation on a Pacific island, in Paul, B.D. (ed) 1955.
                    Health, Culture and Community: 211-235. New York, Russell Sage Foundation
              Schneider, D.M. 1957. Political organization, supernatural sanctions and the punishment for
                    incest on Yap. *Amer. Anthrop.* 59 (50): 791-800
              Underwood, J. H. 1969. Preliminary investigations of demographic features and ecological
                    variables of a Micronesian island population. *Micronesia.* 5 (1): 1-24
              Useem, J. 1946. Report on Yap, Palau and the lesser islands of the West Carolines. *United
                    States Economic Survey*
              Yap State Statistical Office, 1981. *Statistical Yearbook 1980.*

BOOKS
Bayliss-Smith, T.P. 1982. *The Ecology of Agricultural Systems.* Cambridge University Press
Bayliss-Smith, T.P. and Feachem, R. (eds) 1977. *Subsistence and Survival: rural ecology in the Pacific.* London, Academic Press
Brookfield, H.C. with Hart, D. 1971. *Melanesia: a geographical interpretation of an island world.* London, Methuen
Clarke, W.C. 1971. *Place and People: an ecology of a New Guinean community.* Berkeley & London, University of California Press
Conklin, H.C. 1957. *Hanunoo Agriculture.* Rome, U.N. Food & Agricultural Organisation
Fisk, E.K. 1978. *The Adaptation of Traditional Agriculture.* Canberra, Australian National University
Glasse, R.M. and Meggitt, M.J. (eds) 1969. *Pigs, Pearshells and Women: marriage in the New Guinea highlands.* New Jersey, Prentice-Hall
Harris, M. 1979. *Cultural Materialism.* New York, Random House
Hides, J.G. 1935. *Through Wildest Papua.* London, Blackie & Son
Leahy, M. 1937. *The Land that Time Forgot.* London, Hurst & Blackett
Meggitt, M.J. 1974. *Studies in Enga History.* University of Sydney
Miller, G.A. 1981. *Language and Speech.* San Francisco
Radford, R. 1987. *Highlanders and Foreigners in the Upper Ramu. The Kainantu Area 1919-1942.* Melbourne University Press
Rappaport, R.A. 1968/1984. *Pigs for the Ancestors.* New Haven & London, Yale University Press
Steward, J. 1977. *Evolution and Ecology.* University of Illinois Press
Strathern, A. 1971. *The Rope of Moka: ceremonial of exchange in Mount Hagen, New Guinea.* Cambridge University Press
Strathern, A. (Trans) 1979. *Ongka: a self-account of a New Guinea big-man.* London, Duckworth
Vayda, A.P. 1976. *War in Ecological Perspective.* New York & London, Plenum Press
Waddell, E. 1972. *The Mound Builders: agricultural practices, environment and society in the central highlands of New Guinea.* University of Seattle Press
Wurm, S.A. 1979. *New Guinea and Neighbouring Areas: a sociolinguistic laboratory.* The Hague, Mouton
Yen, D.E. 1974. *The Sweet Potato and Oceania: an essay in ethnobotany.* Honolulu, Bishop Museum Press

PAPERS
Allen, B.J. 1983. Human geography of Papua New Guinea. *J. Hum. Evol.* 12: 3-23
Allen, B.J. (ed) 1984. Agricultural and nutritional studies on the Nembi plateau, Southern Highlands. *Papua New Guinea Dept. Geography* Occasional paper no. 4, University of Papua New Guinea
Allen, B.J. and Crittenden, R. 1986. Degradation and a pre-capitalist political economy: the case of the New Guinea highlands, in Blaikie, P.M. and Brookfield, H.C. 1987. *Land Degradation and Society.* London, Methuen
Allen, B.J. et al 1980. Child malnutrition and agriculture on the Nembi plateau, Southern Highlands, Papua New Guinea. *Soc. Sci. Med.* 14D: 127-132
Allen, J. 1977. The hunting Neolithic: adaptations to the food quest in prehistoric Papua New Guinea, in Megaw, J.V.S. (ed) 1977. *Hunters, Gatherers and the First Farmers Beyond Europe.* Leicester University Press
Baines, J. 1983. Dietary patterns of pregnant women and birth weights on the Nembi plateau, Papua New Guinea. *Unpublished MSc thesis,* London School of Hygiene and Tropical Medicine
Baines, J. and Crittenden, R. 1984. Interactions between disease and malnutrition on the Nembi plateau, Papua New Guinea. *Papua New Guinea Medical Journal* 27 (3-4)
Binns, C. 1976. Does food volume limit dietary intake of highland children? *Nutr. Dev.* 2: 4-7
Bourke, R.M. 1984. Systems of agriculture, in Allen, B.J. (ed) 1984 (above)
Bourke, R.M. 1985. Sweet potato (*Ipomoea batatas*) production and research in Papua New Guinea. *Papua New Guinea Journal of Agriculture, Forestry and Fisheries* 33 (3-4): 89-108
Crittenden, R. 1982. Sustenance, seasonality and social circles on the Nembi plateau, Papua New Guinea. *Unpubl. PhD thesis* Australian National University

245

BIBLIOGRAPHY
■
Crittenden, R. 1984. The political economy of land degradation on the Nembi plateau, Southern Highlands Province, Papua New Guinea. *Paper presented to the Land Degradation Workshop* Dept. of Human Geography, The Research School of Pacific Studies, Australian National University

Crittenden, R. and Baines, J. 1985. Assessments of the nutritional status of children on the Nembi plateau in 1978/80. *Ecology of Food and Nutrition* 17: 131-47

Crittenden, R. and Baines, J. 1986. The seasonal factors influencing child malnutrition on the Nembi plateau, Papua New Guinea. *Human Ecology* 14 (2): 191-224

Divale, W.T. and Harris, M. 1976. Population, warfare and the male supremacist complex. *Am. Anthrop.* 78: 521-538

Edmundson, W. 1980. Adaptation to undernutrition: how much food does man need? *Soc. Sci. & Med.* 14D: 119-126

Heywood, P. 1982. Functional significance of malnutrition, growth and prospective death in the Highlands of Papua New Guinea. *J. Food Nutr.* 39 (1): 13-19

Heywood, P. 1983. Growth and nutrition in Papua New Guinea. *J. Hum. Evol.* 12: 133-143

Hope, G.S., Golson, J. and Allen, J. 1983. Palaeoecology and prehistory in New Guinea. *J. Hum. Evol.* 12: 37-60

Todurawai, M. 1983. Provincial brief on the Southern Highlands Province. *Southern Highlands Province Local Government Office*, Papua New Guinea

Spriggs, M. 1982. Taro cropping systems in the Southeast Asian-Pacific region: archaeological evidence. *Archaeology in Oceania* 17 (1): 7-16

Watson, J.B. 1977. Pigs, Fodder and the Jones effect in postipomoean New Guinea. *Ethnology* 16 (1): 57-70

CHAPTER 3: THE RICE GROWERS pages 52-72

BOOKS

Bayliss-Smith, T.P. 1982. *The Ecology of Agricultural Systems.* Cambridge University Press

Belo, J. (ed) 1970. *Traditional Balinese Culture.* New York, Columbia University Press

Boon, J.A. 1977. *The Anthropological Romance of Bali 1597-1972: dynamic perspectives in marriage and caste, politics and religion.* Cambridge University Press

Covarrubias, M. 1937. *Island of Bali.* New York, Alfred Knopf

Geertz. C. 1963. *Agricultural Involution: the process of ecological change in Indonesia.* Berkeley, University of California Press

Geertz, C. 1975. *Deep Play: notes on a Balinese cockfight.* Andover, Mass. MSS modul. Publ. Repr. 72 (Daedalus, Winter 1972)

Geertz, C. 1980. *Negara: The Theater State in Nineteenth Century Bali.* New Jersey, Princeton University Press

Geertz, C. 1980. *Local Knowledge: further essays in interpretive anthropology.* New York, Basic Books

Hobart, M. 1978. The Path of the Soul: the legitimacy of nature in Balinese conceptions of space, in Milner, G.B. (ed) 1978. *Natural Symbols in South East Asia.* University of London, S.O.A.S.

Hobart, M. 1980. *The Search for Sustenance: peasant economy of a Balinese village and its cultural implications.* London

Lansing, J.S. 1974. *Evil in the Morning of the World – phenomenological approaches to a Balinese community.* Ann Arbor, Michigan Papers on South and Southeast Asia No.6

Lansing, J.S. 1983. *The Three Worlds of Bali.* New York, Praeger

Ramseyer, U. 1977. *The Art and Culture of Bali.* Oxford University Press

PAPERS

Bateson, G. 1949. Bali: The value system of a steady state, in Belo, J. 1970 (above)

Birkelbach, A.W. 1973. The Subak association. *Indonesia* 16 (Oct): 153-169

Geertz, C. 1959. Form and variation in Balinese village structure. *Am. Anthrop.* 61: 991-1012

Geertz, C. 1972. The wet and the dry: traditional irrigation in Bali and Morocco. *Human Ecology* 1: 23-39

Howe, L.E.A. 1984. Gods, people, spirits and witches: the Balinese system of personal definition. *Bijdragen* 140 (2/3): 193-222

Kahn, E. 1985. The staffs of life (part 4) – everybody's business. *New Yorker* 4 March 85: 51-75

Swaminathan, M.S. 1984. Rice. *Scientific American* 250 (1): 62-71

BOOKS
Martin, W. 1971 (6th edition). *Switzerland: from Roman Times to the Present.* London.
Elek
Netting, R. 1977. *Cultural Ecology.* Menlo Park, Calif., Cummings Publishing Co. Inc.
Netting, R. 1981. *Balancing on an Alp: ecological change and continuity in a Swiss
mountain community.* Cambridge University Press
Steinberg, J. 1976. *Why Switzerland?* Cambridge University Press
Tyler, J.E. 1930. *The Alpine Passes 962-1250.* Oxford, Basil Blackwell

PAPERS
Hardin, G. 1968. The tragedy of the commons. *Science* 162: 1243-1248
Netting, R. 1974. The system nobody knows: village irrigation in the Swiss Alps, in Downing,
T. E. and Gibson, M. (eds) 1974. *Irrigation's Impact on Society.* Tucson, University of
Arizona Press
Netting, R. 1976. What alpine peasants have in common: observations on communal tenure
in a Swiss village. *Human Ecology* 4: 135-146
Wiegandt, E. 1977. Inheritance and demography in the Swiss Alps. *Ethnohistory* 24: 133-48

CHAPTER 5: NOMADS pages 89-108

BOOKS
Campbell, B. 1983. *Human Ecology.* London, Heinemann
Clements, F.A. 1980. *Oman, the Reborn Land.* London, Longman
Graburn, N.H.H. and Strong, B.S. 1973. *Circumpolar Peoples: an anthropological perspective.*
Pacific Palisades, California, Goodyear Publishing Co.
Ingold, T. 1976. *The Skolt Lapps Today.* Cambridge University Press
Ingold, T. 1980. *Hunters, Pastoralists and Ranchers: reindeer economics and their
transformation.* Cambridge University Press
Khazanov, A.M. (trans. J. Crookenden) 1984. *Nomads and the Outside World.* Cambridge
University Press
Spencer, P. 1968. *The Samburu: a study in gerontocracy in a nomadic tribe.* London,
Routledge & Kegan Paul
Spencer, P. 1973. *Nomads in Alliance: symbiosis and growth among the Rendille and
Samburu.* Oxford University Press
Wielgolaski, F.E. (ed) 1975. *Fennoscandian Tundra Ecosystems.* 2 vols. Berlin, New York,
Springer

PAPERS
Haukioja, E. and Salovaara, R. 1978. Summer weight of reindeer (*Rangifer tarandus*) calves
and its importance for their future survival. *Rep. Kevo Res. Stat.* 14: 1-4
Karenlampi, L. 1971. Studies on the relative growth rate of some fruticose lichens. *Rep. Kevo
Subarctic Res. Stat.* 7: 33-39
Kershaw, K.A. 1978. The role of lichens in boreal tundra transition areas. *The Bryologist* 81
(2): 294-306
Klein, D.R. 1968. The introduction, increase, and crash of reindeer on St. Matthew Island.
Journal of Wildlife Management 32: 350-367
Rainy, M. 1981. The ecology of cattle pastoralism among the southern Samburu.
Unpublished PhD thesis University of Nairobi
Robinson, P.W. 1985. Gabbra nomadic pastoralism in 19th and 20th century northern Kenya:
strategies for survival in a marginal environment. *Unpublished PhD thesis* Northwestern
University
Sjenneberg, S. and Slagsvold, L. 1968. Reindeer husbandry and its ecological principles. *US
Dept. Int. Bureau of Indian Affairs*
Siuruainen, E. 1976. The population of the Sami area of Finnish Lapland. *Acta Univ. Oulu
A40 Geograph. 2*
Siuruainen, E. and Aikio, P. 1977. The Lapps in Finland. *Society for the Promotion of Lapp
Culture Series* No. 39
Thesiger, W. 1950. Desert borderlands of Oman. *Geog. J.* 116: 137-71

PAPERS

Acheson, J. 1975a. The lobster fiefs: economics and ecological effects of territoriality in the Maine lobster industry. *Human Ecology* 3: 183-207

Acheson, J. 1975b. Fisheries management and the social context: the case of the Maine lobster industry. *Trans. Amer. Fisheries Soc.* 104 (4): 653-668

Acheson, J. 1979. Variations in traditional inshore fishing rights in Maine lobstering communities, in Anderson, R. (ed) 1979. *North Atlantic Maritime Cultures.* The Hague, Mouton

Acheson, J. 1981. Anthropology of fishing. *Ann. Rev. Anthropol.* 10: 275-316

Acheson, J. and Reidman, R. 1982. Biological and economic effects of increasing the minimum legal size of American lobster in Maine. *Trans. Amer. Fisheries Soc.* 111 (1): 1-12

Fountain, C. 1984. The high price of exploitation. *Boston Globe Magazine* 9 April 1984

Ryther, J.H. 1969. Photosynthesis and fish production in the sea. *Science* 166: 72-76

CHAPTER 7: THE SEASHORE pages 122-135

BOOKS

Boas, F. 1895. *Social Organisation and Secret Societies of the Kwakiutl.* Washington D.C. Rep. U.S. Nat. Museum

Carey, N. 1983. *The Queen Charlotte Islands.* Anchorage, Alaska Northwest Publishing Co.

Cook, J. 1784. *A Voyage to the Pacific Ocean* Vol. 3. London

Dalzell, K. 1968. *The Queen Charlotte Islands. Vol. 1 1774-1966.* Queen Charlotte City, Bill Ellis Publishing

Dixon, Capt. G. 1789. *A voyage around the world ... 1785, 1786, 1787 and 1788 in the King George and the Queen Charlotte.* London. (NB: this book is often catalogued under the the name of the man who prepared it for publication: W. Beresford.)

Duff, W. 1965. *The Indian History of British Columbia. Vol 1. The Impact of the White Man.* Victoria B.C. British Columbia Provincial Museum

Ellis, D.V. (ed) 1977. *Pacific Salmon – Management for People.* Vancouver

Forde, C.D. 1934/1979. *Habitat, Economy and Society.* London, Methuen

Goddard, P.E. 1924. *Indians of the Northwest Coast.* New York, American Museum of Natural History

Gunther, E. 1972. *Indian Life on the Northwest Coast of North America – as seen by early explorers and fur traders during the last decades of the 18th century.* University of Chicago Press

Halliday, W.M. 1935. *Potlatch and Totem.* London, Dent

Harrison, C. 1925. *Ancient Warriors of the North Pacific.* London, H.F. & G. Witherby

Jones, J.W. 1959. *The Salmon.* London, Collins

Kroeber, A.L. 1939. *Cultural and Natural Areas of Native North America.* Berkeley, University of California Press

McFeat, T. 1966. *Indians of the North Pacific Coast.* Seattle, University of Washington Press

Netting, R.M. 1977. *Cultural Ecology.* Menlo Park, Calif., Cummings Publishing Co. Inc.

Phillips, P.C. 1961. *The Fur Trade* 2 vols. Norman, University of Oklahoma Press

Portlock, N. 1789. *A Voyage Round the World.* London

Swanton, J.R. 1905. *Haida Texts and Myths.* Washington DC, Government Printing Office

Vayda, A.P. 1969. *Environment and Cultural Behavior.* Garden City, New York, Natural History Museum Press

PAPERS

Donald, L. and Mitchell, D.H. 1975. Some correlates of local group rank among the southern Kwakiutl. *Ethnology* 14: 325-346

Langdon, S. 1979. Comparative Tlingit and Haida adaptation on the west coast of the Prince of Wales Archipelago. *Ethnology* 18: 101-119

Lazenby, R.A. and McCormack, P. 1985. Salmon and malnutrition on the northwest coast. *Curr. Anthrop.* 26 (3): 379-84

Piddocke, S. 1965. The potlatch system of the southern Kwakiutl – a new perspective. *Southwestern Journal of Anthropology* 21: 244-264

Snyder, S. 1975. Quest for the sacred in northern Puget Sound: an interpretation of potlatch. *Ethnology* 14: 149-161

Suttles, W. 1968. Coping with abundance: subsistence on the northwest coast, in Lee, R.B. and DeVore, I. (eds) 1968. *Man the Hunter*: 56-68. New York, Aldine

CHAPTER 8: HUNTER GATHERERS pages 136-155

BOOKS

Ardrey, R. 1961. *African Genesis: a personal investigation into the animal orgins and nature of man.* London, Collins

Ardrey, 1976. *The Hunting Hypothesis.* London, Collins

Boas, F. 1911. *The Mind of Primitive Man.* New York, Macmillan

Boas, F. 1940. *Race, Language and Culture.* New York, Macmillan

Campbell, B. 1983. *Human Ecology.* London, Heinemann

Darwin, C. 1871. *The Descent of Man.* London

Ellen, R. 1982. *Environment, Subsistence and System.* Cambridge University Press

Harding, R.S.O. and Teleki, G. (eds) 1981. *Omnivorous Primates: Gathering and Hunting in Human Evolution.* New York, Columbia University Press

Harris, M. 1986. *Good to Eat.* London, Allen & Unwin

Harrison, G.A. and Boyce, A.J. (eds) 1972. *World Population and Settlement: the structure of human populations.* Oxford, Clarendon Press

Harrison, G.A., Weiner, J.S., Tanner, J.M. and Barnicot, N.A. 1982. *Human Biology* (2nd edition). Oxford University Press

Johnston, M. 1931. *Congorilla: adventures with Pygmies and gorillas in Africa.* London, George Harrap

Lee, R.B. 1984. *The Dobe !Kung.* New York, Holt, Rinehart & Winston

Lee, R.B. and Devore, I. 1976. *Kalahari Hunter Gatherers: studies of the !Kung San and their neighbours.* Cambridge Mass., Harvard University Press

Lee, R.B. and Devore, I. (eds) 1968. *Man the Hunter.* New York, Aldine

Lesser, A. 1985. *History, Evolution and the Concept of Culture.* Cambridge University Press

Netting, R. 1977. *Cultural Ecology.* Menlo Park, Calif., Cummings Publishing Co. Inc.

Schebesta, P. 1933. *Among Congo Pigmies.* London, Hutchinson

Silberbauer, G. 1981. *Hunter and Habitat in the Central Kalahari Desert.* Cambridge University Press

Speck, F.G. 1935. *Naskapi, the Savage Hunters of the Labrador Peninsula.* Norman, University of Oklahoma Press

Stocking, G.W. 1968/1982. *Race, Culture and Evolution – essays in the history of anthropology.* University of Chicago Press

Turnbull, C.M. 1961. *The Forest People: a study of the Pygmies of the Congo.* New York, Simon & Schuster

Turnbull, C.M. 1966. *Wayward Servants: the two worlds of the African Pygmies.* Garden City, Natural History Press

Webster, H. 1948. *Magic: a sociological study.* Oxford University Press

PAPERS

Abruzzi, W. 1979. Population pressure and subsistence among the Mbuti Pygmies. *Human Ecology* 7: 183-189

Bailey, R.C. and Peacock, N.R. (in press). Efe Pygmies of northeast Zaire: subsistence strategies in the Ituri Forest, in de Garine, I. and Harrison, G.A. (eds) (in press). *Uncertainty in the Food Supply.* Cambridge University Press

Dart, R.A. 1953. The predatory transition from ape to man. *Int. Anthrop. & Linguistic Rev.* 1: 201-217

Frisch, R.E. 1978. Population, food intake and fertility. *Science* 199: 22-30

Harako, R. 1976. The Mbuti as hunters. *Kyoto Univ. African Studies* 10

Hart, J.A. 1978. From subsistence to market: a case study of the Mbuti net hunters. *Human Ecology* 6: 325-353

Hill, K. 1982. Hunting and human evolution. *J. Hum. Evol.* 11: 521-544

Lee, R.B. 1968. What hunters do for a living, or, how to make out on scarce resources, in Lee, R.B. and DeVore, I. (eds) 1968. *Man the Hunter.* New York, Aldine

Lee, R.B. 1973. Mongongo: ethnography of a major wild food resource. *Ecology of Food and Nutrition* 2: 307-321

BIBLIOGRAPHY

■

Milton, K. 1985. Ecological foundations for subsistence strategies among the Mbuti Pygmies. *Human Ecology* 13: 71-78

Moore, O.K. 1957. Divination – a new perspective. *Am. Anthrop.* 59: 69-74

Shoumatoff, A. 1984. The Ituri Forest. *New Yorker* 6 February 1984

CHAPTER 9: THE POTATO GROWERS pages 156-174

BOOKS

Baker, P.T. (ed) 1978. *The Biology of High Altitude Peoples.* Cambridge University Press

Baker, P.T. (ed) 1982. *Human Population and Biosphere Interactions in the Central Andes.* Mnt. Res. Dev. 2 (1)

Baker, P.T. and Little, M.A. (eds) 1976. *Man in the Andes: a multidisciplinary study of high altitude Quechua.* Stroudsburg, Penn. Dowden, Hutchinson & Ross

Brush, S.B. 1977. *Mountain, Field and Family: the economy and human ecology of an Andean valley.* Philadelphia, University of Pennsylvania Press

Burton, W.G. 1966. *The Potato.* Wageningen, Veenman & Zonen

Cook, N.D. 1981. *Demographic Collapse: Indian Peru, 1520-1620.* Cambridge University Press

Hyslop, J. 1984. *The Inka Road System.* Orlando, Academic Press

Kendall, A. 1973. *Everyday Life of the Incas.* London, Batsford

Lanning, E.P. 1967. *Peru Before the Incas.* New Jersey, Prentice-Hall

Little, M.A. 1981. *A General Prospectus on the Andean Region.* Mnt. Res. Dev. 1 (2)

Murra, J.V. 1980. *The Economic Organization of the Inka State.* Greenwich, Conn., J.A.I. Press

Salaman, R.N. 1949/85. *The History and Social Influence of the Potato.* Cambridge University Press

Thomas, R.B. 1973. *Human Adaptation to a High Andean Energy Flow System.* University Park, Penn., Pennsylvania State University

Ucko, P.J. and Dimbleby, G.W. (eds) 1969. *The Domestication and Exploitation of Plants and Animals.* London, Duckworth

PAPERS

Baker, P.T. 1984. The adaptive limits of human populations. *Man* 19 (1): 1-14

Bolton, R. 1979. Guinea pigs, protein and ritual. *Ethnology* 18: 229-252

Brush, S.B. et al 1980. The dynamics of Andean potato agriculture. *Social Science Unit* International Potato Center, Lima

Hawkes, J.G. 1967. The history of the potato. *J. Roy. Hort. Soc.* 92: 207-24, 249-92, 288-300, 364-5

Lanning, E.P. 1968. Early man in Peru. *Scientific American* 213 (4): 68-76

Mayer, E. 1979. Land-use in the Andes: ecology and agriculture in the Mantaro Valley of Peru with special reference to potatoes. *Social Science Unit* International Potato Institute, Lima

Protzen, J-P. 1983. Inca quarrying and stone-cutting. *Nawpa Pacha* 21: 153-82

Quilter, J. and Stocker, T. 1983. Subsistence economics and the origin of Andean complex societies. *Am. Anthrop.* 85: 545-562

Thomas, R.B. 1976. Human ecological analysis of a high Andean valley, in Baker, P. and Little, M.A. (eds) 1976. (above)

Ugent, D. 1970. The potato. *Science* 170: 1161-1166

Werge, R.W. 1979. The agricultural strategy of rural households in three ecological zones of the central Andes. *Social Science Unit* International Potato Institute, Lima

Winterhalder, B., Larsen, R. and Thomas, R.B. 1974. Dung as an essential resource in a highland Peruvian community. *Human Ecology* 2: 89-104

Yamamoto, N. 1982. A food production system in the southern central Andes. *Senri Ethnological Studies* 10: 39-57

CHAPTER 10: INDIA AND CHINA pages 175-198

BOOKS

Agarwal, A., Chopra, R. and Sharma, K. 1982. *The State of India's Environment: a citizens' report.* Centre of Science and Environment, New Delhi.

Chagnon, N.A. and Irons, W. (eds) 1979. *Evolutionary Biology and Human Social Behavior.* North Scituate, Mass., Duxbury Press

Cherfas, J. and Gribben, J. 1984. *The Redundant Male.* London, Bodley Head
Clayre, A. 1984. *The Heart of The Dragon.* London, Collins/BBC
Daly, M. and Wilson, M. 1978. *Sex, Evolution and Behaviour.* North Scituate, Mass. Duxbury Press
Dumont, L. (revised edition) 1980. *Homo Hierarchicus – The Caste System and its Implications.* University of Chicago Press
Gaur, A. 1984. *A History of Writing.* London
Harris, M. 1986. *Good to Eat.* London, Allen & Unwin
Ho, Ping-ti, 1959. *Studies on the Population of China 1368-1953.* Cambridge, Mass
Hutchinson, J.'1972. *Farming and Food Supply: the interdependence of countryside and town.* Cambridge University Press
Hutton, J.H. (4th edition) 1963. *Caste in India.* Oxford University Press
Loewe, M.A.N. 1966. *Imperial China: the historical background to the modern age.* London
Peter, Prince of Greece and Denmark 1963. *A study of Polyandry.* The Hague, Mouton
Rivers, W.H.R. 1906. *The Todas.* London, Macmillan

PAPERS
Chagnon, N.A., Flinn, M.V., and Melancon, T.F. 1979. Sex-ratio among the Yanomamo Indians, in Chagnon, N.A. and Irons, W. 1979. (above)
Gadgil, M. (in press). Social restraints on resource utilization: the Indian experience, in Pitt, D. (ed) (in press). *Culture and Conservation Commission on Environmental Planning,* I.U.C.N.
Gadgil, M. and Malhotra, K.C. 1983. Adaptive significance of the Indian caste system: an ecological perspective. *Annals of Human Biology* 10: 465ff
Harris, M. 1966. The cultural ecology of India's sacred cattle. *Curr. Anthrop.* 7: 51-9
Keyfitz, N. 1984. The population of China. *Scientific American* 250 (2): 22-31
Odend'hal, S. 1972. Energetics of Indian cattle in their environment. *Human Ecology* 1: 3-22
Odend'hal, S. 1980. Human and cattle population changes in deltaic west Bengal, India between 1967 and 1977. *Human Ecology* 8: 1-7
Sopher, D.E. 1980. Indian civilisation and the tropical savanna environment, in Harris, D.R. (ed) 1980. *Human Ecology in Savanna Environments.* London, Academic Press

CHAPTER 11: COMMERCIAL FARMERS pages 198-218

BOOKS
Bennett, J.W. 1967. *Hutterite Brethren: the agricultural economy and social organization of a communal people.* Stanford Calif., Stanford University Press
Collier, J. 1947. *The Indians of the Americas.* New York, Norton
Ewers J.C. 1955. *The Horse in Blackfoot Indian Culture.* Washington DC, Government Printer's Office
Ewers J.C. 1958. *The Blackfeet: raiders on the Northwest plains.* Norman, University of Oklahoma Press
Hostetler, J. 1974. *Hutterite Society.* Baltimore, Johns Hopkins University Press
La Farge, O. (ed) 1942. *The Changing Indian.* Norman, University of Oklahoma Press
Klee, G.A. (ed) 1980. *World Systems of Traditional Resource Management.* London, Edward Arnold

PAPERS
Alberta, Province of, 1959. *Report of the Hutterite Investigation Commission.* Edmonton
Byfield, L. 1983. Harnessing the Hutterites. *Alberta Report* 31 January: 32
Eaton, J.W. and Mayer, A.J. 1953. The social biology of very high fertility among the Hutterites: the demography of a unique population. *Human Biology* 25: 206-64
Hanson, J.R. 1984. Bison ecology in the northern plains. *Plains Anthropology* 29 (10): 93-113
Hoeppner, K. and Gill, J. 1974. Communal property in Alberta. *Technical Report No. 6C* Alberta Land Use Forum, Edmonton
McKinley, M. 1982. Beware the Hutterites! *Alberta Report* 20 December: 39
Peter, K.A. 1980. The decline of Hutterite population growth. *Canadian Ethnic Studies* 12(3): 97-109
Weatherbe, S. 1984. Scapegoating the Hutterites. *Alberta Report* 9 April: 36

CHAPTER 12: THE CITY pages 219-240

BOOKS

Ball, J.N. 1977. *Merchants and Merchandise. The Expansion of Trade in Europe, 1500-1630.* London, Croom Helm

Campbell, B. 1983. *Human Ecology.* London, Heinemann

Chapman, E.H. 1981. *Cleveland: village to metropolis.* Cleveland, Western Reserve Historical Society

Hall, P.G. 1984. *The World Cities.* 3rd edition. London

Hawke, D.F. 1980. *John D. The Founding Father of the Rockefellers.* New York

Hopper, R.J. 1979. *Trade and Industry in Classical Greece.* London, Thames & Hudson Klee, G.A. (ed) 1980. *World Systems of Traditonal Resource Management.* London, Edward Arnold

Lawrence, A.T. and Schattlinger, J.M. 1979. *Cleveland's Flats.* Cleveland, History Associates

Mumford, L. 1961. *The City in History: its origins, transformations and prospects.* London, Secker & Warburg

Rickman, G.E. 1980. *The Corn Supply of Ancient Rome.* Oxford University Press

Rose, W.G. 1950. *Cleveland, The Making of a City.* New York, World Publishing

Rotberg, R.I. and Rabb, T.K. (eds) 1985. *Hunger and History: the impact of changing food production and consumption patterns on society.* Cambridge University Press

Ste Croix, G.E.M. de 1981. *The Class Struggle in the Ancient Greek World.* London, Duckworth

Short, J.R. 1984. *An Introduction to Urban Geography.* London, Routledge

Tassel, D.D. van and Grabowski, J.J. (eds) 1986. *Cleveland: a tradition of reform.* Kent State University Press

Warren, K. 1973. *The American Steel Industry 1850-1970: a geographical interpretation.* Oxford, Clarendon Press

World Resources 1986. *World Resources: an assessment of the resource base that supports the global economy.* New York, Basic Books

PAPERS

Carter, H. 1977. Urban origins: a review. *Progress in Human Geography* 1 (1): 12-32

Dodsworth, T. 1984. Cleveland, Ohio. *Financial Times* 9 April: 25-28

Long, L. and DeAre, D. 1983. The slowing of urbanization in the U.S. *Scientific American* 249 (1): 31-39

Lynch, M. (in press). Arts and patrons: the growth of Cleveland as a cultural center, in *An Anthology of Essays by the Western Reserve Historical Society* for the Cleveland Heritage Program, Cleveland

Marbut, C.F. 1931. Russia and the United States in the world's wheat market. *The Geographical Review* 21 (1): 1-19

▪ INDEX ▪

253

Efe people, 153, 154-5
elders, Samburu, 91, 92, 96
Enga people, 42, 45
environment, as cultural
  determinant
  on Bali, 57, 69
  on Yap, 11
eskimoes, 141, 147

fat, dietary need for, 147-8
Finland, 104, 105
  see also Lapps
fishing, 142
  British Columbia, 128, see also
    salmon
  Maine, see lobster fishing
forest clearing see swidden
fur trade, NW Amer., 122-5, 132

Gabbra people, 93-4
gatherers, 142
  women as, 145-6, 155
  see also Bambuti; !Kung San
gerontocracy, in Samburu society,
  91
Ghyben-Herzberg Law, 13
gifts
  Toda, 181
  see also moka exchange;
    potlatch
goats, 99, 107, **55**
gods Balinese, 53, 64, 65; see also
  Dewi Sri
  Hindu, 189
  Inca, 159
  Samburu, 91-2
grain
  in human interactions, 222
  in Inca civilisation, 159-60
  in classical Rome, 225-8
  in Greece, 224
  in industrial economy of Europe,
    174
grass supply
  Samburu, 90
  Törbel, 79, 84, 85
Great Plains (prairies), 206, 208,
  219-20, **106-9**
Greece, classical, 223-5
guinea-pigs, Quechua use, 169-71
guns, Amer. Indian use, 202, 203

habitat
  alpine, 73, 83, **27, 30-1**
  arable cropland, India, 183, **92-6**
  coast, NW Amer. Pacific, 126-8,
    63-4
    Maine, 111-3, **56-60**
  desert, Kalahari, 144, **68-71**
    Jiddat-il-Harasiis, 106-7, **50-5**
  forest, equatorial rain-, Zaire,
    149-50, **72-80**
  forest, temperate, British
    Columbia, 127-8, **61-6**

forest, tropical, Papua New
  Guinea, 39, **7-14**
grassland, temperate, Great
  Plains, 198, 200, 206, **106-12**
  Russia, 220
grassland, tropical, 89, **33-40**
  island, Pacific, 12-14, **2-6**
  tropical, Bali, 56-7, **15-20**
  mountain, Andes, 164-5, **1, 81-7**
  Nilgiri plateau, 175-6, **89**
  tundra, 100-1, **44-7**
Haida Indians, 127, 133-5, **61-6**
Harasiis people, 106-7, **50, 53**
harbour gangs, Maine, 110, 119,
  120, **56-60**
Harrijan caste, 59, 186
haymaking, in Törbel, 75, 79, 84,
  85, **26-8**
Hinduism
  on Bali, 57, 64
  in India, 185-6, 188-93
horses, effect on Amer. Indian
  society, 200-1
hunter-gatherers, see gatherers;
  hunters
hunters, 146
  examples, see Bambuti;
    Blackfoot Indians; !Kung San;
    Naskapi Indians
Hutter, Jakob, 207, 208
Hutterite colonies, 206-10, 217-18,
  222, **109-15**
  education, 213-16, **114-5**
  organisation, 210-13

Inca civilisation, 157-61, 163
India, 175-6, 182-5, **88-98**
  caste system, 185-8, **94-6**
  sacred cows, 188-93, **97**
  see also Toda
Indian Act (1874), 133
Indians, American 141, 147-8,
  198-9
  North West Coast, 124-5, 127-30
    potlatch, 130-3
  see also Haida Indians; Blackfoot
    Indians; Blood Indians; Naskapi
Indus Valley civilisation, 157
infanticide, 179, 196
Irish potato famine, 174
iron industry, Cleveland, 232, 233
irrigation, 157
  on Bali, 69-71
  in India, 183-4
  in Törbel, 85, 86
Irula people, 176, 177
Ituri Bambuti, 150, 151, 153, 155,
  72-80

Jiddat-il-Harasiis, 106-7, **50**
Johnson, Martin and Osa, 151-2

Kalahari desert, 144, **67-71**
  people, see San people

Kenya, North, 97
  people, see Samburu
killing cycles, Samburu, 91
Kota people, 176, 177
Krishna, Hindu god, 189
Ksatriyas 59, 186
!Kung San, see San people
Kurumba people, 176, 177

Labour requirements, of
  Blood Indians, 200
  Indian agriculture, 184, **94-6**
  Kalahari hunter-gatherers, 144-6
  NW Pacific coast societies,
    129-30
  rice cultivation, 56, 67
  swidden agriculture, 40
land rights
  Bali, 71
  communal, among Hutterites,
    210, 213
  concept imposed on Blood
    Indians, 203-4
  East Africa, 97-8
  effect of state take-over in India,
    187
  Hutterite, restricted by law, 209
  Swiss alpine village, 74-5, 79,
    87, 88
  Maine coast, 109-10, 118, 120
  Pacific coast, NW American,
    127-30
  Peruvian Andes, 168
  Yap, 17-18, 19
languages
  American Indian, 199
  as social determinant on Bali, 60
  of Bambuti, 153
  Chinese, written form, 194
  Hutterite, 215
  Inca, 158
  in New Guinea, diversity, 37-8
Lapps, 103-5, 106, **44-9**
larch trees, in Törbel, 73, **30-2**
Leahy, Michael, 35-7
lichen, as reindeer food, 101-2
llamas, 166, 167
lobster fishing, 116-18
  See Maine, lobster fishing

magic, function of, 136
  Naskapi, 137-8
Maine, lobster fishing, 109-10,
  112-16, 118-21, **56-60**
maize growing, Inca, 157-8, 159-
  60, 171
male redundancy, in
  food gathering, 146, 155
  human populations, 180
  reindeer, 102-3
  Swiss alpine populations, 88
mangrove, **5**
manifest destiny, in Amer. Indian
  policy, 203

254